How America Gets Away W

How America Gets Away With Murder

Illegal Wars, Collateral Damage and Crimes Against Humanity

Michael Mandel

Pluto  Press

LONDON • ANN ARBOR, MI

First published 2004 by Pluto Press
345 Archway Road, London N6 5AA
and 839 Greene Street, Ann Arbor, MI 48106, USA

www.plutobooks.com

British Library Cataloguing in Publication Data
A catalogue record for this book is available from the British Library

ISBN   0 7453 2152 6 hardback
ISBN   0 7453 2151 8 paperback

Library of Congress Cataloging in Publication Data
Mandel, Michael.
   How America gets away with murder: illegal wars, collateral damage and crimes against humanity / Michael Mandel.
      p. cm.
   Includes bibliographical references.
   ISBN 0–7453–2152–6 (HBK) — ISBN 0–7453–2151–8 (PBK)
   1. Aggression (International law) 2. War (International law) 3. War crimes. 4. Crimes against humanity. 5. United States—Foreign relations—2001– I. Title.

   KZ6355.M36 2004
   345'.0235—dc22

                                                                    2004005804

10   9   8   7   6   5   4   3   2   1

Designed and produced for Pluto Press by
Chase Publishing Services, Fortescue, Sidmouth, EX10 9QG, England
Typeset from disk by Stanford DTP Services, Northampton, England
Printed and bound in Canada by Transcontinental Printing

For Karen, Tevi and Orly

Contents

Acknowledgments

Of the many people who contributed to this book in large and small ways, I am most indebted to Karen Golden, Ed Herman, and Max Mandel for their generous help and encouragement throughout the project, and for the care they took in reading and commenting on the manuscript. I would also like to single out for special thanks my research assistants Melanie Banka, Trung Nguyen, Raha Shahidsaless and Jeremy Wilton; my faculty assistants Lynne Fonseca, Angela Monardo and Roberta Parris; helpful friends, family and colleagues Noam Chomsky, Gail Davidson, Harry Glasbeek, Reuben Hasson, David Jacobs, Giulia Mandel, Lucy Mandel, Mika Mihailovic, Natasa Mihailovic, Chiara Giovanucci Orlandi, Marianne Rogers, Helena Ruken, Michael Scharf, Wolfgang Schulz and Snezana Vitorovich. I'm very grateful to Osgoode Hall Law School of York University in Toronto and to the Facoltà di Giurisprudenza of the University of Bologna for their invaluable institutional support. Finally, for their hard work in turning the manuscript into a book, I would like to thank Anne Beech, David Castle, Robert Webb and Charles Peyton of Pluto Press.

Frequently Cited Sources

***Nuremberg Tribunal Judgement*, 1946** refers to The Judgment of the International Military Tribunal for the Trial of German Major War Criminals, 30 September 1946. Page references are to *The Judgement of Nuremberg, 1946* ('uncovered editions' London: the Stationery Office, 1999). The judgment may also be found reproduced in full as *Judgment of the International Military Tribunal for the Trial of German Major War Criminals* The Avalon Project at Yale Law School <http://www.yale.edu/lawweb/avalon/imt/proc/judcont.htm>.

Pinochet Judgment refers to *Reg. v. Bow Street Magistrate*, Ex p. Pinochet (No. 3) (H.L.(E.)) [2000] 1 A.C. 147.

Amnesty Report refers to Amnesty International, *NATO/Federal Republic of Yugoslavia 'Collateral Damage' or Unlawful Killings? Violations of the Laws of War by NATO during Operation Allied Force*, 6 June 2000, AI Index: EUR 70/018/2000 <http://web.amnesty.org/aidoc/aidoc_pdf.nsf/Index/EUR700182000ENGLISH/$File/EUR7001800.pdf>.

ICTY Report refers to *Final Report to the Prosecutor by the Committee Established to Review the NATO Bombing Campaign Against the Federal Republic of Yugoslavia*, U.N. Doc. PR/P.I.S./510-E (2000), available at <http://www.un.org/icty/pressreal/nato061300.htm>.

***Nicaragua v. United States of America*, 1986** refers to Case Concerning the Military and Paramilitary Activities in and Against Nicaragua (*Nicaragua v. United States of America*) (MERITS), Judgment of 27 June 1986, [1986] I.C.J. Rep. 70.

Milosevic Trial Transcript refers to *Prosecutor v. Slobodan Milosevic*, 'Kosovo, Croatia And Bosnia Herzegovina' (IT-02–54) Transcripts <http://www.un.org/icty/index.htm>.

ICTY Press Releases and Press Briefings are archived by date at <www.un.org/ICTY/latest/latestdev-e.htm>.

NATO Morning Briefings and **NATO Press Briefings** are archived by date at <http://www.nato.int/kosovo/press.htm>.

Security Council Resolutions are archived by year and number at <http://www.un.org/documents/scres.htm>.

Part I
Illegal Wars/Collateral Damage

1
Iraq 2003

America's war on Iraq in 2003 was its third illegal war in just under four years. Each one was a bloody horror, but the Iraq war distinguished itself both for its bloodiness and for the flagrancy of its illegality. It was virtually *certified* as illegal by a defeat at the Security Council so unspinnable that President Bush had to back down from his boast to make the members 'show their cards' by forcing a vote.[1]

The illegality of the Iraq war was not due to some lawyer's technicality. The reasons for it (explored later in this chapter) were the same as the reasons for the defeat at the Security Council: the failure of the United States to demonstrate one decent moral justification for resort to war, with all the death and destruction that were sure to follow. The United Nations weapons inspections had turned up nothing, and, despite crude attempts by the Americans and the British to discredit the inspectors before the war with phony intelligence – 'risk assessment *enhancement*' as the American comic strip *Doonesbury* called it[2] – they themselves would do no better when they scoured the country afterwards. There was admittedly no threat of Iraq attacking the United States or its allies, so there was no plausible claim of self-defense. Those few who believed that the war would be about 'freeing' Iraqis were rapidly disabused of this when, with the regime of Saddam Hussein overthrown, the Americans made it clear that the Iraqis would have a hard time ever freeing themselves from the American military occupation. Nor could concern for Iraqi human rights be taken seriously as a motive from a country that had punished Iraqis for twelve years with an inhuman sanctions regime.

And where was the humanity to be found in a war that had destroyed so many human lives? Iraq Body Count, an international research group dedicated to documenting scientifically the Iraqi civilian casualties, estimated the number of those killed in the war and occupation (as of August 2003) at between 6,100 and 7,800, with 20,000 wounded.[3] Most of these people, about 4,100 to 5,200, had been killed during the invasion. A *Los Angeles Times* survey of Baghdad hospital records counted 1,700 civilians killed in the battle for Baghdad alone.[4] The same records showed 8,000 injured. 'Injured' included losing both your arms and suffering deep burns to 35 per cent of your body, not to mention having your father and mother killed, like twelve-year-old Baghdadi Ali Ismail Abbas. While the war deaths of American and UK soldiers were carefully counted at 164, with 569 injured, the number of Iraqi soldiers killed and wounded would probably never be known.[5] Estimates ranged from 2,300 to *tens* of thousands.[6]

The killing didn't stop with the overthrow of the Iraqi regime. What the Americans called the 'bitter enders' immediately started a guerrilla war against the occupation, attacking American soldiers and many other targets daily throughout 2003. American deaths from these attacks – about 200 in the period from 1 May to 1 December – sent shock waves through the US. But about 3,000 Iraqi civilians were killed during the same period, whether as bystanders in the attacks on Americans or in the inevitable counter-attacks, or in other violence related to the occupation. Jittery American soldiers shot dead five members of the same family on 13 June, then nine Iraqi police and three civilian bystanders on 12 September, and all five occupants of a farm truck carrying chickens on 11 November. The August truck bomb attacks against United Nations headquarters in Baghdad and a Shia Mosque in Najaf took the lives of over 100 Iraqis, as well as those of UN operations chief Sergio Vieira de Mello and top cleric Ayatollah Mohammed Bakr al-Hakim. When attacks against Americans reached a crescendo in November with the shooting down of four American helicopters and about 70 US combat deaths, America responded with 'Operation Iron Hammer,' and the bombing war had essentially re-commenced. 'This is war,' said a US Major-General on 19 November. 'We're going to use a sledgehammer to crush a walnut.'[7] On that day and the next, the Americans killed ten Iraqi 'insurgents,' and another ten Iraqi civilians died in bomb blasts in three separate cities. Three were children killed in an explosion at a school, and it wasn't known whether the bomb had been placed there or one of the children had been playing with 'unexploded ordnance.'[8]

Compounding the violence was the fact, soon evident, that the US had done virtually no planning for actually administering Iraq after it had been conquered. A country reduced it to a fifth of its pre-1991 productive capacity by more than a decade of sanctions quickly descended into the chaos of looting, violent crime and sabotage. Not only the treasures of the Baghdad Museum, but the hospitals, schools and power plants were stripped of everything that wasn't bolted down. The murder rate soared, and oil, water and electricity systems remained a shambles throughout 2003. Already in June, with anti-American discontent and guerrilla attacks steadily rising, US ground forces commander Lt. Gen. David McKiernan had concluded that 'Iraq will be a combat zone for some time.'[9]

In early 2003 a global anti-war movement the likes of which had never before been seen demonstrated in its millions to show that the world did not believe the revolving justifications the Americans kept serving up for the war. A poll released by the American Pew Research Center on the day before the war showed opposition in every country surveyed except for the United States, including America's main ally Britain, where opposition ran at 51 to 39 per cent. Opposition was massive not only in opposing countries like France (75 percent opposed to the war, to 20 percent in favour), Germany (69 to 27 percent) and Russia (87 to 10 percent) but also in 'Coalition of the Willing' countries Italy (81 to 17 percent), Spain (81 to 13 percent), Poland (73 to 21 percent) and Turkey (86 to 12 percent).[10] The world was convinced that this was not a war fought because of some new realities of terrorism, weapons of mass destruction, much less for 'freedom,' but rather for the old familiar reasons of empire: private wealth and public strategic power. Iraq had the second-largest oil reserves in the world, a source of both, and it was clear that the Americans wanted to be the ones in charge, not only of Iraq, but of the whole, increasingly unstable region.[11] '[W]hy does the administration seem unconcerned about an exit strategy from Iraq once Saddam is toppled? Because we won't be leaving. Having conquered Iraq, the United States will create permanent military bases in that country from which to dominate the Middle East.'[12] The ancient coinage of empire, 'credibility,' was at stake: 'Every ten years or so, the United States needs to pick up some small crappy little country and throw it against the wall, just to show the world we mean business.'[13]

The world's representatives at the United Nations and on the Security Council, prodded by opinion on the world's streets, scrutinized America's trumped-up claims that some legitimate collective interest or human good was at stake and rejected them. Despite the enormous pressure it could wield as the richest and most powerful country in the world, the United States was able to muster only four votes for war out of the 15 on the Security Council, the body entrusted by the 191 members of the United Nations (including the US) with the duty to decide matters of war and peace.

In technical terms this was a war of 'aggression' – the legal word for a war that does not fall within the narrow confines of the right of self-defense and has not been authorized by the Security Council as absolutely necessary in the collective interest of international peace and security. What does it mean for a country to wage a war of aggression? If we judge it by the standards laid down by the Nuremberg Tribunal that judged the Nazis after World War II, it is the *supreme international crime*. The first count against the Nazis in the Nuremberg Charter was the 'crime against peace ... namely planning, preparation, initiation [and] waging of a war of aggression, or a war in violation of international treaties' – international treaties just like the Charter of the United Nations. The judges of the Tribunal came from the four victorious powers America, Russia, Britain and France. In one of the best-known passages from the judgment of the Tribunal they declared:

> *War is essentially an evil thing. Its consequences are not confined to the belligerent states alone, but affect the whole world. To initiate a war of aggression, therefore, is not only an international crime; it is the supreme international crime differing only from other war crimes in that it contains within itself the accumulated evil of the whole.*[14]

So according to this foundation judgment of all international criminal law, the Americans, and that means their leaders – Messrs. Bush, Rumsfeld and Powell, General Franks, Ms. Rice, etc., and their associates Messrs. Blair, Hoon, Straw, et al. – are guilty of having committed the supreme international crime in Iraq, the one that contains within itself the accumulated evil of the whole. But even more than this: these leaders are also guilty for every act of violence with which this war was pursued. In the words of the American Chief Prosecutor at the Tribunal, the much-venerated American Supreme Court Justice Robert H. Jackson:

> Any resort to war – any kind of war – is a resort to means that are inherently criminal. War inevitably is a course of killings, assaults, deprivations of liberty, and destruction of property. An honestly defensive war is, of course, legal and saves those lawfully conducting it from criminality. *But inherently criminal acts cannot be defended by showing that those who committed them were engaged in a war, when war itself is illegal.* The very minimum legal consequence of the treaties making aggressive war illegal is to strip those who incite or wage them of every defense the law ever gave, and to leave the war-makers subject to judgment by the usually accepted principles of the law of crimes.[15]

In other words, President Bush and his colleagues are legally guilty of the murder of many thousands of people, not to mention the grievous assault of many tens of thousands more and so on down the list of the most serious crimes in the criminal codes of every country of the world. It's the kind of thing that, when done on a fraction of the scale in the Bush family's Texas, gets you a one-way ticket to the lethal injection chamber. And it doesn't matter that the war was authorized by the American Congress, even if that made it legal according to American law, because the fact that a war is legal according to the law of the country that launches it is irrelevant to international law. The Nazi war was legal according to Nazi law. International law is about *international* norms and *international* treaties, like the Charter of the United Nations (to which, all appearances to the contrary, the Americans are still parties) that made the war unquestionably illegal. According to Principle II of the *Principles of International Law Recognized in the Charter of the Nürnberg Tribunal and in the Judgement of the Tribunal*: 'The fact that internal law does not impose a penalty for an act which constitutes a crime under international law does not relieve the person who committed that act from responsibility under international law.'[16] Principle III adds: 'The fact that a person who committed an act which constitutes a crime under international law acted as Head of State or responsible government official does not relieve him from responsibility under international law.'

But the President isn't headed for Death Row, he's not even going to court. Because, for all we hear about war crimes and international criminal courts, there isn't one that has any jurisdiction over these supreme criminals for their supreme crimes. There is a brand new International Criminal Court at The Hague that is supposed to try people for war crimes, but, in order not to offend the Americans – who aren't even parties to the Court – it doesn't have jurisdiction over the supreme crime of starting an illegal war in the first place, only the lesser ones, crimes against the so-called 'laws and customs of war.' It's as if there were no law against murder, only murdering without reasonable regard for the safety of bystanders. Think of it as a 'loophole.' One Nuremberg prosecutor wrote at the time that, since the laws and customs of war are typically violated by both sides, they are 'at best a fragile barrier between the violence of war and its victims ... [A] modern war, no matter how chivalrous, involves so much misery that to punish deviations from the conventions without punishing the instigators of an aggressive war seems like *a mocking exercise in gentlemanly futility*.'[17]

It's because of this 'loophole' that there was so much talk during the Iraq war about the Geneva Conventions and the 'laws and customs of war' but nothing about the crime of starting the war itself. When the attack was launched, stern warnings were issued to all the 'belligerents' by Human Rights Watch, Amnesty International and groups with lesser prominence, reminding them of their duties under the laws and customs of war.[18] But neither said a single word about the illegality of the war itself or the supreme criminal responsibility under international law of the leaders of the countries that had started it. During the war, too, an enormous amount was said about the lesser crimes. The US was very vocal about the mistreatment of American prisoners of war, who were, according to the US, subject to 'humiliating and insulting circumstances designed to make them objects of public curiosity' contrary to Article 14 of the Third Geneva Convention. Amnesty International agreed that questioning US prisoners on Iraqi TV was wrong, but pointed out that the Americans were violating the very same proscriptions, not only with respect to Iraqi prisoners, but also the steady stream of prisoners it had sent and was continuing to send to Guantánamo Bay, which it had unilaterally declared a Geneva-Conventions-free zone.[19]

The Department of Defense also complained about Iraq's alleged 'perfidy' in using fake surrenders and dressing soldiers as civilians, to draw the invaders into ambush.[20] When a suicide bomber disguised as a taxi-driver blew himself up along with four American soldiers at a checkpoint, Human Rights Watch condemned it as 'perfidy,' distinguishable from permissible 'ruses of war' and even 'suicidal attacks by undisguised military forces' because 'they do not depend on taking advantage of an enemy's willingness to abide by the law protecting non-combatants.'[21] Then an American tank opened fire at a car loaded with people at a checkpoint near Karbala and killed ten civilians, five of them children. There were conflicting accounts of whether there had been adequate warning, but the army spokesman Brig. Gen. Vince Brooks was quick to point to cases of 'perfidy' as the context.

> General Brooks suggested that other checkpoints had been rushed by several Iraqi vehicles at a time; sometimes a car carrying civilians would precede others full of armed combatants. He would not say whether that had been the case on Monday.[22]

At his press conference, General Brooks invoked the soldiers' 'inherent right to self-defense' and said, 'While we regret the loss of any civilian lives, at this point they remain unavoidable, as they have been throughout history.'[23] Amnesty International was also critical of these 'perfidious' practices for the way they endangered civilians, but they also condemned the invading forces for the use of inherently indiscriminate cluster bombs and the bombing of a TV station. Amnesty also questioned whether the required precautions were being taken to protect civilians, and called for investigations into civilian deaths like those at the Karbala checkpoint and the shooting of demonstrators in Falluja.[24]

But never once did Amnesty International, let alone Human Rights Watch, mention the fundamental reason why none of the these incidents really had to be investigated at all – namely that all of this death and destruction was legally, as well as morally, on the heads of the invaders, whatever precautions they claimed to take, because it was due to an illegal, aggressive war. Every death was a crime for which the leaders of the invading coalition were personally, criminally responsible. When General Brooks said the soldiers at the Karbala checkpoint were exercising their 'inherent right to self-defense' he was talking nonsense: an aggressor has no right to self-defense. If you break into someone's house and hold them at gunpoint and they try to kill you but you kill them first, they're guilty of nothing and you're guilty of murder.[25] General Brooks got one thing right: civilian deaths *'remain unavoidable, as they have been throughout history.'* Which means that the people who started this war knew that precisely this kind of thing would happen. And that's why they're guilty of murder (see Chapter 2). The *best* they can say for themselves is that the thousands of dead were the *absolute minimum* that anyone could expect from the war they started.

Despite all this, and despite the evidence of major coalition criminality against civilians reported by independent journalists such as Robert Fisk[26] and John Pilger,[27] when the time came for talking about prosecution, the only subjects were Saddam Hussein and his associates. In fact, because the Iraqi war crimes of 2003 were, after all, rather minor in the context, attention was turned to digging up the graves of all Saddam's crimes from the time of the first Gulf War. There would definitely be trials, it was just a question of where: in The Hague (with Slobodan Milosevic), in the US, or in American-run Iraq.[28] For reasons explored in Chapter 7, it was the last option that had been settled upon by the time of the capture of Saddam in December 2003. But the trials had been announced much earlier by the Bush administration – a few days prior to the war, in fact – and the point of the announcement was obviously not to commit America to trying Saddam – they were trying to *kill* him at that point – but to justify the illegal war.[29] Likewise for the war criminal provisions in the post-war Security Council Resolutions, and indeed all the earnest pondering after Saddam's capture. No mention in any of this, of course, of the enormous complicity of the supreme criminals in these very crimes, and no question of their prosecution for the supreme crime they had just committed, not even for any of the lesser crimes. The Americans were boycotting the International Criminal Court, and when the famous Belgian 'universal jurisdiction' law was invoked by some Iraqis against General Tommy Franks for indiscriminate and even deliberate attacks on civilians, it turned out the law had just been changed so that the charges would now be sent for 'investigation' to … the United States.[30]

So here is the problem with international criminal law: it lets the Americans get away, not only with murder, but with the supreme international crime, and it punishes only the individual evils of the Americans' enemies – even though these are but the inevitable result of this supreme crime that 'contains within itself the accumulated evil of the whole.' It does this so regularly that it cannot be regarded as some minor kink that has to be worked out of the system. Despite international criminal law's banner commitment to 'ending impunity,' its operating principle is really one of *'selective* impunity.'

The question is, what is this war crimes business about that always winds up punishing only the 'usual suspects'? In an attempt to answer it, the rest of Part I explores the criminality of the Iraq war and the two illegal wars that preceded it, as well as the concepts of collateral damage, self-defense and humanitarian intervention. Part II examines the various species of international criminal law in action, especially the International Criminal Tribunal for the Former Yugoslavia, but also the new International Criminal Court and other types of 'universal jurisdiction.'

THE LAW AND THE WAR AGAINST IRAQ

The war against Iraq was denounced as illegal by a great many experts on international law throughout the world. They vastly outnumbered those few, mainly the protagonist governments and their hired guns, who defended its legality. You can pursue the details of these arguments from the sources themselves.[31] It should be enough here to briefly outline the main points.

International law prohibits the use of military force by one state against another, except on one of two conditions: either it is pursuant to a valid authorization by the Security Council of the United Nations, or it is in the exercise of the narrowly defined 'inherent right of self-defense.' The first condition dates from the Charter of the United Nations of 1946, a treaty binding on all its members and the supreme document of international law. The second pre-dates the Charter but is preserved and limited by it. To these two accepted cases, it has been advocated (without much success) that there be added a third, namely 'humanitarian intervention.' The Americans tried to justify their war against Iraq by reference to all three criteria. Self-defense and humanitarian intervention are discussed in detail in Chapters 2 and 3 respectively, so they will be touched upon only briefly here. What needs some attention is the question of Security Council authorization.

Security Council authorization

The Charter of the United Nations is essentially an anti-war document. Its very first words condemn war as a 'scourge':

We the Peoples of the United Nations
Determined to save succeeding generations from the scourge of war, which twice in our lifetime has brought untold sorrow to mankind ...

The principles by which the Charter seeks to save us from war include these:

Article 2

3. All Members shall settle their international disputes by peaceful means in such a manner that international peace and security, and justice, are not endangered.

4. All Members shall refrain in their international relations from the threat or use of force against the territorial integrity or political independence of any state, or in any other manner inconsistent with the Purposes of the United Nations.

The Charter does not ban the use of force completely, but it creates a powerful presumption against it by concentrating the authority for its legitimate use in the Security Council. Even the right to self-defense is only temporary under the Charter, until the Security Council can intervene (see Chapter 2). The idea of concentrating this authority in the Security Council is to fulfill a fundamental objective of the Charter, namely 'to ensure by the acceptance of principles and the institution of methods, *that armed force shall not be used, save in the common interest ...*'[32] The Security Council's quasi-monopoly over the legitimate use of force aims to ensure that it is used in the 'common interest' by the Council's *representative* nature. It is made up of 15 member states, ten of which are elected for two-year terms by a 2/3 vote of the General Assembly of all the 191 members of the United Nations, which represents virtually the entire population of the world. In March 2003, the elected members were Angola, Chile, Germany, Pakistan, Spain, Bulgaria, Cameroon, Guinea, Mexico, and Syria. In addition to these ten, of course, there are the five Permanent Members (the United States, Russia, China, France and the United Kingdom), each with a veto on any decision of the Council. While Resolutions of the Security Council can pass with nine affirmative votes, even 14 cannot act over the objection of one of the Permanent Members. This means that the Permanent Members cannot act without complete support from each other and substantial support from members elected by all the other members of the United Nations; but any one of the Permanent Members can defeat any action of the Security Council. The system is clearly less than perfectly democratic, but it doesn't take much reflection to see that it's better at ensuring force is used only in the 'common interest' than is the Americans acting alone, or even with their self-appointed 'Coalition of the Willing.'

Article 24 of the Charter gives the Security Council 'primary responsibility for the maintenance of international peace and security,' and all Members 'agree that in carrying out its duties under this responsibility the Security Council acts on their behalf.' But even the Security Council has limits on its power. The second paragraph of Article 24 provides that, '[i]n discharging these duties the Security Council shall act in accordance with the Purposes and Principles of the United Nations' and within 'specific powers ... laid down in Chapters VI, VII, VIII, and XII.' What are these 'specific powers'? Chapter VI provides for the 'pacific settlement of disputes.' It requires that the parties to any dispute 'shall, first of all, seek a solution by negotiation, enquiry, mediation, conciliation, arbitration, judicial settlement, resort to regional agencies or arrangements, or other peaceful means of their own choice' (Article 33). If they fail to settle the dispute on their own, Article 37 lays down the absolute requirement that 'they shall refer it to the Security Council.' Chapter VII – 'Action with respect to threats to the peace, breaches of the peace and acts of aggression' – is the part that provides the Security Council with authority to use coercive measures including armed force, but only as 'may be necessary to maintain or restore international peace and security.' It also has the power to 'make recommendations' (Article 39), or to employ 'measures not involving the use of armed force,' which 'may include complete or partial interruption of economic relations and of rail, sea, air, postal, telegraphic, radio, and other means of communication, and the severance of diplomatic relations.' Article 42 provides, finally, for the use of armed force:

> Should the Security Council consider that measures provided for in Article 41 would be inadequate or have proved to be inadequate, it may take such action by air, sea, or land forces as may be necessary to maintain or restore international peace and security. Such action may include demonstrations, blockade, and other operations by air, sea, or land forces of Members of the United Nations.

The American mass media tried its best in early 2003 to portray the Security Council as some dubious, meddling, alien body imposing itself on the United States; but it can be seen from this that nothing is further from the truth. This is not the International Criminal Court that the US has never accepted. The Security Council has been made the supreme international authority over war and peace by a solemn treaty, drafted, signed and still voluntarily adhered to by the United States, along with each of the 191 Member States of the United Nations. It is binding on all members as a condition of their membership: 'All Members, in order to ensure to all of them the rights and benefits resulting from membership, shall fulfill in good faith the obligations assumed by them in accordance with the present Charter.'[33]

Hence the importance of demonstrating that the Security Council has authorized any given use of force. In his pre-war speeches of 6 March and 17 March 2003, President Bush made the issue of 'weapons of mass destruction' the central theme. But, according to Bush, possession of them by Iraq not only posed a threat to the United States, it also put Iraq in defiance of Security Council Resolutions, and these authorized the United States to go to war:

> Under Resolutions 678 and 687, both still in effect, the United States and our allies are authorized to use force in ridding Iraq of weapons of mass destruction. This is not a question of authority, it is a question of will. Last September, I went to the U.N. General Assembly and urged the nations of the world to unite and bring an end to this danger. On 8th November, the Security Council unanimously passed Resolution 1441, finding Iraq in material breach of its obligations and vowing serious consequences if Iraq did not fully and immediately disarm. Today, no nation can possibly claim that Iraq has disarmed. And it will not disarm so long as Saddam Hussein holds power.[34]

Now, in fact, none of these Resolutions, taken singly or combined, can be made to read as authorizing military action by the United States – not on its own or with any number of allies, not in any imaginable circumstances in 2003 or at any time after 1991. You just have to read them to see for yourself.

Resolution 678 of 29 November 1990 explicitly, if euphemistically, authorized the unilateral use of force, but it did so only for very specific purposes, none of which had any relevance to the war of 2003. Resolution 678 was the one that authorized the first Gulf War. It was a brief Resolution, following eleven previous ones dealing with the crisis that started with Iraq's invasion of Kuwait on 2 August 1990. It said that the Security Council

> 1. *Demands* that Iraq comply fully with Resolution 660 (1990) and all subsequent relevant Resolutions, and decides while maintaining all its decisions, to allow Iraq one final opportunity, as a pause of goodwill, to do so;
> 2. *Authorizes* Member States co-operating with the government of Kuwait, unless Iraq on or before 15 January 1991 fully implements, as set forth in paragraph 1 above, the above-mentioned Resolutions, to use all necessary means to uphold and implement Resolution 660 (1990) and all subsequent relevant Resolutions and to restore international peace and security in the area ...

Resolution 660, the one that the 'necessary means' were supposed to enforce, was relatively short and had essentially two operative paragraphs. They said that the Security Council

1. *Condemns* the Iraqi invasion of Kuwait;

2. *Demands* that Iraq withdraw immediately and unconditionally all its forces to the positions in which they were located on 1 August 1990 ...

Resolution 678 said that all necessary means could also be used to enforce 'all subsequent relevant Resolutions,' but this could only help the United States in 2003 if it meant all *future* Resolutions (a rather reckless blank check, it might be thought, for the Council to write). In fact, the phrase specifically refers to the ten listed Resolutions passed between 2 August and 28 November 1990, specified in the preamble to 678 as 'the above-mentioned subsequent relevant Resolutions.' All of these Resolutions had only one object: ending the invasion of Kuwait and all the behavior associated with it. Even the 'restoration of peace and security in the area' was specifically restricted by the preamble: 'Determining that there exists a breach of international peace and security *as regards the Iraqi invasion of Kuwait.*'[35] It did not authorize any state to militarily and unilaterally enforce peace in the Middle East (which might be bad news for Israel).

The main thing to notice about Resolution 678 is that it specifically authorized both 'all necessary means' and their unilateral deployment by individual member states (such as the US). Many protested in 1990–1 that war was not necessary in the circumstances, meaning either that the use of force was invalid under the Resolution, or the Resolution itself was invalid as a breach of the Council's duty under the Charter to exhaust peaceful means. But nobody could doubt, and nobody has doubted, that 'all necessary means' *could* include military force. The next thing to notice about Resolution 678 is that the authorization was expressly for a specific purpose: to eject Iraq from Kuwait. And since Iraq had definitively quit Kuwait (and was declared 'liberated' by President Bush Sr.) on 27 February 1991, the Resolution obviously had not the slightest relevance to justifying the war of 2003.

The third thing to notice is that neither Resolution 678 nor any of the prior eleven said a word about 'weapons of mass destruction.' That was up to Resolution 687 of 3 April 1991, the second Resolution mentioned by President Bush in March 2003. Resolution 687 indeed imposed major disarmament obligations on Iraq, but it did not even *suggest* that any member state could enforce them through the use of force. Not 'all necessary means,' not any means whatsoever. Quite the contrary, it said that a ceasefire would go into effect as soon as Iraq *notified* the UN of its acceptance of the terms of the Resolution. Paragraph 33 declared that '*upon official notification by Iraq to the Secretary-General and to the Security Council of its acceptance of the above provisions*, a formal ceasefire is effective between Iraq and Kuwait and the Member States cooperating with Kuwait in accordance with Resolution 678 (1990).'[36] Iraq promptly gave this official notification, by letter of 6 April 1991 from its Permanent Representative at the UN to the President of the Security Council and the Secretary-General of the United Nations. The letter detailed Iraq's (rather well-founded) objections to the Resolution, but it ended with an unequivocal: 'Iraq ... has no choice but to accept this Resolution.'[37] The ceasefire then went into effect. By paragraph 34 of the same Resolution, the Security Council decided 'to remain seized of the matter and to take such further steps as may be required for the implementation of the present Resolution and to secure peace and security in the region.' Whence the inspections regime and the many other measures of the Resolutions that followed, all of them lacking any hint that any member state could use military force in the event that Iraq did not comply.

So neither 678 nor 687 could possibly be read to authorize the use of force in 2003 by the US and the UK. That leaves 1441, of 8 November 2002. Resolution 1441 made a lot of demands on Iraq, many completely unreasonable, given that the US and its client state Israel vastly out-gun Iraq in weapons of mass destruction, however defined, and that Israel has vastly out-defied Iraq in the matter of Security Council Resolutions. But Resolution 1441 did not say or even imply that any state or group of states could attack the country for failing to comply with any of those demands.

Resolution 1441 said that the Security Council 'Decides that Iraq has been and remains in material breach of its obligations under relevant Resolutions, including Resolution 687 (1991),' and that it 'Decides ... to afford Iraq, by this Resolution, a final opportunity to comply with its disarmament obligations under relevant Resolutions of the Council; and accordingly decides to set up an enhanced inspection regime ...' It also said that non-compliance 'will be reported to the Council for assessment' and directed the Security Council 'to convene immediately' on receipt of the weapons inspectors' report 'in order to consider the situation and the need for full compliance with all of the relevant Council Resolutions.' Resolution 1441 further 'Recalls, in that context, that the Council has repeatedly warned Iraq it will face serious consequences as a result of its continued violations of its obligations.' (The Resolution did not actually *warn* of those consequences itself, as President Bush and the press repeatedly misinformed the public.) All these words were carefully chosen after alternative versions were picked over between 2 October 2002, when the Americans submitted their first draft, and 8 November, when the final very different draft was passed. Their meaning is all too plain: the Security Council was serious about Iraqi compliance with its disarmament requirements, but it was the responsibility of the *Security Council* to decide whether and to what extent there had been compliance, and what to do about it. That means the Security Council *as an institution*, all 15 members voting according to the rules written into the Charter of the United Nations, which require a majority of nine for any action, with no vetoes from any of the five Permanent Members.

What Resolution 1441 lacked, in other words, was any hint of authorization of unilateral military action, much less the explicit 'authorizes member states to use all necessary means' found in 678. This was no slip. These very words were in the draft submitted by the US to the members of the Council on 2 October 2002:

> 10. Decides that false statements or omissions in the declaration submitted by Iraq to the Council and failure by Iraq at any time to comply and cooperate fully in accordance with the provisions laid out in this Resolution, shall constitute a further material breach of Iraq's obligations, and that such breach *authorizes member states to use all necessary means* to restore international peace and security in the area.[38]

But this draft was rejected, and the final, italicized words were nowhere to be found in 1441.[39] The Americans came back on 25 October with a formulation that omitted the objectionable words and concluded with 'shall constitute a further material breach of Iraq's obligations.'[40] Even that was rejected by the other members of the Council, who insisted that the words 'and will be reported to the Council for assessment' be added, making it clear that the Council itself would decide the consequences of any 'material breach.'

There was an attempt to make something out of the words 'material breach' as they appear in an earlier part of 1441: '[The Security Council] *Decides* that Iraq has been and remains in material breach of its obligations under relevant Resolutions, including Resolution 687 (1991).' Since 687 was the ceasefire Resolution, some lawyers argued that the declaration in 1441 that Iraq was in 'material breach' had the effect of releasing the United States from its ceasefire obligations under 687, as if it were a treaty. One big problem with this theory is that for a material breach to suspend a *multilateral* treaty, 'unanimous agreement' by all the parties is required. The ceasefire of 1991 was not just between Iraq and America but between Iraq and *all* the forces aiding Kuwait, a coalition of 34 countries, among them many vocal opponents of the 2003 war, such as France, Germany, Saudi Arabia and Syria. Nobody heard any of them saying that they wanted to rescind the ceasefire.[41]

An even bigger problem with this theory is that it depends on an obviously willful misreading of Resolutions 1441 and 687. Resolution 1441 doesn't say that Iraq has been in material breach of the *ceasefire conditions* of 687, but rather its *disarmament obligations* under 687. The ceasefire conditions were quite distinct from the disarmament obligations themselves. They consisted only of the *notification of Iraq's acceptance* of the disarmament obligations. Ongoing compliance with the actual obligations was not made a condition of the ceasefire. This may sound like a quibble, but it is actually very important. The American argument depends on reading 687 to mean that a resumption of hostilities was to remain perpetually at the discretion of any party to the ceasefire, if they didn't think that Iraq was living up to its disarmament obligations. But 687 says the ceasefire will go into effect the moment Iraq says it agrees to the terms, and leaves it to the Security Council as a body to police those terms. The 'material breach' theory wants us to assume that the Security Council used the wrong language to describe what it really wanted, namely to give any party the unilateral right to re-start the war at any time, thus renouncing Council control over the question of war and peace. But the Security Council acts through Resolutions and we have the authority of no less a figure than George W. Bush himself for the importance of giving their words 'merit and weight':

> This is not only an important moment for the security of our nation; I believe it's an important moment for the Security Council itself.... And the fundamental question facing the Security Council is, will its words mean anything? When the Security Council speaks, will – will the words have merit and weight?[42]

Well said, Mr. President, but to give the Security Council's words 'merit and weight' means concluding that 678, 687 and 1441 could not possibly be read as authorizing America's war.

In fact, even the last, ill-fated Resolution introduced by the US, UK and Spain in February 2003 could not be read as authorizing force, since it merely referred back to 1441 and declared, rather melodramatically, that 'Iraq has failed to take the final opportunity afforded to it in Resolution 1441 (2002).'[43] But everybody knew what the Americans were going to try to do with these words if the Resolution passed, and since the inspectors were calling for more time to carry out the job the Council had given them, France and Russia declared they would veto the Resolution if it came to a vote. The sponsors then desperately tried to get a majority of the Council to agree, pretending the veto was unimportant. This, even though America exercises the veto more than all the other Security Council members put together: 76 out of a total of 138 vetoes since 1966.[44] Without the American veto, Israel would have been sanctioned long ago for violating dozens of Security Council Resolutions over its 36 years of occupation of the Palestinian territories. Without the American veto, Boutros Boutros-

Ghali would not have been replaced by the more US-friendly Kofi Annan as Secretary General.[45] But not only did a *majority* in the Security Council elude the Americans on this Resolution; when they finally backed out of the 'card-showing' contest, the three sponsors had only been able to add Bulgaria to their list, for a grand total of *four votes* out of 15, and only two out of five veto-bearing permanent members.[46]

The Americans are well known to international lawyers for trying 'to distort the words of Resolutions ... in order to claim to be acting on behalf of the international community.'[47] Even before the war of 2003, they and the UK had been bombing Iraq, and killing Iraqis, for a decade to enforce self-declared 'no-fly' zones in Iraqi territory under the supposed authority of Resolution 688 of 5 April 1991. But all that Resolution did was innocently 'appeal' to 'all Member States and to all humanitarian organizations to contribute to ... humanitarian relief efforts' being undertaken by the Secretary General. The American and British forces expanded this to the right to bomb any facilities capable of threatening their military flights over Iraqi territory. It was widely acknowledged that those attacks had no basis in the Resolution, and the Bush administration strikes of early 2001 were protested by European NATO members.[48] All humanitarian pretext for this was dropped in the lead-up to the 2003 war when, as the inspections were being carried out, the bombing was clearly designed to 'soften up' Iraqi defenses for the impending war, well before even the United States had declared that its 'diplomatic efforts' had been exhausted.[49] The Americans engaged in the same Resolution twisting in Afghanistan in 2001 (see Chapter 2) and, before that, in Kosovo in 1999 (see Chapter 3). In 1998, after obtaining a Resolution on Iraq that clearly stopped short of authorizing the unilateral use of force to back up weapons inspections, they simply said, 'We think it does' and bombed away.[50] But where the law is concerned, it doesn't matter what they 'think,' it's what the Resolution actually *says* that matters.

Everything turns on the elemental difference between means and ends. The Charter gives the Security Council a number of options short of military force to get its Resolutions put into effect. In its Resolutions the Council (always with the vote of the veto-wielding Americans) very carefully delineates not only the ends but also the means. Then the Americans come in and argue that, whatever the means chosen by the Security Council, the US is free to use military force. They even write it into their domestic law, though they themselves take care to be very specific about means: 'The President is authorized to use the Armed Forces of the United States as he determines to be necessary and appropriate in order to ... enforce all relevant United Nations Security Council Resolutions regarding Iraq.'[51]

And they do this pretending concern for the 'credibility' of the Security Council.[52] Of course, if this were indeed the law, any other country would have the same entitlement as the US to use military power, but, naturally, only to the extent they had it. Presumably, that's why the Americans like this theory so much more than everybody else does. The new American doctrine of self-defense holds similar attractions.

Self-defense

In the absence of authorization from the Security Council, the United States had to try and squeeze its war into the 'inherent right of self-defense,' a right that, under Article 51 of the UN Charter, allows the use of military force without Security Council approval. Bush put it simply in his press conference of 6 March:

> Secondly, I'm confident the American people understand that when it comes to our security, if we need to act, we will act, and we really don't need United Nations approval to do so. ... when it comes to our security, we really don't need anybody's permission.[53]

The right of self-defense was central to the American justification for war in Afghanistan and is discussed in detail in Chapter 2. The problem with its use in the war against Iraq is that the notion of self-defense in international law, similar to the ordinary criminal law of any country, depends on there being an 'armed attack,' either actual or demonstrably imminent, so that there is no alternative but to respond with force. Furthermore, the United Nations Charter, while preserving the right of self-defense, limits it to cases where the Security Council has not yet intervened and taken measures to restore international peace and security, the idea being that international disputes are to be settled peacefully if possible, and that it is up to the Security Council to seek those peaceful alternatives. The reasons for these limits are moral: self-defense can justify the taking of life only where demonstrably necessary to save life. If there is a non-violent alternative, it must be taken. Hence the role of the Security Council. The law only allows self-help where there is no time to seek a collective peaceful solution.

Now the Americans knew that the accepted doctrine of self-defense under international law posed a problem for them if they wanted to invade Iraq, so as part of their war preparations they elaborated a new doctrine, which they called 'anticipatory' and 'pre-emptive,' but which Noam Chomksy has correctly pointed out is really *preventive*.[54] This was first publicly elaborated in a speech given by President Bush in June 2002 to the West Point Military

Academy graduating class. In that speech, Bush claimed the right to respond militarily to threats before they 'fully materialize':

> If we wait for threats to fully materialize we will have waited too long ... And our security will require all Americans to be forward looking and resolute, to be ready for preemptive action when necessary to defend our liberty and to defend our lives.[55]

In other words, not attacks, not even mere *threats* of attacks, but threats that haven't even fully materialized: *potential* threats. In September 2002, when Bush started to beat the war drums in earnest, the doctrine was elaborated in the so-called 'National Security Strategy of the United States':

> Our enemies have openly declared that they are seeking weapons of mass destruction, and evidence indicates that they are doing so with determination ... And, as a matter of common sense and self-defense, America will act against such emerging threats before they are fully formed. The United States has long maintained the option of preemptive actions to counter a sufficient threat to our national security. The greater the threat, the greater is the risk of inaction – and the more compelling the case for taking anticipatory action to defend ourselves, even if uncertainty remains as to the time and place of the enemy's attack.[56]

In his war speech of 17 March, Bush said:

> The danger is clear: Using chemical, biological or, one day, nuclear weapons obtained with the help of Iraq, the terrorists could fulfill their stated ambitions and kill thousands or hundreds of thousands of innocent people in our country or any other.... In one year, or five years, the power of Iraq to inflict harm on all free nations would be multiplied many times over. With these capabilities, Saddam Hussein and his terrorist allies could choose the moment of deadly conflict when they are strongest. We choose to meet that threat now where it arises, before it can appear suddenly in our skies and cities. The cause of peace requires all free nations to recognize new and undeniable realities.... Terrorists and terrorist states do not reveal these threats with fair notice in formal declarations. And responding to such enemies only after they have struck first is not self-defense. It is suicide.[57]

Not only did Bush provide no evidence that there was any action underway by Iraq to attack the United States or help others do so, or any plan to do so, he never even *claimed* this was the case. He claimed only that the fact that Iraq had such weapons made it a potential threat: 'one day, with the *help* of Iraq, the terrorists *could* fulfill' – 'in one year, or five years' – 'these *capabilities'* – '*could* choose.' Of course evidence for the existence of the weapons was non-existent as well; the inspectors and the US army turned up *nothing*. But even that was beside the point because international law has never accepted and could never accept the legally and morally nonsensical doctrine Bush elaborated.

There are two decisive reasons for this. Above all, the doctrine would justify the deliberate infliction of death and destruction on a massive scale where *no evidence* had been produced to show that this was necessary to prevent any broadly equivalent tragedy from befalling the people doing the inflicting. That would mean treating the lives of the people of the country attacked as less worthy of protection than the lives of the people of the attacking country, because it would displace all the risks onto them: to counter an unsubstantiated risk to the people of the attacking country (here the US), the people of the attacked country would be sentenced to death and destruction. You can imagine that international law cannot proceed on that assumption, even when the lives subject to the unsubstantiated risk are so precious as American lives. Secondly, the Bush doctrine is a disguise for the doctrine of Might Makes Right so thin that a child could see through it, because it would also theoretically give every country the right to attack the US, but no means to do so. The US has threatened the world with weapons of mass destruction for about 60 years now, since it dropped the atomic bombs on the civilians of Hiroshima and Nagasaki. It has the world's largest cache of weapons of mass destruction, however you care to define them. In the wildest delusionary fantasies of the American administration, the capabilities of Iraq to threaten anybody were infinitesimal compared to the threats the US brandishes every day. There is no law or morality without 'universalizability,' which means the US would have to recognize the right of any country to act preventively against the US itself, and you won't find that in any of President Bush's speeches. So self-defense was not available here.

Humanitarian intervention

Though 'Iraqi Freedom' gave the 'Operation' its name, the object of freeing Iraqis came a distant third in the arguments of President Bush for the invasion. In his penultimate war speech of 6 March, Bush said 'The world needs him to answer a single question: Has the Iraqi regime fully and unconditionally disarmed, as required by Resolution 1441, or has it not?'[58] Bush did *not* say, 'Has the Iraqi regime stopped oppressing its people?' On the other hand he pledged, in the event of war, to protect innocent lives, bring food and medicine and, finally, to 'help that nation to build a just government after decades of brutal dictatorship. The form and leadership of that government is for the Iraqi people to choose. Anything they choose will be better than the misery and torture and murder they have known under Saddam Hussein ... We will be changing the regime of Iraq for the good of the Iraqi people.' In his 17 March speech Bush promised Iraqis:

> We will tear down the apparatus of terror and we will help you to build a new Iraq that is prosperous and free. In free Iraq there will be no more wars of aggression against your neighbors, no more poison factories, no more executions of dissidents, no more torture chambers and rape rooms. The tyrant will soon be gone. The day of your liberation is near.[59]

Despite its low ranking in pre-invasion justifications for war, after the occupation turned up no evidence of weapons of mass destruction the 'liberation' of Iraq became the main *ex post facto* argument for war. When mass graves dating from the first Gulf War started to be uncovered, Thomas Friedman wrote in the *New York Times*:

> As far as I'm concerned, we do not need to find any weapons of mass destruction to justify this war. That skull, and the thousands more that will be unearthed, are enough for me. Mr. Bush doesn't owe the world any explanation for missing chemical weapons (even if it turns out that the White House hyped this issue). It is clear that in ending Saddam's tyranny, a huge human engine for mass destruction has been broken. The thing about Saddam's reign is that when you look at that skull, you don't even know what period it came from – his suppression of the Kurds or the Shiites, his insane wars with Iran and Kuwait, or just his daily brutality.[60]

When Tony Blair, under attack at home for misleading the British public on the weapons question, journeyed to Washington to be honored by the US Congress, his fallback was the same:

> Can we be sure that terrorism and weapons of mass destruction will join together? Let us say one thing: If we are wrong, we will have destroyed a threat that, at its least, is responsible for inhuman carnage and suffering. That is something I am confident history will forgive.[61]

'Humanitarian intervention' by military force was an important theme in the 1999 Kosovo war, and its legal status is discussed in detail in Chapter 3. To briefly anticipate that discussion, the main reason a claim of humanitarian intervention could never succeed in the Iraq war is that, as usual, what the Americans were claiming was a *unilateral* right of humanitarian intervention, whereas, if the right exists at all in international law, it exists only as a *collective* right; that is, one that can only be authorized by the Security Council, and, as we've just seen, the Security Council did not authorize this war. The obvious reason for restricting military intervention for humanitarian reasons to cases authorized by the Security Council is to give some assurance that it is not being abused to disguise aggressive war, which is exactly the use the Nazis made of it to justify the invasion of Poland that launched World War II. The drafters of the UN Charter had this and many other examples before their eyes when they gave the Security Council the exclusive responsibility for authorizing non-defensive wars.

There are indeed some proponents of a unilateral right to military intervention for humanitarian reasons, but, as the discussion in Chapter 3 will show, they are few and on virtually non-existent legal ground. And even these proponents lay down conditions that the Americans could never have hoped to meet in the case of Iraq. First there is the question of motivation. The US made it very clear that it would never have invaded Iraq purely to defend the human rights of its people. This was stated explicitly in the speeches of George W. Bush, and most succinctly by Secretary of Defense Donald Rumsfeld during his Iraq victory tour: 'Our coalition came to Iraq for a purpose – to remove a regime that oppressed your people and threatened ours.'[62] In other words, Saddam Hussein could have gone on oppressing his own people forever as far as the Americans were concerned, as long as he was not regarded as a threat to the American people, or, more frankly, their interests. Now, according to the advocates of unilateral humanitarian intervention, mixed motives are acceptable, as long as the non-humanitarian ones don't interfere with the humanitarian ones: 'collateral non-humanitarian motives ... should be such as to not impair or reduce the first paramount human rights objective of the intervention.'[63] But there is plenty to show that the non-humanitarian motives for this war overwhelmed any incidental humanitarian ones. In the first place, the US and the UK seem to have made no plans whatever to actually care for the needs of the Iraqis once they had conquered the country. Though they made sure everything having to do with the oil industry and the secrets of the regime was secure, they evidently couldn't have cared less about the plundering of infrastructure and heritage that occurred 'under their noses.' Robert Fisk reported the following from Baghdad:

> After days of arson and pillage, here's a short but revealing scorecard. US troops have sat back and allowed mobs to wreck and then burn the Ministry of Planning, the Ministry of Education, the Ministry of Irrigation, the Ministry of Trade, the Ministry of Industry, the Ministry of Foreign Affairs, the Ministry of Culture and the Ministry of Information. They

did nothing to prevent looters from destroying priceless treasures of Iraq's history in the Baghdad Archaeological Museum and in the museum in the northern city of Mosul, or from looting three hospitals. The Americans have, though, put hundreds of troops inside two Iraqi ministries that remain untouched and untouchable because tanks and armoured personnel carriers and Humvees have been placed inside and outside both institutions. And which ministries proved to be so important for the Americans? Why, the Ministry of Interior, of course – with its vast wealth of intelligence information on Iraq – and the Ministry of Oil.[64]

One month after the war was declared won, the press was echoing human rights groups and reporting a 'descent into lawlessness' and 'chaos,' and the 'plundering of government property, often under the eyes of American soldiers ... most government ministries have been gutted.'[65] According to the advocates of unilateral military humanitarian intervention, 'the final test will be whether human rights have been effectively restored as a result of the intervention.'[66] But as the occupation wore on, it seemed that human rights had actually been *worsened* by the invasion, even taking into account the end of the Saddam Hussein regime. In the war's immediate aftermath, UNICEF reported that child malnutrition in Baghdad had almost doubled since before the war.[67] Iraqi doctors were reporting an increase in infant mortality from the lack of clean drinking water, due to the unrestored electricity.[68] In one ghastly event, a nuclear power facility was looted for barrels by thirsty villagers who dumped their radioactive waste and used them to carry drinking water.[69] In September, the Iraqi Governing Council said it would be two years before electricity was back to pre-occupation levels *if* someone came up with 8 billion dollars.[70] And even that did not take into account the sabotage that was still blacking out the country in November. And electricity,' as one Baghdad merchant pointed out, 'means safety. It's the chain of life.'[71] In Baghdad the murder rate appeared to have increased to *ten times* its pre-war level – even before the car bombings started.[72] A Gallup poll of September 2003 reported that 94 per cent of Baghdadis still considered the city 'a more dangerous place than before the invasion.'[73]

Another reason the Iraq war would fail as a humanitarian intervention is because of the premium naturally placed by the theory (tendentious as it is) on the right of self-government ('Did the intervenor seek to dominate the target state in some way unrelated to humanitarian concerns?'[74]). President Bush had promised that 'the form and leadership of [their] government is for the Iraqi people to choose. Anything they choose will be better than the misery and torture and murder they have known under Saddam Hussein.' But that promise was quickly broken. As soon as the extent of opposition to the occupation became clear, plans for elections of an interim government were replaced by 'consultations' for an appointed 'Governing Council,' ultimately 'chosen' by the 'staff' of American 'civil administrator' L. Paul Bremer III, also referred to in the press as 'viceroy,' who would have veto powers over any significant decisions.[75] In calling a halt to even local elections, Bremer declared that he was 'not opposed to [self-rule] ... I want to do it in a way that takes care of our concerns.'[76] The question of how long the coalition would stay in Iraq depended only 'in part on how quickly the Iraqi people can write and approve a constitution.'[77] When the Governing Council quickly proved to be a farce that, most importantly, failed to give any legitimacy to the occupation, the Americans decided to dump it and demote the constitution-writing process to an 'interim' one. Instead, there would be an Afghanistan-style assembly in June 2004, which would 'elect' a provisional government, but there would be no actual elections, and the Americans would have an effective veto, via the Governing Council, over the choice of delegates to the assembly. The plan, immediately denounced by the Shiites, was explicitly part of a *longer*, not shorter, exit strategy and any new government was expected to 'invite' the US troops to stay.[78]

Also relevant in judging this war as a humanitarian intervention was American *complicity* in the oppressiveness of the Iraqi regime.[79] Complicity argues against a right to humanitarian intervention on a number of grounds. It speaks to the sincerity of the motives, and above all it speaks to the crucial question of the necessity of the intervention. If the Americans were a big part of the problem, then non-military means of improving the lives of Iraqis were in their own hands. Thus, the relevance of all the reminders during the build-up to the war of how much the US had to do with what Iraq had become, starting with its support for the disastrous Iran–Iraq war of 1980–8. America played both sides of that war to some extent, but mainly kept it going by being a very helpful ally to the regime of Saddam Hussein, providing crucial economic, military and diplomatic support. The costs to both sides were enormous; a median estimate is about 800,000 dead.[80] The atrocities that have since been laid at the feet of Saddam Hussein – the wartime gas attacks against Iran and the Anfal campaign against the Kurds – now fatuously used by presidents and journalists to justify the war of 2003, were committed when the US was Saddam's good friend and benefactor, with a younger Donald Rumsfeld as the US emissary.[81] In those days the American attitude was 'It was just another way of killing people – whether with a bullet or Phosgene, it didn't make any difference.'[82] The Iran–Iraq war was followed by the probably pretextual and certainly wildly excessive Gulf War.[83] A median estimate puts the Iraqi dead at 80,000 to 85,000, including about 3,000 civilians.[84] Civilian life support systems (water, energy, sewerage, agriculture, industry and transportation) were devastated. Then came the separatist uprising of Kurds and Shia, famously encouraged but not aided by the Americans, which led to brutal reprisals, the results of which were being unearthed in 2003 as justification for the latest war. This was followed by the pseudo-humanitarian bombing campaign of the US and the UK, with its regular toll of civilian death, lasting through three American presidencies.[85]

Above all, there were the sanctions. Unlike the bombing, the sanctions had the explicit authorization of the Security Council, having been put in place before the attack that expelled Iraq from Kuwait. But they were maintained for twelve years by the veto power of the United States and enforced by its military and economic muscle. Though they gave the appearance of being renewed periodically by consent of the whole Security Council, what were actually renewed were the time-limited *exceptions* that allowed Iraq to sell some of its oil for food and other humanitarian supplies. Without these renewals, the blanket sanctions imposed in 1990 would have sprung back into effect. It was the US alone that was responsible for the maintenance of the sanctions regime.[86] Already in 1991, then Secretary General Perez de Cuellar, in an often-quoted speech on 'humanitarian intervention,' was warning that the 'primary victims' of economic sanctions in developing countries 'are the most vulnerable sections of the affected population – women and children, the poor and the infirm.'[87] In Iraq it was the children who were hit hardest. In 1996 UNICEF reported that 4,500 children under the age of five were dying monthly in Iraq from malnutrition, polluted water and lack of medicine, all traceable to the destruction that occurred during the war and the sanctions that made it impossible to restore sanitary and health services.[88] The UNICEF report put pressure on the US to ease the sanctions somewhat to allow a limited 'oil for food' program in which Iraq was allowed to sell a small amount of its oil. But even with these limits eased, the devastation of the Iraqi economy by the sanctions was such that UNICEF reported a rate of infant mortality in 1999 that was still double what it had been before the war. The death rate for children under five had risen to 131 per 1,000, from 56 per 1,000 before the economic sanctions. Infants less than one year old were now dying at a rate of 108 per 1,000, up from 47 per 1,000.[89] By 2001, America's NATO allies were publicly stating their disgust at the sanctions.[90] Tariq Ali wrote of them in 2000: 'Clinton and Blair are personally responsible for deaths of hundreds of thousands of small children, callously slaughtered to save their joint "credibility" … Since without America and Britain, the blockade would have been lifted long ago, the role of other Western leaders, craven though it is, need not be reckoned.'[91] The US and the UK tried to blame the effect of the sanctions on the spending habits of the government – 'Saddam's palaces' – but even those who believed that the 'primary responsibility for this disaster is Saddam's' had to admit that 'the UN, an increasingly divided UN we should add, has become a secondary perpetuator of it.'[92] In this case 'divided' meant the US and the UK against the rest. And the simple fact is that, without these sanctions, those children would not be dead. The American-led embargo, wrote John Pilger in opposition to America's humanitarian war of 2003, was 'every bit as barbaric as the dictatorship over which Iraqis have no control.'[93]

The first act of the Iraqi Governing Council 'chosen by Bremer's staff' was to declare the American overthrow of the Saddam Hussein regime a national holiday.[94] Even those who opposed the occupation – the great majority of Iraqis by every indication – even some of those who opposed it violently, were happy to see Saddam gone; and if not Saddam, then at least the sanctions.[95] But, given American complicity in the brutality of this regime, to justify the invasion on this account would be like the guy who hit his head with a hammer because it felt so good when he stopped. If America really had the human rights of Iraqis at heart and did not merely want, as Pilger argued, 'a more compliant thug to run the world's second greatest source of oil,' it would have done things very differently. It would have worked through and not against the United Nations, and its first order of business would have been to lift the sanctions and end Iraq's isolation. It would have sought peaceful means to rebuild prosperity and human rights in Iraq on the basis of the country's enormous natural wealth and advanced level of development; this is called 'engagement' when there is no ulterior motive for going to war. It is difficult to imagine how military action could ever sincerely have been thought useful to the people of Iraq, given the horrifying costs and the 'quagmire' that had to be entailed by the sudden overthrow, by foreign armies, of a strong government firmly based in the country's traditional ruling group (Arab Sunnis, with about one quarter of the total population) – even if that government was hated by the rest of the country. 'No problem of political and social structure, in the Middle East or elsewhere, can be resolved by a war,' wrote Italian journalist Rossana Rossanda the day after the attack on Italian military headquarters that left 19 Italians and 13 Iraqis dead. 'To the contrary. It can only make matters worse.'[96] This simple proposition is so widely understood that the US would not have had a prayer making the case for war to even its own people, let alone the UN, if it had argued on exclusively humanitarian grounds *beforehand*. But a sincere 'humanitarian war,' if such a thing were even imaginable, would have been rather more painstakingly prepared, one imagines, with a view to ensuring that post-war Iraq was indeed a better place to live for the Iraqis who survived it. It would have to have been a *whole lot* better to justify these costs. Even the legal ideologists of humanitarian war say it should be permissible 'only in the face of ongoing or imminent genocide, or comparable mass slaughter or loss of life,' something nobody claimed was the case with Iraq.[97] In other words, a humanitarian war would not have squandered tens of thousands of lives to punish a regime for atrocities far in the past or as an exercise in wishful thinking for the future. Iraq is a good example of why the law does not accept unilateral humanitarian intervention under any circumstances, a matter explored fully in Chapter 3.

That America's war on Iraq was a flagrant violation of the Charter of the United Nations was implicitly corroborated by the pundits who thought it appropriate to conclude from it that the fundamental legal prohibitions in the Charter on making war were no longer valid: 'It is hard to avoid the conclusion that the Charter provisions governing use of force are simply no longer regarded as binding international law.'[98] But what would that leave of a treaty whose very first commitment is 'to save succeeding generations from the scourge of war'? So others have concluded that it is the United Nations Charter itself that is no longer valid, that it has gone the way of the Covenant of the League of Nations.[99] Pentagon guru Richard Perle drew this conclusion and 'thanked God' for it.[100]

This may all be a bit premature, of course, and even wishful thinking on the warmongers' part; but even if it were true, it would take nothing of significance away from the supreme criminality of this war or America's other aggressive wars. The Nuremberg judgment pre-existed the Charter and it was based on a moral logic that cannot be refuted by the mere fact of supreme criminals going unpunished. Murder is still murder, even if America manages to get away with it. What the meaning is of an international criminal law that systematically *lets* them get away with it is a more complicated question.

2
Afghanistan 2001

On 4 February 2002, American forces in Afghanistan killed Daraz Khan because he was tall. They killed him, and two other Afghan villagers who happened to be with him hunting for scrap metal, with a 'Hellfire' missile launched from a pilotless 'Predator' drone. They did it on the off-chance that, because he was tall, he might have been Osama bin Laden. Daraz Khan and his friends together left a dozen wives and children to mourn them.[1] In late May, six-year-old Zargunah was killed while she was trying to hide during an attack on her village near Kandahar by American and Canadian forces acting on incorrect information that there were senior Taliban and al-Qaeda officials there. The Americans nevertheless considered the raid a success because they managed to kill one 70-year-old 'supporter' of Taliban leader Mullah Omar.[2] Earlier in the war, on 18 October 2001, the village of Bibi Mahru on the outskirts of Kabul was hit by an American 'precision' 500-pound bomb. It killed Gul Ahmad, 40, a Hazara carpet weaver, his second wife Sima, 35, their five daughters and his son by his first wife, as well as two children living next door. 'We buried them together in the graveyard. We divided it with separate gravestones but their bodies were all in pieces,' said Mr. Ahmad's first wife, who was living in another village at the time of the bombing.[3] None of these incidents even made it into a *New York Times* review of the 'principal' sites where American bombs killed Afghan civilians: Gardez (23 dead); Khost and Zani Khel ('at least' 85 dead); Madoo and Khan-i-Merjahuddin (103 dead); Asmani and Pokharai ('about' 50); Niazi Qala (52 dead); and Kakrak (54 dead).[4]

America launched a ferocious war on Afghanistan in October 2001 that took a conservatively estimated 20,000 lives in its first six months, about half of them non-combatant men, women and children. By March 2002 the war had already seen 22,000 bombs dropped and missiles fired, of both the 'smart' and 'dumb' variety. These included cluster bombs that spread lethal yellow 'bomblets,' many of which did not explode when dropped, and just lay around to kill and maim civilians who easily mistook them for the food packets of the same color, that the Americans dropped at the same time. The war also saw 'important military innovations' from the 'historic' first use of pilotless 'Predator' aircraft and their 'Hellfire' missiles, like the one that killed Daraz Khan, to 'bunker busters' that could penetrate caves and kill troops where they hid or slept, and 'daisy cutters', 15,000 pound bombs pushed out the back of transport planes to float down on parachutes and incinerate everything within 500 meters of the blast. These weapons were rained down on cities and villages and anywhere else the Taliban might be, or where rival warlords settling scores claimed they were, on power plants and even food depots, because the Taliban might take the food.[5]

By the end of July 2002, civilians directly killed in Afghanistan by the American bombing probably numbered between 3,125 and 3,620. This was the number University of New Hampshire economics professor Marc Herold derived in the most thoroughly documented and best-argued study available.[6] The American Project on Defense Alternatives made a more conservative estimate of between 1,000 and 1,300.[7] But they added that at least 3,000 civilians on top of this were killed through disease, exposure and the disruption of aid. This latter figure was certainly an under-estimate. An article from the *New York Times* tells the story of one tiny region, Abulgan, isolated by the fighting, where in just three villages 600 people were known to have died from malnutrition and lack of medicine: 'These are just three villages out of 55. The total number of dead over the last few months has to run into the thousands.'[8] The British *Guardian* newspaper conservatively estimated that the civilian deaths caused indirectly by the war, not by the bombs alone, but by starvation, disease and exposure – 'Afghanistan was already on a lifeline, and for three months we cut the line' – amounted to between 10,000 and 20,000.[9]

The killing of civilians did not stop with the overthrow of the Taliban and the installation of a new Afghan government, because US troops continued to meet armed opposition. In July 2002, an American AC-130 'Spectre' gunship attacked a Pashtun village with cannon-fire, killing at least 54, mostly women and children, and wounding more than 120. An entire wedding party of 25 was wiped out.[10] Afghan and Iraqi collateral damage started to overlap in April 2003 when American forces still fighting in Afghanistan killed eleven members of one family during a skirmish near the Pakistan border, even as their colleagues were in the process of conquering Baghdad.[11] It continued to do so throughout the year.[12]

Even though they were not given profiles in the *New York Times*, each one of these lives was just as precious to the dead, their loved ones and dependants as the 3,000 killed in New York, Washington and Pennsylvania on 11 September 2001, as were the lives of 10,000 or so Taliban fighters killed in combat or as prisoners, as well as 600 Afghan allies of the US.[13] The Taliban and Northern Alliance fighters also killed hundreds of civilians during the attack. Looting, raping and killing by the triumphant Northern

Alliance made tens of thousands of Pashtuns refugees and continued well into 2002.[14] US losses amounted to about 30, of which 12 were incurred on the battlefield.

Michael E. O'Hanlon of the American Brookings Institution (who points out that there would have been 'at least two wounded for every one person killed') called the war 'a masterpiece of military creativity and finesse' that caused 'relatively modest harm to innocents,' characterizing 1,000 civilian deaths from bombing (the most conservative estimate in circulation) as 'a mercifully low number.' The only real failings of the war, to his mind, were in not capturing or killing Osama bin Laden and the 'image' problem of violating the Geneva Conventions on the treatment of prisoners of war.[15]

We can all marvel at the ability of Americans to rage and weep over 3,000 deaths from a single attack while deeming the death from their own incessant bombings of even 1,000 souls as 'relatively modest harm,' but this point has been made over and over. The point I want to make here is that these events, like similar ones in Yugoslavia before and Iraq afterwards, constitute not only tragedies, but *crimes*, very serious crimes, in fact *supreme international crimes* and *mass murder* by the individual leaders of the United States and its allies. These were the same people who would repeat their crimes in Iraq (Bush, Rumsfeld, Powell, Rice, Blair et al.), plus some who would not come along for the ride in Iraq (Canada's Jean Chrétien, for instance), and those who devised and executed the military strategy, such as General Tommy Franks, and so on down the line. That the US 'image problem' should arise, not from this mass murder of civilians, but from the comparatively minor, if blatant, violation of the Geneva Conventions in failing to afford prisoner-of-war status to captured enemy fighters, is testimony only to the loyalty of the American mass media.

But there is no point in calling for the Bushes and the Rumsfelds of the world to be hauled in front of some international criminal court, like Slobodan Milosevic, because everything there is to know about international law shows us they won't be, not for Afghanistan and not for Iraq. The Americans argue that the simple explanation for this is the world of moral and legal difference between what they do and what real criminals do. Justice, after all, is not only treating like cases alike, but also treating different cases differently. They argue that the war in Afghanistan was, like the others, in 'self-defense' and in full respect of international law (George W. Bush even said in one of his speeches that a goal of the war was to make 'the rule of law' prevail[16]). They argue that they, unlike their enemies, always aim to prevent and minimize human suffering, that 'collateral damage,' though 'regrettable,' is not criminal. They even argue that the war in Afghanistan, like the wars in Iraq and Yugoslavia, was, in part, a 'humanitarian intervention,' in this case to overthrow the odious Taliban regime of fundamentalist women-haters.[17]

But this is what the Revolutionary Association of the Women of Afghanistan says. They're the women who risked their lives to expose the crimes of the Taliban and were celebrated in the American media for doing so.[18] Here's what they said of American humanitarianism on 14 September 2001:[19]

> On 11 September 2001, the world was stunned with the horrific terrorist attacks on the United States. RAWA stands with the rest of the world in expressing our sorrow and condemnation for this barbaric act of violence and terror.... But unfortunately we must say that it was the government of the United States who supported Pakistani dictator Gen. Zia ul-Haq in creating thousands of religious schools from which the germs of Taliban emerged ... If it is established that the suspects of the terrorist attacks are outside the US, our constant claim that fundamentalist terrorists would devour their creators, is proved once more.... The US should stop supporting Afghan terrorists and their supporters once and for all. Now that the Taliban and Osama are the prime suspects by the US officials after the criminal attacks, will the US subject Afghanistan to a military attack similar to the one in 1998 and kill thousands of innocent Afghans for the crimes committed by the Taliban and Osama?

On 11 October 2001 (four days after the US launched its attack on Afghanistan), they said this:

> America, by forming an international coalition against Osama and his Taliban-collaborators and in retaliation for the 11 September terrorist attacks, has launched a vast aggression on our country. Despite the claim of the US that only military and terrorist bases of the Taliban and Al Qieda will be struck and that its actions would be accurately targeted and proportionate, [what] we have witnessed for the past seven days leaves no doubt that this invasion will shed the blood of numerous women, men, children, young and old of our country.

On 10 December 2001 (when a new government of Afghanistan had been installed in Bonn by the US and the UN, with heavy participation from America's Afghan allies in the Northern Alliance) RAWA issued this statement:

> The people of the world need to know the 'Northern Alliance' criminals.... These are the very people who immediately upon usurping power ... proclaimed – amongst other sordid restrictions – the compulsory veiling

of all women. The people of the world need to know that in terms of widespread raping of girls and women from ages seven to seventy, the track record of the Taliban can in no way stand up against that of these very same 'Northern Alliance' associates.... If the United Nations is sincerely concerned in regard to the independence, unity and democratisation of Afghanistan it must under no name or pretext continue its support to the 'Northern Alliance' and swiftly and unequivocally condemn and punish any country which tries to supply funds and arms to these murderers.

In other words, according to these Afghan women, it was the Americans' own fault that 11 September happened, the US war against Afghanistan was aggressive and not defensive, the civilian deaths were to be expected, and the government installed to replace the Taliban was as bad as, if not worse than, what it replaced. As far as can be ascertained, most of the world's people agreed with RAWA's opposition to the war. According to an IPSOS-REID poll of 21 December 2001, only the people of the rich countries of the G-7 supported the war (which was more support than the Americans would have in Iraq), while the rest of the world opposed it.[20]

That the world believed the war in Afghanistan was wrong, however, did not make it any more a crime deserving of punishment than it did in Yugoslavia or Iraq. It also had to be illegal. Was it?

The grounds for a lawful use of military force by one state against another were outlined in Chapter 1. It must either be validly authorized by the Security Council of the United Nations, or it must fall within the strictly limited 'inherent right of self-defense.' (The dubious right of 'humanitarian intervention,' something very important in the Kosovo war and discussed fully in the next Chapter, was argued only faintly as a justification for the attack on Afghanistan.)

Was the attack on Afghanistan authorized by the Security Council? The Security Council passed two unanimous Resolutions on terrorism between 11 September 2001 and America's attack on Afghanistan on 7 October, SCR 1368 of 12 September and SCR 1373 of 28 September. The argument that these resolutions authorized the Americans to attack Afghanistan cannot withstand a simple reading of the resolutions themselves, which contain not even an implicit authorization of war on Afghanistan. The resolutions condemned the attacks of 11 September and took a whole host of measures to suppress terrorism. Resolution 1373 has two dozen operative paragraphs outlining legislative, administrative and judicial measures for the suppression of terrorism and its financing, and for cooperation between states in security, intelligence investigations and criminal proceedings. The resolution sets up a committee of all its members to monitor progress on the measures in the resolution, and gives all states 90 days to report back to it. But military force? Not once does either of these resolutions mention military force or anything like it. They don't even mention 'Afghanistan' by name. Nor do they use the fateful euphemism 'all necessary means,' contained in the first Gulf War Resolution 678 of 29 November 1990, discussed in Chapter 1.

Defenders of the war tried to cut and paste the words of these resolutions to make it seem like they authorized force – just as they would in Iraq in 2003 – but their efforts can only be regarded as fraudulent. For instance, the words 'to combat by all means threats to international peace and security caused by terrorist acts' and 'to take all necessary steps to respond to the terrorist attacks' were emphasized. These words do indeed appear in Resolution 1368, but only as things the *Security Council* is 'determined' and 'ready' to do (not the United States or any other member state) by the non-military means outlined in the resolution, with further measures perhaps to be specified in the future.

> *The Security Council ... Determined* to combat by all means threats to international peace and security caused by terrorist acts ... 1. *Unequivocally condemns* ... [etc.]; 5. *Expresses* its readiness to take all necessary steps to respond to the terrorist attacks ... ; 6. *Decides* to remain seized of the matter.

Similarly, defenders of the war pointed out that, in Resolution 1373, the Security Council *'Decides also* ... that all States shall ... (b) Take the necessary steps to prevent the commission of terrorist acts,' as if there were nothing else in the sentence or the Resolution. But the complete sentence reads: 'Take the necessary steps to prevent the commission of terrorist acts, including by provision of early warning to other states by exchange of information.' The 'provision of early warning' is not generally taken to include an invasion. And in the rest of the Resolution, all sorts of 'necessary means' are specified *except military force*. Did they just forget?

So this was just another case, like Iraq, of the Americans trying 'to distort the words of resolutions ... in order to claim to be acting on behalf of the international community.'[21] They seem to count on nobody actually reading the Resolutions themselves.

Afghanistan was different from Iraq, though. The Security Council Resolutions were passed in the immediate aftermath of the shocking attacks on New York and Washington, and the war followed before a month had passed. Thus the claim of 'self-defense' had a superficial plausibility that the war against Iraq lacked. This was reflected in the Resolutions of September

2001, particularly in one much-discussed paragraph of the preamble to each of them:

> *Recognizing* the inherent right of individual or collective self-defence in accordance with the Charter ...

This is indeed suggestive. It suggests support for military action by the US at a time when Afghanistan was an obvious target. But a mere suggestion of support is a far cry from an *authorization*. Authorization is a legal act, and the Security Council knows how to do that when it wants to – and how not to do it. An example of how to do it is the case of Iraq's invasion of Kuwait. There, the Council affirmed the right of self-defense to occupied Kuwait in the most unequivocally focused way:

> *Affirming* the inherent right of individual or collective self-defence, in response to the armed attack by Iraq against Kuwait, in accordance with Article 51 of the Charter;[22]

That was in August 1990, four days into the invasion. It was the second of twelve resolutions that explicitly authorized everything from diplomacy to sanctions to the threat of war crimes prosecutions, but not military force. Not at least until the very last one on 29 November, which was short and to the point. Resolution 678 had only five operative paragraphs, the central one of which (already quoted fully in Chapter 1) '*Authorizes* Member States ... to use all necessary means to uphold and implement [the]relevant resolutions and to restore international peace and security in the area.' Here was a resolution that did *nothing but* authorize the use of force, while the September 2001 resolutions, with their non-committal preambulatory invocations of the right to self-defense, authorized *everything but* the use of force.

So anyone who can read can see that the passages in the preambles to the September 2001 resolutions are clearly only a non-committal recognition of a legal right that exists even without the recognizing. For all these passages say, it could be Afghanistan that had the right to attack the United States. The legality of the war depended not on the resolutions, but entirely on the only other way to justify the use of military force, the inherent right of self-defense itself – in other words, on whether the attack fitted within that right, something on which the resolutions take no position whatsoever.

By virtue of the veto, nothing can get into a Security Council resolution without the consent of the United States, but the wording also has to satisfy a majority of the other members, including the other four with vetoes. For the US, treating this as a matter of self-defense and not as Security Council authorization would have had the distinct advantage of taking its actions outside all formal supervision or control by the United Nations. The 'inherent' right to self-defense is the *unilateral* one. Being non-specific about the target of self-defense would also fit US designs, clearly expressed in President Bush's speeches, to spread this war far beyond Afghanistan. Before the Iraq fiasco of 2003, it was assumed, because of its powerful means of persuasion, that the US could generally get its way with the other members of the Security Council. Mahajan argued that, in the extraordinary circumstances following 11 September, we had to assume that the US could have obtained Security Council authorization for war if it had wanted.[23] But such speculations have to be revised after March 2003. Authorizing an attack on Afghanistan, even in the circumstances of September 2001, would have been a grave breach of the Security Council's duties to seek, above all, the peaceful resolution of threats to peace. In fact, it's unlikely that the Security Council would have been willing to go further than this non-committal preamble, because granting the US the *carte blanche* it has since claimed would have constituted a major leap into the unknown for traditional rivals Russia and China, and even for traditional ally France (as it was considered at the time). So if the preamble suited the US, it also let the other members of the Security Council off the hook, because it left everything to be decided by the inherent right to self-defense, as if the resolution had never been passed.

But the inherent right of self-defense has very stringent requirements which absolutely ruled out the attack on Afghanistan. The requirements all stem from the fact that the resort to military force, with its terrible, irreversible costs, has to be *necessary*, and demonstrably so. It is not enough that there be a threat to a state's safety: there must also be no plausible, effective, non-military solution to the threat; or at least there must be such urgency for a military response that there is no time to explore non-military alternatives. And the extent of the response has to be measured, so that it is no more than necessary in the circumstances to meet the threat. This makes absolute moral sense. It is in fact impossible to imagine any other rule consistent with respect for humanity. Given the inevitable loss of life and limb, not to mention innocent life and limb, unnecessary wars are an abomination. And all of this has to be demonstrable in the light of day; it can't just be claimed – that is what makes it legal and not merely rhetorical.

This has been the law of the inherent right of self-defense for more than 150 years. It was formulated by the American government itself in the *Caroline Case* of 1841 to justify US rejection of a British claim to self-defense in an attack on an American naval vessel. The British were attempting to obtain the release of a British subject charged with the murder of US citizens in the attack – *murder*, notice, not a violation of the 'laws and customs of war.' US Secretary of State Daniel Webster, in his letter to the British government of 24 April 1841, laid down what he thought the British would have to show to make out the case for self-defense:

> ... a necessity of self-defence, instant, over-whelming, leaving no choice of means, and no moment for deliberation ... that [they] did nothing unreasonable or excessive; since the act, justified by the necessity of self-defence, must be limited by that necessity, and kept clearly within it. It must be shown that admonition or remonstrance ... was impracticable, or would have been unavailing; ... that there could be no attempt at discrimination between the innocent and the guilty; ... that there was a necessity, present and inevitable, for attacking [the ship] in the darkness of night ... while unarmed men were asleep on board, killing some and wounding others ... setting her on fire, and, careless to know whether there might be in her the innocent with the guilty, or the living with the dead, committing her to a fate which fills the imagination with horror. A necessity for all this, the government of The United States cannot believe to have existed.[24]

This rule has never been questioned. It was even applied by the Nuremberg Tribunal in 1946 to reject the Nazi claim that their invasion of Norway was in self-defense:

> The defense that has been made here is that Germany was compelled to attack Norway to forestall an Allied invasion, and her action was therefore preventive. It must be remembered that preventive action in foreign territory is justified only in case of 'an instant and overwhelming necessity for self-defense leaving no choice of means, and no moment for deliberation.' (The Caroline Case...) ... [I]t is clear that when the plans for an attack on Norway were being made, they were not made for the purpose of forestalling an imminent Allied landing, but, at the most, that they might prevent an Allied occupation at some future date ... It was further argued that Germany alone could decide ... whether preventive action was a necessity, and that in making her decision final judgment was conclusive. But whether action taken under the claim of self-defense was in fact aggressive or defensive must ultimately be subject to investigation and adjudication if international law is ever to be enforced.[25]

The same principles were applied in 1986 by the International Court of Justice to reject the American claim of self-defense in an attempted justification of the US terror campaign against Sandinista Nicaragua, which included bombing it, mining its harbors and supporting the counter-revolutionary Contras in a civil war that took tens of thousands of lives.

The US claimed its military activities against Nicaragua were an exercise in 'collective self-defense.' But, according to the Court, the American actions lacked proof of 'necessity':

> Thus it was possible to eliminate the main danger to the Salvadorian Government without the United States embarking on activities in and against Nicaragua. Accordingly, it cannot be held that these activities were undertaken in the light of necessity ... the Court cannot regard the United States activities ... that is, those relating to the mining of the Nicaraguan ports and the attacks on ports, oil installations, etc., as satisfying that criterion.[26]

Reading this case after the attack on Afghanistan is like déjà vu, because the American argument for military force in the case was that the Nicaraguan government was allowing insurgents from El Salvador to operate from its territory, that is, 'harboring' them. But the Court held that, for self-defense to justify an attack upon a state, that state had to be involved in the attack itself, more than by merely 'harboring' the attackers. For the purposes of the law of self-defense, an armed attack required either 'the sending *by or on behalf of a State* of armed bands, groups, irregulars or mercenaries, which carry out acts of armed force against another State ... *or its substantial involvement therein* ... But the Court does not believe that the concept of "armed attack" includes ... assistance to rebels in the form of provision of weapons or logistical or other support.'[27] The point is, simply, that if it was not the government of the state that was carrying out the attack, there might be an alternative for preventing further attacks other than war against that state, with the inevitable bloody consequences for civilians and soldiers alike. The international law of self-defense is the same as the domestic law of self-defense, which does not allow somebody who has been attacked to chase the attacker, six-guns blazing, into somebody else's crowded house, or to burn the house to the ground with everybody inside because the owners may have been sheltering the attacker.

These were the conditions of the 'inherent' right to self-defense before the Charter of the United Nations existed. The Charter reinforces them and even adds others. Article 33, for example, requires that 'the parties to any dispute shall, first of all, seek a solution by ... peaceful means' such as 'negotiation, enquiry, mediation, conciliation, arbitration, judicial settlement,' and so on. Article 51 defines self-defense as a *temporary* right that subsists only until the Security Council intervenes:

> Nothing in the present Charter shall impair the inherent right of individual or collective self-defense if an armed attack occurs against a Member of

the United Nations, *until the Security Council has taken measures necessary to maintain international peace and security.* (Emphasis added)

The article adds that actions by Members in the exercise of the right of self-defense 'shall not in any way affect the authority and responsibility of the Security Council ... to take at any time such action as it deems necessary in order to maintain or restore international peace and security.'

The point of the article is clearly to recognize an attacked state's right to repel the attack, but to leave anything other than immediate solutions to the Security Council. It underlines the rigorous legal distinction between self-defense and reprisal.[28] Like domestic law, international law allows you to defend yourself when the law is not around, but it does not allow you to take the law into your own hands.

Now, it has been argued that this Article must mean that the right of self-defense persists until the measures taken by the Security Council have actually succeeded in restoring international peace and security. Otherwise, it is said, we would have the absurd position of a state being at the mercy of an aggressor just because the Security Council took *some* measures, even though they were clearly inadequate, or measures that were adequate but needed time to be effective.[29] But it is impossible to see how the US could make this argument in the case of 11 September. The attack, even if considered to be an ongoing one, had ceased for the moment. The US needed a month to get its armed forces in readiness. It immediately set about trying to solve the enormous security lapses that had made 11 September possible. The Security Council, with the necessary US vote, took a host of non-military measures aimed at effectively combating international terrorism. It's obvious that the US did not find itself lacking in time to go to the Security Council. Nobody is even claiming that the US encountered any obstacles at the Security Council that would have made it defenseless if it had to work through the proper channels. Nor did anybody claim that the United States had proposed what it thought were more effective, collective measures, which the Security Council rejected. The only way to make sense of what happened is to conclude that the US wanted to have a free hand to act alone and not to be bound to seek non-military alternatives – the very antithesis of international law and the Charter of the United Nations. If Article 51 were interpreted to require the Security Council to have eliminated all potential threats to a country's security before the right of self-defense was superseded, then Article 51 would have no conceivable application, especially to a Permanent Member who could always block any action and then use that as a pretext. Legally speaking, that's a pretty good reason for concluding that it would be wrong to interpret Article 51 in that way.

But even apart from Article 51, the other conditions of the inherent right to self-defense were nowhere to be seen in the case of the attack on Afghanistan. The right of self-defense requires a demonstration that no non-military solution is available. This, like Article 33 itself, imposes an obligation on a state to seek a negotiated solution, before embarking on war. Now in the case of Afghanistan, as early as 19 September, the Taliban supreme leader Mullah Omar, repeating denials of Afghan involvement in the 11 September attacks, publicly offered to negotiate a settlement with the United States that could even include the extradition of bin Laden.

> We have told America that we deny Osama's involvement in the latest incidents in America.... However, we repeatedly put forwards proposals concerning ways of solving Osama Bin Laden's issue. We have told America that if it has any evidence of Osama Bin Laden's guilt, it should be given to the Supreme Court of Afghanistan, so that we can take action in the light of it. America has rejected all this. We have proposed to America to let representatives of the Organization of Islamic Conference come to Afghanistan to assess Osama Bin-Laden's activities for its satisfaction. But this has been rejected by America also.... If the American Government has some problems with the Islamic Emirate of Afghanistan they should be solved through negotiations.[30]

On 20 September, the Grand Council of Afghan clerics to whom the Taliban had submitted the question recommended that the UN 'investigate independently and precisely the recent events to clarify the reality and prevent harassment of innocent people.'[31] Yet in his speech of 20 September, President Bush declared that there would be no negotiation or even discussion:

> And tonight the United States of America makes the following demands on the Taliban: Deliver to United States authorities all of the leaders of al Qaeda who hide in your land.... Close immediately and permanently every terrorist training camp in Afghanistan. And hand over every terrorist and every person in their support structure to appropriate authorities. Give the United States full access to terrorist training camps, so we can make sure they are no longer operating. *These demands are not open to negotiation or discussion.* The Taliban must act and act immediately. They will hand over the terrorists or they will share in their fate.[32]

These demands were obviously impossible to accept for the government of any sovereign state that wished to remain so.[33] Rahul Mahajan and John

Pilger have concluded that in making these demands on Afghanistan, the US *deliberately sought war*. In fact they argue that the US intentionally made it impossible for the Taliban to hand over bin Laden, by refusing to present them with any evidence of bin Laden's involvement – the minimum that any nation demands, even of its friends, when it is asked to extradite a criminal.[34] According to Pilger, since the invasion of Afghanistan had far wider objectives that transcended bin Laden and long preceded 11 September, the US didn't want him before they'd had a chance to make war.[35]

Not that capturing bin Laden could possibly have justified in law or in morals the devastating attack on Afghanistan – remember, we're talking about *killing* tens of thousands of people – much less avoiding seeking a solution through the Security Council. In the first place, bin Laden had plenty of time to evade capture, even with the Americans' unilateral attack, something he appeared, after more than two years of war and occupation (at this writing), successfully to have done. Secondly and far more importantly, one is not allowed to invade a country to effect an arrest. When the Israelis kidnapped Adolf Eichmann from Argentina, they were unanimously condemned by the Security Council, even though they didn't harm a hair on his or anybody else's head. And he was a *Nazi* with the blood of *millions* on his hands.[36] Furthermore, far from showing the required 'necessity of self-defence, instant, over-whelming, leaving no choice of means, and no moment for deliberation,' it is clear that even if the overthrow of the Taliban were a necessary and legitimate self-defense objective, there was ample time to contemplate more effective, collective action that could have avoided the terrible human costs of the Americans taking the law into their own hands. In December 2001 the American Project on Defense Alternatives published a detailed study of the alternative legal options clearly available to the United States that would have spared thousands of innocent lives. They pointed out that the 'negative side-effects' of the campaign had little to do with fighting the al-Qaeda threat, and instead came from the decision to overthrow the government by relying on aerial bombardment. 'Less costly and destabilizing approaches were available,' which might have included limited and selective air strikes, but would have been much more effective if they had focussed on law enforcement and intelligence against the real danger of terrorist operations coming from *outside* Afghanistan. Resolving 'the broader problems of Afghanistan' might have required a major military operation, but this would have been more effective and would have resulted in much less harm to innocents if it had involved more careful planning, perhaps '6–8 months of intensive diplomatic, intelligence, and military preparations.' Above all, this would have required working through the United Nations Security Council to 'facilitate the formation of a more effective and representative government, and end the use of Afghan territory as a base for terrorist and insurgent activities elsewhere.' The 'full panoply of persuasive tools would have had to be brought into play – among these: trade bargains, economic assistance, sanction relief, promises of security cooperation, and debt forgiveness.'[37] The same reasoning, with only slight changes, would also clearly have applied to the invasion of Iraq in 2003.

Events seemed to bear out the futility of the Americans' unilateral military approach as a way of confronting either terrorism or 'the broader problems of Afghanistan.' At the time of writing, two years after they launched their attack, Afghanistan was still a place ruled by fundamentalist warlords, where women were obliged to wear the ghostly *burqa* and marginalized by law, but above all by social conditions, which hadn't changed merely through the banishment of the Taliban.[38] 'After the Taliban is the same as before the Taliban. It's all the same people, with the same guns. What was the American bombing for?'[39] Though the *Loya Jirga* (traditional assembly) held under UN auspices in June 2002 was billed as an exercise in democracy and self-determination, the selection of the government to replace the Taliban was essentially a deal worked out between the United States and its Northern Alliance warlord allies, and then imposed on the Afghans. The interim leader himself, Hamid Karzai, seemed more a representative of the US than the Afghans. American intelligence agencies and oil companies had been working with him since the mid-1980s, and he had even served as a consultant to the American oil company Unocal when it was working on the Caspian Sea oil pipeline project in the mid-1990s, a project that appeared crowned with success on Karzai's accession to office.[40]

To justify the war, cheerleading journalists had made it seem like the overthrow of the Taliban would solve everything: 'When the Taliban finally fall – and they will – billions of dollars in reconstruction aid will flood in ... Far from being a tragedy for Afghans, this war could be the best thing that has happened to them in two decades.'[41] But the incentive to promise big things while bombing the Taliban did not become an incentive to deliver once they were vanquished. The few billions pledged were a spit in the ocean of Afghanistan's needs, and much even of what arrived never got past the warlords' pockets.[42] The only result of the regime change seemed to be a regime friendlier to the US. Long after the US had become enmeshed in the occupation of Iraq, there were still 11,000 US troops in Afghanistan fighting a 'resurgent' al-Qaeda and Taliban, who seemed reinvigorated, not only by popular opposition to the return of the warlords, but also by the Iraqi resistance.[43] Karzai ruled only in Kabul, with a few hundred US soldiers as his personal bodyguards and 5,000 NATO troops as the government's guarantors.[44]

Even as an exercise in 'rooting out terrorism,' the attack on Afghanistan appeared to be a failure. A front-page article in the *New York Times* of 16 June 2002 had American authorities agreeing with what the war's opponents had been saying from the beginning: 'Classified investigations of the Qaeda threat now under way at the FBI and CIA have concluded that the war in Afghanistan failed to diminish the threat to the United States...'[45] Failed even to *diminish* it. Of course, this admission now suited America's plans to take its War on Terrorism to new pastures; hence the doctrine of preventive self-defense announced precisely at this time for use in Iraq in 2003, international law be damned.[46] It was as if the Nuremberg Tribunal's decision on the Nazi invasion of Norway had gone the other way.

The evident failure of America's war on Afghanistan to begin to resolve either terrorism or 'the broader problems' of Afghanistan was relevant to the crucial question, both legal and moral, of alternatives to unilateral military action by the United States. The main point made by the anti-war movement here was once again that of American *complicity*. The violent fundamentalists of Afghanistan were simply, in RAWA's words, America's 'Frankenstein monsters,' backed by the US to the tune of billions of dollars and highly sophisticated weaponry, all for the purpose of bringing down America's Soviet rivals, whose ten-year war in Afghanistan spelled the end of the USSR.[47] The Soviets supported the reformers (whose reforms, incidentally, included significant advances in the status of women), so the Americans backed the fundamentalists (with their well-known opposite attitude to women). After the fall of the Soviets until well into 2001, American interest in Afghanistan centered on access to Caspian Sea oil, and the US supported whatever regime – now the Northern Alliance, now the Taliban – seemed capable of exerting control.[48]

Opponents of the war in Afghanistan mounted a powerful case for linking the phenomenon of terrorism itself to the behavior of the Americans in the world. Lewis Lapham called 11 September 'an attack on American foreign policy, which, for the last thirty years, has allied itself, both at home and abroad, with despotism and the weapons trade, a policy conducted by and for a relatively small cadre of selfish interests.'[49] Naomi Klein labeled the attacks part of 'a war not so much on U.S. imperialism but on perceived U.S. imperviousness [which] has produced a blinding rage in many parts of the world, a rage at the persistent asymmetry of suffering.'[50] The most frequently asked question in America in the days following 11 September 2001 was 'Why do they hate us?' – to which one commentator had the wit to reply: 'They hate us because we don't even know why they hate us.'[51]

This 'asymmetry of suffering' had its basis in a structure of inequality such as the world had never seen before, with America the richest country in the world and Afghanistan one of the poorest.[52] One index of inequality was oil itself, which the Arab world produced and the West, above all the US, consumed.[53] Despite the fabulous wealth of the elite of the oil-rich countries, the average Arab had to survive on about one-seventh the average American's income.[54] The American musician Quincy Jones had an earthy assessment of the war in Afghanistan: 'That's why this fucking war is going on, that's why, because the gap between rich and poor is too large.'[55] This was essentially the message, if in more genteel language, of 100 Nobel Peace Prize winners, who declared that 'the most profound danger to world peace in the coming years will stem ... from the legitimate demands of the world's dispossessed' for 'the wider degree of social justice that alone gives hope of peace.'[56]

Everybody seemed to understand that if you could explain the attack on America by America's own transgressions, then the justification for the retaliation would evaporate, because America would be responsible for starting the whole thing. Donald Rumsfeld acknowledged this indirectly when he said of the deaths of Afghan civilians by American bombs: 'We did not start this war. So understand, responsibility for every single casualty in this war, whether they're innocent Afghans or innocent Americans, rests at the feet of the Al Qaeda and the Taliban.'[57] There was a desperate quest to detach the events of 11 September from America's 'foreign policy.' The American media and the politicians tried their best to explain 11 September as a result of pure 'evil' or 'envy,' or as an attack on the things that were *good* about America. In a famous cartoon by Tom Tomorrow, one of the criteria for being a 'Real American' was to answer 'yes' to the question: 'Do you **GENUINELY BELIEVE** the terrorists are motivated by nothing more complex than a blind, unreasoning hatred of **FREEDOM**?'[58] Bush said that America had been attacked 'because we're the brightest beacon for freedom and opportunity in the world.'[59] Some beacon for freedom, with two million adults behind bars on any given day – more people, even relative to its population, than any country in the world.[60] Maybe if they'd attacked Sweden you could say they were attacking a beacon for freedom, but the United States?

The debate about terrorism didn't start with 11 September. It's an old one by now, with familiar contours. On one side we have a minority of peoples and states, the ones with the most powerful militaries, who can be heard to repeat the formula that individual and not state terrorism is the problem, and that ends never justify means, at least when these means are terrorist (not state terrorist), so that you can condemn the means without even discussing, much less addressing, the ends.[61] On the other side, we have most of the people and states of the world, who find it impossible to detach terrorism from questions of social justice. This was summed up in the General Assembly Resolution of 1972 following the Munich Olympics massacre, which expressed 'deep concern over increasing acts of violence which endanger or take innocent human lives or jeopardize fundamental freedoms,' and which consequently urged states 'to devote their immediate attention to finding just and peaceful solutions to the underlying causes which give rise to such acts of violence.'[62] Even the Americans seem to subscribe to this position when it suits them. The Kosovo Liberation Army, fighting the Serbs for independence, were *officially* branded terrorists by the Security Council. But when the Serbs (America's ultimate quarry) argued that repressive measures were necessary to fight terrorism, the Security Council, with America's affirmative vote, '*underline[d]* that the way to defeat violence and terrorism in Kosovo is for the authorities in Belgrade to offer the Kosovar Albanian community a genuine political process.'[63]

Most people and states, furthermore, appear to consider 'state terrorism' to be 'the most harmful and deadly form of terrorism.'[64] They appear to agree with Chomsky and Herman, who classically labeled it 'wholesale' terrorism, as opposed to the 'retail' terrorism that preoccupies the big powers and their clients.[65] But what else can you call the attack on Afghanistan if not a terrorist act? George W. Bush himself said he was aiming it not only at the terrorists but at anybody who decided not to join his 'crusade.' Remember his words:

> Every nation in every region now has a decision to make: Either you are with us or you are with the terrorists. (11 September)
>
> ...
>
> [T]here is no such thing as a good terrorist. No national aspiration, no remembered wrong can ever justify the deliberate murder of the innocent. Any government that rejects this principle, trying to pick and choose its terrorist friends, will know the consequences. (10 November)

This can only be understood as an attempt to instill fear, not in the terrorists, but in anyone who might stand in the way of American military might as they pursued them. And the means by which the Afghanistan war was undertaken, how can these escape the label 'terrorist'? Tens of thousands of civilians and soldiers killed with the most effective conventional technology of death ever known, Hellfire missiles fired from Predator drones, 'bunker busters,' 'daisy-cutters' and Apache helicopters, flying tanks with rocket launchers and chain guns firing 600 rounds per minute. 'As you might expect, it is a terrifying machine to ground forces.'[66] Or think about the nuclear weapons with which the United States seeks to 'deter' its enemies. Is it only professors of criminal law who realize that the hidden word in 'deterrence' is 'terror'? Far from being a war against terrorism, it was much saner, as Noam Chomsky pointed out, to think of the war on Afghanistan as one being conducted by one of the world's leading terrorist states.[67]

COLLATERAL DAMAGE

One criterion by which America seeks to distinguish its far more terrifying violence from that of the real terrorists, a criterion which has even persuaded some respected intellectuals, is its *attitude to the taking of civilian life*. George W. Bush summed it up in his speech to the United Nations on 10 November 2001: 'Unlike the enemy, we seek to minimize, not maximize the loss of innocent life.' The idea is that there is a transcendent all-trumping difference between 'terrorist attacks' as commonly understood and the 'collateral damage' that the American military regularly inflicts, and that this is the difference between 'premeditated murder' and 'unintended killing,' as American political commentator Michael Walzer wrote in *Dissent*:

> A few left academics have tried to figure out how many civilians actually died in Afghanistan, aiming at as high a figure as possible, on the assumption, apparently, that if the number is greater than the number of people killed in the attacks on the Twin Towers, the war is unjust.... But the claim that the numbers matter in just this way – that the 3,120th death determines the injustice of the war – is wrong. It denies one of the most basic and best understood moral distinctions: between premeditated murder and unintended killing.[68]

The people who attacked the Twin Towers in New York *meant* to kill civilians. That was at least one of the purposes of the attack. Suicide bombers seek the maximum number of civilian deaths; whereas the Americans claim that they mean only to kill 'combatants' and seek to minimize injury to civilians as much as possible, and, indeed, given their objectives, the claim is plausible in many cases.[69] The killings are therefore, according to them, 'unintended' and 'accidental.'

This kind of killing is called 'collateral damage,' the official American military definition of which is 'unintentional or incidental injury or damage to persons or objects that would not be lawful military targets in the circumstances ruling at the time.' According to the military, 'such damage is not unlawful so long as it is not excessive in light of the overall military advantage anticipated from the attack.'[70] It appears that the term was in wide use in the 1950s and 1960s as nuclear war jargon. Thomas Schelling of Harvard University used it in an article in 1960 in which he argued for the dispersal of US nuclear weapons sites away from urban areas to minimize 'collateral damage' from Soviet attacks on them.[71] The term became common currency only during the Gulf War of 1991, but when NATO spokespersons used it liberally in the Kosovo war of 1999, without any trace of shame, to describe civilians, including children, killed by NATO bombs, the opprobrium was so great that they had ultimately to try and distance themselves from it. For most of the war, you could find Jamie Shea, Wesley Clark and the rest, using the phrase routinely at NATO press conferences. For instance, Jamie Shea: 'Targets are carefully selected and continuously assessed to avoid collateral damage' (26 March 1999);[72] Major General Jertz: 'by trying to avoid collateral damage we are not using weapon systems which we could use if we were as brutal and as cruel as Milosevic is' (10 May);[73] and Supreme Commander General Wesley Clark on 13 April, after an American pilot bombed a passenger train crossing a bridge – not once but *twice* – and killed 16 civilians: 'it is one of those regrettable things that happen in a campaign like this and we are all very sorry for it, but we are doing the absolute best we can do to avoid collateral damage, I can assure you of that.'[74]

On the other hand, by the end of the war you could find at least the media-savvy Shea trying to distance himself from the psychopathic coldness of 'this awful term.'[75] Lord Robertson himself put the phrase between quotation marks in his official defense of the war on its first anniversary.[76] Its destiny to live on only in infamy seemed sealed when Gulf War veteran Timothy McVeigh used the term to describe the children killed in his 1995 bombing of a federal building in Oklahoma City, which he considered an act of war against the United States.[77] But you could still find the odd old-soldier usage of it during the Afghan war.[78] By Iraq, it was being used mainly by journalists, often as a condemnation. For example, Robert Fisk reported this sickening scene from Baghdad:

> It was an outrage, an obscenity. The severed hand on the metal door, the swamp of blood and mud across the road, the human brains inside a garage, the incinerated, skeletal remains of an Iraqi mother and her three small children in their still-smouldering car. Two missiles from an American jet killed them all – by my estimate, more than 20 Iraqi civilians, torn to pieces before they could be 'liberated' by the nation that destroyed their lives. Who dares, I ask myself, to call this 'collateral damage'?[79]

Only rarely, and at very low levels, could the term be found in official military discourse.[80] President Bush's speech-writers completely shunned it in favor of solemn pledges to 'protect innocent lives in every way possible.'[81]

On the other hand, intellectuals were keen to defend the moral distinction. In mid-war, law professor Kenneth Anderson argued:[82]

> There is no moral equivalence between stray missiles aimed in good faith, using the best technology available, and deliberate violation of the categorical rules of war, like using human shields, shelling civilians to prevent them from fleeing Basra and rape or summary execution of prisoners.

Yet he had to admit that many people didn't see it quite this way:

> ... it does seem to millions of people worldwide that there is indeed a moral equivalence between the tactics of the Americans – hitting targets from the air and pleading collateral damage as a defense against responsibility – and the tactics of the Iraqis, who, lacking other means to attack, use their own civilians as a material and moral resource, no matter what laws of war it might violate. This was the attitude, it should be said, held by Churchill, who intended a scorched-earth defense of Britain (including the use of poison gas) without much regard for the lives of British civilians, should the invader ever arrive.

Anderson tried to salvage the distinction in the only way he could think of:

> There is, I think, only one way to evaluate these conflicting claims ... To deny the distinction means that you either accept that virtual nonviolence is the only tenable position or that you are indifferent to the lives of civilians, since you are guilty of anything that happens anyway – and in that case, anything becomes a target. The justification for the principle ... is that it appears to be the only principled way of steering between a pacifism that few of us, in real life, would accept, and a brutal realism that denies the moral necessity of even trying to distinguish between combatants and noncombatants.

But these stark alternatives of, on the one hand, unrealistic pacifism and, on the other, placing no limits on the rules of war, are spurious because they ignore the fundamental question of the *legality and morality of the war itself*. It just shows how far wrong international criminal law has gone that anyone could not think this relevant. The question is only difficult for the international criminal law professionals because they take for granted the great big hole in the modern practice of international criminal law: its refusal to distinguish between legal and illegal war-making, between aggression and self-defense. The whole edifice depends on pretending all wars are legal on all sides. But what would have made Churchill's plans morally defensible was that the Nazis were the aggressors and Britain was forced to fight back by any means it could. The Nazis would have borne the blame, not Churchill. You can't possibly judge the morality of collateral damage while leaving out the question of the war itself, however congenial this may be to aggressors with the 'best technology available.' It is the immorality and illegality of a war that makes collateral damage a crime. The real alternatives are to make war only when it is necessary and moral and legal, and not to make it when it is not. Then, if you take as much care as possible to avoid injury to non-combatants, nobody will have the right to criticize you when they are harmed, because their harm will be the responsibility of those who started the war, just like Rumsfeld said.

To return to the argument of Michael Walzer, there is indeed a moral and legal difference between meaning to kill someone and killing someone accidentally, but (a) it's not as fundamental as Walzer would have it; and (b) it doesn't do much to help the inflictors of collateral damage. The principles are exactly the same for national and international criminal law, and for law and morals. Meaning to kill someone (*without* a lawful excuse such as self-defense) makes killing murder. Some kinds of accidental, and indeed intentional, killings are lesser crimes (manslaughter, criminal negligence, and so on) and may even be no crime at all if it should be found that all reasonable care was taken to avoid harm. Take dangerous driving: run somebody down on purpose and it's murder; run somebody down by accident because you weren't driving carefully enough and its manslaughter; run somebody down when you were driving very carefully and it's no offence at all. It was not your *fault*.

But some accidental killing is treated very seriously, even as seriously as murder. Try to run down one person that you mistook for another and that's murder – that's the Daraz Khan situation, described at the beginning of this chapter. You intended to kill the person you killed; you just got the identity wrong. But the identity of the victim is irrelevant *if you had no right to kill in the first place*. A very different question is whether, assuming the Americans had the right to kill Osama bin Laden – which they did not – they took sufficient care to ensure that it was him they were killing. In this case, 'collateral damage' may not be criminal at all. Walzer has missed precisely the point that Anderson has – namely that it depends on the legality of the war, which in turn generally depends on its morality.

What about the more classic case of collateral damage, for example trying to run someone down in a pedestrian mall, with malice towards none of the other pedestrians, trying your best to minimize the harm to them, *but knowing that some will inevitably be killed*? World Court Judge C. G.

Weeramantry thought the answer so obvious that he used it as part of his argument for the illegality of nuclear weapons:

> It is not to the point that such results are not directly intended, but are 'by-products' or 'collateral damage' caused by nuclear weapons. Such results are known to be the necessary consequences of the use of the weapon. The author of the act causing these consequences cannot in any coherent legal system avoid legal responsibility for causing them, any less than a man careering in a motor vehicle at a hundred and fifty kilometres per hour through a crowded market street can avoid responsibility for the resulting deaths on the ground that he did not intend to kill the particular persons who died.[83]

Collateral damage is a very special kind of 'accidental,' 'unintentional' or 'unpremeditated' killing. *New York Times* language columnist William Safire was only half right when he defined it as 'unintended, inadvertent.'[84] It is not 'inadvertent,' meaning, literally, that no thought was given to it. In fact, it is foreseen as *inevitable.* When the Americans planned the war on Afghanistan, they knew that many civilians, very probably thousands of civilians, would die. One of the questions in a CBS/*New York Times* public opinion poll conducted within a week of the attack on the World Trade Towers asked, 'Should the U.S. take military action against whoever is responsible for the attacks ... Even if it means many thousands of innocent civilians may be killed?' Fifty-eight percent of respondents, representing the American population with a margin of error of 3 percent, answered 'Yes.'[85] Not just thousands, *many thousands.* Here's Secretary of Defense Donald Rumsfeld in October 2001:

> Any time that the Department of Defense is engaged from the air or on the ground, we have to know that there are going to be people hurt. Overwhelmingly, they will be people who we intend to hurt. On occasion, there will be people hurt that one wished had not been. I don't think there is any way in the world to avoid that and defend the United States from the kinds of terrorist attacks which we've experienced.[86]

Here he is in December:

> One of the unpleasant aspects of war is the reality that innocent bystanders are sometimes caught in the crossfire, and we're often asked to answer Taliban accusations about civilian casualties ... We know this much for certain – the United States has taken extraordinary measures to avoid civilian casualties in this campaign. That's not true of Taliban or al Qaeda forces....[87]

And here he is again in July, 2002 (after the wedding massacre):

> There cannot be the use of that kind of firepower and not have mistakes and errant weapons exist. It's going to happen. It always has and I'm afraid it always will.[88]

This is not 'inadvertent' killing. It is *deliberate* killing –'killing deliberately "by mistake,"' one Palestinian journalist called it.[89] It is *premeditated* killing in the literal sense that it is clearly foreseen and contemplated beforehand, with the repeated claim that those killed are the *very minimum* to be expected. Otherwise, how could an expert like Michael O'Hanlon of the Brookings Institution characterize 1,000 civilians killed as 'a mercifully low number'?[90] Not, 'Oh my God, we killed innocent people!' but 'What, we only killed 1,000?'

So we are being asked to distinguish between meaning to kill and killing knowingly – both, of course, *without lawful excuse*. Does the law make this distinction? Evidently, not since Moses:

> And if an ox gore a man or a woman, that they die, the ox shall be surely stoned, and its flesh shall not be eaten; but the owner of the ox shall be quit. *But if the ox was wont to gore in time past, and warning hath been given to its owner, and he hath not kept it in, but it hath killed a man or a woman, the ox shall be stoned, and its owner also shall be put to death.*[91]

In March 2002 it wasn't an ox but a dog. That's when a Los Angeles jury convicted a woman of second degree murder when the dog she was walking mauled a neighbor to death. Her husband, who was not present, was convicted of manslaughter. Nobody suggested that she wanted her dog to kill the neighbor or that she set her dog upon her neighbor, or anything like that. It was enough that she and her husband '*knew* their dogs were "time bombs" that could kill someone – but did not care.'[92] When the judge later ordered a new trial in the woman's case (while sentencing her husband to a maximum four years in prison), it was not because she didn't *mean* to kill anyone, but because, in his words, 'I cannot say as a matter of law that she subjectively *knew* that day that her conduct would cause death.'[93] Even so, he added, 'There is no question in this court's mind that in the eyes of the people, both defendants are guilty of murder. In the eyes of the law, they are not.'[94]

Criminal law, like most people, does not think it worth distinguishing between killing knowingly (collateral damage) and killing on purpose, at least when there is no lawful excuse. Both are murder. The criminal law, in fact, punishes collateral damage under two distinct approaches. The first is the universally accepted idea of 'transferred intent':

Suppose that Smith shoots at Black with the intention to kill him. But his aim is bad, and Smith's bullet hits and kills White, a clearly visible bystander, instead. Since the early days of the common law, all Anglo-American jurisdictions hold Smith guilty of murder by the doctrine of transferred intent.[95]

This doctrine has been applied consistently for hundreds of years. For instance, in the old case of *The Queen v. Saunders and Archer* (1573), an English court held it murder where a man tried to poison his wife but by accident poisoned his daughter.[96] Somewhat more recently, in the case of *People v. Sanchez* (2001), a California court held the accidental killing of an innocent bystander in a drive-by shooting to be first degree murder by transferred intent.[97] As for criminal codes, the New York Penal Code provides that it is equally murder when, '[w]ith intent to cause the death of another person, [one] causes the death of such person *or of a third person.*'[98] The Canadian Criminal Code provides the same thing.[99] Some scholars find the doctrine conceptually awkward in artificially 'transferring' the intention to kill one person to a victim for whom the accused may have had no ill will at all. But even those who disagree with the technique of the doctrine agree with its substance – namely that such cases should be punished as severely as murder.[100]

The second approach of the criminal law to collateral damage is almost as universal, and that is treating knowledge as the equivalent of intention for the purposes of the law. The approach of the Bible and the California court in the dog mauling case is common to many jurisdictions. This is also the attitude of the English common law. An example is the decision of the English House of Lords in *Hyam v. DPP* (1974), which upheld a conviction for the murder of two children, where the accused set fire to a house merely intending to frighten their mother. The court decided that murder was not restricted to 'the intention to cause death' but also included 'where the defendant knows that there is a serious risk that death or grievous bodily harm will ensue from his acts.'[101] England's foremost authority on criminal law, Glanville Williams, puts the case this way: 'Where the defendant desires result *x*, and anyone can see, by merely considering *x*, that another result *y* (forbidden by law), will also be involved, as the direct consequence of *x* and almost as part and parcel of it, then the defendant will be taken to intend both *x* and *y*.' He adds that 'certainty in human affairs means certainty as a matter of common sense – certainty apart from unforeseen events or remote possibilities.'[102]

In England this is called 'oblique intention,' and it is accepted by most writers and authorities and in many codes throughout the world. The only objections that have been made to it are similar to those made against the doctrine of 'transferred intent,' namely those relating to ordinary meaning and verbal fitness, not to punitive appropriateness. In other words, it may be awkward or even wrong to *say* of those who only knew someone was going to be killed by their acts that they 'intended' to kill, but there is no objection to punishing them equally as severely as those who do. Professor Wayne LaFave, author of a leading American text, adopts this position:

> Intent has traditionally been defined to include knowledge, and thus it is usually said that one intends certain consequences when he desires that his acts cause those consequences or knows that those consequences are substantially certain to result from his acts.... This failure to distinguish between intent (strictly defined) and knowledge is probably of little consequence in many areas of the law, as often there is good reason for imposing liability whether the defendant desired or merely knew of the practical certainty of the results.[103]

As for murder, LaFave writes:

> Apart from the question of when capital punishment should be permitted, there is no basis in principle for separating purposeful from knowing homicide. Many of the modern codes do not distinguish between them, although a majority do appear to require intent rather than knowledge or at least, to classify intentional and knowing killings differently.[104]

Of the many jurisdictions for which it is all the same, there is, interestingly enough, the Texas of George Bush, father and son. Under Texas law a person commits murder if he or she:

(1) intentionally or *knowingly* causes the death of an individual; [or]

(2) *intends to cause serious bodily injury and commits an act clearly dangerous to human life that causes the death of an individual;* ...[105]

Since the collateral damage inflicted in Afghanistan and Iraq by the former governor has involved so many perfectly predictable cases of multiple killings, of both adults and children, it might be worth pointing out that, under Texas law, murder is punishable by death if:

(7) the person murders more than one person:

    (A) during the same criminal transaction; or

    (B) during different criminal transactions but the murders are committed pursuant to the same scheme or course of conduct; or

(8) the person murders an individual under six years of age.[106]

This isn't some Texas exoticism either. According to the American Law Institute *Model Penal Code*, 1980, criminal homicide is equally murder 'when it is committed purposely or knowingly' (Art 210.2 (1)). Article 2.02 defines 'knowingly' as including the situation where one 'is aware that it is practically certain that his conduct will cause ... a result.'[107] Illinois law goes further yet and provides that '[a] person who kills an individual without lawful justification commits first degree murder if, in performing the acts which cause the death ... he knows that such acts create a *strong probability* of death or great bodily harm to that individual or another.'[108] The *New York Penal Code* is one of those codes that restrict murder to cases where the 'conscious objective is to cause death.' However, it still treats collateral damage as murder by adopting the universal doctrine of 'transferred intent' discussed earlier.[109]

The reason why the law almost always equates knowledge with intent is that the distinction is morally irrelevant for most of the purposes of punishment, which are the defining criteria of criminal law. A person who goes ahead with an unlawful act in the certainty that it will cause death is just as dangerous to life, maybe even more dangerous, than a person who goes ahead in the hope (vain or not) that it will cause death. This first person is worth punishing as severely for the purpose of 'deterrence' or protection of the public as the second, and protection is what most people want from criminal law. Furthermore, it would seem that the person who acts in full knowledge that death will occur is as *deserving* of punishment as one who actually seeks death, because they have both acted with their eyes wide open, voluntarily, and in disrespect of the lives of others, which they have equally sacrificed to their own illegitimate ends. This is not to deny that some people hold, evidently, that the intentional killer (without lawful excuse) is more abhorrent than the mere knowing killer (without lawful excuse), and that is the explanation for the codes that sometimes treat it as a lesser, though always very serious, crime. Still, it is hard to see why. Certainly there are many well-known instances where the distinction is not regarded as at all important. When Timothy McVeigh called the children he killed in Oklahoma City 'collateral damage,' he was not arguing that it was acceptable to kill them knowingly. He was actually arguing in his own defense that he did not *know* there was a daycare center, and that had he, he might have reconsidered his target:

> I recognized that someone might be bringing their kid to work. However, if I had known there was a daycare centre, it might have given me pause to switch targets. That's a large amount of collateral damage.[110]

In other words, McVeigh was not arguing about the difference between intention and knowledge, but about the difference between knowing and not knowing, just like the court in the California dog-mauling case. And when the FBI responded to McVeigh's claim, it wasn't by saying that it was his conscious objective to kill children, but rather that he must have *known* that there was a daycare center in the building from the brightly colored children's pictures in the windows. In other words, he should be executed because he *knew* many children would die.

This exact point is made in the movie *Collateral Damage*, an Arnold Schwarzenegger vehicle made shortly before the attacks of 11 September 2001. The movie is a bunch of clichés if there ever was one, but they are useful clichés meant to reassure the public by repeating back to them what they already know. The 'collateral damage' in the movie is the Schwarzenegger character's wife and son, who die in a Colombian terrorist bombing of an LA office building aimed at visiting Colombian military officials. Schwarzenegger goes on a rampage when an apologist for the terrorist is broadcast on television using the term just like General Wesley Clark might have: 'The deaths of the mother and the little boy are regrettable; it's called collateral damage.' The movie's release was delayed by the attack on the Twin Towers and the Pentagon, supposedly because it involved terrorist attacks against office buildings. But there are quite a few other things in the movie that might have offended official US sensibilities, for instance, the display of official American willingness to kill civilians; indeed the display of some 'terrifying' attack helicopters in action against a 'terrorist camp' full of civilians on the explicitly flimsy pretext of rescuing an American. There was also the cynical deployment of the concept of self-defense by the bad guys: at one point the terrorist says the attack on LA that killed the star's wife and child was an exercise in Colombian 'self-defense.'

Cynicism about the American notion of self-defense was running high in Canada when the cockpit tapes were released of the American F-16 pilot who accidentally killed four Canadian soldiers with a 500lb bomb near Kandahar on 18 April 2002. There was a national outpouring of mourning in Canada for these four, and there's nothing wrong with that. But imagine if Afghanistan had the mass media to mourn the 20,000 plus Afghanis who Canada helped America to kill in the cause of fighting terrorism. The Canadians were involved in a night training exercise, and the pilot saw fire on the ground. It does not appear that he ever seriously thought he was being fired upon, much less that he was in any danger at his altitude, so his routine use of 'self-defense,' and its approval by the controller, are evidence of a complete debasement of the concept to mean its opposite – namely, any reasonably safe opportunity to kill with vastly superior firepower.

Pilot: *I've got some men on a road, and it looks like a piece of artillery firing at us. I am rolling in in self-defense.*

And then, after he dropped the bomb:

Pilot: *Can you confirm they were shooting us?*
Air Controller: *You're cleared. Self-defense.*[111]

Rolling in in self-defense, lacking any hint of urgent necessity, could be the motto of the entire war on Afghanistan.

No doubt one of the biggest affronts to American feelings in the Schwarzenegger movie had nothing to do with 9/11 and everything to do with 10/7 – namely, the use of 'collateral damage' itself as an irredeemably dirty word, synonymous with murder, at a time when US forces were doing so much of it in Afghanistan. According to the Schwarzenegger character, the Colombian terrorist deserved to die because he *knew* innocent people like the star's wife and child would be killed when he tried to blow up the Colombian military officers; not because he wanted them to die. In fact, the only difference Schwarzenegger sees between himself and the terrorist is the willingness to accept *any* collateral damage. When he calls the terrorist a 'coward who kills women and children,' the terrorist replies: 'Well, it seems we're both willing to kill for a cause, so what's the difference between you and I?' Schwarzenegger's comeback is the movie's signature line: 'The difference is, I'm just going to kill you.' At one point Schwarzenegger sacrifices his plan to kill the terrorist and gets himself caught, all to avoid hurting bystanders. If this says anything, it says that popular wisdom, like law, holds collateral damage to be just as hateful as the standard variety of murder.

So law and morals condemn the attack on Afghanistan, like that on Iraq, as severely as the attack of 11 September – indeed more severely, given the disproportion in the actual amount of death and mayhem inflicted. But although a lot of people have been self-righteously slaughtered by the Americans to 'bring justice,' in George W. Bush's words, to the perpetrators of the 11 September crime, it's a sure bet that no Americans will even stand trial for what they have done.

3

Kosovo 1999

As the collateral damage accumulated in the villages and mountains of Afghanistan, far away in Northern Europe, in a modern courtroom in the ultra-civilized Dutch city of The Hague, Slobodan Milosevic, ex-President of Yugoslavia, went on trial for war crimes and crimes against humanity. The court was the International Criminal Tribunal for the Former Yugoslavia (ICTY), the first of its kind since the Nuremberg and Tokyo Tribunals of World War II.

The international criminal justice movement was riding high. Milosevic's trial commenced in February 2002. In April the movement's crowning glory, the new International Criminal Court (ICC) received the necessary sixtieth ratification to allow it to take effect, and it did so on 1 July. But the movement was also encountering some powerful opposition. A couple of days after the Milosevic trial started, Belgian charges against Israeli Prime Minister Ariel Sharon for crimes committed during the 1982 Lebanon war were called into question by the decision of yet a third international court in The Hague (we will sort these courts out in due course), the International Court of Justice (ICJ). The Belgian charges, based on 'universal jurisdiction' would be thrown out in June, and the law authorizing them completely de-clawed by the time of the American war on Iraq in 2003. Over in Chile, former dictator Augusto Pinochet was successfully ending a long entanglement with international criminal law that started with his arrest in London in 1998 for the torture and murder of thousands of Chileans during and following the coup by which he came to power in 1973.

The biggest setback for the movement came in May 2002, when the United States formally withdrew its support for the Court and set about muscling through exemptions for itself from the Court's jurisdiction. US opposition had stiffened during the war over Kosovo when, for a brief moment, the Prosecutor for the Yugoslavia tribunal appeared to be seriously considering charges against NATO leaders for war crimes committed during the bombing campaign, with President Bill Clinton at the head of the list. ICTY prosecutor Carla Del Ponte very quickly backed off on the charges and this taught different lessons to different people. To the movement's many supporters, the willingness of the tribunal even to contemplate charges against US leaders showed how even-handed it was: maybe one day, if the case warranted it, even an American leader could be brought to trial. To the

Americans, however, this was decisive: that an international criminal court could even *appear to consider* bringing Americans to trial was proof that this was a movement to be opposed. To those who brought the charges, Del Ponte's decision proved that powerful countries like the US had nothing to fear from international criminal law and, furthermore, that the trials of America's enemies were an exercise in hypocrisy.

And this was the point Milosevic himself hammered home every day of his trial. How could you charge me with war crimes when the Americans committed these very crimes against civilians in Yugoslavia? Milosevic went so far as to charge the tribunal with having been set up to justify NATO's war crimes against the Serbs. He added that in Kosovo he too was fighting Islamic terrorists, just like the Americans were at that moment in Afghanistan.

These events were not merely linked in time or in the desperate defense strategy of an ex-President on trial for war crimes. From the point of view of international law, the wars in Afghanistan and Yugoslavia had a lot in common. For one thing, they were both supremely criminal. But the issue wasn't only that NATO wasn't on trial, it was that Osama bin Laden wasn't on trial either. The trial before an international criminal court of those suspected of being involved in the 11 September attacks was the main alternative stressed by those opposed to an attack on Afghanistan – in other words, the vast majority of humanity – not to mention the Taliban themselves; but it was rejected out of hand by the Americans as irrelevant. On the other hand, the arrest and trial of Milosevic and other Serb leaders before an international tribunal was absolutely central to the NATO campaign in Kosovo. That Milosevic's Serbia was responsible for war crimes in Yugoslavia was the dominant theme of NATO's approach to the conflict from the very beginning. ICTY prosecutor Louise Arbour worked hand in hand not only with NATO governments, but with NATO military commander Wesley Clark and his colleagues, and one of the key demands that NATO made in the ultimatums that preceded the bombing was that Arbour be allowed to investigate alleged crimes against humanity in Kosovo.

Furthermore, the war in Kosovo was extremely important in setting the precedent for America's illegal wars in Afghanistan and Iraq. It broke a fundamental legal and psychological barrier. When Pentagon guru Richard Perle 'thanked God' for the death of the UN, the first precedent he could cite in justification of overthrowing the Security Council's legal supremacy in matters of war and peace was Kosovo: 'Facing Milosevic's multiple aggressions, the UN could not stop the Balkan wars or even protect its victims ... The rescue of Muslims in Kosovo was not a UN action: their cause never gained Security Council approval.'[1] But Kosovo was also the testing ground for the whole international criminal law movement, because it was here that we had, for the first time in history, an international criminal tribunal established *prior to the war whose criminals it was putting on trial*, and therefore capable of playing a role in that war; what's more, a tribunal with the firepower (NATO's) to enforce its actions. The actions taken by this tribunal – the relentless pursuit and eventual trial of one of the war's protagonists (the 'vanquished') and the absolution of all the others (the 'victors') – provided an unparalleled opportunity to evaluate the new international criminal justice in action.

Not only did the Kosovo war lack Security Council 'approval,' it also lacked the approval of the people of the United Nations. Despite NATO's frequent claims that the bombing was being carried out on behalf of 'the international community,' the people of the world were severely split on the war, with most appearing to have been against it. An opinion poll taken in mid-April 1999 and published by the *Economist* showed substantial opposition to the war even inside the NATO countries, even when the question was the misleading, 'Are you for or against NATO's decision to bomb Serb *military installations?*' According to the poll, a third or more of the population were opposed in Canada, Poland, Germany, France (all NATO) and Finland; they were almost evenly split in Hungary (NATO), precisely evenly split in Italy (NATO), and opposed by a three-to-two margin in the Czech Republic (NATO). In Russia opposition stood at 94 percent, in the Ukraine 89 percent, and in Slovakia 75 percent. [2] Opposition in the world's two most populous states, China and India, was official and assumed to be widespread in the population. [3] A poll taken in Greece, a NATO country, showed 99.5 percent against the war, with 85 percent believing NATO's motives to be strategic and not humanitarian. War criminals? 69 percent of those polled favored charging Bill Clinton with war crimes, 35.2 percent Tony Blair and only 14 percent Slobodan Milosevic – not far from the 13 percent who favored charging NATO General Wesley Clark and the 9.6 percent for charging NATO Secretary General Javier Solana. [4] In the United States itself, despite the relentless pro-bombing coverage of the networks, public opinion started out favorable, but by the end of the campaign had fallen to below 50 percent. [5] A year after the war, 133 developing nations gathered in Havana opposed the very premise of the war – the so-called right of 'humanitarian intervention.' [6] Intellectuals and artists were also divided. Those in favor included such literary luminaries as Susan Sontag, Salmon Rushdie, and, of course, Czech President Václav Havel (Tariq Ali would later term these warrior writers 'the *belligerati*'). But those opposed were no slouches either; their ranks included Alexander Solzhenitsyn, Harold Pinter, Mikos Theodorakis and Nelson Mandela.

The disagreement was not about the immediate harm done by the war. Nobody on either side had any doubt that the bombing inflicted a huge amount of suffering and damage. The 78-day campaign fired about 25,000 of the world's most devastating non-nuclear bombs and missiles at the former Yugoslavia. Somewhere between 500 and 1,800 civilian children, women and men of all ethnicities were killed by NATO's bombs alone. The lower figure is the one conservatively estimated by Human Rights Watch[7] and accepted by NATO with rather suspicious ease. The higher figure of 1,800 was the Federal Republic of Yugoslavia (FRY) government's official figure.[8] The truth is probably closer to the FRY figure.[9] No doubt many more were gravely, and even permanently, injured – given the expert's two-wounded-for-everyone-killed rule of thumb.[10] Less damage than America would do in Afghanistan and Iraq, for sure, but a lot of dead and maimed adults and children nevertheless, to whom we can add a whole population terrorized by a relentless attack that spared no urban center. On top of this, an unknown number of soldiers killed and wounded, somewhere between the FRY's claim of under 600 and NATO's claim of between 5,000 and 10,000 dead.[11] Finally, and most controversially, between 2,100 and 10,500 were killed in Kosovo not by the bombs but by the Serb–Albanian violence on the ground after the bombing had begun.

The bombs also did a huge amount of property and 'infrastructure' damage. There was extensive destruction of bridges, hospitals, schools, factories, livestock, crops, power grids, media facilities, religious buildings, including early Christian and medieval churches, archeological sites and museums. The effects of the war on the environment were disastrous. The repeated bombing of oil refineries, chemical plants (most notably in the Pancevo suburb of Belgrade), electrical networks and fertilizer factories propelled huge quantities of toxins (chlorides, ammonia, mercury, and so on) into the air and the ground, and into the Danube's drinking water.[12] This war was no exception in the way of 'the mortal residues of modern war,' including unexploded cluster bombs and the carcinogenic residue of exploded ones made with depleted uranium.[13] The damage to 'the economy' has been quantified at between US$60 billion and US$100 billion.[14] A lot of money for a country that was already very poor after eight years of economic sanctions and ten years of depression. In 1998 Yugoslavia was ahead of Romania but behind Albania in the race for the poorest country in Europe. In 1999, after the war, it was safely in the lead.[15]

The bombing campaign also saw about 1 million people made refugees from Kosovo. The Organization for Security and Cooperation in Europe (OSCE) put the number at around 860,000 ethnic Albanians and 100,000 Serbs. Probably another million were made internal refugees.[16] Of course, there is a lot of disagreement on whether the refugees were fleeing the bombs or being forced out by organized terror, but there can be no doubt that at least a portion of the Albanians, not to mention the Serbs, were running from the bombs – they would have to have been crazy not to, because they were being killed by them, for instance in the two well-publicized convoy incidents (see Chapter 6).[17] The really important point, though, is that the refugee crisis started *after* the commencement of the bombing. There were no refugees at all during the prior five-month period in which the observers of the OSCE were present and, according to the UN Secretary General's report of 24 December 1998, there had been a significant return of former refugees from the intensified conflict of the year before.[18] After three days of bombing in March 1999 the refugees amounted to only about 4,000; a week later there were 350,000. If it was 'ethnic cleansing' that caused the flight of many ethnic Albanians, it was ethnic cleansing that occurred *after* the NATO bombing started ('The Serbs didn't touch us until NATO attacked'[19]), something conceded even by official US State Department reports.[20]

NATO says the Serbs were planning to do it anyway, with or without the bombing, and that it would have been worse. This claim is vital to the case for the bombing and NATO still clings to it, despite the fact that the only evidence for it is the mythical 'Operation Horseshoe' (see below). Outside NATO itself, even supporters concede that the bombing would at least have *helped* any of the complicated plots they variously ascribed to Milosevic. For example, Michael Ignatieff, without any evidence at all, made this almost indecipherable claim: 'The air campaign did not *cause* the ethnic cleansing, but there seems little doubt that Milosevic anticipated an air campaign and gambled that he could use it as a cover – and as a justification – for an attack on unprotected civilians.'[21] Well, 'cause' is indeed a complicated philosophical concept, but both law and morals have no difficulty holding responsible those who, with their eyes wide open, make a necessary contribution to a crime, even if there are other contributors also to blame. To deny this is like saying, 'we bear no responsibility if we hand guns to acknowledged murderers and then beat them to a pulp, threatening worse, provoking them to carry out murders that we anticipate.'[22] This isn't about whether Milosevic is responsible, it's about whether NATO was *also* responsible; it's about NATO's *complicity*. The point is not that Milosevic was charged with atrocities in Kosovo, it's that *Clinton wasn't too*. Of course, one is only responsible for *wrongful* conduct, and NATO's responsibility turns, like America's would in Afghanistan and Iraq, on the wrongfulness and illegality of the Kosovo war, a question addressed below. But on the question of 'eyes wide open,' NATO clearly felt a refugee flow in the hundreds of thousands to be an 'entirely predictable' result of the bombing, claiming only (and unconvincingly) to have underestimated its extent.[23]

Peter Gowan argues persuasively (see below, this chapter) that the bombing was in fact an 'invitation to genocide' that was unexpectedly not taken up. This would explain NATO's early claims that genocide was occurring as a confident prediction rather than a mere lie meant to play out the Holocaust metaphor. Already on 28 March 1999, George Robertson was claiming the FRY was 'a regime intent on genocide' and that the bombing was intended to stop 'genocidal violence' and 'ethnic extermination.'[24] In an often-cited interview on CBS television US Defense Secretary William Cohen speculated that 100,000 military-aged men 'may have been murdered.'[25] But reporters who went to refugee camps during the war found it impossible to get eyewitness confirmation of these claims. Audrey Gillan of the British *Guardian* reported from Macedonia that neither she nor other reporters could get *anyone* to confirm the existence of the mass killings, systematic rape or even robberies that NATO was talking about.[26]

When the war ended and NATO had free access to Kosovo there was a great rush to unearth atrocities. But it didn't take long for all the prior talk of 'genocide' and 'Holocaust' to die down in the face of a serious evidence problem. Cohen's 100,000 figure was never mentioned again, and the official estimates dropped fast. By September they were down to 11,000. Even that number seemed exaggerated from reports out of Kosovo, for instance by a Spanish forensic team with experience in Rwanda who categorically denied the claims of genocide.[27] The Trepca mines, another 'Auschwitz' according to the British press, turned out to contain *no bodies at all*.[28] A Canadian Broadcasting Corporation story of the murder of a five-year-old Kosovo Albanian girl had to be retracted after the war when her sister admitted to the reporter that she had lied to gain sympathy for the cause.[29] The only corroboration for the figure of 11,000 came from an American Bar Association Report – 'coincidentally' sponsored by the State Department – which, on the basis of interviews with refugees, made statistical projections that were uncannily close to the claims of their sponsors.[30]

By the time Milosevic went on trial in The Hague the prosecution was severely hedging its bets. Now it was only 'at least four and a half thousand people died, but estimates rise to ten.' Even the refugees due to terror had been reduced to 'over three-quarters of a million people ... forcibly moved from Kosovo or *forcibly removed within it*.'[31] Since the total number of ethnic Albanians refugees during the war is generally accepted as about 1.5 million (860,000 external and 665,000 internal), that appears to be an admission that about half of the refugees were simply fleeing the war that NATO had started.[32]

And the main point about all of these deaths and refugee flows is that they occurred *after* the commencement of the bombing. Indeed, of the 385 murders in the original ICTY indictment of Milosevic, 340 were alleged to have occurred after the bombing started (the others were from the controversial Racak incident, of which more later). These deaths couldn't justify the bombing; they were a *cost* of it to be added to all the death and destruction that NATO's bombs did on their own. Even in the Ignatieff scenario (bombing used by Milosevic to carry out his plan), the bombing made a crucial contribution to these deaths. A justification of all of these costs would have to prove that these people would have died anyway, or indeed, that more would have died had NATO not bombed. And if that justification failed, these would not only be costs, but *crimes* in which the NATO leaders were morally complicit and for which they were criminally responsible, on top of what their bombs did by themselves.

Added to these costs would be the pathology of NATO-occupied Kosovo. The withdrawal of the FRY forces left Kosovo to the KLA, restrained only minimally by their NATO sponsors, and what followed was a reign of terror against non-Albanians.[33] The murder rate in Kosovo in this period was about the highest in the world, 20 times the Western European and Canadian rate, and five times the American rate.[34] Nor did this appear to be simple revenge, but rather part of 'a precise political program aimed at the expulsion of the minorities and, definitively, at the homogenization of Kosovo along a single ethnic profile,' 'reverse ethnic cleansing' in aid of the project of an independent Kosovo.[35] 100,000 Serbs left Kosovo before the year was out, joining the 100,000 who had fled during the war, leaving only one-third of the pre-war community.[36] The Roma fared equally badly: an estimated 70 percent of the pre-war 100,000–150,000 had been expelled by September 1999. If there appeared afterwards to have been a reduction in the incidence of human rights abuse, 'this was due principally to the effective reduction of the population belonging to the minorities' – in other words to the very success of 'reverse ethnic cleansing.'[37] Serbs remaining in Kosovo continued to be confined to NATO-guarded enclaves and to be the victims of 'ethnically motivated' murder right through America's wars in Afghanistan and Iraq.[38]

'The West fought a war with Mr. Milosevic and his forces over Kosovo in 1999 and made the lives of Kosovo's Albanians significantly better,' according to *New York Times* correspondent Steven Erlanger.[39] This would be faint praise indeed, given all the lives wiped out or ruined and the destruction caused to each and every ethnic group. But whether the lives of Kosovo Albanians had been made even 'significantly better' was debatable. Albanian refugees returned to a situation of extreme instability characterized by a violent struggle *within* the Albanian community for dominance of the new Kosovo. This struggle saw much violence directed against 'dissidents,' including the murder of two Kosovo Albanian judges in December 1999, and terrorist acts 'of a clear mafia matrix,' as organized crime sought to take advantage of the open border with Albania to evade justice and carry out an illegal traffic in arms, drugs, oil, and so on.[40] The economy of Kosovo also suffered the classic distortions of war and military occupation: not only were the Serbs expelled from factories, but many factories were dismantled and plundered, and their parts sent to Albania by criminal bands.[41] A coercive sex economy thrived 'in the zones with the densest foreign presence, military and civilian, which takes advantage of services that can be defined as "voluntary" or even "mercenary" only with a lot of hypocrisy.'[42]

NATO sought to defend its war as 'a just and necessary action,' a pure rescue operation for the Kosovo Albanians who were at the mercy of a genocidal regime.[43] But most of the world was deeply distrustful of NATO's motives, or more precisely of America's motives, because it was clear from the outset that this operation was conceived and executed primarily by the Americans. The US flew 80 percent of all strike missions, 90 percent of the advanced intelligence and reconnaissance missions, and fired 95 percent of the Cruise missiles. The other 18 NATO members representing 'the international community' merely provided political cover, and even some restraint. They were, in fact, excluded from all targeting decisions and intelligence involving American missiles or planes, in other words 80 percent of what was going on.[44] People had a hard time swallowing the notion of the United States using its military power for humanitarian reasons, given its long and consistent record of purely self-interested aggression, its failure to intervene where its interests weren't at stake, its support for human rights abusers, and its human rights abuses of its own citizens.[45] Michael Ignatieff argues that the 'requirement that "he who casts the first stone should be without sin" is a guarantee of inaction,' and that the 'fact that the West does not live up to its ideals does not invalidate the ideals or invalidate their defense.'[46] But the point was not whether the Americans were hypocrites; the point was whether, with their unbroken record, they should be trusted when they claimed that the kind of damage they did to human life in Kosovo, and would do again in Afghanistan and Iraq, was really for the good of the people they were bombing.

Another powerful reason for opposing NATO's intervention was that the countries doing the bombing bore a large measure of responsibility for the Balkan crisis that the bombing was supposed to solve. This argued against the 'humanitarian intent' of the interveners – they didn't care about the people before, what made us think they cared now? – and, more importantly, it argued against the *necessity* of war by pointing to the peaceful alternatives that had always been in the hands of those doing the bombing. NATO tried, characteristically, to blame the whole thing on one evil person: 'the seeds of tragedy can be traced to the rise to power of Slobodan Milosevic.'[47] But the war's critics hammered away at the widely accepted decisive contribution made by the United States itself, along with the rich countries of Europe, to the disintegration and descent into violence of the former Yugoslavia.

The history of the West's complicity in the 'Balkan tragedy' has often been told, and need not be repeated here.[48] In broad outline, it is a story of the rich countries of Europe and America taking advantage of the sad state of the post-Soviet economies to impose solutions (sometimes known as 'Shock Therapy') through powerful credit institutions like the IMF and the World Bank. These solutions were highly favorable to the Western investors but devastating to the people of the countries concerned, leading to fiscal crises and massive depressions throughout Eastern Europe. Part of the goal was to encourage the fragmentation of the old Soviet bloc to create in its place 'hub and spoke' arrangements dependent on the West. Economic advantages were matched by strategic ones, involving nothing more sophisticated than the old divide-and-conquer strategy and the ancient rule that debt and subjection go hand in hand ('And thou shalt lend unto many nations, but thou shalt not borrow; and thou shalt rule over many nations, but they shall not rule over thee'[49]). Yugoslavia was one of the early victims of shock therapy. By the time of its dissolution crisis in the 1990s, its economy was destroyed and its federal government bankrupted. This would try the civil peace of any country, as Shock Therapy architect Jeffrey Sachs explained:

> Bankrupt governments ... are prone to fail. Rarely does that failure mean a simple reversion to old practices; often it means a more dangerous state of affairs, including criminality, political extremism, civil unrest, hyperinflation, capital flight, and, in the worst cases, civil war.[50]

Economic crisis does not inevitably lead to civil war, but Yugoslavia had the necessary additional ingredients in abundance. It was made up of several distinct and economically unequal ethnic communities, with a very short history of being unified in a federation. On the eve of the dissolution crisis, the Serbs were the dominant ethnic group (about 40 percent of the total Yugoslav population), followed by Croats (22 percent), Slovenes (8 percent) and Albanians (6 percent). But ethnic Serbs were mostly concentrated in Serbia, and the richest republics were Slovenia and Croatia to the north, where Slovenes and Croats were respectively dominant. The poorest region in the country was Serbia's province of Kosovo, where Albanian Muslims constituted the majority. The next poorest was Bosnia-Hercegovina, divided ethnically between Muslims, Serbs and Croats. The economic crisis made it impossible for the federal government to provide the material incentives necessary to satisfy the various constituent elements. The richer republics of Slovenia and Croatia had little reason to stay with a sinking ship that was taxing it for redistribution payments to the poorer regions, while the poorer regions, like Bosnia and Kosovo, had little reason to hang on to what was left.

The contribution of the Western countries to Yugoslavia's civil war did not end with their precipitation of a profound economic crisis; their management of that crisis was characterized by the same self-centered recklessness. With the Cold War over, a united Yugoslavia as a foil for the Soviets was no longer of any value to the Western countries. Now their geopolitical and economic interests were all in favor of disintegration, which they did not leave to chance but rather encouraged despite the obvious dangers of ethnic civil war. Slovenia's independence was relatively painless, as there was only a tiny Serb minority; but in the case of Croatia, Europe underwrote independence despite the profound opposition of a Serb minority that was 600,000-strong – about 15 percent of the population – and that quite naturally preferred to keep its well-defined enclaves united with Yugoslavia and their Serb co-nationals. The result was an absolutely predictable civil war, which, though brief, saw thousands dead on both sides and hundreds of thousands 'ethnically cleansed' – violently forced into refugee status to create 'facts on the ground' for future territorial claims.

The independence of Croatia and Slovenia, and the virtual collapse of the federal state, enormously increased independence pressures on the precariously balanced multi-ethnic Bosnia, which was about 43 percent Muslim, 31 percent Serb and 17 percent Croat. But as much as independence appealed to Bosnian Muslims, it was seen as a threat by the Serb and Croat minorities, who naturally sought closer links to their parent republics. And when the Bosnian Muslims declared independence in April 1992 a vicious war broke out that would last three years and see tens of thousands dead.[51]

The Europeans had been more cautious about Bosnia than they had been about Slovenia and even Croatia. They earnestly sought a solution that amounted to ethnic cantonization with a great deal of autonomy for each community. Agreement between the factions was almost reached on this basis in Lisbon in February 1992 and again in March, before war broke out, and it was almost reached again on several occasions during the first year of the war. These latter peace bids were under the joint auspices of the United Nations and the European Union, represented by the American Cyrus Vance, former Secretary of State under President Carter, and David

Owen, former UK Foreign Secretary under the Labour government of James Callaghan. Owen has written a detailed account of the Vance–Owen Peace Plans.[52] According to him and many other authoritative sources, a major obstacle to achieving a peaceful settlement was American intervention. Both the Bush and Clinton administrations took it upon themselves to sponsor the Bosnian Muslims, and encouraged them to avoid compromises on the promise of support, including military intervention by NATO.

For instance, of the Lisbon agreements of February 1992, the Canadian Ambassador to Yugoslavia at the time, James Bissett, has written, 'the entire diplomatic corps was very happy that the civil war had been avoided – except the Americans. The American Ambassador, Warren Zimmerman, immediately took off for Sarajevo to convince [the Bosnian Muslim leader] Izetbegovic not to sign the agreement.'[53] Zimmerman later admitted this, although he claimed, implausibly, just to be helping Izetbegovic out of an agreement with which the latter was uncomfortable.[54] However, according to 'a high-ranking State Department official who asked not to be identified,' quoted in the *New York Times*, '[t]he policy was to encourage Izetbegovic to break the partition plan. It was not committed to paper.'[55] That was Bush Sr. As for Clinton, in February 1993 David Owen made this public statement:

> Against all the odds, even against my own expectations, we have more or less got a settlement but we have a problem. We can't get the Muslims on board. And that's largely the fault of the Americans, because the Muslims won't budge while they think Washington may come into it on their side any day now … It's the best settlement you can get, and it's a bitter irony to see the Clinton people block it.[56]

The US then engaged in a long tug-of-war with the United Nations over authority to use NATO air strikes, and was ultimately successful in obtaining it, explicitly, in several 'all necessary means' resolutions, but only under United Nations control ('subject to close cooperation with the Secretary-General').[57] The US used this authority to bomb Serb positions in May 1995. The Serbs responded by bombing UN-established 'safe areas' and taking UN soldiers hostage. In August NATO struck again, this time massively. Then the Americans supplied the missing ingredient – not bombs, but pressure on the Muslims: 'In Sarajevo and in New York the Americans were for the first time exerting real pressure on the Bosnian Muslims to agree to an overall settlement package.'[58] There quickly followed a peace agreement in November in Dayton, Ohio, which resulted in a new Bosnia-Herzegovina, not far from what had been agreed to at Lisbon in 1992 or Geneva in 1993, except that it would now become a permanent protectorate run by NATO, and of course it had been brokered by American military power.[59] Boutros

Boutros-Ghali was the Secretary General of the UN from 1992 to 1996. This was his assessment of the American contribution to peace in Bosnia:

> In its first weeks in office, the Clinton administration had administered a death blow to the Vance–Owen plan that would have given the Serbs 43 per cent of the territory of a unified state. In 1995 at Dayton, the administration took pride in an agreement that, after nearly three more years of horror and slaughter, gave the Serbs 49 per cent in a state partitioned into two entities.[60]

KOSOVO

NATO's military support for the (mainly Muslim) Bosnian independence movement greatly encouraged the separatist aspirations of the Albanian Muslims of Kosovo, the southernmost province of the Republic of Serbia. This was a region that had been disputed periodically by Serbs and Albanians since the fourteenth century, but which had a huge Albanian majority (almost 90 percent). The Albanians had demanded and been granted significant autonomy by the Yugoslav constitution of 1974. When the bitter economic crisis of the 1980s hit, tensions were heightened further. A *New York Times* story of 1 November 1987 describes a Kosovo that was highly autonomous but increasingly hostile to Serbs:

> Ethnic Albanians already control almost every phase of life in the autonomous province of Kosovo, including the police, judiciary, civil service, schools and factories.... As Slavs flee the protracted violence, Kosovo is becoming what ethnic Albanian nationalists have been demanding for years ... an 'ethnically pure' Albanian region.[61]

As well as being home to several hundred thousand Serbs, Kosovo was also a place of great cultural and religious meaning to the Serbs as a whole, full of medieval Orthodox Christian monasteries and monuments. US Ambassador Warren Zimmerman conceded that 'Kosovo is to Serbs what Jerusalem is to Jews – a sacred ancestral homeland.'[62] It was also a place of great mineral riches. The Trepca mine complex was not just the site of alleged atrocities, it also 'generated 25 percent of the entire regional industrial output and figured as one of the principal sources of exports for the entire former Yugoslavia.'[63]

The year of the *New York Times* story was also the year of Slobodan Milosevic's 'infamous' speech, which, according to NATO's official story, was the start of all the trouble.[64] In this speech Milosevic promised the Serb minority: 'No one has the right to beat you! No one will ever beat you again.' It's hard to understand how these could be regarded as immoderate words, given what everybody concedes was going on, including the beating of Serbs. Milosevic was elected President in May 1989. Earlier that year a constitutional revision had cut back on Kosovo's autonomy under the 1974 constitution. This was partly in reaction to Albanian separatism, but it was also directly related to the West's economic strangulation of Yugoslavia. In 1988 the IMF made the provision of a loan of US$2.2 million (the biggest in IMF history to that date) conditional on centralized control of the economy. According to Susan Woodward, '[t]he pressures from the IMF and the banking consortium organized by the U.S. State Department to recentralize monetary control and create more effective economic administration' were 'a primary reason for the Serbian constitutional revision reducing its provinces' autonomy.'[65]

From 1989 to 1996 the Albanians, under the leadership of Ibrahim Rugova, employed a mainly non-violent form of opposition to Serb rule. They could not fail to be caught up in the dissolution of Yugoslavia, and in September 1991, shortly after the independence declarations of Slovenia and Croatia, a clandestine vote for independence was held and Rugova was elected president of the proto-Kosovo. The Albanians boycotted Serb institutions and set up parallel ones. The turn to violence came only in 1997, and appears to have had nothing to do with Serb repression. A part of the Albanian independence movement became impatient with non-violent methods; a mood change evidently related to the collapse in 1997 of the economy and government in Albania proper, the disbanding of its army, the looting of its arsenals and the consequent appearance of a mass of cheap arms on the market, which found their way into the hands of the Kosovo separatists. Thus the appearance in late 1997 of the Kosovo Liberation Army. The methods of the KLA were rather different from the non-violence of Rugova: 'The first actions of the [KLA] are the selective assassination of Albanians accused of "collaboration" with the Serbs. Subsequently they go on to attack police patrols and posts.'[66] By February 1998, the KLA had launched a 'full-scale insurrection' in which they took brief control of 40 percent of Kosovo.[67]

THE ROAD TO RAMBOUILLET

In the year before the bombing campaign, violence dramatically increased in Kosovo, though the 2,000 dead on both sides combined were no more numerous than in many contemporary conflicts where the US chose not to intervene.[68] There are enormous controversies about this year, but the facts that are beyond dispute show clearly that, far from seeking to avoid a fight, NATO was bent on provoking one. The KLA itself made major and deliberate contributions to the escalation of the violence, and this was aimed precisely at drawing NATO intervention on their side, on the Bosnian precedent. NATO knew this and encouraged it. This means that the KLA and NATO themselves bear a large share of the responsibility for the violence in Kosovo; and, moreover, that military intervention was not a humanitarian necessity but rather entirely avoidable.

That the KLA was a full party to the spiral of violence was well understood at the UN, where Security Council Resolutions were even-handed in their condemnation of 'the use of excessive force by Serbian police forces against civilians and peaceful demonstrators in Kosovo,' and 'all acts of terrorism by the Kosovo Liberation Army.'[69] Of course, 'terrorist' was even then about as bad a label as you could find in the US lexicon, signifying everything that is hateful and justifying the most extreme responses; so it is remarkable that it is associated in a Security Council Resolution with the KLA, since all Security Council Resolutions have to be agreed to by the United States itself. Yet, at the very moment of this resolution, NATO had already started preparing for military options against the Serbs. In fact, as told by Lord Robertson, American diplomacy consisted of little more than NATO threats to intervene militarily against the Serbs: 'Experience had taught that diplomacy without the threat of force would be wasted on [Milosevic].'[70] But even NATO had to admit that 'any balanced analysis of the situation in Kosovo ... would acknowledge that serious acts of violence and provocation were committed against the Serb population by Kosovar Albanians, and in particular by the KLA.' According to NATO, though, these 'paled in comparison to the premeditated, well-orchestrated, and brutally implemented campaign of violence and destruction conducted by the forces of the Yugoslav regime against the Kosovar Albanian population.'[71] This referred to the Serbs' ferocious military responses against the villages where the KLA had taken control, amounting to 40 percent of Kosovo by the summer of 1998; but it was really no more than the classic response of superior forces to popular guerrilla activity, regularly deployed by Israel against the Palestinians in territories acknowledged to be 'occupied.' The Americans deployed it in Vietnam with a savagery unknown to the Middle East or the Balkans, and without the justification of defending their own territory from a separatist group; they would deploy it within a year in the battle for Kosovo itself, when they attacked Serbia to break the morale of the people and force Milosevic to capitulate.

But what could NATO's threats of military intervention mean, not to the Serbs, but to the KLA? How could the KLA miss the clear signal that their provocations would be 'understood' by NATO, but that retaliation by the

FRY would bring forth dire threats and, ultimately, if only for the sake of 'credibility,' military intervention. According to Michael Ignatieff, writing from a pro-interventionist point of view, this was explicitly discussed by the KLA and the 'Balkan pro-consul' Holbrooke in December 1998, when Ignatieff accompanied Holbrooke on a visit to Kosovo:

> ... the Kosovar's taste for compromise is vanishing fast. There is already talk that the hidden Kosovar strategy is to provoke the Serbs into massacres and reprisals, which would force NATO troops to intervene. The first stage in provoking NATO intervention would be to drive out the unarmed monitors. Armed NATO troops would replace them and impose independence, or at least partition, on Milosevic. Such, at any rate, is the desperate dream. Holbrooke may favor a robust armed deployment himself but he knows how reluctant NATO would be to authorize one, so he does his best to close down the idea that NATO is waiting in the wings to ride to the rescue.[72]

Some 'desperate dream': it would come true within a span of just six months. But NATO 'reluctant'? In December 1998? NATO had already explicitly threatened Yugoslavia with air attacks in September. Though the Security Council had condemned both sides, NATO's threats were reserved for the FRY.[73] Thus the FRY was 'persuaded' to agree to withdraw troops from Kosovo and allow in a 'Kosovo Verification Mission' under the auspices of the Organization for Security and Cooperation in Europe. The agreement was endorsed by Security Council Resolution 1203 of 24 October 1998. This resolution once again condemned violence on both sides and, most notably, given the war footing that NATO had put itself on and the claims that it would later make to 'implicit' authorization for war by the Security Council, it pointedly reaffirmed that, 'under the Charter of the United Nations, primary responsibility for the maintenance of international peace and security is conferred on the Security Council.' The Resolution also repeated 'the commitment of all Member States to the sovereignty and territorial integrity of the Federal Republic of Yugoslavia.'

Calm returned for a while when the Kosovo Verification Mission began to function. According to the Secretary General's Report of 24 December 1998, 100,000 refugees had returned home. However, by the time Holbrooke was meeting with those desperate dreamers in the KLA, violence had returned. What is striking is how well understood it was in UN circles that the pattern was the familiar one of provocations by KLA paramilitaries and response by Serb authorities. Here's an excerpt from the Secretary-General's Report under the heading 'Obstacles to returns/security':[74]

On 20 November, two policemen were killed and three injured in a suspected ambush by Kosovo Albanian paramilitaries in Prilep ... On 14 December ... [t]hirty Albanians were killed and twelve wounded near the Gorozup and Liken border posts in fighting between Yugoslav border guards and a group of armed Albanians. That same day, two masked men entered and attacked patrons in a cafe in Pec, killing six Serbs. On 18 December, the Deputy Mayor of Kosovo Polje was kidnapped and murdered.... Following the 13 October accord ... Kosovo Albanian paramilitary units have taken advantage of the lull in the fighting to re-establish their control over many villages in Kosovo, as well as over some areas near urban centres and highways. These actions by Kosovo Albanian paramilitary units have only served to provoke the Serbian authorities, leading to statements that if the Kosovo Verification Mission cannot control these units the Government would.

RACAK

The die of the Kosovo war was cast on 15 January 1999 at the small village of Racak, just south of Pristina. The ICTY indictment of Milosevic, which came only four months later, put it simply enough: '... on 15 January 1999, 45 unarmed Kosovo Albanians were murdered in the village of Racak.' This is an event well worth pausing over if one wants to understand how international criminal law can be manipulated to legitimate an illegal war. It became known to the world when the Head of the OSCE mission William Walker held a press conference the following afternoon (16 January), and denounced the killings as 'a massacre' and 'a crime against humanity' for which he did not 'hesitate to accuse the government security forces of responsibility.' Two days later (18 January), Chief ICTY prosecutor Louise Arbour arrived at the border of Kosovo demanding entry to investigate the crime, which the FRY government denied her. As chance would have it, she was accompanied by film crews and the scene was broadcast around the world, along with details of 'the mutilated bodies of 45 ethnic Albanians in a gully ... men, women and a child murdered in cold blood.'[75] Racak quickly became the emblematic episode of Kosovo. Bill Clinton played it for all it was worth. On 19 March 1999, in his justification of the war he was about to launch, the President told the world's press: 'We should remember what happened in the village of Racak, where innocent men, women and children were taken from their homes to a gully, forced to kneel in the dirt, sprayed with gunfire – not because of anything they had done, but because of who they were.'[76]

But the Serbs had a different version of events, one that has received some considerable corroboration from independent sources. There is no dispute, for example, that this was a pre-announced police action against Racak and three other villages to track down a KLA group that had attacked a police patrol a week before and killed four policemen. There is no dispute that heavy fighting took place, after which the Serbs withdrew and KLA fighters re-occupied the village. There is no dispute that KLA fighters were also killed in the fighting.[77] According to the Serb version, however, *all* of the dead were either KLA fighters or civilians caught in the crossfire. There was no massacre of civilians, but the KLA had plenty of time to dress their dead fighters in civilian clothes (or to remove them for that matter, leaving only civilians), arrange bodies in the 'gully,' and then call in Walker and the press. There was some corroboration for even the contested elements of the Serb version.[78]

The EU sent a team of Finnish forensic investigators to perform autopsies. They performed or witnessed about 40 autopsies on the Racak bodies, alongside FRY and Belorussian pathologists. The FRY team confirmed the Serb version in most respects, though the change-of-clothes hypothesis was discounted. According to one of the Serb investigators, Dr. Dusan Dunjic,

> Criminological technicians confirmed the presence of traces of gunpowder explosion on the hands of 37 out of the 40 examined bodies. The discovery of traces of gunpowder explosion indicates that directly before death, these people had handled firearms; ... all these facts led the investigating bodies to conclude that this concrete case did not involve a 'massacre' in the village of Racak, but a legitimate battle of the authorities against terrorists.[79]

The EU forensic mission did not make its own findings available to the public, but on 17 March 1999 – that is, on the day before the collapse of the Rambouillet talks (see below) – the head of the EU mission, Dr. Helena Ranta of the University of Helsinki, was asked by the Presidency of the EU (Germany) to give a press conference in Pristina about Racak; in other words, this was not the fortunate 'coincidence' for NATO that a 'Western diplomat' made it out to be: 'The publication of the report in the midst of the talks may be a coincidence, but if it damns the Serbs, it will certainly add to the pressure and form part of the justification for any NATO action.'[80] Nor was OSCE mission head William Walker taking any chances with what Ranta would have to say. Shortly before the press conference, they had an intense meeting that was later described by Ranta as 'a very unpleasant experience indeed.'[81] Ranta seems to have struggled at the press conference not to let her professional duties succumb to political importuning, but she was only partly successful. She underlined the fact that the statement was only her 'personal view' and 'should not in any manner be construed as an authorised communication on behalf of ... the EU Forensic Expert Team.'[82] But she then proceeded to go well beyond what she or her team had observed, and the result was very favorable to the NATO version of events. In several respects, she simply relied on what she had been told by Walker or his officials. For example, on the very important question of whether the 22 men – not 45 men, women and children as reported – had been shot in the gully where they had been found, she said: 'Based on the information obtained from the KVM and KDOM observers the total of 22 men were found in a gully close to the village of Racak. *They were most likely shot where they were found.*'[83] She made this entirely hearsay-based statement despite her earlier caveats that the team's investigations were hampered by the fact that they had only arrived a week after the deaths, that there had been 'no chain of custody' of the bodies from the moment of death, and that, therefore, 'what may or may not have happened to the bodies during that time is difficult to establish ... with absolute certainty.'[84] Notice that even this wasn't good enough for Bill Clinton, who, in his pre-bombing press conference, invented the presence of women and children among the dead in the gully and even had them kneeling in the dirt: *'innocent men, women and children taken from their homes to a gully, forced to kneel in the dirt and sprayed with gunfire.'* At the press conference Clinton was also asked, apropos of the Lewinsky affair, 'What do you think your legacy will be about lying?'[85]

At her press conference in Pristina, Ranta concurred with the Yugoslav pathologists on some matters (lack of mutilation, no change of clothes), but she went beyond observation to conclude, differently from the Yugoslav pathologists, that '[t]here were no indications of the people being other than unarmed civilians.'[86] Still, she cautiously added, 'medicolegal investigations cannot give a conclusive answer to the question whether there was a battle or whether the victims died under some other circumstances.'[87] At least she was cautious in her prepared statement. Her reported ad lib responses to questions from the audience (among whom sat the unpleasant Mr. Walker) included a statement for which she had no professional competence, and very little, if any, basis in personal observation: 'This is a crime against humanity, yes.' This naturally formed the headline of the news stories of the following day.[88] There was another highly misleading element to Dr. Ranta's statement that is so subtle it is impossible to grasp from reading the statement alone. As if to confirm her point about unarmed civilians, Dr. Ranta said that the paraffin tests for gunshot residue used by the Yugoslav and Belorussian pathologists had been scientifically discredited in favor of an electron microscope and x-ray method known as 'SEM-EDX.' Now, what could the following statement in her press release mean to anyone but that the latter tests had been done *on the Racak bodies* and proved negative? 'Test samples for SEM-EDX were taken and they proved to be negative.'[89] But the key word was 'test,' because, as Dr. Ranta revealed to me in July 2001, these tests were not performed on the bodies found in Racak at all. Tests on the bodies from Racak would have been useless if not taken within two to three hours of death, so 'I ordered samples to be taken from certain other sites.'[90] *Not Racak but other sites*, where *other people* had been killed. When she took the witness stand in 2003 at Milosevic's trial, it was evident from the confusion of the prosecutors that Dr. Ranta had not disclosed this particular detail to them either. Nor did she take the occasion to do so on the stand, though she did point out the utter uselessness of the SEM-EDX test by the time her team arrived upon the scene, something completely absent from her crucial press release of 17 March 1999. Dr. Ranta did maintain that, in her opinion, on the basis of the bullet fragments found much later at the site (after NATO's occupation), at least some of the victims were killed where they fell, and thus the event had not been 'staged,' or at least not completely. However, she disclaimed any ability to say whether any had been 'executed' and she had no answer for the point made to her on cross-examination that the many layers of clothing, KLA trinkets and gun-belts worn by some of the autopsied indicated pretty clearly that they were fighters.[91]

In February 2001 several members of Dr. Ranta's team published a report of the 40 autopsies, which seemed to support the Serb position.[92] The report revealed that all but one of the victims were male, all but one were over 15, and only one had been shot at close range. Unlike Dunjic and Ranta, these team members denied any capacity to judge the circumstances of the victims' deaths: 'Determination of reasons for events, their political and moral meanings, or connection of victims to political or other organisations are questions which lie beyond the scope of forensic science.'[93] Finally, they stood up for the professionalism of their Yugoslavian and Belorussian colleagues: 'Having some differences in practical questions between different schools complemented the end result. The autopsy findings were discussed in full professional consensus.'[94]

So NATO's version of the events at Racak has been thoroughly discredited, and the Serb version seems, on the evidence, to have stood up much better, though certainly not completely. But two things are absolutely clear, and critically important for understanding this and subsequent events. First, to the extent there was a massacre, it was provoked by the KLA as part of a deliberate and consistent pattern aimed at bringing on NATO's military intervention. Second, as far as NATO was concerned, Racak was not a reason, but an excuse, more like a *pretext*, for the bombing campaign.

Even supporters of the NATO bombing had to admit that the KLA's tactics were designed to provoke the Serbs into violent overreactions that would bring on the bombs. Michael Ignatieff was already writing in December 1998:

> Hit and run attacks on Serb military and police targets exposed civilians to reprisals. Then they [the KLA] tried to liberate villages and towns, which they had neither the arms nor the men to hold. As soon as they were driven out, the Serbs massacred or evicted the population. It is more than possible, of course, that KLA tactics were not a miscalculation, but a deliberate strategy, designed to incite Serbs to commit massacres that would eventually force NATO to intervene.[95]

'More than possible' is an interesting way of describing something that is otherwise impossible to understand. As the UN Secretary General reported, the KLA had been provoking this kind of massive retaliation all year, indeed since their inception.[96] Had they been doing it for the pleasure of seeing their own people die? Ignatieff, for no apparent reason, seems to think that Racak was an exception, but other commentators have been more logical: '[T]his was entirely consistent with the KLA's pattern of provoking or condoning anti-Albanian atrocities by Serbs in order to stir up international opposition to Milosevic, as the Racak massacre did.'[97]

So if it was a massacre, it was a useful massacre, and one for which the KLA has to bear a heavy responsibility. More importantly, it was an avoidable massacre. It was avoidable by the simple device of NATO's firm refusal to entertain intervention on the KLA's side. But NATO presented Racak as a *reason* for military intervention. And this is the second important point about Racak: it could not in a million years have been a reason for intervention, because, whatever the Americans believed to have really happened at Racak, the responsibility of the KLA at least for provoking it was all too obvious. Or are we supposed to believe that the Americans were the only ones who didn't know what the KLA were up to?

This isn't merely logic; there is also a 'smoking gun' in the person of William Walker himself, the man who denounced the event to the world. From the fact that he was head of the OSCE Verification Mission, ratified by UN resolution, you might think he was some European technocrat representing the 'international community.' In fact, Walker was the opposite of this. He was – before, after and at the time of Racak – a career American diplomat and a full-time employee of the US State Department. His boss was Madeleine Albright and he had spent his whole working life representing American interests. A complete newcomer to the Balkans, his specialty was Central America, where he was in charge of some very sensitive and unsavory missions. In the Reagan years he rose to Deputy Assistant Secretary of State for all of Central America. This was precisely the moment of Reagan's violent crusade against the Sandinistas in Nicaragua, complete with condemnations by the World Court. In fact, Walker was formally a 'subject of investigation' in the Iran/Contra Affair for his involvement with Oliver North in activities that led to North's indictment for the illegal funneling of guns, ammunition and supplies to the Contra rebels who were trying to restore a version of the overthrown Somoza dictatorship.[98] In 1988, Walker was named Ambassador to El Salvador, a country which, at the time, was still in the grip of US-sponsored state terror. Walker was, in fact, famous for another massacre before Racak, a massacre in late 1989, when Salvadoran soldiers executed six Jesuit priests, their housekeeper and her 15-year-old daughter. Walker was not charging anyone with crimes against humanity then: 'I'm not condoning it, but in times like this of great emotion and great anger, things like this happen.' As the *Los Angeles Times* of 14 April 1999 pointed out, 'This reputation as a crusader for human rights represents quite a change for Walker.'[99]

How did Walker get to be head of the OSCE observer mission? The OSCE is European in name only; in fact, it is more like NATO plus Russia. The presidency during the period of the Verification Mission was held by three NATO countries – Germany, Italy and Norway. Walker was put where he was by Madeleine Albright, a fact he grudgingly admitted later on the witness stand at the Milosevic trial.[100] In fact, only one week prior to Racak he gave an on-the-record briefing in which he left no doubt who he worked for, or what his job was:[101]

> Ambassador Walker: *Let me just begin by reminding everyone in the room that even though I was introduced as the head of OSCE, I am a serving career Foreign Service Officer; but in my present capacity, I guess I'm speaking on behalf of the OSCE in Vienna and the KVM mission in Pristina.*

Walker was then asked flat-out whether he was 'spying' for Washington the way Richard Butler, head of UNSCOM, was by then known to have been spying in Iraq (Walker was known to his detractors as 'the Richard Butler of Kosovo').[102] Walker denied that but admitted he reported back to Washington as well as 'all the capitals.' Michael Ignatieff, in his defense of NATO's bombing campaign, concedes that Walker's Racak denunciation 'appeared to bring the Verification Mission squarely down on the side of the KLA at a time when human rights violations were occurring on both sides.'[103] But he claims that Walker was acting on his own in calling the Racak press conference:

> Having seen for himself Walker did not clear his next move with Washington [*notice, not with Vienna, the headquarters of the OSCE, but with Washington*]. At a press conference immediately afterwards, he called the Racak massacre a crime against humanity and left no one in any doubt who was responsible.[104]

Sure. Here was a lifelong diplomat, an employee of the State Department, who had never in his life been known to say anything publicly that the State Department did not want to hear. 'Spring has come early,' Madeleine Albright is reported to have told National Security Adviser Sandy Berger when she first learned of Racak.[105] It was even being openly stated in Washington circles as early as the previous August that Clinton was looking for just such an atrocity-type triggering event.[106]

And Walker cleared his denunciation not only with Washington, but also with NATO command. While he was standing among the bodies at Racak, he pulled out his cell-phone and called Supreme Commander Wesley Clark. It was Clark who revealed this, not Walker. At the Milosevic trial in The Hague three years later, Walker claimed on the witness stand that he had no recollection of telling Clark, but would have to accept Clark's version, as well as that of Richard Holbrooke, Albright's man in charge of Yugoslavia. With the same breath that he swore he could not remember calling Clark and Holbrooke – while conceding that he did – Walker testified that he remembered *not* calling Madeleine Albright:

> Q. [Milosevic] *In your statement, you say that you do not remember having talked to Clark, Holbrooke, Albright, or the OSCE prior to the press conference in Racak. You say, 'I cannot exclude the fact that my memory is lacking on that score.' Let me remind you. Can we see some footage? Can we have the video played, please?*
>
> [*Videotape played*] 'MR. HOLBROOKE: Walker, the head of the Kosovo Verification Mission, called me on a cell phone from Racak.' 'GENERAL CLARK: I got a call from Bill Walker. He said, 'There's a massacre. I'm standing here. I can see the bodies.'
>
> Q. [Milosevic]: *Do you need to comment this at all? I leave it to you to decide.*
>
> A. [Walker]: *I stick by my statement. When I had that interview with BBC, I had no recollection whatsoever of having talked to either of those two gentlemen. As I said yesterday, there were tremendous – there was tremendous commotion and activity going on in the immediate aftermath of my visit to Racak and*

before I made the press conference. Did I talk to those people? Are they telling the truth when they say they talked to me? I have no reason to doubt it. I believe they are both very honourable and truthful people. So I just have to plead a faulty memory when I was talking to BBC. But I'm quite positive I didn't talk to Madeleine Albright, but I have no doubt that people on my staff were calling the various capitals of the OSCE member states to tell them what had been seen on Racak that day. Whether I made some of the calls or whether other people on my staff did, at this point in time, I have absolutely no recollection.[107]

After speaking to Clarke and Holbrooke (but not, in Ignatieff's account, 'clearing it' with them), Walker went back to his office and called the press conference, where he released a written statement entitled 'Massacre of Civilians in Racak,' containing this passage:

Although I am not a lawyer, from what I personally saw, I do not hesitate to describe the event as a massacre, a crime against humanity, nor do I hesitate to accuse the government security forces of responsibility. The FRY government must produce the names of all involved in the police and VJ operations around Stimlje, who gave the orders, who executed those orders. The International Criminal Tribunal for the former Yugoslavia must come in, with visas, at the invitation of the FRY government, or without, to investigate this atrocity, and this must be accomplished in the next 24 hours.[108]

Those were fighting words, and certainly not the kind a career diplomat like Walker uses unless he is sure he has the approval of his superiors. But the reference to the ICTY, with the odd emphasis on visas, reveals yet another convenient memory lapse. The press release was issued on 16 January, but in his testimony at Milosevic's trial, Walker claimed he did not speak to ICTY Prosecutor Louise Arbour until 'the following day' – that is, 17 January:

A. [Walker]: *I believe it was the following day I received a call from Judge Arbour, and we discussed what I had seen briefly and what I had said briefly, and I told her I thought it was very important that either she or people from this Tribunal, investigators, criminal investigators, come to Kosovo and do a thorough investigation. Judge Arbour reminded me that she had not been able to obtain a visa to enter the former Yugoslavia. She asked me if I thought it advisable for her to try to enter. I told her I thought that would be the best thing. I told her that if she was denied entry or her people were denied entry, that that would indicate that the government was not terribly serious about finding out what had happened at Racak. She said that she would personally get on a plane the following day, I believe it was, on the 18th, and try to enter via Skopje, Macedonia, in other words, the southern border. I told her I would send people down.*[109]

Let's try to make sense of this. Walker claims at the trial that Arbour called him after the press conference, on her own initiative, just doing her job as it were, and wanting to investigate the crimes he had announced to the world, and 'reminded' him of her need for visas. But in fact Walker was demanding that she be allowed to enter 'with visas' *at the press conference itself*, which means that Arbour must have been informed *before* the press conference. That's when she must have 'reminded' him about the need for the visas, because he obviously wouldn't need reminding after the press conference where he demanded them on her behalf. She was informed before the press conference, along with the State Department and NATO, and the press statement was worked out, at least in part, with her input. The point of bringing her in was precisely to embarrass the FRY government, and this was discussed with her before the press conference too. The people 'sent down' by Walker also included the international press. That means the whole photo-op appearance of Arbour demanding entry at the Kosovo border was a public relations stunt cooked up to score points against the Serbs. A conscious decision was made by a State Department agent, with clearance from NATO and Washington, to deploy the ICTY prosecutor in this enterprise, and she appears to have lent herself willingly to the cause. We'll pick up this thread later; but for now, could anything be clearer than that, whether Racak was a real or fake massacre, it didn't make one bit of difference to the Americans? That it was just the pretext the Americans had been waiting for and now seized upon to justify a decision taken long beforehand to use force against Yugoslavia? That this was precisely the kind of thing that the Americans had been encouraging the KLA to bring down on themselves (or manufacture in whole or in part)? And if this is all true, how could anyone possibly accept NATO's plea that this war was a humanitarian necessity that they were dragged into in spite of themselves?

RAMBOUILLET

On 30 January, Javier Solana sent President Milosevic what he called 'a final warning,' 'summoning' the Serbs to Rambouillet, France, with a prominent invocation of Racak.[110] It is now widely accepted that Rambouillet was a war conference and not a peace conference, meant to justify a decision already taken to go to war, not to avoid it. That's the conclusion of many independent observers, including David Owen (of the Vance–Owen Peace Plan): 'Rambouillet was structured by the Americans in particular to bring matters to a head and create the political climate for NATO to fulfil its threat to bomb the Serbs.'[111] Key American players have admitted as much. For instance, after the war James Rubin said that while 'publicly, we had to make clear that we were seeking an agreement ... privately we knew the chances of the Serbs agreeing were quite small':

> The other acceptable outcome was to create clarity where previously there had been ambiguity ... That meant the Kosovar Albanians agreeing to the package and the Serbs not agreeing to the package.[112]

The idea that Rambouillet was a hoax is overwhelmingly confirmed by the facts. Though it was the Serbs who were ultimately bombed for the failure of Rambouillet, it was they and not the Albanians who immediately accepted NATO's pre-announced so-called 'non-negotiable principles,' which were

> an immediate end to hostilities, broad autonomy for Kosovo, an executive legislative assembly headed by a president, a Kosovar judicial system, a democratic system, elections under the auspices of the OSCE within nine months of the signing of the agreement, respect of the rights of all persons and ethnic groups, and the territorial integrity of the Federal Republic of Yugoslavia, with Kosovo remaining within the country.[113]

The Serbs had no difficulty in agreeing from the outset to these principles, and maintaining that position throughout. It was on the Albanian side that the objections were raised: first, that the principles did not go far enough towards independence for Kosovo and, second, that they did not require the presence of NATO, for which the KLA had been working so hard. Evidently, with the Serbs agreeing and the Albanians disagreeing, something had to change; so at the very end of the first session, a draft agreement was produced by the US with the big innovation of a 'NATO-led international peace-keeping force.' A further concession was made to the Albanian side: they were promised that after three years there would be 'a mechanism for a final settlement for Kosovo, on the basis of the will of the people.'[114] Everybody seemed to understand this as a referendum on independence that could only go one way, given the ethnic make-up of Kosovo.

The key provisions were under the heading of 'Implementation II,' a late addition to the draft agreement (as is obvious from its title) that would give NATO control of Kosovo: 'The Parties invite NATO to constitute and lead a military force to help ensure compliance with the provisions of this Chapter' (Article I.1.a). 'The appropriate NATO commander shall have sole authority to establish rules and procedures governing command and control of the airspace over Kosovo as well as within a 25 kilometer Mutual Safety Zone (MSZ) ... of FRY airspace within 25 kilometers outward from the boundary of Kosovo ...' (Article X). In addition to this, there was also a breathtaking 'Appendix B' that gave NATO the complete run not only of Kosovo, but of the whole of the FRY. For example, Article 8 provided:

> NATO personnel shall enjoy, together with their vehicles, vessels, aircraft, and equipment, free and unrestricted passage and unimpeded access throughout the FRY including associated airspace and territorial waters. This shall include, but not be limited to, the right of bivouac, maneuver, billet, and utilization of any areas or facilities as required for support, training, and operations.

Much was made of these clauses in the debate over the war. NATO was even said to have put them there to ensure that Yugoslavia would not sign; there were indiscretions to this effect during Rambouillet.[115] According to Lord Roberston, Appendix B contained merely the 'standard' clauses incidental to peace-keeping arrangements, and no specific objection was raised to it at the time.[116] This is true, but it is only a half-truth, because the FRY's objection was a global one to the whole of the implementation section that 'invited' NATO to take over a chunk of FRY territory. That the Appendix B rights over the *whole* territory were entailed as standard equipment to that kind of occupation just proved how impossible it was for any self-respecting state to accept the 'NATO-led presence.'

The FRY voiced no objection to the rest of the agreement – in effect a complete interim constitution for Kosovo with a huge degree of autonomy within the Yugoslav federation (and including a provision dear to American investors that 'the economy of Kosovo shall function in accordance with free market principles'[117]). The *New York Times* reported at this point that 'Mr. Milosevic has shown himself at least as reasonable as the ethnic Albanians about a political settlement for Kosovo.'[118] And indeed, when they paused the conference on the day the draft agreement was tabled, the official statement by the co-chairs admitted that there was 'consensus' on the 'political elements' (namely, everything but NATO and the referendum), and that all that remained to be 'finalised' were the implementation chapters 'including the modalities of the invited international civilian and military presence in Kosovo.' But to the co-chairs these had suddenly become as crucial as the rest: 'It is essential that the agreement on the interim accord be completed and signed as a whole.'[119]

In the period between Rambouillet and Paris, the desperately peace-seeking Americans and British were being condemned at the Security Council for their humanitarian bombing of Iraq, which, during the Rambouillet conference itself, took the lives of at least eleven Iraqi civilians (six on 10 February and five on 15 February).[120] The Serbs, meanwhile, were working furiously on a counter-proposal for an 'international presence' alternative to NATO. But when the talks resumed in Paris on 15 March, it was clear that negotiations were over and the whole thing was now a formality, because the Americans had obtained the Albanian signatures and they didn't have the slightest interest in what the Serbs had to say. The one-sided signing ceremony took place on 18 March 1999 in the presence of the two NATO mediators, but not, pointedly, the Russian Boris Mayorsky, who agreed with the FRY objections to the NATO clauses.[121] The very next day the OSCE ordered its observer force removed, over the protests of the FRY. NATO told the FRY to sign what the Albanians had signed or be bombed. Five days later the bombing began.

What was the urgency? If America wanted to go to war, there was plenty, as there would be in Afghanistan and Iraq in the coming years. Everything was in place, including an enormously complicated multi-billion dollar military operation. Racak was still fresh, the Albanian signatures were on the documents, and nobody had time to scrutinize the events. But if there had been a real desire to make peace, was there no alternative? According to independent observers, significant progress was being made by the observer force right up to the moment of the ordered withdrawal: zero international refugees in the five months preceding the bombardment, only a few thousand internally displaced persons in the weeks before the air bombardment commenced, and success in mediation programs between the various ethnic communities. The main obstacle was the familiar one of repeated KLA provocations.[122] Indeed, the provocations of the KLA continued unabated in the period between the adjournment talks at Rambouillet and their recommencement in Paris on 15 March, in flagrant violation of the conditions set by the co-chairs' statement of 23 February ('honour fully and immediately the ceasefire ... abstain from all provocative actions').[123] The FRY government maintained throughout the war that its opposition to NATO occupation was not opposition to an 'international presence' to implement an agreement on self-rule. Its position was even vindicated in the actual peace accord signed by the FRY on 3 June and ratified by the Security Council on 11 June, which approved the deployment in Kosovo 'under United Nations auspices ... acting as may be decided under Chapter VII of the Charter' of an 'international security presence with substantial North Atlantic Treaty Organization participation ... deployed under unified command and control ...'[124] NATO had insisted on NATO alone, but only until it had bombed the FRY into submission.[125]

NATO claims the Rambouillet talks were a sincere effort to find a peaceful solution, and that it was Milosevic's failure to negotiate in good faith that caused them to fail: 'It is clear the Yugoslav government never seriously sought a negotiated peace at Rambouillet.'[126] But how clear is it, since the Yugoslav government accepted all the so-called non-negotiable principles and the Albanians didn't, and the Albanians only signed when the Albanians and NATO got the additional clauses they wanted inserted? Here is what even the pro-interventionist Goldstone Commission wrote a year after the war:

> In fact, Albright and others had been so firm about the supremacy of NATO over any other institutional actor in this context ... that there was little reason for Serbia to have expected flexibility from NATO.[127]

The very fact that it was NATO and not the FRY that broke off the talks would suggest that it was NATO and not the FRY that was the obstacle to peace. NATO's answer to this was that Milosevic was planning to expel the ethnic Albanians anyway, bombing or no bombing. The plan even had a code name: 'Operation Horseshoe.'[128] The Serbs were pretending to be reasonable at Rambouillet just to buy more time to prepare; NATO saved lives by breaking off the talks and going to war; far from being responsible for what happened on the ground during the bombing NATO was responsible only for ending it. On 11 April 1999 the *New York Times* reported German Defense Minister, Rudolf Scharping as saying, '[o]ur analysis of Operation Horseshoe sadly confirms what we had inferred during the negotiations, which is that Milosevic wanted to win time to prepare a systematic deportation.'[129] But neither the German government nor anyone in NATO ever produced any evidence to support the existence of 'Operation Horseshoe,' apart from a series of maps the German government itself had drawn up. Nor did they get any mention whatsoever in the ICTY indictment of Milosevic. After the war, a retired German general denounced Operation Horseshoe as a complete 'fake.' The maps were fabricated from a general Bulgarian intelligence report about FRY tactics against the KLA that had nothing to do with expelling the civilian population; the name was simply made up by the German Defense Ministry.[130] No doubt the FRY had a contingency plan for occupying Kosovo and driving out the KLA in case of the invasion that NATO had been planning since June, and threatening since September of the preceding year: 'Even living in total peace and security, the U.S. has innumerable contingency plans for actions ranging from nuclear ... to lesser actions.'[131] Indeed, the KLA's operations on the ground during the war were lethal for Serb forces, informing NATO command on their positions and drawing them out into the open so they could be pulverized by NATO's bombs, hundreds at a time.[132]

NATO's claim that it intervened to prevent genocide is also refuted by the very way it conducted the war, withdrawing all of the observers and giving five days of warning, followed by a desultory bombing that stayed away from the scene of the expected genocide for another week. A real rescue operation would have gone in massively with ground troops and without warning. Peter Gowan argues that there was an 'acute, indeed bizarre' contradiction between the 'supposed goal – protecting the Kosovo Albanians,' and the means, 'a bombing campaign ... which left the Serbian security forces free on the ground to do what they wished with the Kosovar Albanians.'[133] The foreseeable results of such a war, planned meticulously for at least a year, were 'large floods of refugees' and 'intense warfare between Serbian security forces and suspected KLA activists in Kosovo.' Furthermore, 'all such wars produce atrocities, rapes, looting and burning: even highly trained soldiers can engage in wanton atrocities in war conditions. The tortures and other atrocities committed by NATO troops engaged in "peacekeeping" in Somalia testify to that ...'[134] What could possibly explain NATO's starting of the war in this particular way?

> There is only one serious explanation: The Clinton administration was giving the Serbian authorities the opportunity to provide the NATO attack with an *ex post facto* legitimation. The United States was hoping that the five days before the launch of the bombing and the first week of the war would give various forces in Serbia the opportunity for atrocities that could then be used to legitimate the air war.... They could predict also that there would be a refugee flow across the borders into Macedonia and Albania. And the U.S. planners were proved right ... As for the Serbian government organizing a genocidal mass slaughter, this did not happen. The Clinton administration organized the launch of the war to invite the Serbian authorities to launch a genocide, but the Milosevic government declined the invitation.[135]

Provoke a war with intended anti-humanitarian consequences? Why would NATO do such a thing? Kosovo's material and strategic value to the West does not exactly leap out at you the way Iraq's does. Some argued that at the bottom of this conflict were the same Caspian Sea oil reserves that made Afghanistan so strategically significant, namely a secure pipeline, this time to the Mediterranean instead of the Indian Ocean.[136] Diana Johnstone argues that another objective was to solidify a strategic alliance with Muslim countries in the region, and even to pay some dues to Arab allies to offset the resentment over Israel.[137] Chomsky, on the other hand, argues that oil pipelines and the like are far too narrow a way to think of a superpower's interests, and that the notion of 'credibility' is far more powerful an explanatory tool. 'Credibility' was indeed the refrain repeated by the NATO leaders whenever pressed for a reason for going to war against the FRY, for instance in President Clinton's war speech:

> We must also understand our stake in peace in the Balkans and in Kosovo. This is a humanitarian crisis, but it is much more. This is a conflict with no natural boundaries. It threatens our national interests. If it continues it will push refugees across borders and draw in neighboring countries. It will undermine the credibility of NATO on which stability in Europe and our own credibility depend.[138]

As Johnstone has remarked, credibility in this context 'has nothing to do with truthfulness and everything to do with readiness to use force.'[139] This means the willingness and ability to crush even mere 'annoyances' like Serbia.[140] Credibility is also the other side of the coin of 'resource control,' as Thomas L. Friedman wrote in the *New York Times* on the very eve of the Kosovo war: 'The hidden hand of the market will never work without a hidden fist.'[141] To credibility one can add the more mundane explanations, the things that are always arguing for superpowers to go to war, if they can just find a suitable excuse. The weapons manufacturers' cash registers rang mightily every time a bomb was dropped on Yugoslavia.[142] The construction companies would make a killing in the reconstruction of Kosovo and, eventually, Serbia. The billion dollars in aid by which donor countries would later extort Milosevic's 'extradition' would naturally wind up in the coffers of donor-country companies like Vice President Dick Cheney's Halliburton, whose subsidiary Brown & Root got the contract for Camp Bondsteel in Kosovo in 1999.[143] The immense costs of reconstruction would also have the benefit of putting Yugoslavia at the mercy of Western lenders.[144] The military itself regarded Kosovo as a huge war game that answered a few simple questions. Could you win a war without sending in ground forces? Without losing one life in combat? Could you get away with violating the Geneva Conventions and fighting a war primarily aimed at breaking civilian morale?[145] Added to these were the 'Wag the Dog' political explanations. In the contemporary Hollywood film of the same name, an American president is involved in a sex scandal (the 'tail') and needs a diversion, so Washington calls on Hollywood to create a fictional war (the 'dog') in Albania, no less. In the case of Kosovo, the real-life President Bill Clinton was being dogged by a series of women he had molested or otherwise taken advantage of, and the fall-out for the whole Democratic Party was enormous. The Kosovo crisis coincided precisely with Paula Jones' lawsuit against Clinton for sexual molestation, and his public investigation, impeachment and humiliation for lewd behavior in the Oval Office with the young intern Monica Lewinsky. At his press conference of 19 March 1999, at which the president devoted *all* of his opening remarks to an explanation of why NATO had to go to war over Kosovo, Clinton answered nine questions from the assembled journalists. Only three were on the subject of Kosovo, the same number as were asked on the subject of his personal morality. The first one started this way: 'Mr. President, when Juanita Broaddrick levelled her charges against you of rape in a nationally televised interview ...'[146] Monica Lewinsky's dress clearly did not itself launch a thousand ships – neither, we can rest assured, did Helen of Troy's face – but she occupied a lot more of Bill Clinton's thinking than Kosovo did.[147] Clinton would have had to be very strong and very committed to resist all the forces for war, from 'credibility,' to the military, to the arms manufacturers. The more complicated and difficult road was the one to peace. It is not that he would have chosen this road without her, but Monica would have argued very strongly in his mind for the easier war option.

In other words, there were lots of motives, all making much more sense of this war than the wildly out-of-character humanitarian one. This is altogether apart from what could have been achieved had the tens of billions spent on bombing, and then reconstructing everything that was bombed, been devoted to 'preventive diplomacy' such as 'genuine support for the nonviolent Kosovar movement' and 'addressing the massive polarization of wealth in Europe, since Kosovo is the most impoverished area in all of Europe.'[148] Not to mention more pressing humanitarian crises, like the AIDS epidemic that kills about two million Africans every year: the US$80 billion spent by America on one year of war in Iraq could have supplied every African in need with all the required antiretroviral drugs for life.[149]

Peter Gowan has a theory about the Kosovo war that has great relevance for the question of how America gets away with murder. Gowan argues that the Kosovo war was essentially fought against the *United Nations legal order*. Gowan's thesis proceeds both from the demonstrable implausibility of the humanitarian thesis and from the difficulty of identifying any interests in the Balkans themselves that were both worth the effort of the bombing and common to all the NATO countries. He concludes that the Balkan wars were primarily about 'political goals outside the Balkans' – goals not of the NATO countries, but of the United States: 'The conflict between the Serbian state and the Kosovar Albanians was to be exploited as a means to achieve US strategic goals outside the Balkans on the international plane.'[150] The strategic goals had to do with the United States' perennial political and economic rivalry with Russia and the Western European states for dominance in Europe. During the Cold War Russia was isolated and the situation of confrontation, combined with US military power, meant Europe had to accept US leadership. With the fall of the USSR, the US was challenged in its leadership role by Germany and France, acting through the increasingly powerful European Union. The US moved to counter this challenge through NATO. It expanded eastward to include Poland, both marginalizing and challenging the Russians. And, most importantly, it sought to develop new tasks for NATO, 'out-of-area' missions that would allow the US to deploy its military assets and once again subordinate Europe politically. The Balkan theater was particularly important for the US, because Europe took the lead at the start of the 1990s, encouraging Croatian and Slovenian independence and then brokering a peace deal in Bosnia. The Americans' determined opposition to and ultimate destruction of the various Bosnian peace plans is seen by Gowan as a quite deliberate strategy aimed at ensuring military solutions in which the US would inevitably play the dominant role, using NATO as the vehicle.[151]

A central objective of the war in Kosovo was the overthrow of the authority of the United Nations: 'instead of thinking that the US was ready to overthrow the authority of the UN Security Council for the sake of the Kosovar Albanians, we assume exactly the opposite: the US was wanting to overthrow that UN authority over NATO and used the Kosovo crisis as an instrument for doing so.'[152] The enthusiasm of the French and British for by-passing the UN, despite their veto powers, was doubtless connected to the fact that in NATO these countries have an effective veto as well, and were no longer hostage to the anti-Western vetoes of Russia and China. The institutional power of Western Europe would thus be actually enhanced. For the US, the legitimation of the use of force outside the structure of the UN Charter would put it in a legal position commensurate with its effective world stature, transforming the international legal order from one based on 'a multilateral order founded at the end of the Second World War and maintained by big-power rivalry until the collapse of the Soviet bloc'[153] to the unipolar world of global capitalism led by Uncle Sam.[154] Michael Ignatieff reports a pre-Kosovo conversation with Richard Holbrooke – America's 'Balkan pro-consul' in the Roman Empire terms Ignatieff uses to describe him[155] – in which Holbrooke says he

> wants to demonstrate that his success at Dayton marked a watershed in the use of American power, not just in the region, but in the world. It showed the tired Europeans and dispirited UN ... what America can accomplish when it uses ruthless means – air strikes or the threat of them, round the clock negotiations and the immense force of Presidential authority – to achieve peace.

'One curious feature of the vision,' comments Ignatieff, 'is how little place it accords the United Nations.'[156]

HUMANITARIAN INTERVENTION

Whether the US went to war in Kosovo for the purpose of radically changing the UN legal order – to allow for 'ruthless means' with 'little place' for the United Nations – it was clear by the time of the Iraq war of 2003 that this was one of the prizes that America tried to extract from it. Hence Richard Perle's claim, quoted earlier, that the 'death' of the UN dates from Kosovo. But implicit in this very idea is the widely accepted view that the Kosovo war itself was illegal, supremely so; that's why it could be regarded as such a rupture with the prior legal regime. Though there were a few more defenders of the legality of the Kosovo war than of the Iraq war, they were still greatly outnumbered by those who argued for its illegality. These included some very eminent authorities, including Louise Arbour's colleague at the ICTY, its first President, Italian law professor Antonio Cassese. In the middle of the war and while still a judge on the court, Cassese published an article that gave voice to the scholarly consensus:

> The breach of the United Nations Charter occurring in this instance cannot be termed minor. The action of NATO countries radically departs from the Charter system for collective security, which hinges on a rule (collective enforcement action authorized by the Security Council) and an exception (self-defence). There is no gain saying that the Charter has been transgressed, in that a group of states has deliberately resorted to armed action against a sovereign state without authorization by the Security Council.[157]

Of course NATO tried to defend its actions on legal as well as moral grounds. In Lord Robertson's corporate non-speak, the NATO countries were 'sensitive to the legal basis for their action.'[158] They concluded that 'a sufficient legal basis existed' in the following 'factors':

> – the Yugoslav government's non-compliance with earlier UN Security Council resolutions, – the warnings from the UN Secretary General about the dangers of a humanitarian disaster in Kosovo, – the risk of such a catastrophe in the light of Yugoslavia's failure to seek a peaceful resolution of the crisis, – the unlikelihood that a further UN Security Council resolution would be passed in the near future, and – the threat to peace and security in the region.

These factors can be grouped into three categories: 1) Security Council Resolutions; 2) impending humanitarian disaster; and 3) threats to peace and security. Common to all three was a big institutional question: while the UN legal order entitled the Security Council to act on any of these bases, it did not entitle any state or group of states to do so. In other words, this was another case of the United States, this time acting through NATO, trying to substitute itself for the Security Council. Nothing could be more obvious in this respect than the invocation of a 'threat to peace and security,' something the Charter gives over explicitly to the Security Council, but only slightly less obvious is the invocation of Security Council Resolutions that do not contain even a hint of Security Council *authorization*. As in the case of Iraq, the Security Council Resolutions made demands (this time on both sides), but they did not back them up with the threat of force. Even supporters of the bombing had to admit that there was no way to read these Resolutions as authorizing the use of force against Yugoslavia for non-compliance, explicitly or implicitly.[159] NATO's invocation of Security Council authority was like saying that any non-compliance with any Security Council Resolution would justify military intervention, no matter how limited the means the Resolution itself envisaged for enforcement. This was precisely the claim the Americans had been using for years to justify bombing Iraq and would use to justify war in 2003. As the British scholar Christine Gray put it,

> It is no longer simply a case of interpreting euphemisms such as 'all necessary means' to allow the use of force when it is clear from the preceding debate that the use of force is envisaged; the USA, the UK and others have gone far beyond this to distort the words of resolutions and to ignore the preceding debates in order to claim to be acting on behalf of the international community.[160]

As might be imagined, this is unacceptable to the vast majority of legal scholars for its *1984*-ish violence to language, and for the usual problems of selective enforcement – the United States has not seen fit to bomb Israel for its complete defiance of 37 years of Security Council Resolutions on the Palestinian territories Israel occupied in 1967. But beyond that, it would put the Security Council virtually out of business, because it could not make the mildest declaration or decision on an international dispute without thereby implicitly authorizing the United States, or anybody with the necessary muscle, to invade and bomb its way to a solution. That's why the notion of 'implicit authorization' even disturbed supporters of the bombing.[161] The Security Council's primary responsibility for the maintenance of peace and security would exist only on paper, which seems to be the option the US prefers to every other, perhaps even to tearing up the paper itself.

Not even NATO claimed the attack on Yugoslavia came within the exercise of the right of self-defense of a Member State, for the simple reason that no NATO country had been threatened or attacked and neither NATO nor the UN recognized Kosovo as independent. NATO didn't even claim that it was coming to the aid of Kosovo's right to self-determination.[162] That was ruled out by the same Security Council resolutions that formed the 'legal basis' to which NATO was 'sensitive,' because they also affirmed the 'territorial integrity' of the FRY. The only legal claim with any coherence at all, leaving aside plausibility for a moment, was the remaining one – the so-called right of 'humanitarian intervention,' to be precise a right of *unilateral* humanitarian intervention that *any* state or group of states could undertake on its own without the requirement of Security Council authorization. Cassese's confident assertion that the war was illegal rested precisely on the widely accepted understanding that no such right existed. Indeed Cassese really wanted to argue that Kosovo created a precedent in favor of it precisely because it was illegal (see below, this chapter).

'Humanitarian intervention' by military force finds no place in the Charter of the United Nations, because for the generation who wrote the Charter the 'scourge' was war *between* states, the violation of national sovereignty that was Nuremberg's 'supreme crime,' the one committed by Nazi Germany that left 50 million dead in its wake. The UN Charter put all its emphasis on outlawing that, whatever the motives. The exception of self-defense against an armed attack proved the rule. The Charter absolutely rejected the use of force in relations between states, enjoining them to settle their disputes 'by peaceful means' and to 'refrain in their international relations from the threat or use of force against the territorial integrity or political independence of any state' (Articles 2.2 and 2.4). It sought to monopolize the use of force (except for temporary self-defense) in the Security Council. Section 2(7) even forbade intervention by the United Nations itself, let alone individual member states, save for exceptions specifically laid down in Chapter VII with respect to threats to international peace and security and self-defense.

The notion of a 'humanitarian war' would have rang in the ears of the drafters of the UN Charter as nothing short of *Hitlerian*, because it was precisely the justification used by Hitler himself for the invasion of Poland just six years earlier. Hitler's address to the Reichstag on 1 September 1939 sounds so much like NATO that it seems there must be some logical structure to justifying aggression:

> ... all German minorities living there have been ill-treated in the most distressing manner. More than 1,000,000 people of German blood had in the years 1919–1920 to leave their homeland. As always, I attempted to bring about, by the peaceful method of making proposals for revision, an alteration of this intolerable position ... An attempt was made to justify

the oppression of the Germans by claiming that they had committed acts of provocation. I do not know in what these provocations on the part of women and children consist, if they themselves are maltreated, in some cases killed.... I have, therefore, resolved to speak to Poland in the same language that Poland for months past has used toward us.[163]

Hitler's pretext for taking over Czechoslovakia had also been expressed as a humanitarian intervention in defense of German minorities who had been 'abused, tormented economically ruined and above all prevented from realizing the right of self-determination of nations also for themselves.'[164] He also saw his stance as a breakthrough in international law, proclaiming to the Reichstag on 20 February 1938 that the 'juridical separation from the Reich as far as international law is concerned' could not prevail against 'the universal rights to self-determination.' Czech President and *belligerato* Vaclav Havel was forgetting his own history when he said, fatuously, during NATO's fiftieth birthday party, that the war over Kosovo was 'probably the first war ever fought that is not being fought in the name of interests but in the name of certain principles and values.'[165] In fact it is nauseating how frequently states *claim* to fight wars for higher values and how rarely the case can be made out.

The Charter's attempt to ban non-defensive wars as illegal was not an innovation in international law. Already after the devastation of World War I there was broad agreement on this principle. It formed the essence of *The General Treaty for the Renunciation of War* of 1928 (popularly known as the 'Kellogg–Briand Pact') concluded between the United States and France, and adhered to by them and 13 others, including Germany and Great Britain. It was eventually ratified by 62 nations. The text read in part as follows:

ARTICLE I
The High Contracting Parties solemnly declare in the names of their respective peoples that they condemn recourse to war for the solution of international controversies, and renounce it, as an instrument of national policy in their relations with one another.

ARTICLE II
The High Contracting Parties agree that the settlement or solution of all disputes or conflicts of whatever nature or of whatever origin they may be, which may arise among them, shall never be sought except by pacific means.

This was the idea that would inform the United Nations Charter, signed in San Francisco on 26 June 1945 after an even more devastating war that ended with the debut of a weapon capable of wiping out the entire human race. And it was the basic idea that informed the Nuremberg trials that commenced that same summer. For the proposition that 'aggressive war' was illegal and criminal when the Nazis waged it, the Nuremberg Tribunal felt it had to do no more than refer to the Kellogg–Briand Pact itself:

> *The nations who signed the pact or adhered to it unconditionally condemned recourse to war for the future as an instrument of policy, and expressly renounced it. After the signing of the pact, any nation resorting to war as an instrument of national policy breaks the pact. In the opinion of the Tribunal, the solemn renunciation of war as an instrument of national policy necessarily involves the proposition that such a war is illegal in international law; and that those who plan and wage such a war, with its inevitable and terrible consequences, are committing a crime in so doing. War for the solution of international controversies undertaken as an instrument of national policy certainly includes a war of aggression, and such a war is therefore outlawed by the pact.*[166]

The question of the relationship between illegal and aggressive wars is a very important one for understanding America's criminality, not only in Kosovo but in Afghanistan and Iraq as well, so it is worth a momentary digression. As is evident from this passage, the Nuremberg Tribunal did not decide whether every illegal war was a war of aggression, although the only example it mentioned of a non-aggressive war was one conducted within the legal confines of the right to self-defense, implying, as would ordinary language, that any non-defensive war would be regarded as 'aggressive.' The Americans, led by Jackson, wanted to include a definition of aggression precisely along these lines, i.e. the use of force except in self-defense. It read as follows:

> An aggressor, for the purposes of this Article, is that state which is the first to commit any of the following actions: 'Declaration of war ... Invasion by its armed forces ... of the territory of another state ... Attack ... on the territory, vessels, or aircraft of another state ... No political, military, economic or other considerations shall serve as an excuse or justification for such actions; but the exercise of the right of legitimate self-defense, that is to say, resistance to an act of aggression, or action to assist a state which has been subjected to aggression, shall not constitute a war of aggression.'[167]

However, the other allies were in favor of leaving out an explicit definition of aggression and the Americans ceded on this point.[168] On the other hand, the Tribunal's Charter as finally drafted did include equally as a 'crime against peace' (alongside a war of aggression) any war 'in violation of international treaties' – for example, the Kellogg–Briand Pact or the present-day Charter of the United Nations.

The Nuremberg Tribunal itself did not have to enter into the question of any distinctions between illegal wars and wars of aggression, because it was dealing with as egregious an example of both as you were likely to get: the Nazi war launched to subjugate all of Europe along with large swaths of the rest of the planet. Of course, the 'lesser' crimes within this 'supreme' crime, including the Holocaust of European Jewry, were also of unimaginable enormity. Yet the Tribunal insisted that the Nazis' worst sin was making aggressive war. There is a powerful logic to this, especially for Polish Jews like myself: if Germany had not made war on Poland, Polish Jewry would not have been consigned to the gas chambers. This is something we should remember when we evaluate the attempts to use the Holocaust to justify 'humanitarian intervention' in violation of international law and state sovereignty. In fact the Holocaust proves the opposite. If the other Western powers had only stopped the Nazis at Germany's own borders – in other words stood up for international law and state sovereignty – which they certainly had the power and opportunity to do in 1938, there would have been no Holocaust. Ninety-seven percent of the Jews slaughtered by the Nazis lived in the countries Germany illegally invaded, including the three million Polish Jews who made up more than 90 percent of the pre-war community. The vast majority of the German Jews who perished were also murdered during the war, having been transported for extermination to occupied Poland.[169]

Not all illegal wars are the equivalent of World War II, just as all crimes against humanity are not the equivalent of the Holocaust. But the hierarchical logic of the Nuremberg Tribunal seems highly appropriate to the kind of illegality at issue in Kosovo (and in Afghanistan and Iraq). Here, too, the war crimes flowed from the crimes against peace, and whatever point there might be of distinguishing between the aggressive and the illegal also vanished. Because, again, this was no mere technical illegality, but rather something fundamental: the launching of a war contrary to the basic peace-seeking principles of the UN Charter for motives of geopolitical and petty political strategy and greed, whether or not it was technically for 'conquest,' with a predictable price in death and destruction as the result.

Legal developments subsequent to the Nuremberg Tribunal have followed the example of the Nuremberg Charter and equated 'aggressive war' with 'illegal war.' The most important was the UN General Assembly Resolution of 1974, which, without a dissenting vote, adopted a definition of aggression that, for all intents and purposes, was the same as that proposed by Jackson at Nuremberg, quoted above. Aggression was defined to include *any* use of armed force by one state against another 'in any manner inconsistent with the Charter of the United Nations.' 'Humanitarian intervention' was specifically ruled out, virtually in Jackson's terms, by Article 5: 'No consideration of whatever nature, whether political, economic, military or otherwise, may serve as a justification for aggression.' [170] The same article deems a war of aggression 'a crime against international peace' that 'gives rise to international responsibility.' A key provision is Article 2, which provides that '[t]he first use of armed force by a State in contravention of the Charter' is presumed to be aggression ('shall constitute prima facie evidence of an act of aggression'), with only one exception: the authority of the Security Council 'in conformity with the Charter' to decide that 'a determination that an act of aggression has been committed would not be justified in the light of other relevant circumstances, including the fact that the acts concerned or their consequences are not of sufficient gravity.' The negative formulation is of enormous significance. It means that a non-defensive war cannot be deprived of its legal characterization as aggression merely by the veto of one permanent member of the Security Council. It will be deemed to be what it is, namely aggression, unless the Security Council intervenes to say it is *not*, meaning that *all* permanent members, as well as at least four of the other ten, would have to agree. It would clearly have been impossible for the US to get such a vote in the case of either Kosovo or Iraq; and, given the non-committal nature of the Resolutions passed in September 2001, it is an open question what would have happened if the case of Afghanistan were ever put to the test, especially at a remove where its full savagery and lack of redeeming value could be appreciated.

In 1986, in the *Nicaragua* case, the World Court recognized the General Assembly's Resolution on Aggression as binding international law when it rejected America's claim to have been acting in self-defense.[171] The case also authoritatively and unequivocally re-affirmed the ban on 'humanitarian wars.'[172] The Americans had argued that their violent intervention was not only an exercise of self-defense, but was also aimed at protecting the human rights of Nicaraguans (threatened by a popular revolution struggling to bring the country out of the repressive backwardness that the United States itself had guaranteed). This too was rejected and the World Court ruled resoundingly against the United States by twelve votes to three.[173] The official decision was that

> the United States of America, by training, arming, equipping, financing and supplying the contra forces or otherwise encouraging, supporting and aiding military and paramilitary activities in and against Nicaragua ... by certain attacks on Nicaraguan territory in 1983–84 ... and by laying

mines in the internal or territorial waters of the Republic of Nicaragua during the first months of 1984 ... has acted, against the Republic of Nicaragua, in breach of its obligation under customary international law not to intervene in the affairs of another State ... not to use force against another State ... not to violate its sovereignty and not to interrupt peaceful maritime commerce ...[174]

The case marked the end of American cooperation with the World Court. In fact, the US unsuccessfully tried to wriggle out of the Court's jurisdiction in the *Nicaragua* case itself by giving notice prior to the decision that it was withdrawing from the Court's jurisdiction. But the Court pointed out that the US had previously committed itself to giving six months' notice and ruled that the case had to proceed.[175] At this point the United States refused to participate in the case any further and formally withdrew its consent to the Court's jurisdiction for all further cases, unless it should specifically consent to a given case beforehand. The lack of World Court condemnation of US lawbreaking since *Nicaragua* doesn't mean the Americans have gone straight, just that the law's arm is not long enough.[176]

The court's rejection of the humanitarian intervention claim of the US was short and to the point:

In any event, while the United States might form its own appraisal of the situation as to respect for human rights in Nicaragua, the use of force could not be the appropriate method to monitor or ensure such respect. With regard to the steps actually taken, the protection of human rights, a strictly humanitarian objective, cannot be compatible with the mining of ports, the destruction of oil installations, or again with the training, arming and equipping of the contras.[177]

The International Court of Justice is the highest authority in international law, so the case bitterly disappointed advocates of unilateral humanitarian intervention. Some have tried to salvage something from the decision by narrowing its precedential value to the facts of the case, claiming that a case for true humanitarian intervention can still be made out if the human rights violations are serious enough and certain other conditions are met.[178] For example Fernando Tesón argues that there is a moral right, under stringent conditions, for states to intervene with armed force to prevent or end very serious human rights violations in other states. He argues that the Charter, despite its words, should be 'interpreted' to make this moral right a legal right.[179] Of course the intervention must be 'truly humanitarian,' which entails compliance with a number of strict conditions. Failing any of them would deprive the intervention of its legality, and it is obvious that the war in Kosovo would have met few, if any:

> *First, the intervening state must aim its military action at stopping human rights deprivations by governments ...*[180]

The NATO bombing campaign seemed aimed at anything but stopping human rights abuses; it seemed aimed instead, especially in the early weeks, at *encouraging* them. Nobody doubts that the situation got predictably worse after the bombing started. Even defenders of the bombing had to admit that NATO's 'strategy at times appeared calculated more to punish and de-claw the Milosevic regime for its past atrocities than to halt the human rights abuses being committed.'[181]

> *Second, collateral non-humanitarian motives (such as desire for border security or strengthening alliances) should be such as not to impair or reduce the first paramount human rights objective of the intervention.*

In fact, it is only the host of 'collateral non-humanitarian motives' examined earlier that could possibly explain the *anti*-humanitarian way that NATO conducted its 'intervention.'

> *Third, the means used must always be rights-inspired.*

A bombing attack clearly aimed at breaking the morale of the civilian population, in flagrant violation of the Geneva Conventions (see Chapter 6), doesn't exactly fit this criterion.

> *... the authenticity of the humanitarian purpose must be ascertained by examining the concrete actions taken by the intervenor ... Did troops occupy the territory longer than necessary?*

The KLA is a separatist movement. It insisted at Rambouillet on a NATO-led presence in Kosovo to ensure its future independence. Four years after the war ended, Kosovo was a NATO protectorate and would remain so for the foreseeable future.

> *Has the intervenor demanded advantages or favors from the new governments?*

How about the overthrow of the government and the handing over of its President for trial as a condition of sanctions being removed? In other words, it was not enough for NATO that the alleged oppression of Kosovo by Serbia end; Serbia itself had to install a subservient ('pro-Western') government and then break its own laws to satisfy NATO's need to see Milosevic brought in chains to The Hague (see Chapter 5).

And the final test will be whether human rights have been effectively restored as a result of the intervention.

While the Albanians are no longer the victims of ethnic violence, a Kosovo largely 'cleansed' of Serbs and Roma hardly bespeaks the restoration of human rights. Here's one rights-based assessment of the situation in Kosovo one year after the war:

[T]here has been a denial of internationally recognized civil and political rights, among which the right to life, the right to physical and mental integrity, the right to liberty and the security of the person, the right to humane conditions of detention and to freedom from torture and from cruel and degrading treatments or punishments and freedom of movement. Moreover, the general atmosphere of terror has given place to other violations in the fields of freedom of association, freedom of assembly, freedom of expression, freedom of thought, conscience and religion, of the right to use one's own language and ... of the right to political participation. Furthermore ... there has been generated a constant negation of economic, social and cultural rights: among others, the right to education, the right to participate in cultural life, the right to health, and the right to social security.[182]

Finally, and most importantly for the war over Kosovo, the decisive question is whether there is a non-violent way of achieving the humanitarian result:

Military intervention, as a remedy against human rights violations, should only be resorted to when all peaceful means have failed or are likely to fail. The reason is simple: war is devastating; innocent people die, countries are ravaged and destroyed.

The evidence speaks rather of a NATO that worked overtime to destroy all of the many chances for a peaceful solution that presented themselves, right up to the moment of the attack.

So NATO's intervention would have failed the legal/moral test of unilateral humanitarian intervention (even if it had existed, which it didn't). Lawyer defenders of the bombing had either to ignore the facts, or the letter or spirit of the Charter, or all three. Some just engaged in creative omission, quoting sections of the Charter but omitting the words that made it clear their enforcement was up to the institutions of the United Nations and not its individual member states.[183] Others engaged in tortuous interpretations, for instance, American law professors Paul Williams and Michael P. Scharf, former State Department lawyers and NATO partisans, who argued that

> ... since [NATO] explicitly rejected claims of independence for Kosovo and publicly reaffirmed the territorial integrity and political independence of Yugoslavia, the purpose of the air strikes could not be construed to either impair territorial integrity or to challenge political independence.[184]

This requires reading 'territorial integrity' and 'political independence' in Article 2(4) as not being impaired when one country bombs another into submission to its will, as long as it doesn't formally annex it; rather different from the ordinary meaning of the words. Different as well from the General Assembly's resolution on aggression quoted earlier. And even the theory of unilateral humanitarian intervention holds that the attackers' 'actions, not their words, must count.'[185] Kosovo has in fact been permanently excluded from Yugoslavia, and is now and for the foreseeable future occupied by NATO troops: 'With each passing month, and every newly paved road, Camp Bondsteel becomes a more permanent part of the Kosovo landscape ... an American emplacement intended for the medium to long term.'[186] This was the only possible outcome of a NATO victory, and it was precisely the state of affairs contemplated by the Rambouillet 'agreement,' the pretext for the bombing campaign.

Williams and Scharf also argue that the strikes against Yugoslavia were legally authorized by the *Genocide Convention*, specifically its requirement that ratifying countries 'undertake to prevent and to punish genocide'[187] – i.e., that the *attack itself* could be considered a prevention and/or punishment of genocide. One little problem with this is that the evidence of genocide was non-existent, as witness the charges against Milosevic when he was finally brought to The Hague (see Chapter 5). But even the most blatant violation of the *Genocide Convention* could not possibly be a legal justification for an armed intervention, because if one takes the trouble to read the *Genocide Convention*, one sees that there are all sorts of ways in which the ratifying states agree to prevent and punish genocide, with the conspicuous exception of armed intervention. States undertake to enact legislation against genocide, and to have people who commit genocide tried by a national or international tribunal; they agree to grant extradition. Most importantly they agree that they 'may call upon *the competent organs of the United Nations* to take such action under the Charter of the United Nations as they consider appropriate for the prevention and suppression of acts of genocide.'[188] Nowhere is NATO or the US listed as a 'competent organ of the United Nations'; nor is any mention made of bombing the hell out of a country alleged to be in violation of the Convention. Williams and Scharf, in the best traditions of American interventionism, 'humanitarian' or otherwise, conveniently ignore this question of means, which is the only real question at stake. Granted the prevention of genocide is a desirable end – hard to find anyone disagreeing with that – does it follow that *any* means are also acceptable? It is no surprise that international law and convention are concerned with means as well as ends. This precise point was also made by the World Court in the *Nicaragua* case:

> Nicaragua is accused by the 1985 finding of the United States Congress of violating human rights ... However, where human rights are protected by international conventions, that protection takes the form of such arrangements for monitoring or ensuring respect for human rights as are provided for in the conventions themselves.[189]

In other words, you cannot use a convention that specifies both means and ends as justifying *any* means, whether those specified in the convention or not. If it were not for the nerve of lawyers this would not have to be spelled out.

As for 'competent organs of the United Nations,' NATO had every opportunity to make all of these arguments to the World Court when Yugoslavia hauled the US and nine other members before it a month into the bombing campaign.[190] But instead of stating its case, NATO chose to deny the jurisdiction of the Court. This was at the very same moment that, on the other side of town, the US was helping the ICTY assert *its* jurisdiction against the FRY leadership. By no coincidence at all, both the World Court (or the 'International Court of Justice,' as it is formally known), a venerable institution dating formally from 1946 (with the UN itself) and effectively from 1922 (with the League of Nations), *and* the ICTY (est. 1993) are situated in The Hague, the ancient capital of the Netherlands and the site of the important peace conferences of 1899 and 1907. The US obviously wanted to give the ICTY some of the luster of the World Court, even confuse them in the public's mind, which happened often, but they are two very different institutions. Only states, not individuals, can appear in the World Court. Its jurisdiction is purely by the consent of all of the parties, and it cannot order criminal penalties against individuals. It is also a far more democratic and representative body. Unlike those in the ICTY, World Court judges are not subject to the veto rights of each of the five permanent members of the

Security Council. The 15 judges are elected by absolute majority of both the General Assembly and the Security Council, and the veto does not apply.

As part of its suit, Yugoslavia requested and received an expedited hearing on 'provisional measures' – essentially asking the Court to order a stop to the bombing in the interim until the full case could be heard. On 2 June the Court issued its decision denying Yugoslavia's request, without deciding the merits of the whole case, which was to proceed at the ordinary snail's pace.[191] But the decision did nothing to vindicate the legality of NATO's air campaign, quite the contrary. Despite heavy NATO presence on the court (five judges appointed by NATO countries) the decision was a clear rebuke by the Court of the questionable humanitarianism and legality of NATO's bombing campaign:

> 16. Whereas the Court is profoundly concerned with the use of force in Yugoslavia; whereas under the present circumstances such use raises very serious issues of international law;
>
> ...
>
> 18. Whereas the Court deems it necessary to emphasize that all parties appearing before it must act in conformity with their obligations under the United Nations Charter and other rules of international law, including humanitarian law;
>
> ...
>
> 31. Whereas, whether or not States accept the jurisdiction of the Court, they remain in any event responsible for acts attributable to them that violate international law, including humanitarian law; whereas any disputes relating to the legality of such acts are required to be resolved by peaceful means, the choice of which, pursuant to Article 33 of the Charter, is left to the parties;
>
> ...
>
> 33. Whereas, when such a dispute gives rise to a threat to the peace, breach of the peace or act of aggression, the Security Council has special responsibilities under Chapter VII of the Charter;

The emphasis on the Security Council was in fact the very crux of the matter. The issue was never one of 'humanitarian intervention' versus 'just standing by'; it was about whether peaceful or violent means should be used and, above all, *who* should decide this. In fact, in the period since the *Nicaragua* case, and especially since the official end of the Cold War, the Security Council had been cautiously experimenting with what is called 'collective' humanitarian intervention – namely, intervention *authorized by the Security Council*. This is what Secretary General Perez de Cuellar was talking about in 1991 when he argued, in an often-quoted statement, that 'the defense of the oppressed in the name of morality should prevail over frontiers and legal documents.' He was talking about the role of the United Nations after the Cold War, when the Security Council 'has now moved to the central position from which it can assert the authority that the Charter has conferred on it.' As with the recent Gulf War, he was insisting that 'all measures of enforcement must be seen to issue from a collective engagement which imposes a discipline all its own.'[192] The collective/unilateral distinction is fundamental to the United Nations system, designed, according to the Charter, 'to take effective *collective* measures for the prevention and removal of threats to the peace' and 'to ensure by the acceptance of principles *and the institution of methods*, that armed force shall not be used, save in the *common interest.*'[193]

There were four cases of collective humanitarian intervention in the first half of the 1990s. In these cases the Security Council authorized the use of 'all necessary means' under 'unified command,' but always subject to the close supervision of the Secretary General. Before the resolutions on Bosnia discussed earlier, there were similar resolutions on Somalia, Haiti and Rwanda.[194] By the time of Kosovo, the power of the Security Council to authorize armed intervention in a conflict within the borders of a sovereign state was well established. Why was it not used in Kosovo?

The usual explanation given by the supporters of the bombing, and the main argument for unilateral humanitarian intervention, is that collective intervention was not available because of a 'paralysis' in the Security Council. Williams and Scharf, for example, argued unctuously that US intervention was worth the risk of setting a precedent for 'other countries to intervene in less altruistic circumstances' because of the 're-emergence of Security Council paralysis in the face of mass atrocities.'[195] Security Council 'paralysis' figures strongly in the precedent that advocates of bombing sought to draw out of the Kosovo war. For instance, ICTY judge Antonio Cassese's unequivocal assertion of the illegality of the war was in no way intended as a criticism; he meant it to establish that, as a result of Kosovo, a rupture with the prior legality had occurred so that a new legal principle might emerge.[196] Cassese argued for a new rule that would add one condition to the failed doctrine of humanitarian intervention, namely that 'the Security Council is unable to take any coercive action to stop the massacres because of a disagreement among the Permanent Members or because one of them exercises its veto power.'[197]

The amazing thing about the 'paralysis' argument is that anyone would have the chutzpah to make it on behalf of intervention by NATO or the US, because they were the ones doing all the paralyzing. It is true that the Soviets used the veto most in the UN Charter's first generation; but from 1966 to

1997 – a rather more relevant period, one supposes, for Kosovo and the 're-emergence' of paralysis to which Williams and Scharf refer – 86 percent of the vetoes cast in the Security Council were cast by NATO countries. From 1966 to 1997 the United States cast 72 out of a total of 132 vetoes, the UK 19 and France 14, while the Soviets cast only 15 and China only three. As the US found itself increasingly in the minority on key issues, its veto use steadily rose from 39 percent of total vetoes between 1966 and 1975 to 57 percent between 1976 and 1985, and to 63 percent between 1986 and 1997.[198] After losing in the *Nicaragua* case, the US vetoed resolutions calling for compliance with the World Court's judgment.[199] In the early years of the new millennium, the US used its veto to shield Israel's brutal occupation of the Palestinian territories from any collective humanitarian intervention; even from something as mild as an international observer force during a period of intense bloodletting.[200] So if there is a paralysis, it is the United States that is mostly to blame. And since we are talking about 'paralysis in the face of mass atrocities,' it's worth mentioning the most notorious example of this – namely the Rwandan civil war of 1994 – because it is widely accepted that in that case it was the United States of Bill Clinton that 'paralyzed' the UN. That's why it is almost impossible to understand the ignorance of a Michael Ignatieff whose *main reasons* for supporting the intervention in Kosovo, despite a lack of Security Council authorization, were Rwanda and Bosnia:

> Sticking only to the most recent and relevant instances, the UN Security Council's failure to prevent genocide in both Rwanda and Bosnia has made it essential that where a veto threatens to make the international community complicit in evil, coalitions of member states should be able to act on their own.[201]

Rwanda and Bosnia? It is true that the powerful evidence that America torpedoed peace efforts in Bosnia is not accepted by everyone – though it appears to be accepted by Ignatieff himself.[202] But where Rwanda is concerned, it is almost impossible to find anyone disagreeing that the US was the problem. The judgment of the Inquiry Commission appointed by the Organization of African Unity in its report, *Rwanda: The Preventable Genocide*, is typical:

> ... throughout the genocide, American machinations at the Security Council repeatedly undermined all attempts to strengthen the UN military presence in Rwanda; in the end, not a single additional new soldier or piece of military hardware reached the country before the genocide ended.[203]

Rwanda was the other country for which an international criminal tribunal was established (see Chapter 4). It was another case of Western greed (again mostly US), and IMF-imposed austerity throwing a match into an ancient and highly volatile inter-communal conflict left over from colonial times. The country was 85 percent Hutu and 14 percent Tutsi, but the Tutsis were the favored elite under Belgian colonial rule. When Belgium's trusteeship ended in 1959, the Hutus staged a revolution that abolished the monarchy and ended Tutsi domination. In the 1980s the country was hit hard by declining international commodity prices and austerity programs imposed by the international financial institutions. The decline in coffee prices was no more an accident of nature than the austerity programs. After establishing quotas and price controls to deal with shortages in the mid-1970s, the coffee importers of the rich countries abandoned them at the end of the 1980s because of downward market pressure on prices. The deregulation led to a drop in wholesale coffee prices of about 50 percent, devastating to the African producing countries. As the economic crisis hit, Tutsi refugees in Uganda founded the Rwandan Patriotic Front (RPF) with the aim of overthrowing the Hutu government in Rwanda. Civil war raged in the early 1990s.[204] In April 1994 the Hutu President was assassinated, the RPF launched an ultimately successful invasion, and a terrible outbreak of ethnic violence occured.[205] By 31 May the UN Secretary General reported to the Security Council that a 'genocide' of minority Tutsis was taking place in which there had already been between a quarter of a million and half a million deaths.

And here's where the United States came in. On 2 May 1994, in the midst of the killing, US President Clinton issued Presidential Decision Directive 25 (PDD 25), which laid down conditions for not only US involvement in, but also support for, UN peacekeeping. According to the released executive summary, the first criterion for US support was 'UN involvement advances US interests.'[206] The United States did not have to resort to its veto to prevent intervention in Rwanda, but its determined opposition was the decisive factor. According to then Secretary General of the UN Boutros Boutros-Ghali:

> It was one thing for the United States to place conditions on its own participation in UN peacekeeping. It was something else entirely for the US to attempt to impose its conditions on other countries. Yet that is what Madeleine Albright did.... Albright employed the requirements of PDD 25 to pressure the other Security Council members to delay the deployment of the full 5,500-man contingent to Rwanda until I could satisfy her that all of the many US conditions had been met.... The US effort to prevent

the effective deployment of a UN force for Rwanda succeeded, with the strong support of Britain.... The international community did little or nothing as the killing in Rwanda continued.[207]

US opposition to intervention in Rwanda is usually explained by reference to American popular outrage the previous October over the killing in Somalia of 18 US soldiers operating under the umbrella of UN peace-keeping. But this cannot explain why the United States would thwart United Nations action, which technically did not require US troop involvement. Furthermore, in the middle of the violence in Rwanda, the Security Council (with the necessary affirmative US vote) passed a Resolution on Bosnia increasing its UN troop presence by 6,500.[208] The only explanation is that the US, in the words of PDD 25, did not deem UN involvement in Rwanda to 'advance US interests,' either because America had no stake in the outcome, or because it actually backed the invading Tutsi forces, and intervention would have prevented their takeover as well as the slaughter. The US had had decent relations with the majority Hutu regime before the invasion, but its relations with the minority Tutsi regime established afterwards have been much closer. America has provided military aid for the Rwandan regime's participation since 1996 in the Congo war, which has benefited so many North American mining interests and taken millions of lives.[209] When *Rwanda: The Preventable Genocide* was released, Western editorialists bristled at any other explanation of the tragedy than simple 'blood lust' or 'something between collective madness and evil.' To them, putting any blame on the US was 'blaming the bystander.'[210] Some bystander.

The value of the Rwandan example is not just to show how selective the US is in its humanitarian intervention, but to show how preposterous it is for the United States to rely on Security Council 'paralysis' to justify its unilateral intervention in Kosovo. In the repeatedly invoked paradigm case, the United States was the problem. In fact, there is nothing like a general paralysis in the Security Council. Quite the contrary: prior to the Kosovo war there had been a spectacular increase in Security Council Resolutions, from 185 in the 1980s to 638 in the 1990s, with the high-water mark of 93 in 1993, the year prior to PDD 25. The 93 Resolutions of 1993 should be compared to the 20 passed in 1989, the last year of the Cold War. Resolutions citing Chapter VII provisions (peace-keeping) increased from 22 in the 44 years spanning the Cold War (1946–89) to 107 in the seven years following the fall of the Berlin Wall (1990–6).[211] Far from there being a paralysis, there had been, prior to Kosovo, an *increase* in peace-keeping and humanitarian activity by the Security Council. The evidence speaks more of an America paralyzing the Security Council precisely in order to undermine the challenge posed by a revitalized United Nations to US claims to represent the 'international community.'

The same thing can be gleaned from the testimony of former UN Secretary General Boutros Boutros-Ghali, who titled his 1999 memoirs *Unvanquished: a U.S.–U.N. Saga*. Boutros-Ghali had much reason to resent the Clinton administration, because it was determined to deny him the traditional second term as Secretary General and conducted a vicious disinformation campaign against him. The US ultimately cast the lone vote against Boutros-Ghali in the Security Council in 1996 (increasing its lead in the 'most vetoes' department). This was the same year the Secretary General publicly denounced the US for its attempts to starve the UN into submission by defaulting on its dues.[212] But Madeleine Albright told Boutros-Ghali he was being fired for refusing in 1993 to grant the Americans the authority to use military force unilaterally in Bosnia.[213] The US was determined, indeed anxious, long before – *five years* before – the threat of a Kosovo 'Holocaust,' to intervene militarily without UN authorization.[214] The confrontation over Sarajevo occurred in August 1993, a full two months before Mogadishu, the occasion for issuing PDD 25. While Boutros-Ghali was unsure of US motives at first ('the Clinton administration's approach [to Bosnia] made sense only as the product of some obscure Machiavellian calculation'[215]), it was clear even before Kosovo that it had something to do with substituting air power for ground troops, and the US for the UN: 'My responsibility was to promote multilateralism; the emerging U.S. policy was unilateralism, with multilateralism providing a fig leaf as needed.'[216]

Boutros-Ghali was replaced by Kofi Annan, whose silence during the Kosovo war on NATO's violation of the UN Charter was deafening. This was no accident. According to Boutros-Ghali, 'The Clinton administration mentioned no one, apparently fearing that its choice would be regarded as America's handpicked puppet. Inside the United Nations, however, everyone knew that the United States' candidate was Kofi Annan.'[217] You won't find it in his official UN biography, but Annan was the UN's special envoy to NATO during the Bosnian war, though in fact it was more vice-versa, as he supported NATO's case for bombing against the restraint of the Secretary General. According to Holbrooke, that is how he 'won the job' as Secretary General.[218]

The Clinton administration chose well with Kofi Annan. From the very moment NATO started planning its military intervention in Kosovo, Annan was at work providing the diplomatic cover. In June 1998 he gave a public lecture that was a very strong and emotional defense of unilateral interventionism, using Kosovo as the example of the next intervention, invoking the Nazi era apropos of it, and explicitly congratulating NATO on its recent threats to the FRY.[219] In January 1999, on the eve of Rambouillet, Annan gave NATO an effective green light for its unilateral military plans. The first-ever visit of a Secretary General of the United Nations to NATO headquarters in Brussels – not Annan's own first visit, of course – took place on 28 January 1999, two days before NATO sent its official Rambouillet 'summons' to the FRY government. Annan addressed the NATO Council in closed session, and it is a pretty easy guess what he told them, because even in his official public remarks there was absolutely no reference to the Security Council's monopoly on the use of force.[220] When he spoke to the press, Annan demoted Security Council approval to something only 'normally' required:

> Asked if NATO could intervene in Kosovo with the express approval of the U.N. Security Council, Annan said: 'Normally, the approval of the Security Council for the use of force is required. I have always said that.' But in what appeared to be a pointed signal to NATO allies not to back off, he told NATO ambassadors: 'Let me ask only that we all – particularly those with the capacity to act – recall the lessons of Bosnia.'[221]

NATO's Secretary General Javier Solana was quite correct in exploiting the visit by saying, 'You have seen from the visit of the United Nations Secretary General to NATO earlier today that the United Nations shares our determination and objectives.'[222] Annan did nothing during the war to disabuse anybody of this impression. Shortly after, he signed a report crudely congratulating the US for what it had done, attacking his predecessor's policies as 'appeasement,' and equating Kosovo to Bosnia and Bosnia to the Holocaust (see Chapter 4).

Whether or not they went to war for the purpose of establishing a new precedent, NATO supporters tried very hard to extract one from it. Tony Blair gave a widely reported speech in Chicago on the eve of the NATO summit – and thus in the midst of a bombing campaign not authorized by the UN Charter – in which he argued that the 'new world' of the 'new millennium' needed 'new rules,' 'new ways' and a 'new framework':

> No longer is our existence as states under threat [*unless you happen to be Yugoslavia*]. ... Non-interference has long been considered an important principle of international order. And it is not one we would want to jettison too readily ... But the principle of non-interference must be qualified in important respects. Acts of genocide can never be a purely internal matter.[223]

The cornerstone of the UN Charter is here reduced to something we don't want 'to jettison too readily.' Not something we don't want to *jettison*, mind you, just something we don't want to jettison *too readily*. This speech was eagerly seized upon by bombing enthusiasts as meaning that '[t]he presumption enshrined in the UN Charter that states should not resort to war except in self defense and that they should be immune from intervention by other sovereign states had now to be revised.'[224] After the war NATO politicians continued to hammer away at the same theme.[225] Kofi Annan started off the new millennium with an appropriately positive assessment in the *Financial Times* entitled 'The legitimacy to intervene.'[226]

Is there anything to be said for this 'new precedent'? Look at Kosovo itself. In fact, the Security Council was intensely involved in the conflict and managed to pass several important resolutions in the year before NATO's attack.[227] And, of course, Resolution 1244 of 10 June 1999 enshrined the peace deal agreed by the FRY and NATO through the mediation efforts of the G-8 Nations. None of these Resolutions authorized an armed intervention; but that is not because the Security Council was incapable of doing so, as the Resolutions of the early 1990s showed. In Kosovo, NATO never even *tried* to obtain Security Council authorization for armed intervention. Interventionists claim that it was pointless because China and Russia were sure to have exercised their veto. But what does that prove? It's like the police wanting to administer their own 'justice' on the street because they don't trust the courts to convict. It's not just that most of us trust the courts more than the police; it's that we feel better when there are some serious checks on the official use of violence.[228]

The proof of this particular principle is in the eating. A veto by China or Russia in the Security Council in the case of Kosovo, if it had been effective in stopping NATO, would have saved thousands of lives, from the very young to the very old, because it would have forced the world to give peace the many chances examined earlier. As the former head of peacekeeping for Bosnia put it, the 'humanitarian disaster unfolded in Kosovo *after* NATO hijacked the decision-making process from the UN.'[229] Furthermore, had Russia or China defeated this initiative of NATO, they would have been representing the considered opinion of most of the world and its leaders. If NATO wanted to dispute this they could have gone to the General Assembly of the United Nations with their case. When the United States wanted the United Nations to get around the Soviet veto in the 1950s in the case of Korea, it went to the General Assembly and passed the 'Uniting for Peace' resolution, which allowed the General Assembly to recommend military action if two-thirds of those present and voting were agreed.[230] But the Uniting for Peace Resolution has not been used since the West lost control of the voting patterns in the General Assembly, and that is undoubtedly why the US didn't try to use it in Kosovo: it would have lost overwhelmingly, because the real international community was against the war.[231]

This is a question not of substance but procedure, not of ends but means – not of whether 'the international community' should intervene when absolutely necessary in the interest of humanity, but rather of *who* is to speak for the international community. It is not only that the particular Security Council failings complained of are the unilateral interventionists' own doing, it is that the alternative is not even an equivalent expression of the 'international community,' much less a better one. The question is not how we can let one or two states thwart the international community by their veto power; the question is how do we know it is the international community when there is the consent of neither the Security Council nor the General Assembly. Nor is the unilateral alternative to the Security Council some more effective way of determining that armed intervention is necessary. Kosovo showed that to most people, too. The unilateral alternative to the Security Council is the rule, not of the best, the most humanitarian or the most representative, but of the most powerful. The only thing everybody is really sure of in Kosovo is that the Americans had their way.

Under the new rules that would be established by the Kosovo 'precedent,' this would be, in effect *institutionalized*. And it would be that much more difficult for world opinion to penetrate the enormous propaganda resources that America can deploy on its own public. As the richest country in the history of the world, America is also blessed with history's most powerful mass media, no innocent bystander, but, on the contrary, a fully-fledged member of corporate America locked in holy matrimony with state and government, sharing identical geopolitical interests. With or without the happy coincidence of the US Secretary of State's chief spokesman being married to CNN's lead correspondent on Kosovo,[232] there is no case that the Americans cannot make plausible to their own people, at least in the short-run, as the war in Iraq showed beyond any doubt. But it could also be seen in Kosovo.[233] Even Cassese, writing in the early stages of the war, seems to have thought he had to take the US position at face value. If you can so easily lead an eminent professor of international law by the nose, how difficult can it be for the casual observer? But when it turns out the self-styled humanitarians were lying, where do you go with Cassese's new rule? How do you enforce it, the part that says intervention is only permissible when necessary in the interests of humanity, and it turns out that it wasn't? Do you go to the World Court? Forget about it, the Americans don't recognize it. The International Criminal Court? Ditto. It was crucial for the American media to discredit the Security Council during the Iraq war, because that was the only institution left with the legal authority to demand that the US prove its case to the world. Abandon that, and the partisan pundits can make any wild claims they want about the law or the facts, without fear that they will ever be tested by any court or assembly with the authority to do so.

The UN Charter was an attempt to put stringent limits on the exercise of military power in the aftermath of an unimaginably devastating war. It did this by basing itself on state sovereignty and an almost perfect legal equality of states, the veto of the five being the only exception. The new interventionists have sought to change the rules by hammering away at the idea of state sovereignty. 'International action to uphold human rights requires a new understanding of state and individual sovereignty,' according to Kofi Annan, but the dichotomy is a false one.[234] It is false, in the first place, because what is intended to replace state sovereignty is not individual sovereignty but the sovereignty of the great powers, which means individual subordination to them and their friends. It is the US that is in charge in Bosnia, Kosovo, Afghanistan and Iraq now; the rest are a distant second. In his wartime speech to the Canadian Parliament Vaclav Havel said that he saw Kosovo 'as an important precedent for the future. It has now been clearly stated that it is not permissible to slaughter people, to evict them from their homes, to maltreat them and to deprive them of their property.'[235] But, Stephen Shalom responded,

> What lesson do we think Turkey's leaders are learning from the attack on Kosovo? Surely not: 'This shows what happens to all who commit atrocities against ethnic minorities.' Isn't it more likely that their conclusion is going to be – as will that of anyone who considers cases like Turkey, Timor, Palestine, and Iraq pre-1990 (when Saddam Hussein was a U.S. ally and murdered Kurds) on the one hand, and cases likely Iraq post-1990 and Kosovo on the other – that serving U.S. interests allows you to do whatever you want with your ethnic minorities and opposing U.S. intervention will get you attacked, regardless of your human rights record?[236]

Secondly, the 'evolution' of sovereignty is only partial, and strangely enough it does not apply to the most 'advanced' countries, because state sovereignty is only going to be abolished for the weak ones: 'A world with a single superpower is a world where only that superpower has a sure claim to "national sovereignty" – an outdated concept for the rest.'[237] There is no question, in other words, of anyone intervening in the United States, a notorious violator of the human rights of its own people, a country of de facto racial segregation, of poverty amidst prodigious wealth, of police brutality, bursting prisons and the death penalty.[238] When it 'intervened' in Kosovo, the United States shared with Japan the dubious distinction of being the only death penalty states in the developed world, and the American execution rate per capita was five times that of Japan. The 98 American executions of 1999 made the United States the fifth biggest overall user of the death penalty in the whole world, after its trading partner China, 'Axis of Evil' members Iraq and Iran, and client-state Saudi Arabia.[239] Moreover, with nearly two million adults in jail on any given day, the United States had the largest prison population in the world, both absolutely and relative to its total population.[240] In 1999 there were 15,530 murders and non-negligent manslaughters officially recorded, a regular Bosnian civil war. That same year 89,110 forcible rapes were recorded.[241] Most respectable criminology attributes this to the massive social, racial and sexual inequality that is the American way of life. But the theorists of humanitarian intervention conveniently define these kinds of oppression to be outside the scope of their doctrine. The 'test' is 'whether human rights violations are sufficiently widespread and pervasive as to justify classifying that society as a repressive state,' but 'repressive state' is arbitrarily defined to exclude the particular repressiveness of the United States. Luckily for them, sky-high rates of violent crime and punishment don't count, not to mention massive economic inequality and the purchasing of elections.[242] Even if the theorists weren't so clever nobody has the power to intervene against America or its clients. Humanitarian intervention is forever doomed to be an 'asymmetrical right ... the right of the powerful to intervene in the affairs of the weak and not vice versa.'[243] This was the precise point made by the International Court of Justice back in 1949 when it rejected Britain's claim that it had a right to temporarily intervene in Albanian waters to look for evidence of violations of international law: 'The Court can only regard the alleged right of intervention as the manifestation of a policy of force, such as has, in the past, given rise to the most serious abuses ... for, from the nature of things, it would be reserved for the most powerful States.'[244]

So the crux of the proposed new exception is that it detaches the end of humanitarian intervention from the institutional means of the Security Council and even the General Assembly. In so doing it frees NATO, or more precisely the United States, from the legal discipline of the United Nations Charter and thus *any legal discipline whatsoever*. This, then, was the legal objective of the Kosovo war – even if it wasn't the main or only political objective; in Cassese's terms, to make 'right out of wrong,' to replace the complicated and nearly democratic mechanism of the Charter of the United Nations with the far simpler Law of the Jungle.

Will the precedent be accepted? Even Cassese, putting a wildly optimistic spin on the response of the international community, felt that it was 'premature to maintain that a customary rule has emerged' after only this one example in Kosovo.[245] Cassese was hopeful, however, because 'only very few states contended that the action on the part of NATO countries was contrary to the United Nations Charter.' That these included Russia, China and India, with well over 2 billion people between them, didn't faze him. But his statement that 'the overwhelming majority of states did not condemn the NATO intervention as illegal' only had to await the following spring to be proved wrong. At the South Summit meeting of developing countries in April 2000, 133 countries issued the following declaration:

> We reject the so-called 'right' of humanitarian intervention, which has no legal basis in the United Nations Charter or in the general principles of international law.[246]

According to standard international law doctrine, such an overwhelming rejection means that unilateral humanitarian intervention is just as illegal now as it was before the war; and that is the view of the preponderance of scholars.[247] Two 'independent commissions' that studied the question also had to admit to a lack of consensus on the precedent. One was a Canadian initiative, the *Report of the International Commission on Intervention and State Sovereignty*, and the other was led by South African Judge Richard Goldstone, whose performance as the first ICTY prosecutor was not praised for its independence (see Chapter 4). These commissions shared the rather thinly spread talents of Michael Ignatieff. Both conceded that you could not get a full-blooded legal precedent from Kosovo, because most of the world still opposed unilateral humanitarian intervention as simply a Western Trojan horse. But both commissions seemed to think it was okay to 'just do it' anyway.[248]

So if Kosovo introduced a new element, it was not an authentic legal precedent, but the beginning of an open abandonment of legality itself as a fundamental point of reference in international relations. This only became really clear in the debate over the Iraq war, when America's political and legal theorists started intoning the Charter's last rites (see Chapter 1). But that was when it also became clear that the other rich countries were having second thoughts about these developments. As long as the vehicle of choice for American military policy was NATO, the lesser members seemed to have had no objections to substituting its authority for that of the UN. But by 2003 it was clear that NATO itself was only a brief stop on the way for the United States. The new doctrine of unilateral, preventive self-defense that emerged after 11 September 2001, under which Bush's America arrogated to itself the right to make war on whoever raised an eyebrow against it, permitted the US to avoid the political limits, minor though they were, that the other 18 members had placed on US war strategy in Kosovo. Afghanistan was strictly an American operation. Even though it was the first time NATO had invoked its Article 5 'solidarity clause,' NATO countries remained in a firmly subordinate position, helping only as they were allowed, and completely under American command. Even as NATO expanded to embrace more former Soviet bloc countries, its increasing military irrelevance led commentators to ask whether we were seeing 'The End of NATO?'[249] – where only six months before the same newspapers were proclaiming it 'the key institution of the current geopolitical West.'[250] And then came Iraq, where the war had to be fought without even NATO's 'solidarity' because of open *opposition* within NATO itself, led by France and Germany. Now the political fig-leaf was supplied by the pathetic, ad hoc 'Coalition of the Willing.' When Richard Perle thanked God for the death of the UN on the eve of America's war with Iraq, 'NATO' was not mentioned once, and was even retrospectively renamed: 'It took a *coalition of the willing* to save Bosnia from extinction.'[251] When, after the Iraq war, Tony Blair tried to get 13 other 'center-left' NATO and non-NATO government leaders at a 'Progressive Governance Summit' to accept a proposal for unilateral intervention, they turned him down and unanimously issued a communiqué affirming: 'We are clear that the UN Security Council remains the sole body to authorise global action in dealing with humanitarian crises of this kind.'[252]

But the question of a new precedent, or even the abandonment of legality altogether, is irrelevant to the nature of what the Americans did in Kosovo, in Afghanistan, and in Iraq, and to what that means for how we decipher international criminal justice. Because the indisputable facts of the war in Kosovo (as with Afghanistan and, as has already been verified at this writing, in Iraq) are that it wrought terrible, heart-breaking destruction of life, limb and livelihood without, as they used to say of pornography, any redeeming value; and that it was *illegal*. And the illegality was no technical 'anomaly' in need of bypassing or overlooking. It was a flagrant violation of the sound and precious anti-war principles of Charter of the United Nations. This is an enormously significant fact to remember as we examine the work of the International Criminal Tribunal for the Former Yugoslavia, for it gets *all* of its authority from the UN Charter. And since the ICTY likes to trace its lineage to Nuremberg, it is also of enormous significance that, in consciously violating the UN Charter, NATO committed what the Nuremberg Tribunal considered to be a 'supreme crime' against peace, the one from which all the others flowed. The ICTY chose to overlook NATO's crimes, and in this and other ways examined in the following pages, it became implicated in them, and in more than just the obvious way that NATO's other allies did. Because law abhors a vacuum at least as much as nature does, and the overthrow of international law and the UN Charter's fundamental principles was too monumental to have been accomplished without some *substitute* legality, and the ICTY obligingly supplied that, too.

Part II
Crimes Against Humanity

4

The War Crimes Tribunal

When Slobodan Milosevic appeared before the judges of the ICTY in July 2001, the first words he spoke were in English: 'I consider this tribunal false tribunal and indictments false indictments.'[1] Before his microphone was shut off by the presiding judge, Milosevic managed to add in his own language:

> This trial's aim is to produce a false justification for the war crimes of NATO committed in Yugoslavia. As I have said, the aim of this Tribunal is to justify the crimes committed in Yugoslavia. That is why this is a false Tribunal.[2]

At the time, criminal lawyers characterized this as a 'poor me, you too' defense, and offered their wise counsel that this wouldn't get him any sympathy from the court. In fact, Milosevic was appealing to everybody *but* the court, and what he said rang true to most of his listeners. What's more, it was not all that far from the opinion of US State Department lawyer Michael Scharf, a self-described 'insider' who was actively involved in the formulation of US war crimes policy, and who had a big hand in drafting the law governing the tribunal.[3] Shortly after the Kosovo war was over, Scharf wrote an article for the *Washington Post* criticizing the victorious governments for not being serious about war criminals except as a public relations device to legitimate the use of force against the Serbs:

> [T]he tribunal was widely perceived within the government as little more than a public relations device and as a potentially useful policy tool ... Indictments also would serve to isolate offending leaders diplomatically, strengthen the hand of their domestic rivals and fortify the international political will to employ economic sanctions or use force.[4]

Apart from the fact that Scharf intended no criticism of the tribunal itself and only its government sponsors, how different is this from what Milosevic was saying?

You could not miss the central role played by the ICTY in the Kosovo war in portraying NATO's unilateral aggression as 'humanitarian intervention' on behalf of 'the international community.' We've already mentioned the way prosecutor Louise Arbour helped NATO play up the Racak incident as an atrocity worthy of war. In the midst of the war itself she would top this with dramatic announcements of indictments against Serb leaders, including Milosevic. There would also be numerous press-conference meetings with various NATO leaders who would theatrically hand Arbour 'dossiers' of Serb war crimes and swear undying allegiance to her cause. And after the war, despite well-documented complaints of NATO war crimes coming from all over the world, Arbour would assign the NATO countries a monopoly over the search for evidence. Later, her successor Carla Del Ponte would issue an amateur whitewash of a report, absolving NATO of all charges without even an investigation. She would then lead the call to punish Serbia with economic ruin if it didn't violate its own laws by handing over Milosevic for trial at The Hague. We'll look at these events more closely in this chapter and the next.

It's easy to see how all this could help legitimate the illegal use of force by NATO. If NATO was pursuing criminals indicted by the Tribunal, it could present its law-*breaking* as law-*enforcement.* And every aggressor wants to demonize its enemy. The ICTY would officially brand them international criminals – and not just any criminals, but *Nazi war criminals.* In fact, if there was one service the ICTY performed for NATO that stood out above all others, it was to confirm NATO's outrageous analogy of Kosovo to the Holocaust.

THE HOLOCAUST ANALOGY

The Holocaust was the dominant metaphor of the war. What had to be stressed was that inaction in the face of Serb atrocities was 'appeasement' all over again, just like the sort that preceded the 'other' holocaust. On 23 March 1999, with the bombing set to start the very next day, Bill Clinton pointedly asked his television viewers:

> What if someone had listened to Winston Churchill and stood up to Adolph Hitler earlier? How many people's lives might have been saved? And how many American lives might have been saved?[5]

The UK's George Robertson repeated the party line a few days later:

> We could not simply stand idly by. We must learn the lesson of the early days of Hitler ... More than most, the British people understand that appeasement did not work in the 1930s. Nor will it in the 1990s.[6]

The Germans, of course, had pulled out the phony 'Operation Horseshoe' in mid-war. As experts on the Holocaust, they could proclaim they had 'serious evidence' of 'concentration camps' and 'systematic extermination that recalls in a horrible way what was done in the name of Germany at the beginning of World War II.'[7] It was enough for the British press to see lines of refugees to invoke the Holocaust in the bombing's very first week: '1939 or 1999?... Nazi style terror came to Kosovo yesterday in a horrific echo of the wartime Holocaust.'[8] Clinton's 'Churchill' speech was made a day after the Academy Awards – reputedly the most widely watched television show in the world. That night Hollywood had lavished Roberto Benigni's *La Vita è Bella* with Oscars for a Holocaust-lite film that portrayed the whole thing as essentially about trains and refugees, a film in which only one actual death occurs and it is off-screen.

But, of course, trains and refugees do not add up to a holocaust. The worst cases of 'ethnic cleansing' in Kosovo, or indeed Bosnia, did not even come close to the extermination program of the Nazis. It does not minimize the suffering of people killed in the thousands, terrorized and expelled from their homes in the Balkan wars, to distinguish that from being hunted down one by one wherever we lived, or wherever we ran, in a methodical plan to wipe an entire people off the face of the earth. The Nazis murdered six million Jews, two-thirds of all the Jews of Europe, 90 percent of all the Jews of Poland. Of the 8,000 Jews in my father's little town of Apt (Opatow), a mere 300 survived the war.[9] In the real Holocaust, as it has been pointed out, 'deportation' didn't mean Jews being put on trains to Israel; it meant Jews being sent to Auschwitz to be gassed.[10]

Nor did European Jewry have a separatist army like the KLA that was carrying out terrorist attacks on German police and trying to take a piece of Germany away from the Germans. Nor was the United States planning a bombing campaign to help them do it. Nor, for that matter, did the West merely 'stand by' and do nothing during the real Holocaust. Instead, it locked its doors to Jewish immigration and sent people back to their destruction. Nor did the 'idol of state sovereignty,' the one NATO wanted to 'dissolve' in Kosovo, pose any obstacle.[11] Hitler broke that barrier himself in 1936 when he occupied the Rhineland and sent his warplanes against the Republic in the Spanish Civil War, and again in 1938 when he forcibly annexed Austria and Sudeten Czechoslovakia, not to mention his conquest of the rest of Czechoslovakia in early 1939. Had the world stood up for national sovereignty and international law, there would have been no Holocaust. And when the Allies were engaged in a fully legal war with Germany in Poland, and they were begged by Jewish representatives to go five kilometers out of their way and bomb Auschwitz, which could have saved hundreds of thousands of Jewish lives, they couldn't be bothered because it didn't fit into their strategic plans.[12] If there was any analogy between Kosovo and the Holocaust, it was that the West didn't give a damn about the Albanians any more than they did about the Jews.

The official admission that Kosovo was neither Holocaust nor attempted Holocaust came when Milosevic was read his charges at The Hague and there was no charge of either genocide or attempted genocide among them – at least as far as Kosovo was concerned – even within the absurdly weak definition of 'genocide' employed by the ICTY. The genocide charges were all for Bosnia; and the only way of explaining the speed with which the press rose to NATO's Holocaust bait in Kosovo was the store of capital that had been built up in the Bosnian civil war.

BOSNIA AND THE BIRTH OF THE ICTY

The nature of the Bosnian civil war made the Holocaust analogy slightly more plausible than it would be for Kosovo. Bosnia was a war over territory, and everyone foresaw some sort of coming division on ethnic criteria, so all sides tried to create 'facts on the ground.' Hence the practice of 'ethnic cleansing,' which essentially meant forced population transfers, usually accompanied by terror. Of course, ethnic cleansing was completely different from the Nazi deportations of Jews, even though it employed some of the accouterments, such as brutal transports and detention camps. One particular difference stands out: the Nazi idea was to rid the *world* of Jews, not a specific contested territory with some final settlement in mind, and hence the transportations were to extermination camps. The term 'concentration camp' was a euphemism for the Nazis, but since them it has stood for what they were trying to hide by the use of it.

The Bosnian government based its international public relations campaign squarely on the Holocaust analogy. The campaign found a very sympathetic ear among the opinion makers of its American allies, and was, indeed, managed by the American PR firm Ruder Finn, which Bosnia hired in June 1992.[13] On 29 July, Bosnia sent the Security Council a list of 94 'concentration camps and prisons' under the control of 'the Belgrade regime and its surrogates,' in which 'tens of thousand of innocent civilians' were held, 'most of whom are women, children and elderly persons.'[14] On 31 July, Bosnia's Muslim President Izetbegovic told British television that the Bosnian Serb leader Karadzic was 'as bad as Hitler,' and asked 'Do the European leaders know about the Serbian concentration camps, about the mass killings?'[15] Gruesome articles immediately started to appear in the Western press. In one, Roy Gutman wrote of 'the Brcko concentration camp' where, 'according to [a] survivor,' 'at least 3,000' Muslims, prisoners and townspeople, were 'slaughtered' in six weeks, nine-tenths of the prisoners immediately; 'the preferred method was slitting throats.'[16] When the self-styled 'Adolf' of Brcko was brought to trial in The Hague some years later, he was convicted of only twelve counts of murder, all by pistol shots, and the number of alleged deaths in the area had dropped to a vague 'in the hundreds,' with a total of 66 bodies exhumed from the mass graves.[17] These were horrible brutalities, the kind that occur in all wars, but Nazi extermination they were not.

However, in the early days of August 1992, the Holocaust imagery poured out of the American press. On 3 August, liberal columnist Anthony Lewis wrote in the *New York Times*:

> Nazis transporting Jews in 1942? No, Serbs transporting Muslim Bosnians in 1992: one glimpse of the worst racial and religious bestiality Europe has known since World War II ... President Bush has been a veritable Neville Chamberlain in refusing to face the challenge in Yugoslavia.[18]

Lewis was evidently rooting for Democratic presidential candidate Bill Clinton, and Clinton showed no less restraint than he would as President: 'If the horrors of the holocaust taught us anything, it is the high cost of remaining silent and paralyzed in the face of genocide.'[19] 'We cannot afford to ignore what appears to be a deliberate and systematic extermination of human beings based on their ethnic origin.'[20] The American Jewish Congress was enlisted to lend its authority with an advertisement entitled 'Stop the Death Camps' that had text such as: 'to the blood-chilling names of Auschwitz, Treblinka, and other Nazi death camps there seem now to have been added the names of Omarska and Brcko...'[21] The *New York Times* ran a lead editorial on 4 August under the title 'Milosevic Isn't Hitler, But...'. The only reason the *Times* could see for distinguishing between Milosevic and Hitler was the fact that Milosevic's lack of military might limited the geographical scope of his 'Final Solution.'[22] Hitler wasn't even bad enough for cold-warrior Margaret Thatcher, who had to add Stalin to the mix: 'The Serbian ethnic cleansing policy ... combines the barbarities of Hitler's and Stalin's policies toward other nations.'[23]

For visuals, the press at first had to rely on old World War II footage from Nazi death camps.[24] But these were quickly substituted by images of actual Serb-run camps filmed by an enterprising British television crew, which made it seem as if the same thing were happening all over again – even though the Nazis were not known for letting Allied news teams into Auschwitz. On 7 August, America's and Britain's front pages carried the photo of an emaciated Bosnian Muslim standing behind barbed wire in the Trnoplje prison camp in northern Bosnia.[25] This would become the poster for the Bosnian Civil War. A controversy arose some years later over who was actually *inside* the fence, the film crew or the prisoners;[26] but it wasn't the positioning of the barbed wire that made the Nazi link false. A lot of horrible things occurred in these camps, but not extermination. In its very first case, the ICTY heard charges of beatings, torture, sexual assaults and murder committed against Bosnian Muslims interned in the Omarska camp during June and July 1992. The Bosnian Serb Dusko Tadic was sentenced to 20 years in prison, though he was personally acquitted of all murders.[27] But that's not the point; the point is that the counts of murder against Tadic only numbered *nine*. And even a hundred murders by a sadistic official wouldn't make this a 'concentration camp' in anything but the literal sense. For a Nazi 'concentration camp' you need gas chambers and crematoria. And did you ever hear of a Jewish concentration camp where Nazis were tortured, raped and killed by Jews? Because at the same time that the Serbs were being 'Nazis' to the Muslims, the Muslims and Croats were being 'Nazis' to the Serbs. At least that was the finding of the same court that convicted Tadic. In November 1998 the ICTY convicted a Bosnian Croat and three Bosnian Muslims for beatings, torture, sexual assault and murder of Bosnian Serbs in the Celebici camp in May, June and July 1992.[28] The sentences, as in the *Tadic* case, were for up to 20 years.

In fact, there was plenty of information available in the summer of 1992 to show the Serbs not only sinning but sinned against as well: 'Nor is the cleared-earth policy an exclusively Serbian practice. Croatian forces have jumped into the fight ... expelling Muslims and Serbs ... And Muslim Slavs ... have also tried to oust Serbs and Croats,' read an August story in *Time*. 'No one's hands are clean in this dreadful war,' said a UN field officer. 'All have done horrible things.'[29] Canadian General Lewis Mackenzie, in charge of UN forces in Bosnia, said there was 'plenty of blame to go around here and if this war is going to stop, both sides have a significant degree of responsibility.'[30] It appears that the Serbs had even been its first victims at the hands of the Croats in 1991.[31] The very origin of the phrase has been attributed to a Croat governor of Western Bosnia in Hitler's puppet state, who urged that his territory be 'thoroughly cleansed of Serbian dirt.'[32]

But in August 1992 the crude propaganda campaign to Nazify the Serbs was a terrific success; and it is precisely here that we find the birthplace of the ICTY and its whole modern war crimes progeny. 'When I came to work on the morning of August 7, 1992, the Department of State was in a frenzy over the ITN broadcast of conditions at the Omarska concentration camp,' writes Michael Scharf.[33] Scharf's job was to draft Security Council Resolution 771 of 13 August, which 'called upon' states and international humanitarian organizations 'to collate substantiated information in their possession or submitted to them relating to the violations of humanitarian law, including grave breaches of the Geneva Conventions being committed in the former Yugoslavia and to make this information available to the

Council.' The Council had already warned, a few weeks earlier, apropos of the deteriorating situation in Sarajevo, that 'persons who commit or order the commission of grave breaches of the Conventions are individually responsible in respect of such breaches.'[34]

Now Scharf didn't have to work from scratch on these resolutions; in fact he 'borrowed' the war crimes wording straight from a Security Council Resolution against none other than Saddam Hussein.[35] Gulf War Resolution 674 of 29 October 1990 was the fruit of a campaign publicly launched by UK Prime Minister Margaret Thatcher within a month of the occupation of Kuwait. Speaking on British television of the Iraqi detention of foreign nationals, she said:

> If anything happened to those hostages then sooner or later when any hostilities were over we could do what we did at Nuremberg and prosecute the requisite people for their totally uncivilized and brutal behaviour. They cannot get out of it these days by just saying: 'Well we were under orders'. That was the message of Nuremberg.[36]

President Bush Sr. picked up the torch in October when stories of Iraqi atrocities were starting to circulate ('newborn babies thrown out of incubators') – these would later be shown to be total fabrications:[37] 'Hitler revisited,' declaimed Bush. 'But remember, when Hitler's war ended, there were the Nuremberg trials. America will not stand aside. The world will not allow the strong to swallow the weak.'[38]

So the whole war crimes initiative started life as part of the tool-kit for labeling Saddam Hussein the new Hitler, in order to build the case for war against Iraq. To make this even clearer, the idea (according to the official history of the ICTY) appears to have originated with the *US Army*. To make it even more ironic, the people who dreamed it up in turn got the idea from the prosecution of war crimes committed by *American soldiers*: 'The US official in charge of the Kuwait dossier was in Vietnam, where he successfully prosecuted 28 marines who had committed acts of murder which could be classified as war crimes.'[39] In other words, the idea of prosecuting the Iraqi leader for (trumped up) war crimes came from experience with (genuine) war crimes committed by Americans. In fact the Americans seemed to have warmed to the idea of an international tribunal because of the bad press they had received from prosecuting Panamanian President General Manuel Noriega in the US on drug charges, after the US invasion of tiny Panama. That 'supreme crime' took hundreds of civilian lives and was condemned by the General Assembly of the United Nations as 'a flagrant violation of international law and of the independence, sovereignty and territorial integrity of States.'[40] This time (1990) the US preferred an international tribunal for Saddam Hussein, to 'diminish the impression of western victors taking revenge on the vanquished.'[41]

When the Americans decided to end the Gulf War without overthrowing Saddam they also lost interest in putting him on trial for war crimes – more proof of which was cart and which was horse. But the precedent was a very handy one for the military confrontation brewing in the Balkans. The Europeans – especially the Germans, who had started the whole thing by precipitating Croat separatism – were very happy to use the media campaign to blame everything on the Serbs. German Foreign Minister Klaus Kinkel gave a rabid speech at the EU–UN conference in London later the same month that the barbed-wire footage was televised. Invoking the 'terrible images that can be seen daily on television screens all over the world,' he proceeded: 'Where does the main source of the evil lie? The answer is obvious: in Belgrade!' And he concluded: 'Those responsible for all crimes and violations of human rights, both inside and outside of the camps, must be brought to account. An international court of criminal justice has to be created.'[42] The French foreign minister Roland Dumas made sure to link what was going on to the Nazis by nominating Elie Wiesel ('who won a Nobel peace prize for his work on behalf of the living memory of the holocaust') for the job of visiting the camps.[43]

Wiesel had already involved himself in the anti-Serb campaign, though he had the scruples to stop short of the Holocaust analogy ('Omarska is not Auschwitz'[44]). He was invited in the late summer to visit the Serb-run camps, but he didn't go until November. When he wrote about his experience four years later, not only were they 'not Auschwitz,' they seemed nowhere near as bad as a standard US maximum security jail. For instance, of the camp he calls 'the notorious Manjaca camp' Wiesel wrote:

> The prisoners tell us that the food is not too bad, the conditions in general bearable ... What are their main complaints? To be out of touch with their relatives, their people. To be cut off from the outside world. To live on the sidelines, to feel superfluous ... There is a young German among them ... He was taken prisoner by the Serbs. Why? How does this war concern him? 'Oh, I didn't come to fight' he answers, shrugging his shoulders, 'but to write a book.' ... And that's why the Serbs arrested you? 'Well, it's that ... they caught me with a Kalashnikov [rifle] in my hand.' I am bewildered: 'And it was with a Kalashnikov that you were going to write a book? Have pens gone out of fashion?'[45]

Wiesel would become a strong Clinton supporter and a prominent Kosovo *belligerato*. He also claimed joint authorship of the idea of a war crimes tribunal with Secretary of State Lawrence Eagleburger:

> In December [1992], I had along talk with my friend Larry Eagleburger, Secretary of State under George Bush, about the means available to put an end to the slaughter in the former Yugoslavia ... It was then that we had the idea of an international tribunal. We agreed that not to prosecute the criminals would amount to condoning their crimes. In extreme situations, speaking out is a moral obligation. An initial list of names was drawn up. Eagleburger showed it to his European counterparts.[46]

Wiesel's memory is evidently less than perfect. Eagleburger and candidate Clinton had publicly launched the war crimes idea at the beginning of August, some four months earlier.[47] Klaus Kinkel, just quoted, put it forward at the UN–EU London conference. But the conference concluded without taking up his suggestion. Its main concern was with peace, and its most important decision was to set up the permanent peace conference at Geneva with Vance and Owen as Chairs. The only reference to criminal proceedings was the rather non-committal one that the co-chairmen would 'carry forward a study of the creation of an international criminal court.'[48] Far more important for Vance and Owen than a criminal court was the carrying forward of the peace process, which made real gains in the fall of 1992. But a big obstacle to peace was the Americans, who had already blasted one possible peace deal in February 1992, before the outbreak of the Bosnian war, and would repeat this feat over the next three years.

Now the point of all this is that the Americans used even the idea of a criminal court as a way of opposing the peace process and justifying the military solution that they favored. And it's here that Wiesel's friend Larry Eagleburger comes in. In fact, Wiesel's 'long talk' with Eagleburger came in Geneva at a particularly delicate stage in the peace negotiations. The list of names was not merely shown to Eagleburger's 'European counterparts,' it was announced in public, to the press, as a blistering attack on the entire Serb leadership – in fact a declaration that they would all be prosecuted as war criminals at a second Nuremberg. And this in turn was part of an announcement that the Americans were going to start bombing, and that the people of Serbia had only themselves to blame if, in terms George W. Bush would use in 2001, they 'shared their leaders' fate.' Here's the key part of Eagleburger's speech:

> It is clear that the international community must begin now to think about moving beyond the London [peace] agreements and contemplate more aggressive measures. That, for example, is why my government is now recommending that the UN Security Council authorize enforcement of the no-fly zone in Bosnia, and why we are also willing to have the Council re-examine the arms embargo as it applies to the Government

of Bosnia-Herzegovina. Finally, my government also believes it is time for the international community to begin identifying individuals who may have to answer for having committed crimes against humanity. We have, on the one hand, a moral and historical obligation not to stand back a second time in this century while a people faces obliteration. But we have also, I believe, a political obligation to the people of Serbia to signal clearly the risk they currently run of sharing the inevitable fate of those who practice ethnic cleansing in their name.[49]

Eagleburger then named ten individuals who, according to him, should be charged with war crimes. Seven of them were low-level (four Serbs, two Croats and one Muslim); but there were also three big names, all Serbs: Milosevic, Karadzic and Mladic. In other words, *the proposal for a war crimes tribunal was used by the Americans to justify their intention to go to war, collateral damage and all, by branding their proposed enemies as Nazis*. It was also an obvious attempt to *derail the peace process*. British PM John Major was said to be 'incensed,' though Owen called the charges merely 'unhelpful,' which was putting things diplomatically considering that the Vance–Owen peace plan depended on the involvement of leaders named by Eagleburger as war criminals. The question now arose of whether they should even be allowed into the United States to participate in peace talks.[50]

This was fine by the supporters of the international criminal justice movement. They have always found it impossible to understand how anybody could think the minor matter of peace more important than punishing war criminals. Louise Arbour would express this view when she indicted Milosevic. Her predecessor Richard Goldstone had fretted in 1994 over the precedent that might be set by US and UN negotiations for an amnesty-for-peace swap with the military leaders in Haiti. 'This is an example of the wrong way to deal with these crimes,' he told the press then. 'It doesn't serve justice and it ignores the victims.' His Deputy Prosecutor Graham Blewitt added: 'If people look at this as being an avenue for obtaining peace it hinders our work.'[51] Michael Scharf called the UN amnesty-for-peace approach 'infamous.'[52] Journalist Carol Off approved of Goldstone's approach: 'He was right. War criminals were not chattels to be traded for peace.'[53] Off was openly scornful of Boutros-Ghali's opposition to moves like Eagleburger's: 'It was no secret that the Secretary-General didn't want the war crimes issue to undermine the peace process. If peace required negotiating with mass murderers, it was important to find other ways of describing those mass murderers in public statements.'[54] Yet when Eagleburger made his speech, *tens of thousands* of Bosnian deaths had yet to occur. Would it not have been worth sacrificing a few trials in The Hague to prevent that?

Besides, the idea that the Eagleburger speech was simply an exercise in let-justice-be-done-though-the-heavens-should-fall by a principled man who just couldn't 'stand by' is in the William Walker realm of fantasy. Though Eagleburger and Wiesel both claim it was a spontaneous result of their fortuitous meeting and their moral outrage, it was no less calculated than Walker's outburst at Racak. State Department insider Michael Scharf describes it this way:

> The speech was generally assumed to have been largely impromptu and some press reports implied it had not even been cleared with the White House. Nothing could be further from the truth. The 'naming names' speech was in fact 'cleared' throughout the government in advance, and I, myself, made certain revisions to ensure that the statement contained the requisite legal caveats and qualifiers.[55]

The very notion of an American administration unable to stand by in the face of crimes against humanity is absurd. Not only did America work overtime to make sure that *everybody* stood by while Rwandans slaughtered each other, its history is full of active slaughtering, a prime example of which is the Vietnam War, which bears mentioning if only to shed light on Eagleburger's own credibility as a morally driven actor.

If you think Christopher Hitchens does a good job incriminating Henry Kissinger for hundreds of thousands of deaths in South-east Asia, then you may be interested to know that morally outraged Larry Eagleburger worked at the American State Department from 1968 through 1984 as Kissinger's right-hand man. This was a period that included such barbarities as the Vietnam War, the installation of Dictator Augusto Pinochet in Chile, and the terror war against Nicaragua. During the Iran–Contra affair, Eagleburger was the third-ranking person in the State Department – in other words, William Walker's boss. Hitchens points out in his book that the American-supported Indonesian invasion of East Timor took between 50,000 and 80,000 lives while Henry Kissinger was Secretary of State, and Hitchens even quotes a declassified memo of a meeting of 18 December 1975 to show Kissinger's consciousness of guilt. Lawrence Eagleburger was at that meeting, showing no moral outrage, only supplying excuses. After he left the State Department Kissinger would profit handsomely from his relations with the brutal Indonesian regime, through his consulting firm Kissinger and Associates. Eagleburger was President of Kissinger and Associates from 1984 to 1989, before returning to the State Department under George Bush

Sr. to help out with the invasions of Grenada and Panama and the Gulf War, and then to express his moral outrage at the Serbs.[56]

The Eagleburger speech was also timed to coincide with the meeting of a 'Commission of Experts' appointed by the Security Council to investigate Balkan war crimes. Law professor Sherif Bassiouni was the American nominee to the commission. An American of Egyptian-Muslim extraction, and extremely committed to prosecuting Serbs, Bassiouni was another one of those 'no peace without justice' visionaries. According to him, UN resistance to the aggressive American approach was due to that foolish idea 'that the top priority of the Security Council is to achieve a political settlement, and that everything that impedes this goal should really be checked,' and to the 'great apprehension that the commission might be an impediment to a political settlement.'[57] *This, with many thousands of deaths in the Bosnian civil war still in the future.* The Americans provided the commission with seed money of $500,000 despite a legal opinion by the UN Office of Legal Affairs that this was forbidden – but when would that ever bother the US? When Bassiouni took over as chair, he went out and got $800,000 in private funding from the likes of billionaire anti-communist George Soros. Bassiouni then set up a documentation center at his own De Paul University, with protection from the FBI. More money and secondments from the US followed. By 1994 Bassiouni's commission had compiled a war crimes dossier of 65,000 pages in length, with hundreds of taped interviews, which would become the database for the ICTY's prosecutions.

In the meantime, the actual tribunal had been established by Security Council Resolution 827 of 25 May 1993, its statute substantially reflecting the views of the American State Department as contained in a draft their lawyers had submitted to the Secretary General.[58] The Resolution also contained a helpful provision allowing unlimited direct governmental and private support for the tribunal.[59] This made it possible for the US, at the time in its funding war with the cash-starved UN, to contribute directly to the Tribunal without having to cut the UN in on the action. 'Privatization of both the United Nations and justice itself,' Diana Johnstone has aptly called it.[60] The US took advantage of this to make sure the ICTY was up and running as fast as possible, basically covering its budget in the early years and ensuring that it didn't suffer from the general austerity at the UN caused by the US delinquency.[61] American personnel dominated the prosecutor's office: the Tribunal's 1995 report has 21 of 35 seconded personnel coming from the US alone, with another twelve from other NATO countries, plus two Swedes.[62]

US generosity to the ICTY tribunal compared very favorably with neglect of the ICTY's sister tribunal, the International Criminal Tribunal for Rwanda

(ICTR), with jurisdiction over the terrible ethnic violence that took place in Rwanda during 1994. No doubt a revisionist history will attribute both tribunals to the same 'anti-impunity' impulse. But in fact the Rwanda tribunal is further proof of American insincerity in international criminal law. The Americans were the driving force behind the Yugoslav Tribunal, but they had the Rwanda one thrust upon them. Before the massacres even took place in Rwanda, Bassiouni had already completed and submitted his massive brief on Yugoslav crimes, millions of dollars had been spent by the US on the ICTY, the legal framework had been enacted, and all the judges had long been selected.

The ICTR was an initiative of the ultimately victorious Tutsi RPF and their Ugandan sponsors, who started calling for a war crimes tribunal for their enemies in May 1994, before the killing had even stopped – in other words, as part of *their* wartime propaganda. The tribunal was ultimately established in November of that year by Security Council Resolution 955. The final resolution was opposed by the new Rwandan government, but only because it would lack the ability to impose the death penalty and potentially covered crimes committed by them as well as the former regime.[63] They needn't have worried, though, as the ICTR studiously avoided prosecution of anyone associated with the new regime. According to Louise Arbour herself, this was precisely to avoid RPF wrath. Questioned on why she didn't investigate RPF killings within her jurisdiction of up to 30,000 Hutu in reprisals, Arbour answered: 'How could we investigate and prosecute the RPF while we were based in that country? It was never going to happen. They would shut us down.'[64] These were the people, remember, who wouldn't allow justice to be compromised for mere peace. When, in 2003, Arbour's successor Carla Del Ponte intimated that she might have to start investigating the RPF, the Rwandan authorities made sure that the statute was amended so that separate prosecutors would now be assigned to each tribunal. Del Ponte was taken off the ICTR and re-assigned to the ICTY alone. She agreed to the new assignment while protesting rather too much that the split would 'seriously undermine' prosecutorial 'independence.'[65] The Americans' relative lack of interest in the Rwandan tribunal – despite the apparently greater extent of the criminality – was also shown by their relatively miserly contributions to what came to be known as the ICTY's 'poor cousin.'[66]

So Rwanda was not even an afterthought, it was an inconvenience. The war crimes idea had little to do with a general American inability to 'stand by' in the face of atrocities, and everything to do with their Balkan power-play against the Serbs. The Serbs knew this all along, of course, and launched numerous objections to the establishment of the tribunal. They complained that such an organ should not have been established by the Security Council, where the Americans played such a dominant role, but should have been established by treaty or by the General Assembly of the United Nations.[67] The Americans objected that a treaty would have required Yugoslavia's signature, and a General Assembly tribunal would have taken too much time.[68] Such urgency would be hard to understand if it was justice and not war that the Americans were seeking with this tribunal. And why limit it to Yugoslavia? In an official letter of protest, the FRY government listed 'many armed conflicts in the world' where atrocities had been committed, 'whose perpetrators have not been prosecuted or punished by the international community (Korea, Viet Nam, Algeria, Cambodia, Lebanon, Afghanistan, the Belgian Congo, Iraq, Panama, etc.).'[69]

The issue of Security Council control was no technicality. Not only did this mean that the Americans would have a veto over every detail of the tribunal's powers, it meant that they would also have a veto over every judge and every prosecutor. The Security Council's control over the choice of ICTY judges was indirect, by having control over the list from which they would be elected by the General Assembly. That this was not a meaningless power can be gleaned from the fact that the Security Council whittled down the original nominees (any state could submit two nominees) from 41 to 23.[70] But control over the Prosecutor was direct: he or she would be nominated by the Secretary General and then elected by the Security Council itself, meaning that each permanent member of the Security Council would have a veto. The Prosecutor's role would be more crucial than the judges, as time would tell, deciding which crimes would be prosecuted (for example the Serbs') and which would not (for example NATO's), among the many committed on all sides.

The first prosecutor was Richard Goldstone. He was chosen by a process of elimination. Bassiouni was opposed by Britain as a 'fanatic' and a 'threat to the peace process.' The Russians refused anyone from a NATO country for fear of bias against the Serbs. The Americans too, according to Clinton Secretary of State Warren Christopher, preferred that the tribunal not be seen 'as an American show,' even though they were determined to make it into one.[71] Goldstone was a liberal white South African judge – a Westerner from a non-Western country – moderate enough to be trusted by both sides in the transition from apartheid.

It didn't take long for Goldstone to be completely in thrall to the Americans. On arriving in New York, after a brief meeting with the Secretary General and then the Security Council, the Prosecutor was given directly over to his handler by Madeleine Albright. In Goldstone's own words:

Again, I was warmly welcomed by Madeleine Albright, who had played the leading role in having the tribunal established ... She appointed one of her senior advisers, David Scheffer, to take special responsibility for moving the work of the tribunal forward. David became a friend and adviser to me, especially with regard to my contacts with the various branches of the United States administration. His commitment to the work of both tribunals was deep and supportive.[72]

When he arrived at The Hague, Goldstone found the Prosecutor's office had already been assembled for him, with the majority of the personnel coincidentally hailing from the US: 'I had the distinct impression that [Deputy Prosecutor Graham] Blewitt was concerned that I might wish to reorganize the Office of the Prosecutor. Nothing was further from my mind.'[73] Goldstone was very appreciative: 'The Americans were performing essential services that had enabled the initial investigations to begin even before my arrival.'[74] He developed a 'warm friendship' with State Department legal adviser Conrad Harper, who was helpful in procuring evidence from CNN and a commitment of private money from George Soros, sealed at a reception at Soros' Manhattan residence for Goldstone and three ICTY judges.[75] People started to complain: 'Goldstone, it was believed, was on-side with the U.S. administration. People from the State Department were on his staff.'[76] Goldstone was ultimately upbraided by the Secretary General: 'Boutros-Ghali also informed me that some of the permanent representatives at the United Nations had complained that I spent too much time with the Americans, and he agreed with these sentiments. ... My attitude made it quite clear to the Secretary-General that I did not intend to change my policy.'[77]

Not coincidentally, the tribunal's early years were marked by an anti-Serb bias that mirrored American policy very well; so well, in fact, that tribunal supporters started to fear for its credibility. It was clear to them at least that 'the fix [was] on.'[78] Of the first 75 indictments, 55 were issued against Serbs, 17 against Croats and 3 against Muslims.[79] By March 2002, by my count, it was 79 Serbs, 22 Croats and 8 Muslims. By then NATO had carried out its bombing of Yugoslavia, and the really glaring omission was the leaders and generals of the NATO countries.

Goldstone left The Hague after only two years on the job to go back to South Africa. His successor was Louise Arbour, a Canadian judge (and former law faculty colleague of mine) who Goldstone recommended to Madeleine Albright, after he discovered that his and Arbour's 'sensibilities were somehow pitched in the same key.'[80] Everyone knew it was Madeleine Albright's appointment to make: '[I]f the appointment carried, it would be almost exclusively because of Madeleine Albright.'[81] At their first meeting Albright insisted on talking to Arbour alone, and they 'sniffed each other out' for 15 minutes. The only thing we know of their conversation is Arbour's remark afterwards of Albright: 'I liked her very much'[82] – which is perhaps enough. One commentator said of the meeting and subsequent events: 'Arbour comes across as little more than a puppet of Albright.'[83]

Arbour was an energetic, young (well, my age) French Canadian judge; another moderate with no clear-cut ideology. As a lawyer she had acted for the rapist in a famous rape case, and as a judge she had come down on the side of the Nazi in a pivotal war crimes case. On the other hand, she had also led an inquiry into brutality against women prisoners and sided with the women. 'In fact, it was precisely because Arbour had no history of activism that she was attractive to Albright.'[84] Once Albright was content, it was easy to persuade the Russians, who were happy she was not an American, the French, who were happy she was bilingual, and the British who were happy she wasn't Bassiouni.

Arbour took over the prosecutor job in October 1996. NATO's friend Kofi Annan (another Clinton–Albright choice) took over as United Nations Secretary General on 1 January 1997. On 1 May 1997, Tony Blair was elected Prime Minister of Britain. All of this heralded a new working relationship between NATO and the prosecutor's office that was sealed in blood, on 10 July 1997, with an unprecedented commando raid into Serbian Bosnia by British forces under NATO command, who arrested one Bosnian Serb indictee and killed another who tried to escape. The very next day (coincidence?) General Wesley Clark, the US Military's chief political and strategic planner from early in the Clinton presidency, formally took control of NATO as its 'Supreme Commander' for Europe:[85]

> Arbour will not say what influence she had on the British decision to act, or what role Wesley Clark played in these developments. But it couldn't have been closer to her heart's desire if she had planned and executed the raid herself. She was on a roll.[86]

THE ICTY AT WAR

But the role that the ICTY was born to play came in the Kosovo war. This had nothing to do with trying and punishing criminals, and everything to do with lending crucial credibility to NATO's cause. Starting in the fall of 1998, the ICTY became a virtual press office for NATO, issuing press releases containing official statements that demonized the FRY as an outlaw state whose leaders were inveterate war criminals, up to their old tricks in

Kosovo. There was an exclusive concentration on the Serbs as criminal non-compliers with international law, to the complete neglect of similar behavior by the KLA, Bosnian Muslims and Croats, and ultimately NATO itself.

NATO started planning its military intervention in June 1998, ordering military exercises to 'pressure' the Serbs. Madeleine Albright was already calling the Serb response to the KLA offensive 'ethnic cleansing' and 'slaughter'; Tony Blair was saying Milosevic would only respond to the 'credible threat of the use of military force.'[87] So it didn't hurt NATO strategy when, in July, Chief Prosecutor Louise Arbour announced to the press that she was investigating 'crimes against humanity' in Kosovo.[88] In mid-August 1998 NATO announced it was 'reviewing' its 'military planning for options to bring an end to the violence and create conditions for negotiations.'[89] In early September Prosecutor Arbour and the Court's Chief Judge, Gabrielle Kirk McDonald, started to obsess publicly about the FRY's understandable refusal to cooperate with the tribunal and hand over suspects in connection with charges stemming from the war in Croatia. The ICTY released a letter from Arbour that drew a direct comparison to one of America's favorite 'rogue' states and its most notorious incident of terrorism to date – the bombing of a Pan American passenger flight that took 270 lives, mostly American, when it crashed over Lockerbie, Scotland in 1988. Referring to the Security Council Resolution recently threatening Libya with further sanctions if it didn't hand over the Lockerbie suspects, Arbour wrote: 'This resolution stands in stark contrast with the lack of action by the Council regarding a case which offers much similarity to the Lockerbie case.' In her letter Arbour also lent credibility to the NATO allegations that the Serbs were committing 'war crimes and crimes against humanity' in Kosovo by announcing that she had 'launched an investigation' (important words, as events would show) on behalf of 'the international community'.[90]

The recipient of the letter was the Court's President, Gabrielle Kirk McDonald, a judge who owed her appointment to The Hague to intense lobbying efforts by the Clinton State Department.[91] She duly forwarded the letter to the Security Council, reiterating the charges and significantly cranking up the rhetoric, adding that Yugoslavia had 'demonstrated its disregard and its disrespect for its obligations under international law' and 'contempt for the authority of the Security Council.' The 'reprehensible conduct of the Government of the F.R.Y. in violating the United Nations Charter, resolutions of the Security Council and the Dayton Agreement, should no longer be tolerated.'[92]

The Security Council remained neutral and passed a moderate call for cooperation with the ICTY by all parties.[93] But NATO explicitly threatened war, and McDonald took the occasion to up the ante even further with an inflammatory address to the Security Council on 2 October 1998:

> No State should be permitted to act as if it is 'above the law'.... Therefore, it is imperative that the F.R.Y. be brought into the fold of nations who believe in world peace and respect the authority of the Security Council ... There comes a time when such defiance cannot be ignored. That time is now.[94]

The next step was for Arbour to demand entry into Kosovo to investigate war crimes, adopting NATO's tone of treating President Milosevic as a stubborn recalcitrant who didn't know his place: 'The jurisdiction of this Tribunal is not conditional upon President Milosevic's consent, nor is it dependent on the outcome of any negotiations between him and anyone else.'[95] The FRY replied that Arbour could come and speak to officials and attend a conference, but not otherwise conduct investigations in Kosovo. Arbour declined in protest and McDonald abandoned all restraint, calling the FRY a 'rogue State' (she thought the phrase so important that she repeated it at the top of her press release): 'This conduct is a further example of the FRY's utter disregard for the norms of the international community. Essentially, it has become a rogue State, one that holds the international rule of law in contempt.'[96]

In November the ICTY and the Americans were able to obtain from the Security Council a specific condemnation of the FRY for non-compliance over the Croatian charges, but no sanctions were attached and the paragraph on Kosovo was mild and neutral.[97] In a speech two days later to the United Nations General Assembly, McDonald wanted to increase the dose yet again, but she had no place to go but the Holocaust:

> Following the ravages of World War II, the Nuremberg Tribunal was created to put the world on notice that the international community would not allow such atrocities to go unpunished. Hence the phrase, 'Never again.' Yet, 'again' and 'again' such barbarity comes back to haunt us ... The heinous crimes committed by the Nazi regime were allowed to happen because many bystanders looked the other way. They knew what was happening, but they feigned ignorance ... Thus, I ask you: Will you passively stand by and permit one State to flout the express directives of the United Nations? By omission, will you not become participants?[98]

So in the space of a few months, the ICTY had officially endorsed NATO's branding of the FRY as a rogue state and the situation as equivalent to the Holocaust. But the ICTY's really big moment came with Racak. Remember that the action took place on the afternoon of 15 January 1999. It was denounced by the uncharacteristically morally-outraged and free-speaking William Walker as a 'massacre' and 'a crime against humanity' on 16 January. That very same day Arbour issued a press release calling it a 'massacre of civilians':

> I have launched an investigation into the most recent massacre in Kosovo ... I have spoken to Ambassador Walker and sought his assistance.... In light of the information publicly available, the recent massacre of civilians falls squarely within the mandate of the ICTY, and the Federal Republic of Yugoslavia is required to grant access to investigators from my office ... To the families of the victims of the massacre at Racak, and other atrocities committed in the previous months, I express my sincere regret that we are not able to bring, at this time, the comfort of truth and the expectation of justice.[99]

Whatever the facts of Racak, there is no doubting that the use of it as a way to Nazify the Serbs and justify military intervention by NATO was the reason for its denunciation. Arbour played a willing and collaborative role in this PR stunt (not the crime, but the use of it). In fact it's impossible otherwise to understand such a breach of prosecutorial ethics. She had spoken to no one but the Albright underling Walker; she had seen nothing for herself, but she was already rushing to tell the press it was a massacre of civilians for which she would seek justice. Carol Off spoke to Arbour and her staff about Racak, and what Off described is not horror that such a crime could occur, not moral outrage, not even a thirst for justice, but pure publicity hunting:

> The point was not that she had to see the massacre site in Racak. The point was that the world's media had to see her *attempting* to get there – to send the message that this *was* a crime scene, and that there *was* a prosecutor in the field of international justice demanding to examine it first-hand. If Arbour wasn't allowed, the world would know that it was because Milosevic had something to hide. 'Racak focused public attention on our work, on our relevance,' Arbour says of the event. 'In very simple two-line statements you could get the message out.' Arbour's photo was suddenly on the front page of the *New York Times*, 'above the fold!' exclaimed her excited office staff.[100]

It seemed like a good idea to everyone to make the issue one between Arbour and Milosevic. That's why she went to Kosovo to demand the entry she knew she would be denied; that's why Walker sent the press to meet her; that's why Arbour's good friend and NATO's 'supreme commander' General Wesley K. Clark went knocking on Milosevic's door the very next day to demand that Milosevic either allow Arbour to enter Kosovo or face bombing. Milosevic refused, saying Racak had been staged.[101] From that moment, NATO's 'credibility' and the ICTY were welded together, as in this syndicated American television broadcast of 18 January 1999:

> Well, this strikes at the heart of NATO's credibility, of the standing of the war crimes tribunal, of the cease-fire agreement negotiated between Mr. Holbrooke and Mr. Milosevic in October, and of the leadership of the United States.[102]

NATO then used the tribunal at every step of the way to war. In his 'summons' of Milosevic to Rambouillet on 30 January, Javier Solana put Racak and the ICTY front and center: 'NATO recalls that those responsible for the massacre at Racak must be brought to justice and that the authorities of the Federal Republic of Yugoslavia must cooperate fully with the International Tribunal for the former Yugoslavia.'[103] During Rambouillet itself, the ICTY kept a low profile; but the moment the talks collapsed – or rather were canceled by NATO – the ICTY, like NATO, went on the attack again. On the very day the Albanians signed and the bombing was assured, the ICTY released a formal complaint by the Prosecutor to the Security Council about non-compliance over Racak, a complaint that had been kept firmly under wraps by the ICTY since 2 February.[104]

Now the ICTY was at war. NATO wasted no time in making good Nazifying use of it. Two days into the bombing, UK Defence Minister George Robertson was comparing Milosevic to Hitler, and saying in the same breath that he would 'face justice in The Hague': 'We ... are meticulously collecting evidence on what is going on in Kosovo ... That information will be passed to the international war crimes tribunal and when the time comes, these people will face justice in The Hague.'[105] As for the Tribunal itself, its first job turned out to be a little damage control. On the day the war began it came out with a press release discussing Croatian crimes against Serbs in the war of 1991, but it had nothing to do with providing balance. Quite the contrary, it was a rather desperate *repudiation* of a *New York Times* article based on leaked documents suggesting that the ICTY was going to charge Croatians with these crimes – something rather embarrassing to NATO of course, because Nazis can't be victims of war crimes: 'The Prosecutor does not comment on the existence or progress of any investigation, and this has been the policy of the Office from its inception,' she said, but the leaked documents 'do not contain the official position of the Office of the Prosecutor.'[106] *The Prosecutor does not comment on the existence or progress of any investigation, and this has been the policy of the Office from its inception?* So how come it had been shooting its mouth off about alleged Serb crimes in Kosovo for the better part of a year?[107] And what were we to call it when, two days later, Arbour took what she herself described as 'the unusual step of addressing herself directly to President Milosevic and other senior officers, reminding them of their obligations under international law,' on account of her 'grave concern' that 'serious violations of international humanitarian law continue to be committed in Kosovo'?[108]

Five days later the Chief Prosecutor, continuing her policy of 'not commenting on the existence or progress of any investigation,' released to the media the text of the letter which left no doubt that the recipients were 'under investigation,' including a copy of her Tribunal's statute for easy reference. ('Lest you be in any doubt as to the relevant law, a copy of the salient portions of the text of Statute of the International Tribunal is attached for your information.') The 13 named and numbered recipients were the entire FRY political and military hierarchy, with Milosevic at the top of the list.[109] As usual, Judge McDonald couldn't resist going even further beyond anything resembling her judicial role, and issued her own press release repeating admittedly unverified 'allegations' by refugees, and once again invoking the Holocaust, while reminding Milosevic how comfortable the Tribunal was with charging heads of government with genocide: 'I would also remind President Milosevic ... that just eight months ago, the International Criminal Tribunal for Rwanda convicted the former Prime Minister of Rwanda of genocide.'[110]

But Arbour's press briefing of 31 March was very rich in content and had two other items of even more significance than the crudely packaged accusations against Milosevic. The first had to do with NATO-inflicted 'collateral damage' that, even this early in the war, had begun to make itself felt. The first confirmed civilian death had occurred on the second day of the war, when 16-year-old Senad Dacic was killed by a cluster bomb in Montenegro which also wounded two of his friends. The bombing of Belgrade had begun. Arbour was being pressed from various quarters to start charging NATO leaders with their crimes as well, something which she admitted she had the power to do – though in such a roundabout way that it was clear she couldn't bring herself to say 'NATO' and 'war crimes' in the same breath, even theoretically, without a swipe at the Serbs:

> I have received requests from persons and groups urging me to indict various NATO and other officials for war crimes in relation to the air strikes conducted in Serbia ... There is no doubt in my mind that the jurisdiction of the Tribunal over Kosovo is well known to all, and indeed has never been contested by anyone except the FRY ... I will review all information provided to me, which may suggest the commission of crimes

within the jurisdiction of ICTY. I will only disregard unsubstantiated conclusions and political diatribe.

But the bombshell of the press release was the announcement of the indictment and warrant for the arrest of Serb paramilitary leader Zeljko Raznjatovic (better known by his pseudonym 'Arkan') for undisclosed crimes allegedly committed in Bosnia years before. The indictment had been issued secretly on 30 September 1997, and Arbour said it had been kept secret to enhance the chances of arresting Arkan. So why publicize it now, admittedly reducing those same chances? The justification was really lame: she had received 'reports of his alleged involvement in Kosovo' and wanted to 'put on notice those who might be inclined to retain his services, or to obey his orders, that they too will be tainted by their association with an indicted war criminal.'[111] Now Arkan certainly knew that the ICTY was after him, so the publicity could have zero deterrent effect on him. Anyway, he had other rather more significant things to worry about than The Hague – he would be gunned down by hit men in a Belgrade hotel before a year had passed. As for the others, there could be few decision-makers who didn't know who Arkan was; and anyway, you don't get legally implicated for war crimes merely by hanging out with criminals. So the idea had to be, as Arbour said herself, 'to taint by association,' but the tainting was of the whole Milosevic regime, and the intention of the press release could only have been to brand the FRY a bunch of war criminals and thus legitimate NATO's bombing campaign.

Both Arbour and Goldstone before her had always worked very closely with NATO and the US State Department. By the time of Racak, Clark (NATO), Walker (State Department) and Arbour (ICTY) were cooking up public relations exercises together to put the Serbs on the defensive. Given NATO's violent protagonism in the Balkans this was highly questionable, but the association could not be said to be wrong in itself: until the bombing started on 24 March 1999, NATO itself had been working with the Security Council, and the ICTY was a Security Council organ. Arbour had Security Council authorization from late 1998 to investigate in Kosovo – authorization that the FRY government was thwarting as best it could.

However, when NATO started to bomb Yugoslavia, Arbour's cozy relationship with NATO and the State Department took on an entirely different meaning. The attack on Yugoslavia was a blatant violation of the UN Charter, almost universally recognized as such by experts in international law, including the Tribunal's own first president, Judge Antonio Cassese. So there was good reason for a self-styled Nuremberg successor like Louise Arbour to consider NATO guilty of Nuremberg's 'supreme international crime.' Furthermore, from very early on in the bombing, the 'inevitable collateral damage' started to occur. When NATO took its attack to Serbia's 'infrastructure' the bodies began piling up. At least four civilians were killed on 2 April, and five on 4 April. On 5 April NATO bombs hit a residential area in Aleksanic in Serbia, and killed ten civilians, ranging in age from the 26-year-old Marina Paovic to the 93-year-old Gvozden Milivojevic. This was the first 'accident of war' NATO actually confessed to. As early as 3 April Arbour was served with a formal complaint by the entire Faculty of Law of Belgrade University, demanding that she immediately indict Solana, Clark and all others responsible for 'brutally violating all norms of international law' and committing every crime in Arbour's jurisdiction.[112]

In other words Arbour, McDonald and the whole ICTY were on notice from the beginning of the bombing campaign that NATO was being legitimately accused of war crimes within their jurisdiction. This should have changed everything in their behavior; but it didn't. In fact, the ICTY moved even closer to NATO. In mid-April Arbour made a public round of visits to European NATO leaders.[113] By now she had abandoned all restraint herself, and was openly talking about the case she was building, with NATO's help, against the FRY leaders; she meant everyone to know that they were guilty of the crimes NATO accused them of:

> The Tribunal's investigators are now assembling a body of direct witness testimony ... Refugee accounts are critical, but they are not enough on their own. The victims did not see the command structures or the people giving the orders at the highest levels. We therefore need the sophisticated kind of assistance that only states can provide. I find the discussions I had in Bonn and London to be extremely encouraging. We have been steadily building our co-operation with a number of countries, and their decisions to increase our access to sensitive information takes us another important step forward. It should also send a signal to leaders and commanders on the ground that are implicated in the commission of war crimes that they will be brought to justice.[114]

As Arbour moved closer to NATO, NATO escalated its bombing campaign, and the civilians paid an ever-steeper price. American cluster bombs were responsible for five civilian deaths in Serbia on 10 April, including the first baby, one-year-old Bojana Tosovic. Then two of the most notorious incidents of the campaign occurred. On 12 April a civilian train on the Grdelica Bridge was hit twice by NATO bombs, killing 17 passengers ranging in age from six to 65. On 14 April the war's biggest single incident of 'collateral damage' occurred when NATO attacked a refugee convoy on the Djakovica–Decane road in Kosovo, killing 73 civilians – mostly Albanians, from children to the elderly, many mutilated beyond recognition. NATO at first denied it, but then had to admit responsibility.[115]

Despite this Arbour kept popping up on TV with one NATO leader or another. One televised appearance with British Foreign Secretary Robin Cook, at which he dramatically handed her a 'dossier' of Serb crimes, raised eyebrows among Canadian colleagues of the Prosecutor. 'Is war crimes prosecutor Louise Arbour becoming a pawn of NATO?' asked Toronto's *Globe and Mail*.[116] And the US continued to bear gifts of big money and key personnel to help the ICTY 'carry its message of impartial justice.'[117] On 28 April Arbour announced that the State Department had loaned her a new spokesman, Paul Risley, who had spent the past five years in media relations for the US government and would see the ICTY through to the ouster of Milosevic in October 2000.[118] Arbour then announced that she was off to Washington in search of 'usable court products.' In a State Department press conference of 10 May, Madeleine Albright was bursting with pride as she delivered the court products and more money (and more propaganda: 'tens of thousands of males are missing ... literally thousands of stories of the summary execution of fathers, brothers, husbands and sons'):

> We are the Tribunal's leading financial supporter, and we have asked Congress to help us increase the resources we provide. When conditions permit, the Federal Bureau of Investigation has agreed to provide a forensic team for investigation inside Kosovo. We share with the Tribunal as much information as we can, and we fully endorse its determination to follow the evidence as high as it leads.[119]

Now at this point, NATO had been pummeling civilian targets in the FRY for a full month. Civilian deaths from NATO's bombs were, even by conservative estimates, in the hundreds. NATO had hit a Belgrade TV Station – an act they admitted was intentional – killing 16 on 23 April; a residential neighborhood in Surdulica, killing eleven, on 27 April; a civilian bus on a bridge near Luzane, killing 39, on 1 May. On 7 May they hit not only a marketplace in Nis, killing 14 with cluster bombs, but also the Chinese Embassy in Belgrade, killing three Chinese citizens. This caused outrage in China and a siege of the American Embassy in Beijing, and it was the only attack of the war for which the US apologized.

In fact, starting on 7 May, Arbour received a multitude of complaints from various parties around the world (including me and my colleagues) demanding that she charge NATO leaders with war crimes. She acknowledged this, but barely, in a speech she made on 13 May to launch the campaign for the ratification of the Statute on the International Criminal

Court. But the main point was to reassure everyone that this was in the realm of pure theory:

> Having said that, I am obviously not commenting on any allegations of violations of international humanitarian law supposedly perpetrated by nationals of NATO countries. *I accept the assurances given by NATO leaders that they intend to conduct their operations in the Federal Republic of Yugoslavia in full compliance with international humanitarian law.*[120]

She never mentioned NATO again. It would be for her successor in office to acquit them later on a similar basis – 'accepting assurances' at face value that flew in the face of the evidence.[121]

Arbour had other things on her mind. Since the beginning of the war she had been skirting around questions of the indictment of Slobodan Milosevic himself. She had been threatening to indict him since the third day of the bombing and everybody knew it was just a matter of time. On 7 April her deputy denied there was any 'pressure' to indict Milosevic, but allowed that 'discussions [were] ongoing with countries involved in the NATO exercise about the possibilities.'[122] In fact, on 12 April a law was introduced in the American Congress, declaring that it 'shall be the policy of the United States to support fully and completely the indictment of President Slobodan Milosevic as a war criminal,' instructing the CIA to provide the ICTY with 'any information the intelligence community collects or has collected in support of an indictment and trial of President Slobodan Milosevic for war crimes, crimes against humanity, or genocide.'[123]

On 28 April Arbour denied that anyone had 'asked her to *refrain* from indicting Mr. Milosevic.'[124] On 22 May she proved it by issuing the indictment itself, making it public on 27 May.[125] Milosevic and four other top officials were each charged with three crimes against humanity: murder, persecution and deportation. The press release put the number of murders at 'over 340' and the deportations at 740,000, 'about one-third of the entire Kosovo Albanian population.' The crimes were alleged to have been committed 'between 1 January and late May 1999,' but, in fact, apart from Racak, *all* the crimes detailed in the indictment were alleged to have occurred on dates *after* the bombing had started.[126]

Now, as Noam Chomsky has pointed out, the indictment followed the State Department's line perfectly, 'seeking to foster the interpretation of the NATO bombing as a response to crimes beginning almost three months earlier, while offering evidence of crimes that followed the bombing.'[127] And, of course, the indictments themselves were a beautiful piece of propaganda, not only detaching Serb crimes from the KLA crimes they were mixed up with, but detaching Security Council condemnations of the Serbs from condemnations of KLA terrorism contained within the very same Resolutions. But this was nothing compared to the really extraordinary thing, which was the *timing* of the indictments: they came at a time when there had been absolutely no opportunity to investigate their plausibility. The indictments were issued on 22 May for events that were supposed to have occurred between six and eight weeks earlier, at a place that had been and was still under an intense aerial bombardment. As with Racak, Arbour had done no investigations of her own and had heard only one side of the story – NATO's – and even that must have been rather incomplete. And this was a question not just of 'opening an investigation,' as with Racak, but of actually issuing indictments. Also, unlike at the time of Racak, the prosecutor had received numerous well founded complaints that NATO was committing war crimes itself, and there was no doubt that it was killing a lot of people in an illegal war – one certified as such in a scholarly article by the ICTY's own first President, Judge Cassese. Wait till you see how the ICTY tiptoed around those complaints. And hadn't Arbour heard the one about truth being war's 'first casualty'? For a serious prosecutor, these allegations might have been grounds to open an investigation once the bombing had ended, but indictments in the middle of a war?

According to Arbour's press release, the indictments were 'the product of intense efforts by a large number of people in my Office.'[128] So what was the rush? There was no possibility of arresting anyone until the war was over. Everybody knew that further investigations would be required. The prosecutor herself admitted as much ('It does not represent the totality of the charges that may result from our continuing investigations of these accused ... We are continuing to develop an evidentiary base ... We are still actively investigating other incidents in Kosovo ...'[129]). Indeed, Arbour's successor Carla Del Ponte made the same admission when she came on the job in September 1999, saying that her 'primary focus' would be 'gathering additional evidence' to substantiate the Milosevic charges.[130] And when Milosevic finally appeared before the court in July 2001, he was read an indictment that had hundreds of murder victims added to the original, more than doubling the total.

Arbour herself gave no justification for the great rush except for some silly boasting about 'real time law enforcement':

I have been stressing for several months now our commitment to functioning as a real time law enforcement operation. I believe that it is an extraordinary achievement, by any law enforcement standard, for us to have brought to successful confirmation, an indictment against the five accused, for crimes of this magnitude committed since the beginning of this year.[131]

Why 'real time law enforcement' should be a concern of a judicial body, as opposed to a police force, was never made clear. How issuing indictments that could not be acted upon until the war was over could be considered 'real time law enforcement' was even less clear. Furthermore, 'real time law enforcement' was obviously of no concern to the ICTY once the war was over, because Carla Del Ponte's 'primary focus' of gathering evidence against Milosevic clearly conflicted with enforcing the law against the 'reverse ethnic cleansing' taking place in Kosovo under NATO's watchful eyes. There was simply no legitimate reason to issue these indictments while the bombs were falling. So what was the point?

Arbour gave a hint in her press release when she tried to ward off criticism that indictments might interfere with a negotiated solution:

> Finally, I am mindful of the impact that this indictment may have on the peace process in the Federal Republic of Yugoslavia.... No credible, lasting peace can be built upon impunity and injustice. The refusal to bring war criminals to account would be an affront to those who obey the law, and a betrayal of those who rely on it for their life and security. Although the accused are entitled to the benefit of the presumption of innocence until they are convicted, the evidence upon which this indictment was confirmed raises serious questions about their suitability to be the guarantors of any deal, let alone a peace agreement. They have not been rendered less suitable by the indictment. The indictment has simply exposed their unsuitability.[132]

This was that same old saw about justice having to be done though the heavens fall – even if they should happen to fall on Serb and Albanian civilians – but with this twist: the very moment Arbour chose to disqualify the Serb leadership as partners for a peace agreement was the one in which such an agreement was being concluded by the EU under the auspices of the Russians and the Germans. It was immediately understood to be 'an indictment whose timing was diplomatically devastating.'[133] Some people argued that this was evidence of the *independence* of the court, on the assumption that the Americans were genuinely interested in a negotiated settlement, and that this made it more difficult for Milosevic to agree. Michael Scharf repeated this line in a post-war op-ed piece in praise of the Tribunal: 'Indeed while the United States and Britain initially thought an indictment of Milosevic might interfere with the prospects of peace, it later became a useful tool in their efforts to demonize the Serbian leader and maintain public support for NATO's bombing campaign against Serbia, which was still underway when the indictment was handed down.'[134] But what an absurd spin this is, since all the evidence against Milosevic was provided by the Americans and the UK themselves. Chomsky acidly called it 'the indictment that Washington hoped would not be issued when it provided information and intelligence previously withheld.'[135] Albright's 'Ambassador at Large for War Crimes,' David Scheffer, 'obviously in favor of a speedy indictment,' admitted to having supplied Arbour with sensitive intelligence material; he also came to see her at The Hague *three days* before the indictment was issued.[136] And the indictment's blow to the peace deal coincided with an intensification of bombing that seemed aimed at the same thing.[137]

The denials all round that there was any 'pressure' are not in the least inconsistent with what was obviously a *collaboration*. In fact, the only account that makes any sense is Carol Off's, which she appears to have got from Arbour herself – namely that Arbour *had cleared the whole thing with NATO*. From the moment the bombing started, Arbour was asking for 'court products' from people who knew exactly what she wanted them for: 'Arbour didn't tell them directly that she was planning to indict Milosevic and a number of his associates, but they certainly could have guessed that she was heading towards a showdown.'[138] The five-day gap between the signing and release of the indictment was in fact meant to give Clinton and Blair (but not, apparently, the other NATO leaders) time to approve it:

> Arbour was told by her private sources that President Bill Clinton and Prime Minister Tony Blair had a ten-minute phone conversation in which they decided this was ... okay. Maybe it was even good. But the German chancellor, Gerhardt Shroder, was angry: 'Sometimes there are goals – such as peace in Europe – that take precedence over other considerations.'[139]

The Russians were not informed beforehand. When the indictment was released, Chernomyrdin, at that very moment en route to Belgrade, turned his plane around and declared: 'Today, we reached the finishing line in the negotiating process, but somebody needed to put obstacles on the road to a peace dialogue.'[140]

Madeleine Albright immediately seized upon the indictment to justify the US refusal to tolerate a negotiated settlement on the Russian–German model. She was on television bright and early the next morning. 'We are not negotiating with Milosevic ... The indictments, I think, clarify the situation because they really show that we are doing the right thing in terms of responding to the kinds of crimes against humanity that Milosevic has perpetrated.' Asked what she would do if Milosevic 'promised to meet all the

NATO demands in exchange for a meeting with President Clinton,' Albright answered, 'I think you are raising a completely hypothetical situation. He has to accept the terms, then the bombing campaign will stop. Milosevic is an indicted war criminal.'[141] NATO then struck hard at Serbia, aiming straight for the morale of its citizens. More hits were seen on 30 May than on any other day of the war. Official targets included Belgrade's electricity towers, and several radio and TV stations. It also included an attack on a Surdulica 'ammunition storage depot' that hit a hospital and killed 21 civilians, and a broad-daylight attack on the bridge crowded with civilians at Varvarin, which took nine civilian lives.[142]

Arbour's predecessor, Richard Goldstone, had played the same game with indictments and Milosevic back in 1995, except in reverse. The Americans' preferred solution was a military one that excluded the Bosnian Serb leadership (Karadzic and Mladic) and made Milosevic the Serb interlocutor. Goldstone delivered the goods in the form of selective indictments. On his own account: 'When it was announced that the Dayton talks were to take place, we decided to hasten the indictment.'[143] The indictment of Karadzic and Mladic, that is. The man the tribunal would later charge as the mastermind of the Bosnian 'genocide' was, strangely, missing. Goldstone says politics didn't influence his decision not to indict Milosevic, but Scharf disagrees: '[I]t is hard to believe Goldstone did not intentionally delay pursuing an indictment of Slobodan Milosevic. Clearly such an indictment would have wrecked any prospect for peace at Dayton.'[144] Goldstone, too, was entirely dependent on the US State Department for his information; the CIA even 'managed' the telephones in the prosecutor's office.[145]

So the ICTY provided many valuable services to the Americans in corroborating the claim that the illegal bombing campaign, far from being the supreme international crime, was actually a law-enforcement mission against war criminals who were right then perpetrating unspeakable acts – Nazis in fact, and the ICTY itself drove this point home at every opportunity. When NATO commenced its attack on Yugoslavia, a visitor to the Anne Frank House in Amsterdam would be offended by a prominent photograph of Louise Arbour posted near the exit, with accompanying text making it seem as if she was carrying on the job of punishing Anne Frank's murderers ('It was hoped after Nuremberg that there would never again be a need for such a tribunal,' etc.).

Anne Frank's memory would come in for more abuse at the hands of the Blair government in England during what critics called the 'Blair Holocaust Project,' after the popular movie of the time. This was a local version of the international Holocaust Remembrance Day proclaimed in Stockholm in January 2000.[146] The whole thing appears to have been the brainchild of the

US and the UK, precisely as they were conceiving their attack on Yugoslvia in mid-1998, and invitations to the Stockholm Conference were sent out just weeks after the Kosovo war ended. The international day ultimately focused on the real Holocaust, but the Blair government decided that the British version would be more 'relevant' and subtitled it *Remembering Genocides: Lessons for the Future*, explicitly linking it to the mass murders that NATO would like people to remember, but excluding those it would like them to forget, like Hiroshima and Nagasaki, Vietnam and Iraq:

> [T]he type of behaviour demonstrated in Nazi Germany was not a phenomenon limited either to Germany or the mid-Twentieth Century. Events in Cambodia, Bosnia Herzegovina, Rwanda and Kosovo, to name but a few, amply demonstrate the propensity of human beings to murder en masse ...[147]

Lest anyone miss the point about the UK's recent humanitarian intervention, the official program for the day included a film about *Zlata's Diary*, a book written by the teenager Zlata Filipovic during the siege of Sarajevo in the Bosnian civil war.[148] The program described her as 'a contemporary Anne Frank,' though, as one critic said in disgust, the real Anne Frank didn't survive to reap her royalties and go to Oxford.

5

The Trial of Milosevic

There were two items of unfinished business left on the ICTY's Kosovo agenda. One was the delicate question, taken up in the next chapter, of how to deal with the war crimes committed by NATO in its bombing campaign. The other was the dramatic one of bringing Slobodan Milosevic in chains to The Hague: the Holocaust metaphor absolutely demanded a prisoner in the dock, preferably behind bullet-proof glass and wearing headphones. But Milosevic was still the lawfully elected president of the FRY; he would have to be toppled. The NATO countries, though, had an unbeatable election campaign platform: if Milosevic was not ousted and handed over, the country would never emerge from the ruin to which it had been reduced by NATO's bombs and sanctions. Yugoslavia's children would face the same fate as Iraq's.

Before the Kosovo war was over, a law was introduced in the US Congress imposing a complete economic blockade on the country until the US President should certify that it met certain conditions, among which was 'Cooperation with the International Criminal Tribunal for the former Yugoslavia, including the transfer of all indicted war criminals in Yugoslavia to The Hague.'[1] Not only would the US boycott Yugoslavia; it would exercise its considerable economic muscle in the various international financial institutions, such as the IMF, to force others to do the same. The law further authorized the US President to spend $100 million in support of opposition groups in Yugoslavia, and thus allowed the US shamelessly to hand out wads of overt and covert cash and logistical support to groups willing to oppose Milosevic. This was decisive in constitutional lawyer Vojislav Kostunica's victory over Milosevic in the elections of September 2000.[2] But Kostunica's victory depended on opposing both Milosevic and NATO, as the joint sponsors of Yugoslavia's ruin. The ICTY was identified with NATO, so there was to be no thought of handing over Milosevic without a lot more pressure. Milosevic's ouster was rewarded by the US with $45 million in emergency food aid to get Serbia through the winter; but the price of Yugoslavia's survival was made very clear, and the Americans set a legal deadline – 31 March 2001. If the President didn't certify by then that the FRY was 'cooperating,' $100 million of US aid would be cut off and the

American directors of those 'international financial institutions' would be instructed not to support 'loans and assistance' to the FRY.[3]

The job of collecting NATO's pound of flesh from Yugoslavia fell to Louise Arbour's replacement as Chief Prosecutor, former Swiss Attorney General Carla Del Ponte. Del Ponte was well-known to the Americans for her successful collaboration with the FBI in the late 1980s on the 'Pizza Connection' case – an international drug trafficking/money laundering scheme involving the Sicilian Mafia, American pizza parlors and Swiss banks.[4] There is said to have been a private meeting between Del Ponte and Madeleine Albright at Heathrow Airport in July 1999 to discuss Del Ponte's then-secret work on a corruption scandal involving Russian President Boris Yeltsin.[5] Indeed, the day before Del Ponte was appointed to the ICTY, with the scandal still under wraps, Yeltsin effectively handed over power to Vladimir Putin. But the meeting also took place precisely when a replacement was being sought for Arbour and no doubt would have been another 'sniffing-out' exercise of the sort that Albright had engaged in with Arbour a few years earlier – Albright might have been interested in Del Ponte's thoughts on the charges before the tribunal against Albright for murder and other crimes against humanity.

In January 2001 Del Ponte went calling on Kostunica with fresh arrest warrants. She was met with public protests and a lecture from Kostunica on the 'selective justice' of the Tribunal, which he declared 'an institution more political than judicial.'[6] Kostunica protested that NATO wasn't being prosecuted for its supreme and lesser crimes against Yugoslavia. And why couldn't Milosevic be prosecuted at home? This was perfectly acceptable under the Tribunal's statute, which made jurisdiction 'concurrent' with the national courts; indeed, the new International Criminal Court actually gave *priority* to national courts. But Del Ponte would have none of this. She made the US economic blackmail of Serbia her very own cause. Should Yugoslavia fail to hand over Milosevic, its children would not be permitted to eat: 'I believe at that point the international community will have to consider the sanctions hypothesis. To make the programs of financial assistance to Belgrade conditional. No cooperation with the Tribunal, no assistance.'[7]

As 31 March approached everyone knew what was going to happen.[8] A new government had taken over the Republic of Serbia, the main constituent of the Yugoslav Federation, which now consisted of only Serbia and Montenegro. Prime Minister Zoran Djindjic, later assassinated, was decidedly 'pro-Western.'[9] Yugoslav officials started to drop hints of an imminent arrest of Milosevic; there was only the minor detail of a lack of proof.[10] Sure enough, as the clock approached midnight on 31 March, Milosevic's Belgrade villa was surrounded by Serbian police, and after a few dramatic hours of negotiations – Milosevic is supposed to have said 'They'll never take me alive' and, naturally, Del Ponte is supposed to have said 'I want him alive' – by 5 a.m. of the morning of 1 April, Milosevic was being whisked away to a Belgrade jail, his surrender having been negotiated without bloodshed, with only a few desperate shots fired from the pistol of his distraught daughter. Milosevic was not charged with war crimes, however, but with corruption in the amount US$200 million he was supposed to have diverted to himself and his party.[11] Hardly the kind of thing that would have warranted his being taken into custody *at that moment*, even if there was any hard evidence – and over the next three months none whatsoever was brought forward to substantiate the charges. Everyone knew Milosevic's arrest was, in the words of the Italian Prime Minister Amato, 'strongly influenced by the American position which was explicit: if you haven't arrested Milosevic by 31 March, we will cancel the aid.'[12] Despite this, there was a well-scripted international chorus of celebration for the victory of – of all things – 'the rule of law.'[13] The Americans patted the Yugoslavs on the head for the arrest but reminded them there was much more to be done for the rule of law if they didn't want to starve. Robin Cook declared, with a heavy heart: 'We want to help the government of Serbia reconstruct their economy and put behind them the devastation of the Milosevic years. But we can only do that if they cooperate with the international tribunal in The Hague.'[14]

Colin Powell and George Bush gave the certificate of good conduct provided for by the law, which released US$50 million and access to the international monetary institutions. But now another deadline was set, this time for 29 June, when an international donors' conference was to take place. About US$1 billion would be at stake; though only US$200 million would be American, the US promised to derail the whole conference if Milosevic was not in The Hague.[15]

But there was a huge legal problem standing in the way of the rule of law: the Yugoslav constitution forbade the extradition of nationals. 'A Yugoslav citizen may not be deprived of his citizenship, deported from the country, or extradited to another state.'[16] This was typical of most legal systems in the world, which, when met with a request for extradition of their own citizens, take the option of local prosecution offered by the ancient maxim: *aut dedere aut judicare*, 'either extradite or prosecute.' To make extradition of a Yugoslav citizen legally possible would require, in effect, an amendment to the constitution by a new federal law. But for that, Kostunica needed the votes of his federal coalition partners from Montenegro, who had been elected overwhelmingly from Milosevic's own party. As the deadline got closer, it became clear that there were not enough votes to pass the law. A week before the deadline, Kostunica withdrew the legislation and decided to try and proceed by government decree – a very dubious tactic, constitutionally speaking. The decree, issued on 23 June, provided for a standard, if vertiginously expedited extradition procedure: there would be a hearing, but the losing side would have only three days to appeal to the Supreme Court.[17] Since a mere decree could not override the constitution, lawyers for the opposition went straight to the Federal Constitutional Court, which ordered a suspension of the operation of the decree until the constitutional doubts over its validity could be resolved (it would later be declared unconstitutional[18]). That was on 28 June, the day before the international donors' conference. Kostunica said the decision of the Court should be respected and withdrew from the scene. But the government of Serbia wasn't going to allow a mere Balkan constitution to offend the Americans. Condemning the Court for its ties to Milosevic and, strangely (for a criticism of a legal decision), 'a sellout of Serbia's future,' Djindjic passed his own 'decision' the very same day to extradite Milosevic without any formalities whatsoever.[19] As the clock edged towards midnight, Milosevic was unceremoniously taken from his jail cell and flown by helicopter to a 'UN base' (read *NATO* base) in Bosnia, where he was transferred to a British RAF plane and flown to the Netherlands. He was in the ICTY jail by 1.15 a.m. of 29 June. Not bad work.

There followed yet another well-rehearsed NATO-country chorus of celebration for 'international justice and the rule of law.'[20] The Sunday *New York Times* said it was the rule of law (along with 'prosperity') that distinguished us from the Nazis, the Communists and people like Milosevic:

> Communism promised equality. Hitler promised the 1,000-year Reich. Milosevic promised glory. All the West offers, alongside the prosperity of the boardwalk, is the rule of law. It's enough.[21]

An editorial from Toronto's *Globe and Mail* gives the flavor of the absurdities that were being tossed about at the time:

> Most important, the extradition of Mr. Milosevic is a vindication of the whole idea of international law. Now, former dictator Augusto Pinochet is facing a possible trial in Chile on human-rights charges, and earlier this month a Belgian judge sentenced four Rwandans to long prison terms for their role in the 1994 genocide. 'The long arm of international law is becoming stronger,' South African judge Richard Goldstone, the first UN war-crimes prosecutor, said yesterday. That is something to cheer about.[22]

Pinochet would be free as a bird within a year. He'd had a lot more due process than Milosevic: 16 months of legal proceedings, including *three* hearings in the House of Lords, before the United Kingdom's anti-impunity government decided not to respect extradition requests from four European countries with whom they had treaties. Milosevic's lawyers put it succinctly enough: 'The process of extradition without the presence of attorneys is tantamount to an abduction.'[23] And of course, the United States had flown 15,000 feet over international law in Kosovo itself, and would be at it again in Afghanistan before six months were out, and in Iraq in under two years. The Hutus may have been prosecuted for their crimes in Rwanda, but the ruling Tutsi friends of the Americans had scared off the fearless Hague prosecutors from even looking into what they had done to the Hutus. What a long, strong arm you have, international law!

And speaking of the law, what about the Yugoslav constitution? What about the decision of the Constitutional Court? The 'international community' was well scripted on that one, too: the Court was 'made up of judges appointed under [Milosevic's] regime.'[24] Indeed, they were Milosevic's 'cronies.'[25] But, naturally, the same could be said of all the judges in all the Constitutional Courts of all the NATO countries, let alone the ICTY itself. Louise Arbour had just been rewarded for her work on behalf of NATO with a seat on the Canadian Supreme Court, thanks to one of our would-be indictees, Canadian Prime Minister Jean Chrétien. The United States Supreme Court had, just the previous December, ordered Florida to stop counting votes so that Republican George W. Bush could be President, even though he got fewer than his Democratic rival Al Gore. That court was made up of seven Republican appointments and only two Democrats. Two of the Republicans had been appointed by winner George W. Bush's 'dad.' And hadn't President Kostunica – someone who had notoriously *not* been 'appointed under Milosevic's regime' – denounced the move as 'illegal and unconstitutional'?[26] In any event, even a broken clock is right twice a day – one of the Bush Sr. appointments in the Supreme Court had voted for Gore, after all; and when the Yugoslav Constitutional Court explained its decision ruling the Djindjic decree unconstitutional, the argument was juridically beyond reproach, especially when compared to the legal absurdities coming out of the ICTY itself (see below).[27]

Leaving aside the prohibition on the extradition of citizens, the constitution forbade *any* action interfering with the liberty of the person except where prescribed by federal law.[28] Government decrees such as the Djindjic decision do not have the character of 'law' in Yugoslavia (as in many other countries), but are merely executive acts, and this one was clearly beyond the power of the (non-federal) government of Serbia under the federal constitution. By this principle, even non-citizens could not be deported in the absence of a law. As for the explicit prohibition of the extradition of citizens, the government of Serbia argued that the ICTY warrant was binding by virtue of section 16 of the constitution, which made ratified international treaties 'part of the internal legal order.'[29] The Charter of the United Nations was a treaty, of course, and it made Security Council decisions binding on members. This was the strongest of the government of Serbia's arguments in favor of their 'extradition' of Milosevic, but the Constitutional Court had a better one. It pointed out that Security Council Resolution 827 creating the ICTY did not simply provide that there should be compliance with ICTY requests, but rather that

> all States shall take any measures necessary under their domestic law to implement the provisions of the present Resolution and the Statute, including the obligation of States to comply with requests for assistance or orders issued by the Trial Chamber under article 29 of the Statute.

Thus requests for compliance were not, even on their own terms, self-actuating and automatically part of Yugoslavia's legal system; they required some form of Yugoslavian legal implementation. And the court pointed to the legislation enacted by many other countries in pursuance of this requirement. Without such legislation there would be a complete absence of due process (as in Milosevic's own case), and that itself would violate many norms of international human rights law. Thus, Yugoslavia might well be in breach of some of its international obligations by not extraditing Milosevic, and in compliance with others, but that was a different question from whether the obligation was automatically part of Yugoslav law, and therefore able to supersede the constitutional protections. The separation of international and domestic law is well established throughout the world's legal systems.[30]

So, far from a triumph of 'the rule of law,' Milosevic's extradition seemed more a defeat for it at the hands of naked power. But no matter, Milosevic was in The Hague and the Brussels donors' conference went off as planned. Attendees pledged US$1.28 billion (the US contributed US$181.6 million of this), though most of it went to the debt owed to these very same donors (the World Bank's US$150 million went entirely to its own outstanding debt), and thus the exercise was described as 'a mere drop in the ocean' for Yugoslavia, now at 'near-beggar status.'[31]

MILOSEVIC AT THE HAGUE

Why was it so important for the US and its NATO allies that Yugoslavia hand Milosevic over to The Hague for trial? Milosevic was a spent political force; Yugoslavia had been punished and was now totally dependent on 'the kindness of strangers'; and Bosnia and Kosovo were safely in the control of NATO. The Americans obviously didn't give two hoots about international criminal law or the authority of tribunals – even this one. There were lots of indictees roaming around the Balkans from the other wars besides Kosovo; the US wasn't threatening anyone with starvation for them. What point could there be in demanding Milosevic's hand-over, except a symbolic one? But what was it meant to symbolize? There was only one possible explanation. A senior Russian legislator offered it when Milosevic was arrested in April: 'They want to take him to The Hague to legitimate NATO's aggression of spring 1999 against Yugoslavia.'[32] Diana Johnstone had the best way of putting it: 'It was not enough to bomb Serbia and detach part of its territory. The Serbian people must be made to believe – or to pretend to believe – that they deserved it. The crime must be made to fit the punishment in the New World Order.'[33]

This was the point Milosevic himself would make again and again at his trial: 'This trial's aim is to produce a false justification for the war crimes of NATO committed in Yugoslavia.'[34] But there was one big problem in justifying the massive bombing of Yugoslavia: *no genocide in Kosovo*. Not even an attempted one. 'Genocide,' the legal word for Holocaust, was fundamental to NATO's justification for war; but when the fog had lifted, the numbers didn't come anywhere near it. 'Even if they were twenty thousand,' wrote Guido Rampoldi of Rome's *La Repubblica*, 'it would not give any reality to the hyperbole thrown out during the war by some Western governments ... [t]he allusions to Milosevic–Hitler, the careless meanderings with the word "genocide"...'[35] Despite 78 days of 'grim efficiency' by the 'genocidal' Serbs, the prosecution at Milosevic's trial could commit itself to only the non-committal 'at least four and a half thousand people died'[36] – *died*, not 'were murdered' – and even that was about twice the number of actual bodies ever found. After thousands of witness interviews, a frantic exhumation program conducted by NATO investigators, and despite this being Del Ponte's 'primary focus,' the final amended indictment could charge Milosevic with the murder of only a deliberately vague 'hundreds' of Kosovo Albanian civilians.[37] Adding up the specific numbers mentioned in the indictment gives an approximate figure of 758, of which 607 (73 female) are individually named in the Appendix.[38] By NATO's own admission, its bombs killed at least 500 civilians, and most estimates put the number well beyond 758.

But above all, no charge of genocide or even attempted genocide. Clearly something had to be done. A genocide charge was desperately needed and Del Ponte started dropping hints in April that there would be one, but it was going to have to come from Bosnia. Not that the claim of genocide in Bosnia could be made out without an extreme debasement of the coinage. Even such an ardent *belligerato* as Elie Wiesel had opposed the use of this term:

> In my view genocide is the intent and desire to annihilate a people.... The Holocaust was conceived to annihilate the last Jew on the planet. Does anyone believe that Milosevic and his accomplices seriously planned to exterminate all the Bosnians, all the Albanians, all the Muslims in the world?[39]

But the judges of the tribunal were already working their alchemy and would soon 'rule' that genocide had indeed occurred in Bosnia.

The helpful ruling was made one month after Milosevic's arrival in The Hague, in the case of General Radislav Krstic. It concerned the notorious incidents in the little town of Srebrenica in July 1995.[40] Srebrenica lies at the border of Bosnia with Serbia. With a 25 percent Serb minority, it was hotly contested throughout the Bosnian war, with atrocities and 'ethnic cleansing' committed on both sides in 1992 and 1993. The Srebrenica enclave came under UN protection in April 1993 as a 'safe area' for Muslims. There was sporadic fighting but relative calm from then until mid-1995, a time of great crisis in the war over the territorial claims of both sides. Fighting broke out in June, with Serb forces attacking the UN peacekeepers and a Muslim village, and Muslims attacking a nearby Serb village. In July, the vastly superior Serb forces overran the enclave with minimal resistance. In a matter of a few days the Serbs had transported the women, children and elderly out of the enclave and captured between 10,000 and 15,000 military-aged men, killing thousands of them according to most accounts, though serious questions have been raised about the evidential basis for the conventional view.[41]

Shortly after the war in Kosovo four years later, Kofi Annan issued a report blaming the UN for not intervening forcefully enough at Srebrenica to protect the victims, specifically for not authorizing the use of NATO airpower.[42] Annan repudiated his predecessor's preference for a peaceful solution, which he characterized, in a crude reference to the Holocaust, as 'appeasement' in the face of a 'Serb campaign of mass murder' in the service of a 'Greater Serbia.'[43] But 'Smaller Yugoslavia' would be far more accurate.[44] Nor did Annan's report contain a word of condemnation for the West's huge responsibility in precipitating the war, or of the United States for destroying every chance for peace. Once again, there was the deceptive and ultimately meaningless designation of Srebrenica as 'a horror without parallel in the history of *Europe* since the Second World War.'[45] Coming from an African in the face of even just the Rwanda massacres of 1994, this was nothing short of a disgrace.

Timing is everything in politics as well as in comedy, and the timing of the report was perfect to legitimize the use of force in Kosovo, which, despite the lack of any basis at all, was equated with Bosnia – just another manifestation of the same 'unscrupulous and murderous regime' for which 'all necessary means' were legitimate:

> The cardinal lesson of Srebrenica is that a deliberate and systematic attempt to terrorize, expel or murder an entire people must be met decisively with all necessary means, and with the political will to carry the policy through to its logical conclusion. In the Balkans, in this decade, this lesson has had to be learned not once, but twice. In both instances, in Bosnia and in Kosovo, the international community tried to reach a negotiated settlement with an unscrupulous and murderous regime. In both instances it required the use of force to bring a halt to the planned and systematic killing and expulsion of civilians.[46]

Here we have not only an outrageously revisionist view of Rambouillet, but the actual adoption of NATO's propaganda that it represented the 'international community,' even though its war was opposed by two permanent members of the Security Council, not to mention most of the member states of the United Nations. This is something that might have been expected to weigh on the Secretary General of the United Nations; instead he wound up sounding like Jamie Shea.

But even the Secretary General would go no further than to label Srebrenica an 'attempted genocide.'[47] For the judges in the case of Radislav Krstic it was the real thing. Krstic was in command of the Bosnian Serb military division responsible for the capture of Srebrenica. He was convicted of genocide, persecution and murder, and sentenced to 46 years imprisonment. According to the Trial Chamber, it was not clear that when the Bosnian Serb forces took over Srebrenica they intended a massacre, but at some point they decided to kill all the military-aged males of the enclave. They separated the women, the children and the elderly and transported them out to a Muslim-held area. Then, according to the Trial Chamber, they set about executing the others.[48] There is some serious inconsistency in the judgment on the question of the actual number of victims. In the conclusions, the figure was 'likely to be within the range of 7,000–8,000 men.'[49] But on the way to this, it was a different story altogether. The number of bodies exhumed amounted to only 2,028, and the court conceded that even a number of these had died in combat.[50] In fact, it could only go so far as to say the evidence 'suggested' that 'the majority' of those killed were executed:

'The results of the forensic investigations *suggest* that the *majority* of bodies exhumed were not killed in combat; they were killed in mass executions.'[51] The highest expert estimate of those who went *missing* after the takeover and had not yet been accounted for – remember that these were military-aged men and the war would continue for another four months – was 7,475, and the tribunal found that the evidence as a whole only '*strongly suggests* that well in excess of 7,000 people went missing following the take-over of Srebrenica.' The evidence was found only to 'support the proposition that *the majority* of missing people were, in fact, executed and buried in the mass graves.'[52] A *majority* of a *maximum* of 7,000–8000 would put the *maximum* executed closer to 4,000.

Not that it matters that much. The mass murder of 4,000 people is a horrifying crime, whether committed by Serbs in Bosnia or the Americans in Afghanistan or Iraq. It's the kind of thing that happens in war, and that's precisely why the crime against peace is the 'supreme international crime.' For murdering 4,000 people, they could have sent Krstic (not to mention Clinton) away for a lot of life terms, so why exaggerate the numbers? Because the tribunal wasn't really interested in the murder charges. They were after the big prize of *genocide*, a much more difficult case to make in these circumstances, so the higher the number of dead the better. My computer tells me that the tribunal used 33 times more space in their judgment trying to establish the genocide charge than the murder charge, even though the result for Mr. Krstic would have been the same.

But how could this be genocide? You would expect genocide to mean *the killing of a people*, the way 'homicide' means the killing of a person and 'suicide' the killing of oneself. In fact, the statutory definition of genocide in the law governing the tribunal is rather wider than the word itself would suggest:

> … any of the following acts committed with intent to destroy, in whole or in part, a national, ethnical, racial or religious group, as such: (a) killing members of the group; (b) causing serious bodily or mental harm to members of the group; (c) deliberately inflicting on the group conditions of life calculated to bring about its physical destruction in whole or in part; (d) imposing measures intended to prevent births within the group; (e) forcibly transferring children of the group to another group.

A literal reading of this law (which merely follows the UN *Genocide Convention* of 1948) might make any single ethnic killing, or maybe two, a 'genocide' – at least if it were done as an end in itself, to destroy the group in part 'as such.' This would be light years away from the UN General Assembly Resolution of 1946 that first recognized genocide as an international crime, defining it as 'the denial of the right of existence of entire human groups.'[53] It would be even farther from the Holocaust of the Jews, which was what motivated the escaped Polish Jew Raphael Lemkin to coin the term and to campaign for its legal recognition:

> By 'genocide' we mean the destruction of a nation or of an ethic group. This new word, coined by the author to denote an old practice in its modern development, is made from the ancient Greek work *genos* (race, tribe) and the Latin *cide* (killing), thus corresponding in its formation to such words as tyrannicide, homocide, infanticide, etc.... It is intended ... to signify a coordinated plan of different actions aiming at the destruction of essential foundations of the life of national groups, with the aim of annihilating the groups themselves.[54]

The Tribunal in the Krstic case occupied a middle ground between this literal, everyday meaning of genocide and the extremely minimal possibilities of the statutory definition, deciding that genocide had to include the intent to destroy at least 'a significant part' of the group. But as the defence argued, and the court accepted, there was no evidence that the Srebrenica massacres were part of a plan to kill even a significant part of the Muslims of Bosnia, much less to kill all of them. The defense argued that even killing 7,500 men in Srebrenica could not prove an intent to destroy a significant part, much less the whole, of a Bosnian Muslim community that numbered 1.4 million. This was especially so since the invaders had actually transported the women, children and elderly out to safety in a Muslim-held area, 'as opposed to all other genocides in modern history, which have indiscriminately targeted men, women and children.' The defense argued that,

> had the VRS actually intended to destroy the Bosnian Muslim community of Srebrenica, it would have killed all the women and children, who were powerless and already under its control, rather than undertaking the time and manpower consuming task of searching out and eliminating the men of the column.

They argued that the facts, including the sparing of the wounded, 'instead prove that the VRS forces intended to kill solely all potential fighters in order to eliminate any future military threat,' and 'as a retaliation for failure to meet General Mladic's demand of surrender to the VRS of the BiH Army units in the Srebrenica area.'[55] But the Tribunal judges would have none of this; instead they set themselves to watering genocide all the way down to 'ethnic cleansing,' the way the Western propagandists had during the Bosnian war ('As a result, there are obvious similarities between a genocidal policy and the policy commonly known as "ethnic cleansing"'[56]). As if that weren't enough, the Tribunal then even watered down 'ethnic cleansing' itself.

According to the Tribunal, there was sufficient genocidal intent if what was sought was to kill all the people of a given group *in one area*, even though it wasn't part of any plan to kill them all elsewhere. For this they relied mainly on their own dubious previous judgments and – something not likely to please Ariel Sharon – a 1982 UN General Assembly Resolution that the murder of at least 800 Palestinians in the Sabra and Shatila refugee camps that year was 'an act of genocide.'[57] According to the Tribunal,

> ... the killing of all members of the part of a group located within a small geographical area ... would qualify as genocide if carried out with the intent to destroy the part of the group as such located in this small geographical area. Indeed, the physical destruction may target only a part of the geographically limited part of the larger group because the perpetrators of the genocide regard the intended destruction as sufficient to annihilate the group as a distinct entity in the geographic area at issue.[58]

The court then went the final step and dispensed with the 'annihilation' element altogether, finding genocidal intent in killing to achieve the permanent removal of a group *from one area to another*. How did the killing of only the military-aged men accomplish this? Here the court could be found repeating the age-old shibboleth of patriarchy: in patriarchal society, the men are more important than the women. But then why not kill all the males, the elderly and the boys as well? Why concentrate on those of military age? The Tribunal's answer to that one really gave the whole game away, because it was precisely the argument made by the defense: military-aged men were a *military threat* because they might re-take the area:

> Granted, only the men of military age were systematically massacred, but it is significant that these massacres occurred at a time when the forcible transfer of the rest of the Bosnian Muslim population was well under way. The Bosnian Serb forces could not have failed to know, by the time they decided to kill all the men, that this selective destruction of the group would have a lasting impact upon the entire group. *Their death precluded any effective attempt by the Bosnian Muslims to recapture the territory.* Furthermore, the Bosnian Serb forces had to be aware of the catastrophic impact that the disappearance of two or three generations of men would have on the survival of a traditionally patriarchal society, an impact the Chamber has previously described in detail. The Bosnian Serb forces knew, by the time they decided to kill all of the military aged men, that the combination of those killings with the forcible transfer of

the women, children and elderly would inevitably result in the physical disappearance of the Bosnian Muslim population at Srebrenica....[59]

So genocide was transformed in this judgment, not into mere ethnic cleansing, but into the killing of potential fighters during a war for military advantage. How far was this from Donald Rumsfeld's description of American objectives in Afghanistan?

> Q: *Mr. Secretary, you've talked with some clinical detachment about measures of success there. Isn't one of the measures to kill as many of the al Qaeda and Taliban forces as possible? General Myers talked about the 5,000 dead Americans. I mean, is part of this just killing off these guys?*
> MR RUMSFELD: *Oh, you bet. And they're trying to [do] it every day, and in fact, they're doing it every day. And you've – those trucks that you saw and those buildings you see hit are not empty.*[60]

In the Krstic case, the concept of genocide, except as pure propaganda, lost all contact with the Holocaust – a program for the extermination of a whole people, essentially innocent bystanders, where women and children were separated not for transportation to Israel, but for gassing, so that the strong could be worked to death, with the result that two thirds of the Jews of Europe – one out of every three Jews on the planet – were murdered *as an end in itself*. It was this disgraceful sleight of hand by the Tribunal judges that made possible the charges of genocide against Milosevic, to hide the fact that in Kosovo there wasn't even an *attempt* at the Tribunal's counterfeit form of genocide, much less the real thing. Milosevic's trial was preceded by procedural maneuvers aimed essentially at the same objective. After laying the charges for Croatia and Bosnia (including genocide), Del Ponte sought to have them all combined into one huge trial, something the rules of the Tribunal forbade unless they were 'part of a common scheme, strategy or plan' (Rule 49). Del Ponte argued that, for all their differences, the crimes in Croatia, Bosnia and, at a distance of three years, Kosovo, all formed 'part of a plan for a "greater Serbia."' The Trial Chamber ruled the connection to be 'too nebulous' and ordered separate trials (no doubt having a personal interest as trial judges in avoiding a mega-trial), but they were overruled by the Appeals Chamber, which didn't bother to explain why.[61]

Thus Slobodan Milosevic went on trial for genocide, with the Kosovo–Holocaust analogy more or less intact, and all the papers could trumpet that here was the first head of state who ever went on trial for it; never mind how many real genocides by heads of states had gone unpunished, let alone the crimes – from Hiroshima and Nagasaki through Vietnam to the Gulf Wars and Afghanistan – that the American sponsors of the ICTY had committed that were exponentially more heinous than what passed for genocide in the ICTY's cheapened definition.

Of course, before the trial could even get started, 11 September 2001 completely stole the tribunal's thunder, and the practical effect of the state of war that ensued was to bathe the Milosevic trial in almost total obscurity. This was not a bad thing for defenders of either the Kosovo campaign or the whole enterprise of international criminal law, because anything resembling close public scrutiny of the trial was something their causes could well do without.

VICTOR'S JUSTICE

'Victor's justice' is what critics called the Nuremberg and Tokyo war crimes tribunals. They were set up and staffed by the victorious allies to judge the crimes of their defeated enemies. The new international criminal law was supposed to be different. Michael Scharf said in defense of Milosevic's judges that they represented the whole international community, not just his victorious adversaries, because they were elected by the General Assembly of the United Nations, 'not the NATO-dominated Security Council.'[62] He neglected to mention that the list of nominees had, by the law he drafted, to be approved by the 'NATO-dominated Security Council.' So it was not the luck of the draw that determined that the court that Milosevic found himself before at The Hague was presided over by Judge Richard G. May of the United Kingdom. Since Britain was the second most active NATO participant in the bombing of Kosovo, the impression of victor's justice could hardly have been stronger. Indeed, May had been something of a Labour Party activist before going to the Bench, having stood for Labour in the constituency won by Margaret Thatcher in 1979.[63] But this was a court already top-heavy with judges from NATO countries. In 1997, five out of the eleven judges were from NATO countries; after the elections of 2001, the expanded court that would judge Milosevic had seven of its 16 permanent judges, and two of its six temporary judges, hailing from the alliance that had bombed Kosovo.[64] Not bad for an alliance with only 19 out of 191 UN member states, all of whom were eligible for the court. Not only that, NATO has always managed to have the president of the court come from a NATO country (two from the US itself and one from each of Italy and France), as well as two of the three presiding judges, the ones like May who get to do all the talking and conduct the proceedings. The other two judges in Milosevic's court, O-Gon Kwon and Patrick Robinson, were no strangers either, being nicely divided between the American dependency

South Korea and the British dependency Jamaica. Both were selected with Kosovo and Milosevic specifically in mind.[65]

Milosevic frontally challenged the impartiality of the Tribunal, and naturally the challenge was rejected. He did this on his very first appearance in court, three days after his 'extradition.' The words he used then for the Tribunal were 'false Tribunal,' 'illegal organ,' 'so-called Tribunal' and 'illegitimate one.'[66] When he next appeared before the Court later that summer, before his microphone was shut off, he told the judges flat-out: 'you are not juridical institution; you are political tool.'[67] To these informal charges were joined formal ones, presented not by Milosevic but by his court-appointed lawyers. Their arguments steered clear of offending the court and stuck to such safe but absurdly wide-of-the-mark points as that the ICTY warrants had been served on the Federal government of Yugoslavia but executed by the Serbian government. Milosevic repudiated these arguments and the counsel as well, as just part of the Tribunal team against him:

> [I]t is my understanding that your explanation, when appointing the amicus curiae, was that thereby a contribution would be made to a fair trial, if in such an illegal proceedings one can talk of a fair trial. I think in doing so, you have added a new concept to a set of new concepts, because now we are in a situation when two teams are working for the cause of the same party. So this could now be termed as the 'Hague fair play.'[68]

Then he told the Tribunal what he thought of their 'impartiality' and Del Ponte's: only allies of NATO could ignore the crimes NATO had committed and judge him instead:

> MR. MILOSEVIC: I wish to request from you to disqualify the Prosecutor for obvious reasons, among which I should mention only two. The first we heard yesterday loud and clear when the Kosovo indictment was being read, that all the events took place between the 24th of March and the beginning of June. And the second reason is that the whole planet knows that it was precisely on the 24th of March that a criminal aggression by NATO was carried out against Yugoslavia and went on until the beginning of June.... What we heard is worse than what we could hear from the enemy, that is, from the NATO spokesmen. So this is complete partiality. And if the Court can turn a blind eye to the fact that from the 24th of March until the first week of June this aggression took place, that there were a large number of victims, that 22,000 tonnes of bombs were dropped and that all this is being attributed to Yugoslavia, which committed a crime against itself instead of NATO doing it, then I think that even this court, which is an illegal one, must take those facts into consideration. And if

it refuses to take them into consideration, then it becomes clear that this is no court but just a part of the machinery to commit a crime against my country and my people ... and if you are really a part of that machinery, then please read out those judgements that you have been instructed to read and don't bother me and make me listen for hours on end to the reading of texts written at the intellectual level of a seven-year-old child – or rather, let me correct myself, a retarded seven-year-old.[69]

So, before any evidence had even been introduced, Milosevic had declared that this was a false court set up to blame him for NATO's crimes. And in the long course of his trial (at this writing it is well past its second birthday, with at least two more to go), the court does not seem to have tried very hard to give a different impression. That's unusual for a court, which, in ordinary circumstances bends over backwards to demonstrate impartiality. But these were not ordinary circumstances. Milosevic's challenge to the authority of this 'so-called Tribunal' was very far from the usual defense tactic of trying to curry favor with the judges. In extraordinary circumstances like this, a court's first public relations job is to establish its authority, to show who is boss. On the other hand, the extent of the Court's violation of the rules of procedure, and even decorum, adds weight to Milosevic's charge that their real job was to defend NATO.

It wasn't long before observers from the left, right and center were expressing amazement at the heavy-handed ways of the court and the prosecution. Canada's best-known criminal lawyer, the politically conservative Edward Greenspan, writing in the politically conservative *National Post*, after just one month of the Milosevic trial, pronounced it a 'lynching,' a 'show trial' and a 'kangaroo court.'[70]

Normally, lynchings are done outdoors. Here, the lynching has been brought indoors. Instead of a tree and a rope, there are May and Del Ponte ... A kangaroo court is one in which legal procedures are largely a show, and the action 'jumps' from accusation to sentencing without due process. No matter how long a trial takes, if the result is inevitable, then it's a show trial.[71]

Greenspan's reaction was due primarily to the misbehavior of presiding judge Richard May. Greenspan was clearly no friend of Milosevic ('even a thug is entitled to a fair trial'), but he reminded readers that tradition required May to bend over backwards to *help* an unrepresented accused:

In democratic legal systems where there is an unrepresented accused, the court has a duty to extend its helping hand to guide an accused in such a way that any defences are brought out with its [*sic*] full force and effect....

[N]o judge should become the captain of the prosecution's ship, especially where Mr. Milosevic is without counsel. May seems to be inadvertently proving Milosevic's point about the trial being a charade.

One thing that particularly shocked Greenspan was the way May disrupted Milosevic's cross-examination of witnesses, imposing time limits and incessantly interrupting Milosevic's questions:

> It is a well-known principle that no judge can arbitrarily set a time limit on, or interfere with, a cross-examination.... Here's an example. One and a half hours into Milosevic's first cross-examination, May impatiently asks: 'How much longer do you think you're going to be with this witness?' (Why would he ask this, unless he's got a squash game to get to?)... What's the rush? It looks like May has forgotten that Milosevic is entitled to due process.... May seems bored. The first witness of what is to be a lengthy trial, and the judge is putting time limits on Mr. Milosevic. May doesn't even feign impartiality or, indeed, interest.

Greenspan was also offended by May's admonition to Milosevic not to use cross-examination 'as a way of harassing or intimidating witnesses.' Greenspan was used to judges giving him free rein to use 'brutality' in cross-examination:

> I don't know why May thinks cross-examination should be free from any kind of brutality. Brutality is calculated to unnerve, confuse but ultimately to expose. Cross-examination is a duel between counsel and the witness. The only weapon the defence has is the right to ask questions.

But you don't have to take Greenspan's word for it. You can watch for yourself on the internet, where you will find video archives of all the proceedings.[72] If you watch, you will find that, despite his obvious inexperience as a cross-examiner, and despite the lawyer-like crudeness of some of his attempts to confuse and discredit witnesses, and, above all, despite the constant harassment from the bench, Milosevic in fact managed to make some good use of his cross-examination. Here's an account by a Canadian journalist, once again no friend of Milosevic:

> [The witness] describes how all the houses in her village were burned, how Serb soldiers entered those houses and murdered innocent civilians.... She talks about her convoy of 30 tractors, how the column was attacked by Serbian artillery, was shelled by the Yugoslav air force. Milosevic is suddenly very attentive. 'How did you know these were Yugoslavian planes? Could you see the markings on them? Tell me, do you remember how many times the planes bombed that column? Why did you say you

saw Yugoslavian insignia on the aircraft? Who told you to say that?' Selmani counters valiantly. 'I saw the insignia on the planes because they were flying very low. We could basically distinguish the NATO planes because they flew very high.' Milosevic snorts. But he's discovered a fatal flaw in this testimony and he pounces: 'Do you know NATO took responsibility for that particular bombing? And that it expressed regret that it had happened?' The witness is flustered. She knows only what she knows. Her evidence had sounded completely credible but now it's been compromised. Still, she pushes back. 'I saw it, the Yugoslav flag. Red, white and blue. And this was your entire plan. To do this sort of thing and blame NATO.' Milosevic pulls a face and tosses his spectacles. 'Oh, fine.' As if to say: We know what we have here. Another lying Albanian.[73]

When Milosevic tried to press his advantage against this witness, May simply cut him off. He gave Milosevic one last question but he wouldn't even let the witness answer it:

JUDGE MAY: *This must be your last question, Mr. Milosevic.*
MR. MILOSEVIC: *I would like you to give me an answer. Since you could not have seen Yugoslav aeroplanes and since it is well-known, generally known, who did this, who told you to state that it was Yugoslav aeroplanes that you had seen? Who told you to say that?*
JUDGE MAY: *She has answered that question. She said nobody did, and that is what she saw, and that's her evidence. No point arguing about it.*[74]

Some witnesses, so-called 'protected witnesses,' had been allowed to testify with their identities hidden. This witness was not one of them, but May's constant interruption of Milosevic's cross-examination of her prompted him to quip, 'Mr. May, it appears to me that every witness is a protected witness as far as you're concerned, different forms of protection, that is.'[75] This witness, like many, was also a so-called '92 *bis* witness,' after the rule number allowing them to rely on statements made outside of court to investigators. They come into court and the prosecution summarizes their evidence and then leads them through some of its main points. Milosevic is then given a limited time (say 45 minutes) to cross-examine, but the statements can be voluminous and the witnesses have already been spared the duty of recounting from their own recollection what they have seen or heard. The 92 *bis* statements have obviously been coached and even formulated by others. For instance, this particular witness of the plane logos exhibited in her written statement a totally implausible knowledge of the technical names of various types of automatic weaponry.

In a fair trial, given the seriousness of the charges he was facing, Milosevic would have been allowed even wider than normal latitude in cross-examination. But May obviously regarded it as his job to protect the witnesses from embarrassment over the inconsistencies between their testimony and the statements they had made to tribunal investigators. For instance, KLA commander Shukri Buya got into trouble when, in testimony on the fighting that had preceded the Racak incident, his evidence that Serbian security forces had opened fire first seemed to be contradicted by his 92 *bis* statement that his own forces had fired warning shots into the air so as to alert their colleagues to the approaching Serb forces.[76] Milosevic tried to exploit this apparent inconsistency in his cross-examination: if the Serbs had already opened fire, why was it necessary to fire warning shots?

> MR. MILOSEVIC: Q. *You said that from this heavy machine-gun they shot a burst of gunfire in order to respond to provocations, because the Serbs had been shooting. And two lines up you say that these three bullets were fired as a signal, as an alert. You say that this automatically represented an alert, an alarm, for the soldiers in Racak. This is again on p. 12, that this automatically was an alarm for the soldiers of the KLA in Racak. Did you shoot by way of an alarm or in response to gunfire? Before that, you said that the Serbs had come silently, without a sound.*
>
> JUDGE MAY: *You can't have questions of this length. It's quite impossible to follow. Now, either ask short questions, or we'll have to bring this to an end. He's dealt with it. He's explained what he said happened, how the Serbs fired first and then they fired as an alarm.*[77]

'He's dealt with it.' But the point is not whether the witness has 'dealt with it'; it's whether he is *lying* about it, and a cross-examination tries to demonstrate this by forcing him to deal with the contradictions in his testimony. Of course, if the judge has already made up his mind about the verdict, he won't be interested in whether the witness is lying or not.

Another example is the testimony of the witness Agim Jemini, who claimed, as mayor of the village of Celine, to have witnessed the murder of his mother and father and other members of his family by Serb soldiers. In cross-examination Milosevic brought out that Jemini was a member of the political party of Hashim Thaci, the KLA leader. Though Jemini claimed to have joined after the war, Milosevic pointed out that he was rather young for someone not active in the KLA to have been mayor of his town, and he made some mileage out of the witness's implausible claim that he couldn't remember when precisely he had joined. At one point Milosevic really had the witness on the ropes, all tangled up in his own contradictions. Jemini claimed to have been able to observe what was going on from his hiding place in an attic by removing roof tiles. Jemini had just testified that he could overhear Serb conversation, because the soldiers were only 15 meters away. Wasn't he afraid to expose himself to danger if they were so close that he could hear their conversation? The witness tried to boast his way out of this by saying he wasn't afraid and could have killed the Serbs if he'd wanted, even though he claimed not to have had any weapons:[78]

MR. MILOSEVIC: *So that means that there was a military command 15 metres from you, a full yard of people, of soldiers, as well as the second storey of the house, and yet you still take the roof tiles off the roof in order to look. So weren't you afraid that you would be noticed?*

THE WITNESS: *Yes. However, we thought we were capable of that, and we felt ourselves superior to the Serbian army, which had broken up all rules and sent soldiers to occupy the second floor of my house.*

MR. MILOSEVIC: *All right. I'm talking about your fear now. You hid out of fear, not because you wanted to be above, on a storey above. Weren't you afraid to remove the roof tiles of a house in which there were a lot of troops as well as a yard full of troops? Weren't you afraid of being noticed?*

THE WITNESS: *Yes. At that moment, fear appeared to be going away, because we were expecting to be killed from moment to moment, having seen what was happening around the village ... In fact, there were two of them were only a few metres away. We were on top of that. We could have done everything; we could have killed them. We could have killed the command and everybody else. We didn't do that because we did not believe in that kind of method in this kind of civilisation.*

MR. MILOSEVIC: *Were you armed?*

THE WITNESS: *No.*

MR. MILOSEVIC: *So how could you have killed them if you were not armed, killed the commander and the soldiers and so on?*

THE WITNESS: *There were ample opportunities to kill them. There were other methods. You can't kill people using weapons alone.*

MR. MILOSEVIC: *Well, what other methods were at your disposal? Could you please tell us?*

By now the witness was in deep trouble, but Judge May intervened to save him:

JUDGE MAY: *This is all hypothetical. Mr. Milosevic, you've got two minutes left. Is there anything else you want to ask this witness?*

MR. MILOSEVIC: *I have many more questions left. And I can't see why do I have to cross-examine this kind of witness for less than 40 minutes, Mr. May. He is coming out with all kinds of things here.*

JUDGE MAY: *We have judged it – we judge that 45 minutes is sufficient. Now, if you have anything else to ask him, you should ask it now.*
MR. MILOSEVIC: *I have at least 30 more questions. But let me try and complete this.*

Milosevic then tried to force the witness to confront the contradiction between the fact that the witness's mother was unafraid to be out in the open with Serb police present, and the fact that he, supposedly a non-KLA member, was in hiding:

MR. MILOSEVIC: *... And then you say that they saw your mother in the yard and said, 'Well, what are you doing there, old woman?' And at that time you were hiding with your cousin in the attic. So my question is: Why were you hiding under the roof when even your mother, a female therefore, stood in the yard, baked the bread, and went on her normal business?*
THE WITNESS: *It is not true that life was carrying on as normal. She had come over to bring us some food. However, being aware of the plans of the Serbian offensive, I told her to return and join the rest of the population, to join everybody else, my wife, the children. So I wanted the same of my parents. I was aware of the impending offensive of the day ... My mother returned with her bread in her hands, and when she came, there were Serbian police brought a truck which was driving by our yard. They saw my mother, and in barbarian Serbian language, they spoke to her and she was scared away.*
JUDGE MAY: *What – we're bringing this examination to an end. You're now past your time.*

Having denied Milosevic any further questions, May decided to take some of the court's precious time and ask some questions of his own – so the witness got to repeat his written statement about what happened to his mother.

JUDGE MAY: *What – we're bringing this examination to an end. You're now past your time. But tell us this, Mr. Jemini: What happened to your mother?*
THE WITNESS: *My mother and father and the cousins were in the basement. So when my mother went there ... Some moments later, however, all of them were put together at the house opposite, about five or six metres away, the one that is five or six metres away, and then they make them face the wall and, from a pistol gun a pistol arm was shot in the air first and then with an automatic gun rifle, they were shot at and they fell. That is the moment when calamity fell.*

When Jemini finished his account, Milosevic tried to point out yet another contradiction between this and the original statement, but May now remembered that there was no more time:

MR. MILOSEVIC: Q. *Please. I would like to remind you of the part of your statement, p. 4, paragraph 8 –*
JUDGE MAY: *We have gone past the time which we can sit and I brought your cross-examination to a close. Mr. Milosevic, you must concentrate on asking relevant questions, and you must stop arguing with the witnesses. That way, you'll get through very much more. We're going to adjourn now. I'm afraid there's no time for re-examination or anything else.*

If there is one episode in the trial that epitomizes the whole travesty, it is the testimony of William Walker on 11 and 12 June 2002. He was the US State Department trouble-shooter put in charge of the OSCE observer mission in Kosovo, the one who had, with the help of Louise Arbour, spun the Racak incident into a pretext for war, by denouncing it, 'spontaneously,' as a crime against humanity.[79] A lot turned on his credibility. Walker testified for about an hour and three-quarters. As another '92 *bis*' witness, he was allowed to rely in addition on an extensive prepared written statement and voluminous exhibits attached to it. Walker's testimony was broad-ranging, covering Milosevic's 'general attitude,' his apparent control of the events in Kosovo, his propensity for lying (for which Walker gave two examples: Milosevic had understated the size of the Albanian population of Kosovo and had denied the existence of a letter Walker claims to have received[80]). The key was, of course, Walker's eye-witness account of what he had seen at Racak the day after the killings, which included his 'layman's observations' of whether it was a massacre or not.[81] Remember that the Racak killings constituted 45 counts of *murder* against Milosevic, each one carrying a potential term of life imprisonment, and you can appreciate that, in pure criminal law terms, due process would have required that he be allowed the widest possible latitude in cross-examination. Nor was Walker a traumatized atrocity victim; he was a diplomatic smoothy, now in a cushy job as 'vice-president of an international energy company.' There would be absolutely no excuse for 'protecting' this witness.

During nearly two hours of testimony Judge May didn't interrupt Walker or his lawyers *even once*. But as soon as Milosevic took over, May started in on him. Milosevic asked, 'How long are you going to limit my cross-examination to?' May answered imperiously:

JUDGE MAY: *Three hours, no more.[82] If you refrain from arguing with the witness, if you refrain from repeating the questions, if you ask short questions, you will be able to get much more done. So you follow that line.[83]*

When Milosevic tried to respond, May played the angry parent and told him he was deducting it from his allowance:

MR. MILOSEVIC: *Well, I don't know that I've argued with witnesses. But let me say before I start that I expected that you would shorten the time for my cross-examination, in view of yesterday's proclamations with respect to Rule 92 bis, because Drewienkiewicz testified for two days, Maisonneuve also took two days, and their chief, according to you, should be exposed to cross-examination for three hours only, and I think that that is –*

JUDGE MAY: *… further time, which is taken off your time for cross-examination. Now, move on.*

MR. MILOSEVIC: *All right. Very well, Mr. May. I just said this for it to come out in the record, and not to waste time.*[84]

May then proceeded to interrupt Milosevic *over 60 times* during his cross-examination of Walker. And I'm excluding just polite interchanges; I'm talking about real interference, like the following, all of which consisted of interruptions of questions put by Milosevic to the witness:

JUDGE MAY: *The witness has dealt with that. This is what I mean about your arguing with witnesses. Again, this is a point you can make to us, but it is pointless to continually ask the same question of a witness. Now, ask some other questions. Get on to something else.*[85]

…

JUDGE MAY: *The witness has said what he saw. He can't assist any further. If you make allegations of that sort, you'll have to provide some substance for them. Now, have you got any other questions you want to ask?*[86]

…

JUDGE MAY: *We have dealt with this. Those are simply your allegations, and if you make allegations of that sort, you must support them with evidence.*[87]

…

JUDGE MAY: *Now, what is the question for the witness? He can only repeat what he was told, and he's given his evidence about it. Quotations from statements of other witnesses isn't going to assist. Now, can we move on?*[88]

…

JUDGE MAY: *No assumptions. We will are dealing with the witness's evidence, and he's given it as to what he knew and when. Now, rather than continuing this argument, you would be sensible to move on. Your time is limited. What is your question for the witness?*[89]

…

JUDGE MAY: *Mr. Milosevic, this is a waste of time. The witness has given his account of what he saw and heard. If you want to get this evidence in front of us, you can call the witnesses, but it's a waste of time to go on putting this kind of thing. These are the opinions of people who appear on television ... Move on to the next question.*[90]

...

JUDGE MAY: *You are wasting time. You are arguing with the witness, which you've been told not to do. It's just a waste of time. Now, move on to something else.*[91]

The effect of all this harassment of Milosevic was not only to prevent Walker from getting caught in any lies, but also to put him at his ease by showing him that the Court was on his side, that they did not think anything Milosevic said reflected at all adversely on Walker's credibility. Now it would have been fair for May to have formed this opinion (provisionally, at least), but it was completely unacceptable for him to convey that to Walker, or indeed to bolster his confidence by comradely interjections like 'I think you've answered the point,'[92] or 'Is there anything you can usefully add to that, Ambassador?'[93]

'Ambassador,' of course. The prosecution had 'established' in one of its more relevant bits of examination in chief that Walker was 'entitled' for life to be called 'Ambassador' because he had once served as one.[94] May started out calling him 'Mr.' (the way he designated Milosevic, who had once served as President) but soon slipped into 'Ambassador' and stayed there. May's aid and comfort also included the pre-emptive discrediting of evidence tending to discredit Walker's testimony. For instance, when Milosevic sought to put press stories from *Le Figaro* and Associated Press about Racak that contradicted Walker's account, May told Milosevic he would have to call the journalists as witnesses, and then helped Walker through his response to the question:

JUDGE MAY: *... You can call them to give evidence. I don't imagine there's much point putting it to this witness. He's given his evidence about what happened. Can you comment at all, do you think, usefully, Ambassador, on what's been read out?*
THE WITNESS: *No, I can't. I've already testified to what I knew and when I knew it.*
JUDGE MAY: *Is it just the opinion of some journalist?*[95]

When Milosevic tried to cross-examine Walker on a Serb report that contradicted Walker's own account of Racak, a simple 'I don't recall' was enough to get him off the hook:

JUDGE MAY: *Yes. Did you see the – Ambassador, did you see the report of the Ministry of the Interior Police on Racak at any stage?*
THE WITNESS: *I don't recall if I did or not, sir.*
JUDGE MAY: *No. There's no point asking the witness about it.*[96]

One of the most outrageous episodes of a thoroughly outrageous performance by the Court was when Milosevic reminded Walker of the time in 1989 when, as the American Ambassador to El Salvador, he was called upon for an official comment on the massacre of six Jesuit priests by uniformed soldiers of the US-backed government. Walker certainly wasn't jumping to any conclusions then the way he would at Racak. Indeed, according to Walker, just because the killers were in uniform didn't mean they were government soldiers; they could have been in disguise, after all. Milosevic wanted to force Walker to deal with the evident inconsistency: in Racak, he was claiming to have been so disgusted that he simply had to speak out and publicly denounce the killings as a crime against humanity perpetrated on innocent civilians. His 'spontaneous' decision, within minutes, to do so, was based partly on the fact that the victims were in civilian clothes and thus could not be KLA fighters. Milosevic's point in this line of questioning was obvious: he was trying to show Walker to be a professional liar, who would say anything that his government wanted him to say. Many journalists had asked the same questions about Walker and Racak, and Milosevic put several newspaper articles to him in cross-examination, asking, in his inexpert way, for some response from Walker. After interrupting Milosevic *seven* times during this line of cross-examination alone, May made no effort to conceal the fact that he had already made up his mind on the issue, feigning (one assumes, out of charity) an inability to grasp the obvious relevance of this line of questioning:

JUDGE MAY: *Mr. Milosevic, we've now spent the best part of quarter of an hour to 20 minutes on events in another continent a decade before. If it was an attempt to attack in some way the witness's credibility, you've had the opportunity of putting your case and the witness has dealt with it. Now, move on to some other topic more related to the indictment.*

MR. MILOSEVIC: *Mr. May, since you have limited my time, please allow me to use it the way I consider best. This is a witness who was obviously in charge of carrying out – how should I put this? – some sort of covert operations.*

JUDGE MAY: *Yes, when we come to that, you can put all that. But you're not wasting the time of the Court with events so long ago and of such little relevance. Now, let's move on.*

MR. MILOSEVIC: *On the 11th of December, 1989, St. Louis Post-Dispatch, in a long article – I'm going to quote only a short excerpt:* [In English] '[Previous translation continues] ... Jesuit colleges in the United States, accused the US Ambassador in El Salvador of trying to discredit the witness. In –'

JUDGE MAY: *No. Your attempt to discredit this witness with events so long ago the Trial Chamber has ruled as irrelevant. Now, move on from El Salvador.*

You've been given your clear instructions. If you want to continue with the cross-examination, you must follow them, because the time of the Court is limited, and it cannot be taken up with irrelevant matters such as this. Now, move on to events closer to the indictment.[97]

When Milosevic tried later to return to the question of the uniforms, he was cut short:

MR. MILOSEVIC: *... Now tell me this, please: As you are an experienced man and react in several places, in El Salvador, you explained that the fact that they were in uniform did not mean that they were members of the army, although a uniform does denote the army. Now, here civilian clothing in Racak was the criterion you used to say that they were civilians, although it is common knowledge that terrorists wear civilian clothing and that they need not be wearing uniforms. How, then, is it possible that one and the same man is using different criteria?*
JUDGE MAY: *This is an absurd question, absolutely absurd. Now, you're wasting everybody's time with this. Have you got any other questions?*[98]

May was obviously keen on Milosevic giving Walker a clear shot at a direct question on whether Racak was a hoax. If May wanted to dispose of the hoax theory, it would be very useful to have a straight question and a firm denial.

JUDGE MAY: *In particular, Mr. Milosevic, may I remind you that you made a number of allegations to other witnesses that this incident was to be used as a pretext for what happened thereafter and that Ambassador Walker was involved in that. So if you're going to put it to him, make sure you do before your time is up so he has a chance to answer it.*[99]

The uncooperative Milosevic preferred to attack Walker's credibility by catching him first in some obvious lies, like the ones quoted in Chapter 3 where he denied clearing the Racak denunciation with his superiors.[100] Walker had at first claimed not to have called Wesley Clark and Richard Holbrooke from Racak before the press conference. Milosevic played videos of Walker's denials and the statements by Clark and Holbrooke to the contrary. When Walker added that he didn't know who his staff had called, Milosevic tried to link this with Walker's claims that Milosevic himself knew of everything that was going on in Kosovo:

MR. MILOSEVIC: *All right, Mr. Walker. You do not know that. You did not know about the report of the 16th by your mission and about many other things you say that you cannot –*
JUDGE MAY: *No. This is all comment, Mr. Milosevic. What is your question?*

MR. MILOSEVIC: Q. *My question is: How then do you know and claim that I had to have been informed about each and every detail which took place in Kosovo? How can you say that, then? How can you claim that? How do you know what I did when you don't know what you did yourself?*[101]

Milosevic then tried to confront Walker with the many KLA crimes against Serbs and Albanians and the failure of Walker's mission to do anything about them, the obvious point being to try to show bias and thus attack Walker's credibility as a truthful witness. But May was getting anxious that he wouldn't get the questions and answers needed for the judgment. When Milosevic came to the link between al-Qaeda and the KLA, May cut to the chase:

MR. MILOSEVIC: *All right. And do you know that, for example, Al Qaeda within the KLA, that this fact was presented in the report of the American –*
JUDGE MAY: *He says he's not aware – the witness has given his answer about these matters, as far as he knows. It's as far as he knows. Now, Mr. Milosevic, there is a bigger question: You put to other witnesses that this incident at Racak was used as a pretext for NATO intervention. Now, if that is your suggestion, you want to make that suggestion, you must make it to this witness so that he can deal with it, because he was the one who raised Racak as an incident. Now, is it your case that this was used as a pretext for NATO intervention or not? If it is, you must put it to the witness so he can deal with it.*
MR. MILOSEVIC: *Of course that is what I assert, and I assume that that can be derived from all my questions, that Racak was used and that it was rigged and that it was used as a trigger to start NATO aggression against Yugoslavia.*
MR. MILOSEVIC: *Is that right, Mr. Walker?*
A. *That is not my interpretation of what happened, no.*[102]

But Judge May needed clearer answers than that, so he decided to take over the questioning:

JUDGE MAY: *Were you involved in any such conspiracy or plan?*
THE WITNESS: *No, sir, I was not.*[103]

May spent the rest of Milosevic's cross-examination rephrasing Milosevic's questions so that he (May) could get the answers he needed. For instance:

JUDGE MAY: *What is being suggested goes further than that, that this whole incident, this execution of 40-odd civilians, was in some way manipulated and rigged, is the interpretation we have from Mr. Milosevic, as a pretext for NATO to intervene, which means, if it were true, that you would have to be one of the organisers of such a plot. Is there any truth in the suggestion that this incident was rigged in some way or manipulated?*
THE WITNESS: *No, Your Honour.*[104]

With these answers safely on record, May brought the cross-examination to an end a few minutes later with a curt, 'Your time is now finished.'[105]

By July 2002 the obliging mainstream press had stopped paying attention to the legal dueling at The Hague. Perhaps this was because, at that very moment, the American government was trying to play down the whole war crimes thing as it pulled out of the International Criminal Court and flagrantly violated its Statute and the Geneva Conventions on the treatment of prisoners of war at Guantánamo Bay. Interest would occasionally flare up for a star witness, like retired General Wesley Clark, who took the witness stand in December 2003 while seeking the US Democratic presidential nomination. For Clark's testimony, Judge May dispensed with all pretence of due process and 'pre-emptively' banned cross-examination on anything that might tarnish NATO's version of the war. So, even though NATO's Supreme Commander was allowed to claim that he went to war to prevent what he called a 'final solution' in Kosovo – which, he clarified on questioning, meant to him 'a large-scale ethnic cleansing operation'[106] – Milosevic was not allowed to cross-examine him on the more likely US reasons for the war or its legitimacy or legality, or Clark's own status as a war criminal, no matter how *relevant* such questions might be:

> JUDGE MAY: *Mr. Milosevic, before you begin cross-examining, you should know that there are parameters in this case beyond which you cannot go. We've already made an order which restricts the scope of cross-examination … It is limited to the statement which the witness has given, which means that you are restricted in a way that you are not restricted with other witnesses, because then you're allowed to ask any relevant matters.*[107]
>
> …
>
> MR. MILOSEVIC: *So I cannot ask him anything at all about the war waged by NATO against Yugoslavia. Is that what you're saying?*
> JUDGE MAY: *Yes.*
> MR. MILOSEVIC: *Well, Mr. May, that really is an example showing that this is truly nothing more than a farce.*[108]

The farce would soon have to do without Judge May, however. He bowed out at the end of the prosecution's case in early 2004 for what appeared to be very serious health reasons, having first pushed through a rule change empowering the (American) Tribunal President to assign the case a substitute judge. But though May had done his best to leave his colleagues with a sure-fire record, the general impression was one of a shambles. On the charge of genocide in Bosnia, Carla Del Ponte had to admit, 'I don't have the smoking gun,' which was the understatement of the year.[109] As for Kosovo, May's colleagues would still have to deal with some very tricky questions.

For instance, how to get around the testimony of former head of State Security Radomir Markovic? Here was a *prosecution witness* who repudiated the statement he had purportedly made to investigators while he was being held for 17 months in a Serb jail. Markovic stated categorically that Milosevic had nothing to do with any crimes committed against Albanians in Kosovo or their cover-up, and indeed that he had tried to prevent them and punish their perpetrators.[110] Markovic said that the statement attributed to him was in fact 'a liberal interpretation of the employee, of the officer who made this report. He emphasised certain things that I did not speak about.'[111] Markovic also testified that he had been pressured during his long imprisonment to accuse Milosevic of crimes:

> THE WITNESS: *They spoke to me about the difficult position I was in. They warned me against the possible consequences and offered me an option in the form of accusing Milosevic, as the person who issued orders for those criminal offences, which would relieve me of liability before a criminal court.*
> MR. MILOSEVIC: *Is it true that they offered you a new identity, money, and sustenance for you and your family only so that you would falsely accuse me? Is that correct?*
> THE WITNESS: *Yes, that's correct.*[112]

But this was the chronicle of a verdict foretold – not only, as Greenspan had it, from the opening of the trial, but long before then, from Lawrence Eagleburger's 'spontaneous' denunciation of Milosevic, through the 'spontaneous' actions of Walker and Arbour, no matter how many legal principles they would have to blast through to get there. Even in the freak eventuality, with Judge May gone, of an acquittal, the damage to the Balkans had long been done. And we have yet to get to the most fundamental legal principle that had to be blasted through, the one symbolized by the famous blindfold on Lady Justice. This was also Milosevic's main point: whatever he might be found guilty of, rightly or wrongly, the Americans and NATO themselves were guilty of, too. And it was the ICTY's servile behavior in the face of the criminality of those who set it up in the first place that best proved Milosevic's claim that this was a 'false tribunal':

> For two days Milosevic showed slides of innocent victims of NATO's bombings: 'He's not crazy,' said Richard Dicker, a lawyer with Human Rights Watch, who has been attending the trial. 'What we have heard in the last two days is a very shrewd, canny political offensive. Indeed, he's trying to turn everything upside down, casting himself as the victim, NATO as the criminal and the court as accomplice to the crime.' Of course, little of his political broadside is likely to help him in his trial ... It is Mr. Milosevic, not NATO, on trial.[113]

6
America Gets Away With Murder

With so many people around the world opposed to the Kosovo war, it was only a matter of statistical probability that there would be some lawyers among them. These lawyers could not fail to notice at least two things. First, the central propaganda role that had been assigned to Louise Arbour and the ICTY in vindicating NATO's outrageous Holocaust analogy by masquerading as a second Nuremberg Tribunal. Second, that NATO's bombing campaign was itself Nuremberg's 'supreme' crime against peace, and involved many of the other ones as well – the war crimes and crimes against humanity explicitly covered by the ICTY's statute and committed right in its jurisdiction, one of only two places in the world where international criminal law really applied – even to the Americans.

To lawyers opposed to the war, the ICTY was a big part of the problem, so why not make it part of the solution? Why not insist that Arbour prosecute NATO for its supreme and lesser criminality? Not that she was at all likely to do so, given the track record, but the main idea for most of us who brought charges against the NATO leaders was not to see Clinton and the rest behind bars; it was to use the Tribunal to show the weakness of NATO's moral and legal case for the bombing as law *enforcement* against war criminals. We would show that NATO was no better, legally speaking, than its enemies, and even worse – they don't call it the 'supreme crime' for nothing. The idea was to neutralize the phony criminal law approach – designed, it was clear, to *justify* war – so that the peace camp would have a better chance of ending it. Of course, since we were 99 percent sure that the Tribunal would reject our claim, no matter how clear NATO's guilt, some of us were reluctant to use this strategy for fear that it might *bolster* NATO's case for war. But we concluded that the case was so strong that any failure to prosecute would rebound against the Tribunal's own credibility, and thus NATO's case for war and the precedent it was seeking to set. In other words, our case was as much against the Tribunal as it was against NATO, a simple matter of calling the Tribunal's bluff that it was a real 'juridical institution' and not just a 'political tool.'

THE CASE AGAINST NATO

The ICTY received many complaints from groups and individuals throughout the world demanding prosecution of NATO leaders. The first formal one came from the entire faculty of the University of Belgrade Faculty of Law on 3 April 1999.[1] Another came from the Movement for the Advancement of International Criminal Law, directed by Glen Rangwala of Cambridge University in England. Another complaint, by Greek composer Mikos Theodorakis (of *Zorba the Greek* fame), was subscribed to by 6,000 Greek citizens. A complaint against the Norwegian Foreign Minister was signed by 1,000 Norwegians. Our own complaint was the work of an ad hoc assembly of law professors from my own faculty at Osgoode Hall Law School, joined by lawyers from Toronto and Montreal and by the Association of American Jurists, a pan-American group with members throughout the hemisphere. All of the complaints covered more or less the same ground. Our own charged 68 individual NATO leaders with crimes under the jurisdiction of the Tribunal. The would-be indictees included all of the heads of government, foreign ministers and defense ministers of the 19 NATO countries, starting with Bill Clinton – the 'style of cause' was *Re: William J. Clinton et al.* – Madeleine Albright and William S. Cohen, and on down the list. We also included NATO Secretary General Javier Solana, eight generals including 'Supreme Commander' Wesley K. Clark, closing out the list with Jamie Shea, the smirking face of NATO at the televised press conferences.

The case was based on two distinct kinds of crime within the jurisdiction of the Tribunal: 'crimes against humanity' and 'crimes against the laws and customs of war.' We would have much preferred to include a count of 'aggressive war,' the Nuremberg Tribunal's 'supreme international crime,' from which all of the death and destruction on both sides in Kosovo flowed, but it was no accident that this crime had been excluded from the Statute. According to drafter Michael Scharf:

> There was a clear consensus that the U.S. would not support the inclusion of 'Crimes Against Peace' in the Statute of the ICTY, notwithstanding the Nuremberg precedent … In the final analysis, the United States government, which had been accused by human rights groups and several governments of committing 'Crimes Against Peace' with respect to recent military interventions such as the '89 invasion of Panama, did not want the ICTY to exercise jurisdiction over this offense, leading to precedents that might hamper similar U.S. military action in the future.[2]

Of course, the crime against peace is the one that the United States keeps on committing – not only in Kosovo in 1999, but in Afghanistan in 2001 and Iraq in 2003. America's desire to keep it off the law books, which it also pursued successfully against the International Criminal Court, is, well, understandable. If Milosevic had written the ICTY statute, no doubt it would have looked very strange, too.

But, even apart from aggressive war, there was plenty to go on against NATO.

Crimes against humanity

Article 5 of the Statute gave the ICTY jurisdiction over 'crimes against humanity' committed in 'armed conflict ... and directed against any civilian population,' and it listed a series of crimes, including murder and 'other inhumane acts.' We concentrated on murder, especially in light of Arbour's mid-war indictment of Milosevic for the murder of 'over 340' victims. The NATO campaign took a *minimum* of 500 civilian lives, from ages one to 93, and the number was probably much closer to Yugoslavia's claim of 1,800 civilian dead.

To be guilty of murder, of course, one doesn't actually have to kill anyone *oneself*. Milosevic was not alleged to have killed anyone himself. Liability under the Statute was much wider than this, as it is in ordinary criminal law. Article 7 made anyone 'individually responsible' who 'planned, instigated, ordered, committed or otherwise aided and abetted in the planning, preparation or execution' of the crime and, as Milosevic could tell you, there were no exemptions for state officials, however exalted their positions.

It is not enough for a conviction for murder that someone has been killed, even if the killing is the responsibility of the accused person. All crimes have three essential components: (1) a criminal act, (2) a criminal intent, and (3) a lack of lawful justification or excuse. In murder the criminal act is killing. The criminal intent, as the discussion in Chapter 2 was meant to show, includes not only the intention to kill but also other states of mind deemed equally condemnable: for instance, the *knowledge* that death will occur as a result of one's unlawful act, and even the *purely accidental* killing of one person during the unlawful attempt to kill another. Article 7 of the Tribunal Statute confirmed this, and even went beyond it in cases where a superior, lacking knowledge, had 'reason to know' (in other words *should have known*), that a 'subordinate was about to commit such acts or had done so and the superior failed to take the necessary and reasonable measures to prevent such acts or to punish the perpetrators thereof.'

So the key question was: What was going on in the minds of these NATO leaders when their forces were doing all of this killing and maiming? Of course, they intended to kill soldiers; this they didn't deny. Lacking a lawful justification or excuse for their attack, this was murder, too – should have been, at least, if not for the fact that the ICTY statute restricted crimes against humanity to crimes against civilians. The NATO leaders, however, firmly denied that they intended to kill civilians, and they denied it more vehemently every time civilians were killed. They claimed that they tried their best to avoid killing civilians. There is a lot of evidence to show that these denials were false, and it is examined below. But even if they were true, they should not have got the NATO leaders off the hook. There was enough criminal intent to convict NATO leaders in what they *admitted*, which was that they *knew all along that civilians would die from their air campaign*. Whenever there was an incident involving civilian death, they didn't say, 'Oh my God, we killed civilians! This won't happen again.' No, time after time they said that this was inevitable in war, that they knew it would happen and that they were going to continue bombing in spite of it. They said it when men and women, children and old people, were ripped apart in the most horrible ways imaginable by their detestable weapons. When the 12 April attack on the bridge at Grdelica killed 17 train passengers, the NATO leaders all came out with their well-rehearsed comments. 'We make every attempt possible to minimise civilian casualties, but in actions such as this there will be civilian casualties,' Tony Blair told the UK House of Commons;[3] and Bill Clinton, ever the hard-nosed realist, even in the face of somebody else's children being killed:

> [T]here is no such thing as flying airplanes this fast, dropping weapons this powerful, dealing with an enemy this pervasive, who is willing to use people as human shields, and never have this sort of tragic thing happen …You cannot have this kind of conflict without some errors like this occurring. This is not a business of perfection.[4]

In May, Madeleine Albright and Robin Cook took to the op-ed pages to 'deeply regret' the 'innocent casualties' that were 'impossible to eliminate.'[5] No doubt virtually identical statements could be found in all the languages of NATO, because there was not a peep of dissent from any of the NATO governments, and Javier Solana repeatedly assured everybody of the 'solidarity' in the alliance on the subject of collateral damage.[6]

Jamie Shea's press conferences were a prime source of evidence for NATO's 'state of mind' on collateral damage. For example, asked on 1 June if intensified bombing was 'causing more risks of collateral damage,' Shea pleaded that 'NATO planners take every conceivable precaution' and reminded the questioner of the 'enduring and fundamental difference between unintentional civilian casualties' and the fact that 'Milosevic's forces have intentionally killed thousands of civilians.' Neverthless, he conceded:

Now you are going to ask me, are innocent people going to die in a conflict like this one? The answer is undoubtedly yes ... And if anybody is in danger in Yugoslavia today, it is because Milosevic has chosen to put over a million of his own people, Kosovar Albanians, in danger. That is the bottom line. So there are going to be incidents in the future, unfortunately yes, when Belgrade will allege that we have killed innocent civilians. Some of these stories will be false, some will be exaggerated, but some will be true, but that doesn't diminish the fact that this is a conflict and that we have right on our side.[7]

So the NATO leaders knowingly killed and maimed civilians (or 'aided and abetted' in it, etc.), and they continued bravely on in their strategy in the face of the inevitability of this. The only things they could offer in excuse were that they tried to 'minimize' the collateral damage (a claim analyzed below), and that they were justified in their campaign.

The claim that they were justified in their bombing campaign was as crucial as the claim that they were minimizing collateral damage. A bank robber who shoots up a bank is no less guilty of murder if he only kills to the minimum extent necessary to get away with the cash. Minimizing collateral damage is only an excuse in a legal war. To repeat the point hammered home by Judge Jackson at Nuremberg: '[I]nherently criminal acts cannot be defended by showing that those who committed them were engaged in a war, when war itself is illegal.'[8] In Kosovo, NATO's killing was illegal because the war was illegal. It was illegal essentially because it was immoral, and it was immoral because it was *unnecessary*, and demonstrably so, to achieve the humanitarian goals it claimed to be seeking, or any goal beyond NATO's and America's narrow geopolitical ones.[9] That's what these people died for. They didn't just die in vain, they were murdered, and murdered on a larger scale than was sufficient to indict Milosevic in the middle of a war. So if the ordinary laws of murder and other violent crimes were applied, there's no doubt the NATO leaders would have been easily convicted. The case against them was as strong as the justification for the war was weak. The only way out was the unconvincing claim, offered by the ICTY and examined below, that the kind of murder NATO committed was not in the ICTY's jurisdiction.

Crimes against the laws and customs of war

Besides crimes against humanity, the Statute of the ICTY Tribunal also incorporated as crimes 'grave breaches' of the Geneva Conventions of 1949 (Article 2) and violations of the 'laws and customs of war' (Article 3). The grave breaches of the Geneva Conventions of 1949 included among other things 'wilful killing,' 'wilfully causing great suffering or serious injury to body or health,' 'extensive destruction and appropriation of property, not justified by military necessity and carried out unlawfully and wantonly.' The violations of the laws and customs of war included (but were 'not limited to'): 'employment of poisonous weapons or other weapons calculated to cause unnecessary suffering; wanton destruction of cities, towns or villages, or devastation not justified by military necessity; attack, or bombardment, by whatever means, of undefended towns, villages, dwellings, or buildings; [and] destruction or wilful damage done to institutions dedicated to religion, charity and education, the arts and sciences, historic monuments and works of art and science.'

The Geneva Conventions of 1949 were somewhat less robust in their protection of civilians than their Additional Protocols of 1977, which have never been ratified by the United States. For example, the 1949 Conventions define the civilians protected under them as 'those who, at a given moment and in any manner whatsoever, find themselves ... in the hands of a Party to the conflict or Occupying Power of which they are not nationals.'[10] But, in fact, this posed no real obstacle to the prosecution of NATO leaders; official commentary, and the ICTY itself in its early judgments, had defined 'in the hands of' very widely, to include 'in the power of.'[11] NATO could boast from early in the war that the entire territory of Yugoslavia was in its 'power,' in the very real sense of being at the mercy of its air force.[12] With over 38,000 sorties, NATO never lost a plane in combat. The civilian population of Yugoslavia was very much in NATO's 'hands.'

Engagement of Article 2 of the ICTY statute meant an even lower standard of 'criminal intent' than in the cases of crimes against humanity, signified by use of the word 'wilful.' In criminal law, willful *always* includes knowledge, and often even reaches down as far as 'suspicion.' It also includes the concept of 'willful blindness' – what Oliver North of Iran–Contra fame used to call 'plausible deniability,' where details of criminality are withheld from a higher-up so that he or she can claim not to have known.[13] NATO liked to pride itself on the fact that it consulted *lawyers* over targeting strategy.[14] By this they wanted to show the world that they really cared about civilians, because everybody knows how profoundly moral lawyers are, especially the ones you hire to tell you how to present guilt as innocence. But all the use of lawyers really showed was how conscious NATO was of the facts that made their bombing criminal. Besides, *if* their lawyers told them it was legal – as opposed to saying 'this is how you can *argue* it was legal' – and *if* they believed them, well their lawyers should also have told them that ignorance of the law is no excuse.

Even the real or potential limitations of Article 2 did not apply to Article 3, an open-ended prohibition on violations of the 'laws and customs of war.' The laws and customs of war are almost universally held to include the 1977 Protocols to the Geneva Conventions.[15] This is partly because of their wide formal adoption – Protocol I has been ratified by 161 of the 191 member states of the UN.[16] Indeed, of the NATO countries involved in the Kosovo war, only the US and Turkey had not formally ratified Protocol I, and even the United States officially accepts their binding character as customary law in the relevant parts.[17] But it is mainly because these Protocols merely embody fundamental and widely accepted principles that they have become part of the laws and customs of war. Primary among these is the principle of *discrimination*, meaning that distinctions are to be made between combatants and non-combatants (civilians), and between military and non-military objectives. The latter are not to be the object of attack. Other principles are *necessity* and *proportionality*: a military action must be reasonably necessary to achieve a distinct military advantage, and it must not be excessive in relation to the military advantage sought to be gained.[18] This is simply morality applied to warfare.

For the purposes of the case against NATO, the relevant provisions of the 1977 Protocols were to be found in Part IV of Protocol I ('Civilian Population'). Article 48 enshrines what it calls the 'Basic Rule':

> In order to ensure respect for and protection of the civilian population and civilian objects, the Parties to the conflict shall at all times distinguish between the civilian population and combatants and between civilian objects and military objectives and accordingly shall direct their operations only against military objectives.

Under Article 51, 'Acts or threats of violence the primary purpose of which is to spread terror among the civilian population are prohibited.' So are 'indiscriminate attacks,' including 'those which employ a method or means of combat the effects of which cannot be limited,' or 'an attack which may be expected to cause incidental loss of civilian life, injury to civilians, damage to civilian objects, or a combination thereof, which would be excessive in relation to the concrete and direct military advantage anticipated.' It's not only attacks against civilians that are prohibited, but also attacks against 'civilian *objects*.' Article 52 provides that attacks 'shall be limited strictly to military objectives,' defined as 'those objects which by their nature, location, purpose or use make an effective contribution to military action and whose total or partial destruction, capture or neutralization, in the circumstances ruling at the time, offers a definite military advantage.' Article 55 requires care to be taken 'to protect the natural environment against widespread, long-term and severe damage,' and prohibits 'methods or means of warfare which are intended or may be expected to cause such damage to the natural environment and thereby to prejudice the health or survival of the population.' Article 57 imposes specific duties on those planning attacks to take 'constant care ... to spare the civilian population, civilians and civilian objects.' They are to 'do everything feasible' to ensure that only military objectives are attacked; to 'take all feasible precautions' to minimize 'incidental loss of civilian life, injury to civilians and damage to civilian objects'; to refrain from launching any attack 'which may be expected to cause incidental loss of civilian life, injury to civilians, damage to civilian objects, or a combination thereof, which would be excessive in relation to the concrete and direct military advantage anticipated'; and to suspend such an attack if 'it becomes apparent' that that is the case. Where they have a choice of objectives, 'the objective to be selected shall be that the attack on which may be expected to cause the least danger to civilian lives and to civilian objects.'

Chapter 3 recounted the extensive destruction of civilian life, limb and 'objects' wreaked by NATO's attack on Yugoslavia. Despite the presence of lawyers, the attack also displayed a basic contempt for the rules of war. The exclusive use of high-altitude bombing led to the label 'cowards' war,' because all the risks were displaced onto the civilian population to ensure the safety of NATO military personnel.[19] NATO admitted to using inherently indiscriminate cluster bombs.[20] As for 'civilian objects,' the generals tired quickly of 'tank-plinking' in Kosovo, and within two weeks of the start of bombing they were systematically attacking 'infrastructure' targets in the Serbian cities and countryside.[21] Left in ruins by NATO's 25,000 bombs and missiles were bridges, hospitals, schools, factories, livestock, crops, power grids, media centers, religious buildings including early Christian and medieval churches, archeological sites and museums, as well as air, water and land polluted by the repeated bombing of oil refineries, chemical plants and fertilizer factories.

In mid-May, the United Nations High Commissioner for Human Rights, Mary Robinson, complained that targeting seemed 'unfocused':

> The range of targets seems very broad. And quite clearly civilian residences, hospitals and schools have felt the effects of the bombing. There are too many mistakes. It is not acceptable that civilians are so much in the front line.[22]

It wasn't long before people were drawing the conclusion that the war was directed primarily against civilian morale, 'to spread terror among the civilian population,' in the words Article 51.2 of Protocol I: 'We are beating the daylights out of the country's civilian population,' wrote one American journalist, 'we are deliberately doing things guaranteed to bring about suffering and death among innocent people ... We're sacrificing Serbian newborns to avoid casualties among volunteer American soldiers.'[23]

NATO also convicted itself out of its own mouth. For instance, in an interview given towards the end of the war Air Force Lt. Gen. Michael C. Short, the commander of NATO's air war, confirmed that his goal was to break civilian morale. His only complaint was that the political leaders had not allowed him to do it earlier:

> As an airman, I would have done this differently. It would not be an incremental air campaign or a slow buildup, but we would go downtown from the first night ... If you wake up in the morning and you have no power to your house and no gas to your stove and the bridge you take to work is down and will be lying in the Danube for the next 20 years, I think you begin to ask, 'Hey, Slobo, what's this all about? How much more of this do we have to withstand?' And at some point, you make the transition from applauding Serb machismo against the world to thinking what your country is going to look like if this continues.[24]

In the same interview, Short confirmed that the high-altitude strategy was explicitly meant to displace the risks from the pilots: 'I wanted to destroy the target set and bring this guy [Milosevic] to the negotiating table without losing our kids.... I told them in no uncertain terms that we were not going in below 15,000 feet.' Short meant 'our kids' literally: his son, Christopher, was one of the bomber pilots.

And then of course there were the daily televised briefings of NATO spokesman Jamie Shea, a rich mine of evidence for the conscious violation of the rules of war by NATO. Naturally, he frequently denied aiming at civilian morale – for instance, when asked by a Reuters correspondent about a strike on power plants in Nis:

> There is of course also an aspect of civil inconvenience from this, I acknowledge that but it is not our intention, I want to make this clear to, in any way, render the life of Serbs even more difficult than it is already. Our intention is simply to target the military power apparatus which is responsible, not only for the repressions in Kosovo but also for the dire situation of the Serb people themselves.[25]

But as NATO's real strategy became clearer and the questions became more insistent, Shea and his colleagues began to admit that the strikes had at least what we might call a 'dual use.' For instance, at the press briefing of 3 May one reporter asked, 'Isn't it much harder for NATO to keep up this kind of fiction that it is not at war with the Serbian people, but that it is only attacking military and strategic assets?' Major General Jertz was frank in his reply:

So according to a plan, working systematically this plan, yes we did start with attacking these electricity plants, on the other hand we will just have to continue systematically if Mr Milosevic is not willing to really do what he is supposed to do, take the telephone and tell us that he wants stopping to be bombed, for the sake of his own persons and for the sake of his own people.[26]

When asked whether NATO would regret it if 'one of the side effects of shutting the power off to 70 per cent of the country was to undermine the confidence of the people in the regime of Slobodan Milosevic,' Jamie Shea answered, 'Yes, I would hope that he would start getting some echoes up from the grass roots over the next couple of weeks ...'[27] When reporters asked what military advantage could be gained from temporary power outages when the military had back-up generators, his answer was that Milosevic had to decide whether to use his fuel for military or civilian purposes:

If President Milosevic really wants all of his population to have water and electricity all he has to do is accept NATO's five conditions and we will stop this campaign. But as long as he doesn't do so we will continue to attack those targets which provide the electricity for his armed forces. If that has civilian consequences, it's for him to deal with ...[28]

Even Jamie Shea had difficulty explaining away the vile bombing of a bridge crowded with civilians in the middle of a market day, killing nine people. All he could muster was that Milosevic was responsible for the war and had done much worse:

Fred Colman (USA Today): Two questions on the bombing of the bridge at Varvarin: first of all, can you confirm that the attack took place at 1.00 p.m., or at least in the middle of the day; and second, if it did take place in the middle of the day, how does that square with your repeated assertions, NATO does everything to avoid civilian casualties, since clearly you are going to take more civilian casualties in the middle of the day, than you would in the middle of the night?

Colonel Freytag: I confirm to you again the time; it was 11.01 zulu time, which is 1 p.m.

Jamie Shea: Fred, I've got some civilian casualty figures for you this afternoon. 550,000 internally displaced persons in Kosovo; 883,500 refugees in neighbouring countries, 75 per cent of which are women and children; 193,845 Kosovar refugees elsewhere in the world from Austria to Australia, spread across the globe. Currently, 1,582,345 displaced persons and refugees resulting from the Serb actions in Kosovo, 93 per cent of the original population of Kosovo; 225,000 men missing, but at least 6,000 killed in summary executions, ten mass graves. That is, I think, the vital casualty statistics as far as NATO is concerned, and that is the generation of Milosevic's bullets, not NATO's bombs.

Dimitri Khavine, Russian Line: Although the figures you have released are very impressive and terrible, still can we hope to get some explanation tomorrow, or the day after tomorrow, about the timing of this strike, because it's very important to understand the targeting policy? Why it was stricken just exactly in time when the civilian casualties are most probable. Could we hope to receive the explanation?

Jamie Shea: Dimitri, I hope you'll ask Belgrade to give some timings about some of these other civilian casualties that I have referred to.[29]

The next day, questioners returned to the same theme, with the same response:

Jake Lynch (Sky News) ... And secondly Jamie we haven't yet heard any reason why the bridge at Varvarin was hit at lunchtime and not in the middle of the night and if there is no military reason for that, it can't possibly be so, can it, that NATO takes every precaution to avoid civilian casualties?

Jamie Shea: Jake, we take the same precautions at midday as we do at midnight.[30]

These statements were nothing short of admissions of criminality. Deliberate attacks on civilian objects as part of a strategy of extortion against the civilian population is considered a very serious war crime not only because of the extortion itself, but also because civilians are far more likely to be killed and maimed than when you stick to military targets. The crime and the collateral damage are two sides of the same coin.

So the evidence showed a raft of confessed criminal activity, covering most of the crimes in the ICTY's books, committed in broad daylight before millions of witnesses. We thought we had a pretty good case. We filed our complaints in early May, but only got to meet with Louise Arbour the day before the bombing ended. In the meantime she had issued her indictment against Milosevic, which was such a gross violation of her obligations as a prosecutor that some of my colleagues thought we should pull out of the process altogether. But we decided that the important thing was to make our case; besides, the indictment of Milosevic had set a standard for prosecution that was so low that it would be even more difficult for her not to follow through on NATO.

We carried on as long as possible, as if this were a serious tribunal. We filed evidence and arguments, and when Carla Del Ponte was appointed we spent some more time in The Hague arguing with her and her top legal adviser. In December 1999, Del Ponte let it slip in an interview that she was studying our case.[31] This provoked righteous anger on the part of American authorities, who expressed confidence that nothing would come of it. 'My guess,' said top Pentagon lawyer Richard Black, 'is the U.N. will be reluctant to go toe to toe with the United States on this issue. I don't think they're strong enough today.'[32] Earlier in the war, a US legislator had bristled: 'You're more likely to see the UN building dismantled brick by brick than to see NATO pilots go before a UN tribunal.'[33] These predictions were all proved accurate when Del Ponte immediately backtracked and unctuously apologized for even *suggesting* that she might be *thinking* about *investigating* NATO.[34]

Consequently, Del Ponte surprised nobody in June 2000 when she announced to the Security Council that she was, in effect, dismissing the case against NATO. The decision was greeted with a diplomatically phrased condemnation of the Tribunal by Russia and China, the two permanent members who were not in NATO and who had opposed the war. The Russian representative expressed 'serious reservations about the politicization of its work and its bias vis-à-vis the Federal Republic of Yugoslavia,' noting that 'the Tribunal had taken no action against the North Atlantic Treaty Organization (NATO), even when faced with the deaths of innocent civilians and the destruction of non-military targets resulting from that organization's bombing campaign.'[35] For her part, Del Ponte 'completely rejected' the accusation of politicization. According to the *Washington Post*, Del Ponte said she was 'stupefied' by the Russian accusations.[36] This was rather odd, considering that these accusations had been repeatedly made of the Tribunal throughout its existence. I had publicly written a letter to Del Ponte in March, on behalf of myself and several other complainant groups, using much stronger terms, terms like 'farce,' 'disgrace,' 'a violation of your legal and moral duties.' Del Ponte had even responded by saying that she was 'disappointed in the tone' of my letter.

But there were greater oddities yet. There was the nature of Del Ponte's announcement itself, in which she said she was absolving NATO *without even opening an investigation*:

[T]here is no basis for opening an investigation into any of the allegations or into other incidents related to the NATO air campaign.[37]... I am very satisfied that there was no deliberate targeting of civilians or unlawful military targets by NATO during the bombing campaign ... The prosecutor judged these to be genuine mistakes on the part of NATO.[38]

It was left for a presumably very gullible world to try and figure out how the Prosecutor could have been 'very satisfied' and 'judged these to be genuine mistakes' without even *opening an investigation*.

Then there was the oddity of the timing of the announcement. Del Ponte announced her decision to the Security Council on 2 June, but her committee's report was only released on 13 June. Why did she anticipate the results? For this there can be only one explanation: she knew that Amnesty International was releasing its own report on 7 June with the very different conclusion that NATO was guilty of multiple war crimes, and the Prosecutor wanted to beat them to the punch and present the world with a fait accompli.[39] Thus, for example, NATO Secretary General Lord Robertson had a ready answer to Amnesty the very day they released the report: the ICTY prosecutor had 'told the UN Security Council last week' that she was 'very satisfied there was no deliberate targeting of civilians or of unlawful military targets by NATO during the bombing campaign' and that there was 'no basis for opening an investigation into any of those allegations or into other incidents related to the NATO bombing.'[40] When asked to comment on the different conclusions reached by her office and Amnesty, Del Ponte replied: 'I can only assume our experts are more expert than the experts at Amnesty International. And, especially, my people have much more experience in [investigating] ... crimes against humanity.'[41] Well, that's a laugh if ever there was one. Amnesty has been in the human rights abuse investigation business since 1961. It was awarded the Nobel Peace Prize in 1977. It has more than one million members in 150 countries. Its credibility has had to be earned in a 40-year uphill battle, and unlike the ICTY it is legally and financially independent of all governments and international institutions (nor has it ever had a helpful little hyperlink to NATO on its homepage, like the ICTY had[42]). Furthermore, throughout the conflict over Kosovo, Amnesty had been very strong in its criticism of *all* the parties.[43] It had even welcomed Milosevic's indictment, while reminding the Tribunal not to forget about the KLA and NATO.[44] On reputation for impartiality and credibility alone, one would have to take Amnesty's word against the ICTY any day of the week. But the reports speak for themselves.

Amnesty's report argued that 'civilian deaths could have been significantly reduced if NATO forces had fully adhered to the laws of war,' and it asked that the ICTY 'investigate all credible allegations of serious violations of international humanitarian law during Operation Allied Force [with a view to] bringing to trial anyone against whom there is sufficient admissible evidence.'[45] Amnesty identified three basic types of war crime committed by NATO. First, attacking civilian targets such as the Belgrade RTS radio and television building. Second, failing to suspend attacks even after it became clear that they would cause loss of civilian life excessive in relation to the concrete military advantage to be anticipated, for example in the killing of civilians on bridges (Grdelica, Luzane, and Varvarin). Third, taking insufficient precautions to minimize civilian casualties, for example in bombings that killed displaced civilians (Djakovica and Korisa). On the 'cowards' war' question of bombing from 15,000 feet, Amnesty concluded that 'aspects of the Rules of Engagement, specifically the requirement that NATO aircraft fly above 15,000 feet, made full adherence to international humanitarian law virtually impossible.'[46] Amnesty also found a lack of discrimination contrary to the Geneva Conventions in the use of cluster bombs: 'The use of certain weapons, particularly cluster bombs, may have contributed to causing unlawful deaths.'[47] The Amnesty Report ended with nine case studies, including the five selected by the ICTY Report, making for striking comparisons.

Compared to the Amnesty Report, the ICTY Report comes as something of a shock – not for its conclusion, which was expected, but for the crude and even amateur way it plays the apologist for NATO. If it feels more like it was written by a lawyer for NATO than a judge, well, it was – if only an *ex*-NATO lawyer, Canadian Armed Forces Frigate Captain William J. Fenrick (Ret.). Fenrick had been involved in the project from the beginning, leaving his position as Director of Law for Operations and Training in the Canadian Department of Defense to help the Americans set up the Tribunal in 1992 as a tool to demonize the Serb leadership. Fenrick was in on this at the ground floor, and subsequently became senior legal advisor to the Tribunal when it was officially launched in 1995. The ICTY Report is unsigned, attributed to an anonymous 'committee,' but amateur sleuths will notice that it quotes great swaths of an article authored by Fenrick in 1997, word for word and without quotation marks.[48]

On the other hand, the report goes beyond even the shamelessness of a lawyer's brief to achieve the status of virtual NATO press officer that the ICTY had always been tending towards. At the end of the document, Del Ponte's 'more expert' war crimes investigators declare their more expert investigative technique to be reading NATO's press releases and taking them at face value:

The committee has conducted its review relying essentially upon public documents, including statements made by NATO and NATO countries at press conferences and public documents produced by the FRY. It has tended to assume that the NATO and NATO countries' press statements are generally reliable and that explanations have been honestly given.[49]

Can you imagine what kind of law enforcement a country would have if the police took their suspects' explanations at face value? Can you imagine how many indictments would have been issued against the Serb leadership if the ICTY had stopped at the FRY press releases? It's not as if NATO had a proven record for veracity – or its leaders; remember that at the top of the list of our indictees was the guy who had sworn up and down to everyone that he had not had 'sexual relations with that woman.' The Amnesty Report, while relying for its conclusions only on facts admitted to by NATO, also documents plenty of cases of NATO lying. For example, NATO lied three times about the deadly attack on the refugee convoy at Djakovica: first in claiming the Serbs themselves had bombed the convoy; second in saying there had been only one bombing attack when there had been several attacks on the same convoy and other attacks on other refugee convoys the same day; and third, in presenting an exculpatory tape recording from another incident as if it were from the Djakovica bombing.[50] Amnesty characterizes NATO's explanations of its attempts to prevent civilian casualties as a question of 'rhetoric vs reality.'

In fact, the ICTY Report went to some lengths to try and *hide* NATO's dishonesty. When recounting the convoy incident, the report quoted at length another report by Human Rights Watch, but only to the extent that the Human Rights Watch report quoted NATO's defense of the incident. It snipped out the three previous paragraphs where Human Rights Watch described NATO's explanations as 'convoluted' and 'endless damage control,' and NATO's claims as having 'no basis.'[51] Nor did the ICTY Report quote the following passages from Human Rights Watch:

> [A]lmost half of the incidents (forty-three) resulted from attacks during daylight hours, when civilians could have been expected to be on the roads and bridges or in public buildings which may have been targeted ... Around-the-clock bombing in these and other cases rather seems to have been part of a psychological warfare strategy of harassment undertaken without regard to the greater risk to the civilian population ... In this case [Belgrade TV], the purpose of the attack again seems to have been more psychological harassment of the civilian population than to obtain direct military effect. The risks involved to the civilian population

in undertaking this urban attack grossly outweighed any perceived military benefit.[52]

Nor had NATO proved its trustworthiness by coming clean even to the ICTY itself. Here we have the most persuasive reason for the failure to open an investigation, namely that NATO would not allow one. 'The committee must note, however, that when the ICTY requested NATO to answer specific questions about specific incidents, the NATO reply was couched in general terms and failed to address the specific incidents.'[53] In fact, as far as the record goes, the ICTY sent one letter to NATO on 8 February 2000, and NATO replied ('in general terms,' etc.) on 10 May.[54] That was good enough for the ICTY to pronounce NATO's absolution on 2 June.

The report is so muddled in its reasoning, so blissfully untroubled by inconsistency and double standards, that you have to wonder whether it was written in one of those famous Hague 'coffee shops.' For example, when they said that 500 deaths were too few to be considered crimes against humanity, did they forget that Milosevic had been charged with murder for only 340? 'If one accepts the figures in this compilation of approximately 495 civilians killed and 820 civilians wounded in documented instances, there is simply no evidence of the necessary crime base for charges of genocide or crimes against humanity.'[55] And what about paragraph 56 on high-altitude bombing? 'However, it appears that with the use of modern technology, the obligation to distinguish was effectively carried out in the vast majority of cases during the bombing campaign.'[56] They obeyed the law in the *vast majority* of cases? But what does this mean in a bombing campaign of 38,000 sorties? Seventy-five percent would mean 9,500 sorties for which they did *not* comply with their legal obligations. Ninety percent? That would mean 3,800. Ninety-nine percent? That would leave 380 sorties – rather more than enough to snuff out 500 to 1,800 civilian lives, if you are using the most powerful conventional weapons in the world.

Even with all this, the ICTY had major problems defending the decision not to open an investigation, because the orthodox legal tests laid down by the Statute and deployed so handily to prosecute the Serbs became extremely inconvenient where absolving NATO was concerned. For instance, the Statute of the Tribunal seemed clearly to rule out any 'discretion' on the part of the prosecutor not to prosecute in cases where there was credible evidence of guilt – a so-called 'prima facie case.' The Statute had, in fact, adopted the European principle of 'obligatory prosecution' (*l'obbligatorietà dell'azione penale*, in its Italian version). In *common-law* jurisdictions (the Anglo-Saxon countries: the USA, UK, and Canada, for example), where prosecutors are not supposed to be judicial officers independent of the government, there is indeed a 'discretion' as to whether or not to proceed on a prima facie case. But this Statute embodied the *civil-law* concept prevailing in Europe of the prosecutor as independent judicial officer. The first two prosecutors, even though they hailed from common-law countries, were actual judges, and the third prosecutor was a prosecutor from a civil-law country. The absolute obligation to enforce the law is prized in civil-law countries as a guarantee of prosecutorial independence and equality before the law.[57] The Statute could not have been clearer: 'Upon a determination that a prima facie case exists, the Prosecutor *shall* [the discretion-word would be *may*] prepare an indictment containing a concise statement of the facts and the crime or crimes with which the accused is charged under the Statute.'[58]

As for the 'prima facie case,' this had been defined in the case of Milosevic himself at the traditional level. In approving the Milosevic indictment, Judge David Hunt defined the question as follows:

> I must be satisfied that the material facts pleaded in the indictment establish a *prima facie* case and that there is evidence available which supports those material facts. A *prima facie* case on any particular charge exists in this situation where the material facts pleaded in the indictment constitute a credible case which would (if not contradicted by the accused) be a sufficient basis to convict him of that charge.[59]

The words 'if not contradicted by the accused' are extremely important, because, of course, Milosevic had 'contradicted' the charges against him – denied them flat-out in fact – and had provided plausible alternative versions. According to the rule, the conflicting stories would be for the trial judges to decide in public, not the prosecutors in private. This was the rule the ICTY relied on to allow Milosevic to be indicted in the middle of the war. It was a pretty low legal threshold.

Now, the thing about that threshold is that it was the threshold for *actually issuing an indictment*, not merely opening an investigation. That the *investigation* threshold was even lower is demonstrated by Arbour's approach to Racak. On 16 January, one day after the incident took place, Arbour issued a communiqué stating that she had 'launched an investigation into the most recent massacre in Kosovo,' and was demanding access to the site.[60] Arbour had not even been on the scene – she had not even been denied access to it[61] – and her only informant was William Walker. But she didn't feel she needed to set up a committee. She didn't need a year to make up her mind. She had a bare allegation by an obvious partisan and she was not only 'launching an investigation,' she was calling it 'a massacre of civilians.' Within two weeks, she and the President of the Tribunal were asking the Security Council for sanctions against Yugoslavia for failing to cooperate

(NATO's refusal to cooperate with the ICTY would elicit considerably more understanding). When she requested sanctions from the Security Council, Arbour lowered the threshold even further. It was now enough that there be 'credible evidence *tending* to show that crimes within the jurisdiction of the Tribunal *may* have been committed in Kosovo.'[62] So the mountain of evidence in the public domain that had convinced so many independent observers, including Amnesty International, that NATO was not only worth investigating but was actually guilty, should have been more than enough to *obligate* the Prosecutor to *issue an indictment*, let alone 'launch an investigation.'

Avoiding this required a major overhaul of the rules. First the duty had to be re-'formulated' as a 'discretion':

> Thus formulated, the test represents a negative cut-off point for investigations. The Prosecutor may, in her discretion require that a higher threshold be met before making a positive decision that there is sufficient basis to proceed under Article 18(1).[63]

And what criterion, according to the ICTY Report, was the Prosecutor to apply in the exercise of her new-found 'discretion'? The Milosevic standard – NATO *shall* be prosecuted if it *may* have committed crimes – became reversed: there shall be *no* prosecution if NATO *may not* have committed crimes. For instance, on the question of damage to the environment, NATO was not to be investigated because '[t]he targeting by NATO of Serbian petrochemical industries *may well* have served a clear and important military purpose.'[64] This, of course, is the familiar 'reasonable doubt' standard, applied, one way or another, in criminal trials throughout the world. People should not be convicted where there is a reasonable doubt that they are innocent, if they 'may well' be innocent – in other words, if there is a good chance, on the evidence, that they may not be guilty. However, it is not the standard applied by police and prosecutors. There the standard is the opposite: if the accused *may well* have committed an offense you launch an investigation. Can you imagine how few investigations would be launched if, relying solely on the evidence of statements by the suspects, it appeared that they 'may well' not have done it? This isn't some inexplicable legal formula; it represents a real logical threshold.

Thus a duty became a discretion, and the discretion became exercisable only when there was proof beyond any doubt that the accused were guilty. On this basis, Milosevic never could have been investigated, much less charged.

If there is one example that best illustrates how these devices were deployed, as well as the lap-dog approach of the Committee to NATO's criminality, it is the Grdelica Gorge incident. On 12 April, a NATO warplane launched a guided missile attack that hit a passenger train crossing a bridge, killing 17 civilians. Many of the bodies were charred beyond recognition (they can be seen, along with many other examples of what a humanitarian bombing really looks like, in the two-volume *NATO Crimes in Yugoslavia*[65]). Those identified ranged in age from six to 65. NATO's explanation was that the pilot was attacking the bridge and not the train, and did not see the train until it was too late because the train was going too fast.[66] According to the ICTY Report, '[i]t does not appear that the train was targeted deliberately.'[67] Why? More work for the face-value principle: General Wesley Clark, NATO's Supreme Allied Commander for Europe, said so. The ICTY reproduced Clark's explanation in full:

> [T]his was a case where a pilot was assigned to strike a railroad bridge that is part of the integrated communications supply network in Serbia.... [A]s the pilot stared intently at the desired aim point on the bridge and worked it, and worked it, and worked it, and all of a sudden at the very last instant with less than a second to go he caught a flash of movement that came into the screen and it was the train coming in. Unfortunately he couldn't dump the bomb at that point, it was locked, it was going into the target and it was an unfortunate incident which he, and the crew, and all of us very much regret. We certainly don't want to do collateral damage.[68]

But there was also a second missile that General Clark had to explain:

> The mission was to take out the bridge. He realized when it had happened that he had not hit the bridge, but what he had hit was the train. He had another aim point on the bridge, it was a relatively long bridge and he believed he still had to accomplish his mission, the pilot circled back around. He put his aim point on the other end of the bridge from where the train had come, by the time the bomb got close to the bridge it was covered with smoke and clouds and at the last minute again in an uncanny accident, the train had slid forward from the original impact and parts of the train had moved across the bridge, and so that by striking the other end of the bridge he actually caused additional damage to the train.[69]

Clark then showed the cockpit video of the plane that fired on the bridge:

> Look very intently at the aim point, concentrate right there and you can see how, if you were focused right on your job as a pilot, suddenly that train appeared. It was really unfortunate. Here, he came back around to try to strike a different point on the bridge because he was trying to do a

job to take the bridge down. Look at this aim point – you can see smoke and other obscuration there – he couldn't tell what this was exactly. Focus intently right at the centre of the cross. He is bringing these two crosses together and suddenly he recognizes at the very last instant that the train that was struck here has moved on across the bridge and so the engine apparently was struck by the second bomb.[70]

The ICTY certainly had its work cut out if it was going to dismiss this incident as unworthy of investigation, and it wasn't made any easier by the fact that a German computer whiz, Mr. Ekkehard Wenz, acting entirely independently, had analyzed the video and the technical information provided by NATO and discovered that the video shown by Clark *had been sped up by about five times*. Moreover, Wenz discovered that the plane was of a type which carried both a pilot and a gunner, not just the lonely, very busy pilot that Clark described. Wenz concluded that the attack on the train must have been deliberate.[71] After a German newspaper report, NATO finally admitted months later that the video had indeed been sped up.[72] The ICTY Report did not dispute Wenz's points – nor, naturally, did the incident shake its faith in the trustworthiness of NATO's press releases – but it argued that this still did not prove Wenz's case:

> If the committee accepts Mr. Wenz's estimate of the reaction time available, the person controlling the bombs still had a very short period of time, less than seven or eight seconds in all probability to react. Although Mr. Wenz is of the view that the WSO intentionally targeted the train, the committee's review of the frames used in the report indicates another interpretation is equally available. The cross hairs remain fixed on the bridge throughout, and it is clear from this footage that the train can be seen moving toward the bridge only as the bomb is in flight: it is only in the course of the bomb's trajectory that the image of the train becomes visible. At a point where the bomb is within a few seconds of impact, a very slight change to the bomb aiming point can be observed, in that it drops a couple of feet. This sequence regarding the bombsights indicates that it is unlikely that the WSO was targeting the train, but instead suggests that the target was a point on the span of the bridge before the train appeared.[73]

Notice the bizarre standard used by the Report: 'another interpretation is equally available' – only '*equally* available' to Wenz's conclusion that 'the WSO *intentionally targeted the train*.' In other words, according to the Committee there was a fifty-fifty chance that 17 civilians had been murdered in cold blood by NATO, and they still claimed it wasn't worthy of an investigation. Now think what a different complexion the 'equally available interpretation' would have put on the whole bombing campaign.

Wenz argues, on the other hand, that everything points to an attempt to 'fabricate an accident.' The bombs were not laser-guided but 'TV-guided' (that is, from a television in the bomb, which makes for much greater control), and there was a third bomb that did not hit the bridge at all, suggesting that the bridge was not the target. In fact, the bridge was subsequently repaired by Yugoslavia, not rebuilt, which means that NATO used some very expensive bombs to hit a bridge twice without destroying it: 'it is not very likely that truss bridges were intended to be dismantled brace by brace with $800,000 missiles.'[74] Above all, seven or eight seconds from the appearance of the train was plenty of time for a Weapons Systems Operator, with only that duty, to change the path of the target (in the whole video the target is changed six times in 23 seconds). In an email message to me Wenz put it this way: 'Sit back, close your eyes and count slowly from twenty-one to twenty-eight. Enough time?' Thus, Wenz's view is that the Weapons Systems Officer had plenty of time after he saw the train to put the bomb wherever he wanted.

So, the ICTY analysis of the first bomb is unconvincing. But its analysis of the second bomb is non-existent:

> The train was on the bridge when the bridge was targeted a second time and the bridge length has been estimated at 50 meters. It is the opinion of the committee that the information in relation to the attack with the first bomb does not provide a sufficient basis to initiate an investigation. The committee has divided views concerning the attack with the second bomb in relation to whether there was an element of recklessness in the conduct of the pilot or WSO. Despite this, the committee is in agreement that, based on the criteria for initiating an investigation, this incident should not be investigated. In relation to whether there is information warranting consideration of command responsibility, the committee is of the view that there is no information from which to conclude that an investigation is necessary into the criminal responsibility of persons higher in the chain of command. Based on the information available to it, it is the opinion of the committee that the attack on the train at Grdelica Gorge should not be investigated by the OTP.[75]

This is the empty babbling of whitewashers who have run out of paint. We are talking here about *opening an investigation* in a case where the committee was *divided in its views*, where one cannot even imagine a plausible innocent explanation. Milosevic had lots of explanations for Racak that were, in fact, quite plausible. Louise Arbour did not wait to hear them before she launched her 'investigation' the next day. On the other hand, listen to what Amnesty said about this same incident:

NATO's explanation of the bombing – particularly General Clark's account of the pilot's rationale for continuing the attack after he had hit the train – suggests that the pilot had understood the mission was to destroy the bridge regardless of the cost in terms of civilian casualties. This would violate the rules of distinction and proportionality. Yet, even if the pilot was, for some reason, unable to ascertain that no train was travelling towards the bridge at the time of the first attack, he was fully aware that the train was on the bridge when he dropped the second bomb, whether smoke obscured its exact whereabouts or not. This decision to proceed with the second attack appears to have violated Article 57 of Protocol I which requires an attack to 'be cancelled or suspended if it becomes clear that the objective is not a military one ... or that the attack may be expected to cause incidental loss of civilian life ... which would be excessive in relation to the concrete and direct military advantage anticipated.' Unless NATO is justified in believing that destroying the bridge at that particular moment was of such military importance as to justify the number of civilian casualties likely to be caused by continuing the attack – an argument that NATO has not made – the attack should have been stopped.[76]

The Grdelica Gorge incident is just one of many cases demonstrating the fraudulent nature of the ICTY Report. Another is the deliberate attack by NATO on the RTS (Serbian Television and Radio Station) in Belgrade on 23 April, in which 16 people were killed. This was the case where the ICTY conceded that it would have been a crime if the station were taken out for 'propaganda' reasons alone, the basis on which some NATO officials, including Tony Blair justified the attack ('Strikes against TV transmitters and broadcast facilities are part of our campaign to dismantle the FRY propaganda machinery'), but concluded on the basis of statements by *other* NATO officials that it *may* not have been, and thus decided not to open an investigation.[77] Naturally, these other statements came from NATO *press releases*:

The attack on the RTS building must therefore be seen as forming part of an integrated attack against numerous objects, including transmission towers and control buildings of the Yugoslav radio relay network which were 'essential to Milosevic's ability to direct and control the repressive activities of his army and special police forces in Kosovo' (*NATO press release, 1 May 1999*) and which comprised 'a key element in theYugoslav air-defence network (*ibid, 1 May 1999*). Attacks were also aimed at electricity grids that fed the command and control structures of the Yugoslav Army (*ibid, 3 May 1999*).[78]

The ICTY Report also tried to shift the blame for the incident to the FRY for allegedly allowing the civilians to stay at the station after they had been warned.[79] Indeed, the head of the station was later jailed by the new regime in Serbia for endangering employees, though the finding was only that he was aware that the station *could be* a target.[80] But this was all beside the point: if a robber were to come to your house and tell you to leave, and you stubbornly or stupidly did not, and he killed you, find me any judge (who hasn't been bribed by the robber) who would say the robber was not guilty of murder.

Amnesty International concluded, on the other hand, that 'the attack on the RTS headquarters violated the prohibition to attack civilian objects contained in Article 52(1) and therefore constitutes a war crime.' They argued that even if it could be considered a military objective ('stretch[ing] the meaning ... beyond the acceptable bounds of interpretation'), the attack 'would have violated the rule of proportionality':

> NATO deliberately attacked a civilian object, killing 16 civilians, for the purpose of disrupting Serbian television broadcasts in the middle of the night for approximately three hours. It is hard to see how this can be consistent with the rule of proportionality.[81]

One way of explaining the differences between the conclusions of Amnesty International and the ICTY was that they were applying different standards: Amnesty was applying the law and the ICTY was applying something of its own invention. Take Del Ponte's insistence, when the report was released, that NATO had not 'deliberately' targeted civilians. Not only did this replicate the artificial distinction between killing *intentionally* and killing *knowingly* that we labored earlier; it flew in the face of the wording of the Geneva Conventions and the ICTY's very own statute. This was not a slip on Del Ponte's part; it was fundamental to the reasoning of the report. For instance:

> 54. During the bombing campaign, NATO aircraft flew 38,400 sorties, including 10,484 strike sorties. During these sorties, 23,614 air munitions were released (figures from NATO). As indicated in the preceding paragraph, it appears that approximately 500 civilians were killed during the campaign. These figures do not indicate that NATO may have conducted a campaign *aimed at causing* substantial civilian casualties either directly or incidentally. (Emphasis added)

Try to ignore the faulty logic: a campaign aimed at terrorizing the population, *but without appearing to do so*, would want desperately to reduce those killings to those that could be explained as accidents. 'Make it look like an accident' must be the oldest gangster cliché in the movies. Or in NATO's own terms: 'Avoiding unnecessary suffering among the Serb population was also vital in maintaining public and international support for NATO's actions.'[82] Or in the more sophisticated terms of the (anti-Milosevic) Yugoslav intellectual Aleksa Djilas: the 'main purpose was to intimidate the population ... but they had to do it in such a way that Western public opinion would accept it.'[83] The ICTY was either being hopelessly naïve, or expecting us to be, in perishing the thought that behind NATO's hideous weaponry was also a gangster mentality.

But the main point of this example is the notion that the killing of civilians had to be the *aim* of the attack for it to qualify as a war crime. This is just rubbish, as a simple reading of the Geneva Conventions, and even the ICTY Statute itself, shows. These documents go much further and even speak in terms of *negligence*; in other words, what one 'should have known' as a 'reasonable person.' The 1977 Protocols use classic negligence terminology: *constant care shall be taken – do everything feasible – take all feasible precautions – may be expected to cause the least danger* [not '*is* expected to cause'] *– take all reasonable precautions.*[84] The ICTY Statute explicitly makes superiors responsible not only for what they knew, but for what they 'had reason to know.' That's what prompted General Michael Short to say in his May 1999 interview that, when a pilot would ask him, 'Boss, I see village and I see tanks parked next to the houses in the village. What do you want me to do?', Short would answer, 'Tell them to hit the tanks,' adding 'And if he hits a house by mistake, that's my responsibility.'[85] Except that the ICTY wouldn't make him take the responsibility, because they ruled out negligence as a basis of liability, on grounds which are nowhere explained: 'The mens rea for the offence [of unlawful attack under Article 3] is intention or recklessness, not simple negligence.'[86] In fact, this was a very helpful little amendment if the ICTY was going to acquit NATO without asking for an explanation. Since the ICTY was going to accept every claim of innocence made by NATO at face value, negligence was the only ground left for prosecution. This is because negligence says: we don't care what you knew; it's what you *should have known* that counts. That's been the battle cry of rape victims who have sought, successfully in many jurisdictions, to write into the law that men claiming 'mistaken belief in consent' be required to show that their mistake was 'reasonable.'[87] The section of the 1977 Protocol on grave breaches requires 'wilfulness' (not 'intention') on the part of perpetrators, but not superiors, who are held to a negligence ('ought to have known') standard.[88] Even the 'wilful' part is not connected to the actual killing of civilians, but rather the nature of the attack. For example, Article 85:

> 3. ... the following acts shall be regarded as grave breaches of this Protocol, when committed wilfully, in violation of the relevant provisions of this Protocol, and causing death or serious injury to body or health:
>   (a) making the civilian population or individual civilians the object of attack ...

Notice how naturally this covers the case where civilian morale was being aimed at and the 'inevitable collateral damage' occurred, the kind one 'should have known' about. Where does it say anything about 'intention' or even 'recklessness' as to the consequences themselves?

But even the exclusion of negligence could not justify the Prosecutor's grant of immunity to NATO for unlawful attacks in which it was *known* or *suspected* that civilians would be killed or wounded, even if you couldn't prove they aimed to kill civilians. The notion of 'recklessness,' conceded by the ICTY as sufficient, always includes not only knowledge but even much less – for example, foresight of a probability or even a possibility.[89] And the numerous statements from NATO leaders cited earlier show they knew exactly how their strategies would destroy civilian life and limb. However horrible it was, they claimed this was the absolute minimum everybody *knew* would be the cost of what they were doing. They were anxious to claim they knew what they were doing because they didn't want to be seen as having messed up.

The mental element played a big role in the analysis of cluster bombs. Here there was an awkward precedent: cluster bombs had figured importantly in the indictment of Milan Martic by prosecutor Goldstone in 1995. The ICTY correctly pointed out that in that case the thesis of the prosecution was that the use of cluster bombs could only be understood as a deliberate, and not merely negligent attack on civilians.[90] If the ICTY were not using a 'reverse reasonable doubt' standard, it might have considered 'opening an investigation' into why, if not deliberately to kill civilians, NATO was using cluster bombs to attack cities in a war described more than once by NATO leaders as having to do with breaking the will of the Yugoslavs. If you're going to demand proof beyond a reasonable doubt that NATO deliberately killed people before you open up an investigation, this is naturally very congenial to those who can afford to do their civilian killing from the safety of 15,000 feet. But the law didn't require an intention to kill civilians, only the knowledge that such deaths would occur; or even recklessness or, strictly speaking, negligence with respect to them. When cluster bombs are used near populated areas, everybody knows what the result will be.

Targets

The ICTY engaged in some rather crude selective quoting and outright misrepresentation to handle NATO's attacks on civilian targets. The strategy was to take fairly straightforward rules and suggest there was some kind of confusion, the result being to expand the range of permissible targets. For instance, to get around the rigors of Article 52 of the 1977 Protocol ('Attacks shall be limited strictly to military objectives ...', quoted fully above), the ICTY Report resorted to unofficial commentaries, which it then misquoted and misrepresented. A favorite commentary used by the ICTY Report was a book by British army officer and military lawyer A. P. V. Rogers, *Law on the Battlefield*.[91] In one instance the report quotes a very long list of potential military objectives from the book, which, importantly for NATO's war on Yugoslavia, includes 'bridges ... communications installations, including broadcasting and television stations and telephone and telegraph stations used for military communications.' The ICTY Report follows the list by saying, as does Rogers, 'The list was not intended to be exhaustive.'[92] The Report pointedly does *not* quote what Rogers said in his next breath, which rather directly contradicted what the report was trying to claim his authority for: 'The mere fact that an object is on the list, such as a railway or main road, *does not mean that it is necessarily a military objective.*'[93] In a similar fashion, the ICTY Report relied on a target list prepared in 1956 by the International Committee of the Red Cross, which, through careless punctuation in one version (a semicolon instead of a comma), made it seem that 'installations of broadcasting and television stations' were legitimate targets even if they were not 'of fundamental military importance.' It was for the 'lesser experts' of Amnesty to point out, first, that the French version got the punctuation right, and second, that the draft list was never officially adopted, and the whole idea of 'drawing up lists of military objectives was abandoned in favour of the approach eventually adopted by Protocol I in Article 52' of the 1977 Convention.[94]

Amnesty also added a rather significant quote from Rogers that never made it into the ICTY Report:

> If the target is sufficiently important, higher commanders may be prepared to accept a greater degree of risk to the aircraft crew to ensure that the target is properly identified and accurately attacked. No-risk warfare is unheard of.... However, if the target is assessed as not being worth that risk and a minimum operational altitude is set for their protection, the aircrew involved in the operation will have to make their own assessment of the risks involved in verifying and attacking the assigned target. If their assessment is that (a) the risk to them of getting close enough to the

target to identify it properly is too high, (b) that there is a real danger of incidental death, injury or damage to civilians or civilian objects because of lack of verification of the target, and (c) they or friendly forces are not in immediate danger if the attack is not carried out, there is no need for them to put themselves at risk to verify the target. Quite simply, the attack should not be carried out.[95]

This highly relevant and very recent article by their favorite authority seems to have escaped the attention of the ICTY's experts when they came to discuss the 'cowards' war' question of NATO's high-altitude bombing – even though they admitted having seen Amnesty's report before they released their own. But how did Mr. Fenrick miss this passage from his *own* article, the one on which the ICTY Report was otherwise based?

Military casualties incurred by the attacking side are not part of the [proportionality] equation. A willingness to accept some own-side casualties in order to limit civilian casualties may indicate a greater desire to ensure compliance with the principle of proportionality.[96]

Not to mention this one:

If weapons systems with large CEPs [Circular Error Probable] are directed against military objectives in highly populated areas, one might conclude that the real object of attack is the civilian population, not the military objective.[97]

One might indeed.

The illegality of the war

One question that Amnesty did not deal with, and on which the ICTY took a firm stand, concerned the implications of the illegality of the war. We had stressed the importance of this to both prosecutors. Our argument was that the illegality of the war and the lack of any real (as opposed to claimed) humanitarian justification, made the killing of civilians *murder*, and therefore a 'crime against humanity.' It should have made the killing of soldiers such a crime as well, but the Statute restricted crimes against humanity to crimes against civilians. However, the ICTY resolutely rejected this proposition:

Allegations have been made that, as NATO's resort to force was not authorized by the Security Council or in self-defense, that the resort to force was illegal and, consequently, all forceful measures taken by NATO were unlawful.... That being said, as noted in paragraph 4 above, the crime related to an unlawful decision to use force is the crime against peace or aggression.... [T]he ICTY does not have jurisdiction over crimes against peace.... The ICTY has jurisdiction over serious violations of international humanitarian law as specified in Articles 2–5 of the Statute. These are *jus in bello* offences.[98]

It is true that the ICTY Statute had not included Nuremberg's 'supreme international crime' because it didn't suit the purposes of the sponsors (see above); but this didn't mean the tribunal was obliged to construe the statute as conferring immunity for crimes that *were* in the Statute, such as murder and other crimes against humanity, committed in the course an illegal war (without lawful justification or excuse) exactly as if it were a legal one. The prosecutor tried to insinuate that an argument against such immunity had been rejected by Nuremberg:

> There were suggestions by the prosecution before the International Military Tribunal at Nuremberg and in some other post World War II war crimes cases that all of the killing and destruction caused by German forces were war crimes because the Germans were conducting an aggressive war. The courts were unreceptive to these arguments.[99]

In fact this was more than a 'suggestion' by the Nuremberg prosecution; it was the foundation of its whole case for making 'aggressive war' a crime. And far from being 'unreceptive,' the Nuremberg Tribunal proceeded to declare aggressive war 'the supreme international crime.' Here's what the US chief prosecutor Jackson said in his opening statement on 21 November 1945:

> There was a time, in fact I think the time of the First World War, when it could not have been said that war inciting or war making was a crime in law, however reprehensible in morals. Of course, it was under the law of all civilized peoples a crime for one man with his bare knuckles to assault another. How did it come that multiplying this crime by a million, and adding firearms to bare knuckles, made a legally innocent act? The doctrine was that one could not be regarded as criminal for committing the usual violent acts in the conduct of legitimate warfare. The age of imperialistic expansion during the eighteenth and nineteenth centuries added the foul doctrine, contrary to the teachings of early Christian and International Law scholars such as Grotius, that all wars were to be regarded as legitimate wars. The sum of these two doctrines was to give war making a complete immunity from accountability to law. This was intolerable for an age that called itself civilized.... The common sense of men after the First World War demanded, however, that the law's condemnation of war reach deeper, and that the law condemn not merely

uncivilized ways of waging war, but also the waging of uncivilized wars – wars of aggression.[100]

Jackson's argument was aimed at defending the charge of aggressive war against the claim that it was *ex post facto* law, and therefore a violation of important legal principles. He wanted to show that it had long been a crime to wage an unlawful war, and he was arguing in this passage that this was just a logical application of the ordinary criminal law against violence when there was no defense available of a lawful war. Another American prosecutor at Nuremberg put it this way:

> War, whether or not it is waged chivalrously, inherently involves a series of acts which for millennia have been denounced as crimes under every civilized legal system: deliberate mass killings, assaults, burning – acts that have been criminal even without the abominable sadism which the Nazis added.... Thus, for example, the deliberate killing of Frenchmen even in the course of a war involved a violation of the French laws of murder where the French had been victims of aggression. Under this approach, the Kellogg–Briand Pact and similar agreements are important, not because they directly made aggressive war a crime, but because, by destroying it as a defense, they made the instigation of aggression subject to the universal laws against murder. It is these ancient laws which are the basis for the punishment of aggression prescribed by the [Nuremberg] Charter.[101]

Of course, the principles of the Kellogg–Briand Pact were repeated and strengthened in the Charter of the United Nations, giving enormous contemporary significance to the Nuremberg Judgment.

Now it's true that the prosecution at Nuremberg did not use this argument to try and define 'crimes against humanity,' and it is clear that when, in addition to the crime of aggressive war, the Tribunal convicted the accused of crimes against humanity, they relied on 'the abominable sadism which the Nazis added.' But this had nothing to do with the nature of crimes against humanity and everything to do with the particular structure of the Charter of the Nuremberg Tribunal, including as it did the distinct count of 'aggressive war,' and even restricting jurisdiction over crimes against humanity to those committed in connection with the crime of aggressive war.[102] Given that technical legal division of labor, it would have been redundant to repeat as crimes against humanity the necessary incidents of waging aggressive war. This was also the precise and narrow ground on which the Tokyo Tribunal based its decision to side-step the explicit prosecution argument that all killing during Japan's aggressive wars should constitute murder:

Counts 39 to 52 inclusive ... contain charges of murder. In all these counts the charge in effect is that killing resulted from the unlawful waging of war at the places and upon the dates set out ... In all cases the killing is alleged as arising from the unlawful waging of war.... No good purpose is to be served, in our view, in dealing with these parts of the offences by way of counts for murder when the whole offence of waging those wars unlawfully is put in issue upon the counts charging the waging of such wars.... For these reasons only and without finding it necessary to express any opinion upon the validity of the charges of murder in such circumstances we have decided that it is unnecessary to determine counts 39 to 43 [etc.]....[103]

So the fact that neither the Nuremberg nor the Tokyo Tribunals bothered to count the everyday murder of illegal wars as a 'crime against humanity' was due to the presence of the distinct charge of illegal war. It was a technical question, not one of substance, much less of principle or morality. When crimes against humanity came to be defined in the ICTY Statute, there was nothing to indicate an intention to restrict them in any way. According to 'insiders' Morris and Scharf, the only things meant to be excluded were, naturally, *lawful* acts, those

carried out in accordance with the relevant standards of national and international law ... In this regard, the United States expressly stated its understanding that the definition of crimes against humanity contained in Article 5 would apply to the acts referred to therein only 'when committed contrary to law.'[104]

In its very first case, the ICTY Appeals Chamber also expressed the view that the crimes against humanity in the Statute should be given as wide a meaning as they could logically bear, refusing to restrict them to cases involving 'discriminatory intent.' One passage from the judgment had a startlingly natural applicability to NATO's bombing campaign: *'For example, a discriminatory intent requirement would prevent the penalization of random and indiscriminate violence intended to spread terror among a civilian population as a crime against humanity.'*[105]

Does this mean that the only interpretation possible was that the illegality of the war had rendered the clearly foreseen civilian killings a crime against humanity? Law is not like that. An honestly impartial tribunal – a real 'juridical institution' that wasn't 'just a political tool' – could possibly have reached the same conclusion as the ICTY did on this question, that without a specific head of 'crimes against peace,' the Statute meant to punish only 'added sadism'; in other words, an impartial tribunal could possibly have concluded that they would have to ignore the illegality of the war and immunize NATO leaders from all the crimes they committed as long as they were necessarily incidental to their illegal war strategy. An impartial tribunal might have concluded that the murder of civilians incidental to an illegal bombing campaign, lacking any of the justifications or defenses of the ordinary criminal law, was beyond their jurisdiction. But one imagines that an impartial tribunal not concerned with the 'optics' of lingering too long over this unpleasant detail would have struggled a lot harder with the question. In fact, an impartial *prosecutor* would undoubtedly have left this delicate question for the Court to decide. The ICTY, however, had long proved itself to be anything but impartial.

In the end, whether this was the 'right' interpretation of the Statute is of secondary importance. Because the point was never, realistically, to see NATO leaders behind bars, but rather to show what a farce it was to prosecute only the Serbs when America was as guilty and guiltier. And if that farce can only be defended by an unblinkingly loyal concession to the Americans' evident determination to exclude the 'supreme international crime' from the ICTY's catalog of crimes – and thus to incorporate Jackson's 'foul doctrine' into their governing law – then the ICTY hardly comes out smelling like a rose.[106] The waging of aggressive war was made an independent head of prosecution in the Nuremberg Tribunal not because of something odd about the Tribunal, but because of the *inherent criminality* of aggressive war ('a series of acts which for millennia have been denounced as crimes under every civilized legal system'). To exempt this inherent criminality is no less 'a mocking exercise in gentlemanly futility' than to exempt aggressive war itself.

The ICTY provided a rare opportunity of actually bringing America before the bar of international justice, if only in the sense that the Tribunal had formally to try and justify America's impunity. For reasons outlined in the next chapter, this is unlikely ever to happen again. Despite this and despite what we've just seen, some people have inexplicably tried to draw from our experience with the ICTY the conclusion that even a superpower can be subject to the rule of international criminal law, if only a proper case can be made.[107] It seems that if you want to carry on with this enterprise and continue self-righteously pursuing the acceptable targets of international criminal law, you simply have to keep up the appearance of its potential even-handedness. But is this possible?

7

Rounding Up the Usual Suspects while America Gets Away with Murder[1]

THE INTERNATIONAL CRIMINAL COURT

The holy grail of the international criminal law movement was a permanent international court with jurisdiction over war crimes wherever they should be committed. On 1 July 2002 it was finally achieved with the coming into force of the Rome Statute of the International Criminal Court. Every step of the way had been a joyous international media event, from the huge founding conference in Rome in the summer of 1998 to the deposit of the requisite sixtieth state ratification in April 2002. The judges were sworn in with all due pomp in March 2003, and the prosecutor was elected in a live UN web-cast in April. By that time, 89 states – slightly less than half the UN members – had ratified the treaty.

The grand words of the ICC Statute's Preamble included an affirmation that 'the most serious crimes of concern to the international community as a whole must not go unpunished' and a determination 'to put an end to impunity for the perpetrators of these crimes and thus to contribute to the prevention of such crimes.'[2] Kofi Annan concluded the 1998 Rome conference with the ringing declaration that 'Now at last ... we shall have a permanent court to judge the most serious crimes of concern to the international community as a whole.'[3] But guess what crime was missing? That's right, Nuremberg's 'supreme international crime,' the crime against peace of aggressive war, the one that America was just about to commit in Kosovo and would go on to repeat in Afghanistan and Iraq before the ICC even had its first prosecutor.

The Rome Statute included the familiar triumvirate of crimes that are found in the ICTY and ICTR statutes: genocide, crimes against humanity and war crimes, with many detailed and complicated definitions. But, like those statutes, and *unlike* the Nuremberg Charter, it left 'the crime of aggression' out of the picture, except as a conspicuously empty *heading*, an agenda item, over which jurisdiction was renounced until further notice. By the terms of the statute, the Court would not be allowed to exercise jurisdiction over the crime of aggression unless the statute was amended. No amendment could even be proposed until *seven years* had passed, and it would have to be ratified by seven eighths of the state parties to take effect. Even then – and here's the real kicker – *it would only take effect against state parties who accepted it*: 'In respect of a State Party which has not accepted the amendment, the Court shall not exercise its jurisdiction regarding a crime covered by the amendment when committed by that State Party's nationals or on its territory.'[4] In other words, no jurisdiction over the supreme crime until almost everybody agrees, and then an exemption for any signatory who wants it. It is no secret that this huge hole in the statute was intended as an inducement to the United States to ratify it. According to the President of the Conference, Italian Judge Giovanni Conso: 'The United States did not want this crime to be included in the Statute,' and it was 'to convince the United States' that the formula was adopted of a 'two-phase solution in which the crime of aggression was included as a heading while the definition and the elements constituting the crime were to be elaborated on at a later stage.'[5]

But the United States was not convinced enough to become a party to the statute, and ended up being one of only seven countries actually to vote against it, joined by China, Libya, Iraq, Israel, Qatar and Yemen. One hundred and twenty states voted in favor and 21 abstained. The United States would accept no crime of aggression unless prosecution was conditional upon prior Security Council certification, 'the vital linkage' according to Clinton's 'Ambassador at Large for War Crimes' David J. Scheffer.[6] In fact, this was the US position on every aspect of the Court's jurisdiction; it wanted the court to be a kind of permanent ICTY, 'a standing tribunal' in Scheffer's words, 'that could be activated immediately' by the Security Council on a case-by-case basis.[7] Or, as he told a US Congressional committee in his report on the Rome conference: 'The United States has long supported the right of the Security Council to refer situations to the court with mandatory effect, meaning that any rogue state could not deny the court's jurisdiction under any circumstances.'[8] Naturally, that would neatly exempt 'rogue states' who happen to be Permanent Members of the Security Council. The United States even proposed a last-ditch amendment that would have exempted *all* rogue states, by requiring 'the consent of the state of nationality of the perpetrator be obtained before the court could exercise jurisdiction.'[9] But this amendment was overwhelmingly rejected and the law as drafted gave the court jurisdiction over war crimes when *either* the offender *or* the victim was a party to the statute, and even when the victim only *subsequently* accepted the court's jurisdiction. If Yugoslavia, Afghanistan or Iraq were either a party to the statute or willing to accept the jurisdiction of the Court, then the US would have been subject to prosecution whether or not it joined the statute.[10] The consent of the Security Council would not be required in such a case. The American desire for a permanent ad hoc court was addressed, but only in the form of a separate, *additional* power of the Security Council to refer a case for prosecution, whether or not a party to the statute was the perpetrator or victim. There was nothing in this to protect the US from prosecution under the other provisions of the statute.[11]

The American insistence on Security Council consent was not, naturally, out of any love for Security Council authority, but because of the US veto, which means that nothing can lawfully be done by the Security Council without explicit US consent. Security Council control over the crime of aggression was presented by the Americans as the position of all the permanent members, but the only one to vote against the statute besides the US was China. France and the UK had both signed and ratified by the time the statute went into effect, while Russia had signed and not withdrawn. Yet, according to commentators, 'it is almost certain' that if the crime is ever added it will be in the form America wants it in, 'namely that a charge of aggression may not be brought unless the Security Council has first determined that the state concerned has committed the act of aggression which is the subject of the charge.'[12] In other words, perpetual impunity for the supreme crime for the world's leading practitioners of it.

The Americans won some other very important concessions at Rome, even while staying out of the statute. One was the now notorious section 98, paragraph 2, which allows the US (and others), whether parties to the statute or not, to negotiate agreements that override the authority of the court to demand that criminals be handed over, a luxury that was not available to Milosevic. This clause was also 'included at the insistence of the United States.'[13] The Americans started actively seeking such agreements as soon as the statute went into effect. By April 2003 they had concluded more than two dozen of them, almost all with total dependencies of the sort that made up the bulk of the 'Coalition of the Willing' in the war on Iraq.[14] An Act introduced in the US Congress in June 2000, and signed into law by President Bush in August 2002, contains a 'Prohibition Of United States Military Assistance To Parties To The International Criminal Court,' unless they enter into section 98 agreements.[15] In July 2003, the US carried through on this threat by cutting off military aid to 35 countries then receiving it.[16] The law also prohibits cooperation with the ICC by all levels of government, and gives the President the authority 'to use all means necessary and appropriate to bring about the release from captivity' of any American 'being detained or imprisoned against that person's will by or on behalf of the International Criminal Court' (using the words it claimed were unnecessary in Iraq to authorize the use of military force).[17] For this reason, the American branch of the Coalition for the International Criminal Court calls the Act the 'Hague Invasion Act.'[18] To make the point even clearer, the law prohibits the use of bribes or inducements to obtain release, leaving only force. Amnesty International, Human Rights Watch and the Coalition for the International Criminal Court have condemned these Article 98 agreements as 'US Impunity Agreements,' claiming they are illegal because they are inconsistent with the ideals of the Rome Statute. But the inclusion of 98(2) was no slip, and none of the critics have been able to point to anything in the statute forbidding what the Americans are doing.[19]

Another important victory at Rome for the Americans was Article 16, which allows the Security Council itself to bar any given proceedings for 12 months at a time, renewable indefinitely. Article 16 requires action from the Security Council as a whole, so the US has to get the other permanent members to go along with it to block any prosecutions. However, the US 'has ways.' Apart from its usually persuasive quid pro quo, it can use its veto to demand prosecutorial immunity as a condition of allowing *any* given Security Council Resolution to pass. This strategy was also mandated by the American Servicemembers' Protection Act.[20] The US first tried this out with great success in July 2002. That's when the UN's 1,500-strong peacekeeping force in Bosnia was about to expire unless renewed. The US, which was then contributing a paltry 704 members to the 45,000 UN peacekeeping personnel around the world, nevertheless threatened to pull the plug on the whole operation – in other words not just to pull out its own personnel, not just to withdraw financial support, but to prevent *anyone* from participating, unless there were a blanket ICC prosecution prohibition. Obviously this was not merely about protecting US forces from prosecution. According to one 'senior UN-based diplomat': 'This is about making a point about who's in charge.'[21] The US ultimately won its immunity in Resolution 1422 of 12 July 2002, which added gratuitously that it was intent on renewing it each 1 July (the effective date of the ICC) 'for as long as may be necessary.'[22]

The US had more successes yet at Rome. Scheffer could boast to the Senate that among the long list of 'objectives we achieved in the statute of the court' were 'viable definitions of war crimes and crimes against humanity' and 'acceptable provisions based on command responsibility and superior orders.'[23] In the 'viable definitions' category, the US was able to postpone (to the same future world as the crime of aggression) the banning of nuclear weapons, and even cluster bombs and land mines, while ensuring that chemical and biological weapons were made criminal with immediate effect. They thus enshrined one of their favorite propaganda tools – the notion that 'weapons of mass destruction' only include 'the nuclear weapons of the poor' and not the vastly more terrible genuine articles in their own arsenals.[24]

The provisions on 'command responsibility' and 'superior orders' referred to by Scheffer were in the realm of the *mens rea* requirements for the liability of political superiors, discussed in Chapter 6. These were significantly raised from the broad liability for 'recklessness' and even 'negligence' in the Geneva Conventions and the ICTY and ICTR statutes, to limit liability to cases where the superior 'either knew, or consciously disregarded information which clearly indicated' the criminality of subordinates.[25] There was also a nice new negative definition of 'armed conflict' that conveniently excluded the kind of systematic violence that powerful states perpetrate on their own populations. Article 8.2(e) ('Other serious violations of the laws and customs applicable in armed conflicts not of an international character') 'does not apply to situations of internal disturbances and tensions, such as riots, isolated and sporadic acts of violence or other acts of a similar nature,' but does apply 'when there is protracted armed conflict between governmental authorities and organized armed groups or between such groups.'[26] This is reminiscent of the reason, according to the Tokyo Tribunal Judge B. V. A. Röling, why the US insisted on linking 'crimes against humanity' to 'crimes against peace' in the Nuremberg and Tokyo Charters: 'The connection was desired because some people, such as Stimson, the American Secretary of War, were afraid that without this element the new crime would be applicable to the mistreatment of blacks in the US!'[27]

Despite all these successes, the Americans have steadfastly refused to ratify the statute. This was not at all an aberration of the Bush administration. Not only were all the loopholes negotiated during Clinton's presidency; not only was it Clinton's delegates to Rome who cast their all-but-isolated vote against the statute, but it was Clinton who, in his last words on the subject, stated: 'I will not, and do not recommend that my successor submit the Treaty to the Senate for advice and consent until our fundamental concerns are satisfied.'[28] Clinton did however, *sign* (not ratify) the Treaty on the last day possible (31 December 2000) 'to reaffirm our strong support for international accountability and for bringing to justice perpetrators of genocide, war crimes, and crimes against humanity' (notice the omission of the supreme crime), claiming thus to 'sustain' America's 'tradition of moral leadership.'[29] The signing was purely an exercise in public relations, because it did not in any way bind the US to the Treaty. Technically the Vienna Convention on Treaties does entail some minimal obligations on the part of signatories, even without ratification, 'to refrain from acts which would defeat the object and purpose of a treaty ... until it shall have made its intention clear not to become a party to the treaty.'[30] But all this did was give the Bush administration something to do to symbolically *dissociate* itself from the statute. In May 2002, weeks before the ICC was to go into force, the Bush administration made 'its intention clear not to become a party to the treaty,' in effect 'unsigning' the Rome Statute.[31]

So with all these concessions and loopholes, what was the US's problem with the Court? Or to put it the way Louise Arbour did in 1999: 'I would have thought that the 19 countries of NATO should be able to ratify a Treaty under which they would have *considerably less exposure to scrutiny, let alone prosecution, than they have before ICTY.*'[32] The objections raised by the Americans were of two sorts. First there were some unconvincing legalistic reasons. For example, the United States complained that the treaty applied to non-parties – an odd reason, one might think, to offer for not becoming a party. David Scheffer told the Senate Committee that this was 'contrary to the most fundamental principles of treaty law';[33] but this was contradicted by America's own law and practice from Nuremberg to the ICTY. The US is a party to many treaties that grant criminal jurisdiction over non-parties, and it has even exercised this jurisdiction itself.[34]

The Americans also railed against the denial of due process rights, such as the right to trial by jury.[35] These were the very same rights the Americans had been happy to deny those charged before the ad hoc tribunals they set up for Yugoslavia and Rwanda, or indeed the widely condemned military tribunals they set up in the United States for foreigners charged with 'terrorism' – tribunals which also provided for the death penalty, a punishment denied to the ICC.[36] The insincerity of the American objections to the ICC could only really be appreciated in retrospect, after the United States had defied the Security Council in March 2003 and gone to war with Iraq. That put into high and comic relief the central claim made by the Bush administration when it 'unsigned' the Rome treaty in 2002: '[W]e believe the International Criminal Court undermines the role of the United Nations Security Council in maintaining international peace and security ... the treaty dilutes the authority of the U.N. Security Council and departs from the system that the framers of the U.N. Charter envisioned.'[37]

Pseudo-legal arguments apart, the US's objection to the ICC boiled down to a claim that the Court, free of the discipline of the Security Council (with an American veto), *might actually prosecute Americans.* This was apart altogether from the question of whether the Americans charged might be guilty. In other words, it was not about 'wrongful convictions,' in the sense of convicting an innocent person. The Bush administration put the argument in terms of pure sovereignty:

> While sovereign nations have the authority to try non-citizens who have committed crimes against their citizens or in their territory, the United

States has never recognized the right of an international organization to do so absent consent or a UN Security Council mandate.[38]

'Absent *US* consent,' they might as well have simply said, because that is what the US veto on the Security Council amounts to. The same point about sovereignty, of course, could be made by every Serb on trial in The Hague, not to mention the government of every country that the US has invaded for the supposed good of its own people.

Or consider Henry Kissinger, who took a sudden interest in universal jurisdiction when the anti-impunity brigade took an interest in *him*. His biggest complaint about the ICC is that it would be 'an *indiscriminate* court' – as if he were talking about a cluster bomb and not the blindfolded lady of justice. He thought it 'amazing' that the ICTY could actually be used against the country that set it up:

> For example, can any leader of the United States or of another country be hauled before international tribunals established for other purposes? This is precisely what Amnesty International implied when, in the summer of 1999, it supported a 'complaint' by a group of European and Canadian law professors [*ahem!*] to Louise Arbour, then the prosecutor of the International Criminal Tribunal for the Former Yugoslavia (ICTY). The complaint alleged that crimes against humanity had been committed during the NATO air campaign in Kosovo. Arbour ordered an internal staff review, thereby implying that she did have jurisdiction if such violations could, in fact, be demonstrated.... Most Americans would be amazed to learn that the ICTY, created at U.S. behest in 1993 to deal with Balkan war criminals, had asserted a right to investigate U.S. political and military leaders for allegedly criminal conduct.[39]

The Clinton administration came to the same conclusion about the ICC, for different reasons – this was the administration, of course, that liked to claim sovereignty had gone out of style. Their defense of US immunity from prosecution was an *altruistic* one: the world needs an interventionist United States and how could Americans carry out their humanitarian mission if threatened by prosecution? Here's the way David Scheffer put it:

> The illogical consequence ... will be to limit severely those lawful, but highly controversial and inherently risky, interventions that the advocates of human rights and world peace so desperately seek from the United States and other military powers. There will be significant new legal and political risks in such interventions, which up to this point have been mostly shielded from politically motivated charges.[40]

'Other contributors to peacekeeping operations will be similarly exposed,' noted Scheffer.[41] But none of them were afraid to ratify the treaty. And those who ratified the treaty were obviously willing to accept a little less zealous policing by the US in the interests of a little more law abiding. American police forces made the same argument in the due process debates of the 1960s, and nobody besides the police themselves thought of leaving the decision entirely up to them.

But it was not merely the danger of *charges* that Scheffer was warning against, it was the danger of *'politically motivated* charges.' The opponents of the court repeated this like a mantra. Clinton, on signing the treaty: '[W]e have worked effectively to develop procedures that limit the likelihood of politicized prosecutions.'[42] Bush spokesman Marc Grossman, on unsigning it: 'We also believe that the ICC is built on a flawed foundation, and these flaws leave it open for exploitation and politically motivated prosecutions.'[43] What do they mean by 'politically motivated prosecutions'? Law Professor and Pentagon adviser Ruth Wedgewood translates this as: 'The worry of the United States is that in an unpopular conflict, there is a real chance that an adversary or critic will choose to misuse the ICC to make its point.'[44]

And here the US *is* onto something. In fact, the most popular recognized purpose of all criminal law, local or international, is 'educative.' Look in any textbook on criminal law and you'll find a passage similar to this one from the Canadian Law Reform Commission:

> We still need to do something about wrongful acts: to register our social disapproval, to publicly denounce them and to re-affirm the values violated by them ... Such violation requires public condemnation, and this is preeminently the job of criminal law. This ... is the moral, educative role of criminal law.[45]

In other words, the main official goal of criminal law is precisely to 'make a point.' The point is usually one about 'responsibility' – namely, who (or what) is to blame for this tragic event. The criminal law tries hard to blame the individual criminal and to let all the powerful social forces, with their powerful social actors, off the hook; to present what is really an unequal clash of interests as a neutral contest between right and wrong. The United States tried to make exactly this point when it set up the ICTY in the first place, in Scharf's words, 'as little more than a public relations device' to legitimize the use of force against Yugoslavia.[46] It was precisely to make the opposite point, to *de-legitimize* the use of force, that we brought charges against NATO. It's in America's interest to prevent the proliferation of anti-American point-making opportunities, as former Secretary of State Lawrence Eagleburger explained when he testified before Congress. The morally driven

Eagleburger, who just couldn't help denouncing Milosevic, peace process be damned, opposed the ICC as 'both illegitimate and illogical' on the grounds that an impartial international justice could cut both ways:

> I think we must continue to remind the rest of the world that we are going to continue to make our decisions on the basis of our best interests and that if, for example, we decide we want to act in a certain area, we should not have our GIs subject to the jurisdiction of this Court if somebody wants to make a point against the United States and its actions. And ... if we continue along this path, we will find ourselves being charged with war crimes by those who have no business in the business of charging war crimes because they themselves may well be war criminals or they will be neutrals who resent the power and influence of the United States and will be prepared to act against us if they can.[47]

In other words, why should a country as powerful as the United States submit itself to the democratic judgment of some impartial tribunal? Do you think they're crazy? What do they care what the rest of the world thinks when the only audience that counts is the captive one in US Network Newsland?[48] For Eagleburger, support for the ICTY then and opposition to the ICC now are perfectly consistent: both positions best serve US 'interests.' In accordance with this principle, the flexible people at the White House have now decided that individual states and not international institutions are the appropriate vehicle for international justice:

> We believe in justice and the rule of law. We believe those who commit the most serious crimes against humanity, the most serious crimes of concern to the international community should be punished. We believe that states, not international institutions are primarily responsible for ensuring justice in the international system.[49]

The Americans have ways

Friends of both the US and the ICC have been trying to cajole the US into joining the ICC treaty by arguing that it is indeed in America's 'interests' to do so, because this would increase American *influence* with the Court. Michael Scharf tellingly invokes the experience with the ICTY:

> ... the best way to protect the United States from the specter of indictment of US personnel by a potentially politicized tribunal is not to assume the role of hostile outsider, but rather to sign the Rome Treaty, to play an influential role in the selection of the Court's judges and prosecutor, and then provide U.S. personnel to work in the Office of the Prosecutor, as

the United states has so successfully done with respect to the Yugoslavia War Crimes Tribunal.[50]

This from a *defender* of the ICTY – an 'insider' who wrote the statute, no less. But never mind that, there is a crucial difference between the ICTY and the ICC that diminishes significantly the value to the US of joining. The United States has a formal veto over the individual judges and prosecutors of the ICTY through the Security Council's determining role over personnel.[51] That's how Madeleine Albright got to 'sniff out' Arbour and Del Ponte. The ICC is much more democratically structured. Judges and prosecutors are elected by the State parties, on a one-state-one-vote basis, with no vetoes.[52] As a party to the treaty the US would have one puny vote out of 89. It has far more influence staying outside the court than joining it, at least until it gets the terms it wants. The Americans know that the Court will ultimately come to see things their way:

> As the largest economy, a traditional strong supporter of ad hoc tribunals, and as the only member of the Security Council able to mount and sustain transcontinental military operations with the necessary air transport, technical means of intelligence and logistics, the US is highly relevant to the future efficacy of the ICC.[53]

In other words, to paraphrase Stalin, how many divisions does the ICC have? Britain is a state party, but the bravery it displayed in the bloody commando raids to affect arrests in NATO-controlled Bosnia, like its bravery in bombing Yugoslavia, Afghanistan and Iraq, would evaporate in no time if it didn't have the warm protective cover of America's real military might. Those who implore the US to join the Court in its own interests have to admit these people have a point, as Michael Scharf did in a footnote:

> Even if the United states does not ratify the Rome Treaty, however, the ICC's Assembly of State Parties, which selects the prosecutor and judges, is likely to be dominated not by states with animosity toward the United states, but by America's closest allies, the Western European 'like minded states' which have emerged as the staunchest supporters of the ICC.[54]

Scharf knew what he was talking about. When the ICC judges were elected in March 2003 this appeared in the *New York Times*:

> Supporters argue that the fact the 18 judges are largely from Western-style democracies that are American allies may also calm critics. 'With these judges it will be harder now to paint this court as an anti-American cabal and this will put the lie to the willful distortions Washington has put

out about this court,' said Richard Dicker, a director of Human Rights Watch in New York.[55]

Of the 18 judges (all of whom were nominated by their governments), five came from NATO countries (the UK, France, Germany, Italy and Canada) and three more from Bush's 'Coalition of the Willing' (Costa Rica, Latvia and South Korea).[56] In other words, almost half were nominated by states in formal military alliance with the United States. Of the others, one (South Africa) had already signed a section 98 agreement with the US, three (Brazil, Bolivia and Trinidad and Tobago) had the US as their main trading partner, and two (Mali and Ghana) were desperately poor. Countries like this are not anxious to upset the United States just to 'make a point.' One of Clinton's Bosnia lieutenants put it nicely when he criticized the Bush administration for unnecessarily muscling through the peacekeeper exemption at the Security Council: 'Above all, the administration could make it clear that there will be consequences if any country tries to use the court to make a point about U.S. foreign policy.'[57]

One indication of the orientation of the Court is the choice by the judges themselves of their first president, Philippe Kirsch of Canada. Kirsch had been with the project from the beginning, and his election was no surprise. He had had the leading role at the Rome conference as chairman of the Committee of the Whole. But Kirsch was at Rome as a representative of the Canadian Department of Foreign Affairs, where he had been a loyal employee for 25 years and had reached the highest levels.[58] From there he left for The Hague to represent Canada before the International Court of Justice. In fact, he was Canada's *lawyer* in the case brought by Yugoslavia against NATO in May 1999 for the illegal bombing campaign.[59] Kirsch was defending and advising the very people that we and Amnesty International believed should be charged with war crimes in the bombing that was the subject of our charges. In other words, *he was helping them commit the supreme international crime and a host of lesser ones as well* – helping them, of course, only to the extent that a lawyer helps anyone. So here is yet another NATO lawyer, just like William Fenrick who authored the ICTY Report absolving NATO. How likely is he to see things differently from the NATO countries, to judge them criminals for doing what they used to do when he was on their team?

And, speaking of NATO, it should be pointed out that, not only is the Court to be located in the The Hague – traditional for an international court – but it is for the foreseeable future going to be entirely dependent on the kindness of the Dutch government – a member not only of NATO, but also America's 'Coalition of the Willing.' The Dutch government has promised to build new premises for the ICC, but until they are ready sometime in 2007, the court will be located in temporary premises in the Dutch Ministry of Foreign Affairs – which would make for some interesting intra-NATO discussions if the American President ever thought of using the 'necessary means' Congress authorized in the 'Hague Invasion Act.'[60] Should we seriously expect charges against Holland or its NATO/Coalition-of-the-Willing partners to be pressed by its freeloading tenant?

Experience with the ICTY shows that the most important post of all is that of the prosecutor, the person with the responsibility for choosing who, among the *many* guilty parties in any war, will be charged with war crimes. In the ICC, the prosecutor has been given the 'discretion' (formally denied to the ICTY prosecutor) to refuse to initiate an investigation or prosecution, even when there is 'reasonable basis to believe that a crime within the jurisdiction of the Court has been or is being committed,' if it would not be 'in the interests of justice' to do so.[61] Added to this are some serious new 'confidence-building' barriers to prosecution. Before the prosecutor can even *initiate an investigation*, it has to be approved by at least two judges out of a three-judge panel with the same discretion as the prosecutor; and before a charge can be laid, at least two out of three judges have to certify its 'admissibility,' which includes a judgment as to whether it is being 'genuinely' investigated by local State authorities ('complementarity') and whether it is 'of sufficient gravity to justify further action by the Court.'[62]

Nevertheless, given the heat they had been taking from the United States over 'politically motivated prosecutions,' the state parties were so anxious to avoid even the impression of controversy that they delayed the nomination of a prosecutor until they had secured unanimous approval for a candidate. When the day came to elect the prosecutor, there was only one candidate and the vote was unanimous: 78 yays, no nays and no abstentions. What were they looking for in this candidate? Here are comments reported at the time of the installation of the judges:

> In private, a court official elaborated: 'He or she must be solid on substance, skillful at handling the press, and be politically savvy. It has to be someone who can instill confidence, especially among countries that are not yet members, not least the United States.' ... Some diplomats and legal experts here have speculated that an ideal prosecutor, in fact, would be an American ...[63]

He wasn't an American, but few outside the US could have been a safer bet for the US than Argentine Luis Moreno Ocampo, who just happened at the time to be a visiting professor at Harvard Law School. Though he had a history of prosecutorial activism, it was far in the past – against the

Argentine Junta Generals in the mid-1980s. By the time he took up his post with the ICC, Ocampo was the President of the Argentinian chapter of 'Transparency International,' an 'anti-corruption' organization operating in many countries on behalf of some of the world's largest businesses.[64] Its list of donors included the US Agency for International Development, which helped overthrow Milosevic, the World Bank, the MacArthur Foundation (US), George Soros' Open Society Institute (both major private funders of the ICTY), the Ford Foundation (US), and a number of private companies including some of America's biggest, like General Electric and Ford, top weapons manufacturers Boeing and Lockheed Martin, the oil giants Exxon Mobil and Texaco, and, rather embarrassingly for an anti-corruption group, corruption's new poster corporation, Enron Inc.[65] Ocampo's first interview a day after his appointment contained this ominous passage: 'We have to show how seriously we are working, and slowly people who today are reluctant will start to trust us.'[66] That would be the United States. Ocampo can draw on plenty of advice on how to do this:

> In addition, inviting the direct involvement of NATO and other military personnel in the ICC's own work (even from countries that are not yet state parties), through secondment, advisory councils, and rosters of expert witnesses, would help to build [American] confidence in the ICC.[67]

And, by the way, don't charge them or anyone involved in their military adventures with war crimes.

So this is a Court desperate for credibility, not with the world, but with the world's supreme international criminals. The Americans were very wise to stay out of this Court, because it is going to spend the rest of its life trying to convince them that they have nothing to fear from it. One can't possibly look to a Court like this for anything but a roundup of the usual suspects.

NUREMBERG

Hypocrisy, if 'vice's homage to virtue,' is also just a fancy word for lying. One claims to be acting for some principled reason, but in fact has something less noble in mind. So America's posture vis-à-vis the ICC also sheds retrospective light, if more were needed, on the political nature of the ad hoc tribunals: it can no longer be seriously maintained by anyone that they were sponsored by America as part of any new universal anti-impunity sentiment, as opposed to window-dressing for its old-fashioned, self-centered imperialism. This may well be bred in the bone of international criminal law, because even the venerated Nuremberg Tribunal was a product of similarly narrow political calculations. It actually represented the victory of a *soft line* on Nazism, which saw a powerful reconstructed capitalist Germany, led by the same social strata of conservatives that backed the Nazis, as an essential element of America's post-war geopolitical strategy, and especially its coming struggle with the Soviets. It was a loss for the *hard line*, which wanted Germany effectively plowed with salt and reduced to a state of permanent dependency.

At first the hard line had the upper hand. The Soviets had been pushing for it since Stalingrad, the turning point of the war, where they had taken mind-boggling losses to defeat the Germans. Roosevelt shared their view, though Churchill was opposed, as was evident at the first face-to-face meeting of the 'Big Three' leaders in Teheran in late November 1943. The differences over the matter of war crimes were displayed at a late-night dinner hosted by Stalin over multiple vodka toasts. Roosevelt's son Elliott, an accidental guest at the dinner, quotes Stalin's 'umpteenth toast' as follows:

> I propose a salute to the swiftest possible justice for all Germany's war criminals – justice before a firing squad. I drink to our unity in dispatching them as fast as we capture them, all of them, and there must be at least fifty thousand of them.

According to this account, Churchill objected vigorously:

> 'Any such attitude,' he cried, 'is wholly contrary to our British sense of justice! The British people will never stand for such mass murder. I take this opportunity to say that I feel most strongly that no one, Nazi or no, shall be summarily dealt with, before a firing squad, without proper legal trial, no matter what the known facts and proven evidence against him!'

At this point, President Roosevelt intervened and suggested a 'compromise': 'perhaps we could say that, instead of summarily executing fifty thousand war criminals, we should settle on a smaller number. Shall we say forty-nine thousand five hundred?'[68] Churchill, who more or less corroborates the account, then bolted from the table and only returned when Stalin and Molotov personally chased after him to tell him all was in jest.[69]

But, as Churchill suspected, Stalin was not jesting, and Roosevelt appeared indeed to be much closer to Stalin than to Churchill on this issue. Within his own government, the Secretary of the Treasury, Henry Morgenthau Jr., was proposing a similar plan that included 'the complete demilitarization and deindustrialization of Germany and the severe punishment of all Germans involved in perpetrating war crimes.'[70] Morgenthau proposed that a list be drawn up of Nazis who would upon apprehension and identification be 'put to death forthwith by firing squads made up by soldiers of the United Nations.'[71] He also advocated military commissions to try persons for killing civilians as hostages or on grounds of nationality, race, color, creed or political conviction. The normal punishment would be death, unless there were exceptional extenuating circumstances. To this end, Morgenthau called for the detention of all SS members and all high officials of the police, SA or other security organizations, high government and Nazi officials, and all leading public figures closely identified with Nazism.[72] The soft line on Germany was represented by Secretary of War Henry Stimson, who attributed Morgenthau's plan of reducing Germany to 'a subsistence level' and a 'condition of servitude' to Morgenthau's 'Semitic grievances.'[73] Stimson was in favor of due process trials, with 'dignified' proceedings that did not deprive Germans 'of the hope of a future respected German community.'[74] The soft-liners were 'ardent anti-Communists [who] favored a softer policy towards Germany owing to their distrust of the Soviet Union.' They feared that 'destruction of Germany's economy would make that country dependent on Russia. Such an arrangement might lead to Soviet dominance over all of Europe.'[75]

Roosevelt at first sided with the hard-liners.[76] On Morgenthau's urging, Roosevelt wrote harshly to Stimson in August 1944:

Too many people here and in England hold to the view that the German people as a whole are not responsible for what has taken place – that only a few Nazi leaders are responsible. That unfortunately is not based in fact. The German people as a whole must have it driven home to them that the whole nation has been engaged in a lawless conspiracy against the decencies of modern civilization.[77]

But an unfavorable press gave Roosevelt cold feet, and by the time of his death he had come around to 'Stimson's scheme to boost Allied, and ultimately American, prestige by means of war crimes trials.'[78] The Truman administration, which had set its sights on its new Soviet adversary, found limited trials and the Stimson plan far more to its liking: 'American occupation authorities had a variety of goals. In addition to fulfilling official policy directives calling for denazification, decartelization, demilitarization and democratization, U.S. officials also had numerous unstated, but at times equally significant objectives ranging from reviving the German and European economies to reducing the costs of the occupation for the American taxpayer to containing communism.'[79] Prosecutor Telford Taylor, in a memo of June 1945, argued that the idea of the trials was above all 'to make a point,' or several: 'To give meaning to the war against Germany. To validate the casualties we have suffered and the destruction and casualties we have caused.' These 'larger objectives' required procedures 'which will help make the war meaningful and valid' primarily 'for the people of the allied

Nations.'[80] For his part, Stalin was also attracted to the propaganda value of the trials and decided to go along with what had become inevitable.[81]

The execution of even 50,000 top Nazis and regime supporters would not have expiated German guilt for the years of torture and murder inflicted on millions of defenseless victims, but the victory of the soft line was an enduring outrage against their memory. Only 22 political and military leaders were tried before the International Military Tribunal, and only 11 of those were executed. The US, British and French allies set up various tribunals, executed about 500 and sentenced about 1,000 to life or lesser terms. As the Cold War settled in, the sentences became lighter, and from 1949 a program of clemency was instituted to re-integrate the new German state into the western defense system. By the early 1950s nearly everybody not sentenced to death was free, and nobody was in prison when the decade ended. In his careful study of the whole process, Arieh Kochavi concludes that 'geopolitical interests dominated the western Allies' treatment of war criminals' and that the punishments 'bore no relation to the horrible crimes that had been perpetrated.'[82] So, despite the romanticism and, indeed the criticism ('victor's justice'), the Nuremberg trials were a 1 percent solution – effectively a way of *letting Nazis off*, not of punishing them.

TOKYO

A pillar of the Truman administration's anti-Communism was the atomic bomb, and modern scholarship tends to take the view that dropping it on Hiroshima and Nagasaki had nothing to do with ending the war and everything to do with intimidating the Soviets.[83] One of those who subscribed to this position was the Dutch jurist B. V. A. Röling, a member of the International Military Tribunal for the Far East, which tried 28 Japanese political and military leaders in Tokyo as war criminals and executed seven. In a 1977 interview with future ICTY president Antonio Cassese, Röling said: '[I]t appears from the history of Japan's capitulation that the death of millions of Americans and Japanese could have been prevented without the atomic bombs, just by accepting the Japanese condition: the maintenance of the imperial system.'[84] Röling believed the Americans had used the bomb because so much had been invested in it and 'to impress the Soviets with their new power.'[85] According to Röling, the trial in Japan was aimed at displacing the blame for Pearl Harbor, which many attributed at the time to American negligence or even connivance, onto the Japanese, 'to assert that they had acted in so villainous and scandalous a way that honourable Americans could not possibly have expected the attack.'[86] The hypocrisy of the Americans in putting the Japanese on trial, after incinerating 200,000 civilians 'to make a point' to the Soviets, was well understood at the time. Röling reports that he 'sometimes had contacts with Japanese students.'

> The first thing they always asked was: 'Are you morally entitled to sit in judgement over the leaders of Japan when the allies have burned down all of its cities with sometimes, as in Tokyo, in one night, 100,000 deaths and [culminating in] the destruction of Hiroshima and Nagasaki?' ... I am strongly convinced that these bombings were war crimes ... It was terror warfare ...[87]

Unlike the Nuremberg Tribunal, the Tokyo Tribunal had judges from eleven different countries, and there were even two dissenting judgments, though their publication was suppressed at the time. Röling only partially dissented, but there was a full dissent from the Indian judge Radhabinod B. Pal running 1,235 pages in length.[88] It was mostly a learned attempt to demonstrate, contrary to the thesis adopted by both the Nuremberg and Tokyo judgments, that 'aggressive war' was *not* already a crime by the time of the war, and thus that the trials *did* violate the principle against *ex post facto* law. But what clearly animated Judge Pal, and what his dissent has come to stand for, was an opposition to 'victor's justice':

> 'It does not quite comply with the idea of international justice that only the vanquished states are obliged to surrender their own subjects to the jurisdiction of an international tribunal for the punishment of war crimes.' ... It has been said that a victor can dispense to the vanquished everything from mercy to vindictiveness; but one thing the victor cannot give to the vanquished is justice.[89]

Judge Pal could not 'perceive much difference' between the way the criminally 'atrocious methods' of World War I had been justified 'and what is being proclaimed after the Second World War in justification of these inhuman blasts' at Hiroshima and Nagasaki.[90] His conclusion: 'When the conduct of the nations is taken into account the law will perhaps be found to be *that only a lost war is a crime.*'[91]

THE PINOCHET CASE

The international criminal justice movement has always tried to overcome the stigma of victor's justice while making sure not to tamper with its reality. One example of this is the case of former Chilean dictator Augusto Pinochet, whose arrest on an international warrant in London in October 1998 appeared to be a stunning success for the movement, fresh from its summer accomplishments in Rome. Here, finally, was an *un*usual suspect:

a US-installed dictator, no less, who had just retired after 25 years as the darling of the international Right. The arrest was widely hailed as 'a victory for the rule of law.'[92]

Here we have the 82-year-old Chilean ex-dictator, in quasi-retirement, his immunity from punishment apparently guaranteed by various provisions of the constitution he had written himself, but most importantly by the fact that he had appointed the entire senior judiciary.[93] He decides to visit Britain for back surgery in September 1998, having done so twice without incident in the previous four years. At the very moment he is visiting Britain, two Spanish judges are investigating him in connection with the torture and disappearance of Spanish and non-Spanish citizens – only a few of the 3,000 murdered and tens of thousands tortured in Chile during his regime. The Spanish judges get word of Pinochet's presence in Britain and issue an international warrant for his arrest on murder and torture charges, which British police duly execute according to the British extradition treaty with Spain.[94]

Pinochet, however, has powerful supporters in England, including former Prime Minister Margaret Thatcher, who put together a defense team and throw up every conceivable legal obstacle to his extradition. Even though Pinochet is no longer Head of State (having been voted out by the first election he allowed to be held after 16 years of military rule), and is on a purely private visit, his 'diplomatic immunity' is quickly litigated all the way to the House of Lords. They rule him extraditable in a cliff-hanger 3–2 decision, broadcast live around the world in November 1998.[95] But, for the first time in the history of the Lords, the decision is wiped out because one of the judges is an unpaid director of a charity branch of Amnesty International, an intervenor in the case.[96] You'd think this would have been canceled out by the fact that *all* of the judges had been appointed by the Tory government of John Major, on such friendly terms with Pinochet that he couldn't be arrested on his two previous visits.[97] On 24 March 1999, a new panel of seven Law Lords rules by a 6:1 majority that Pinochet must indeed face extradition to Spain.[98] This, of course, is the very day that NATO, with major UK participation, commences the bombing of Yugoslavia. However, the Law Lords also rule that Pinochet is immune from prosecution for crimes committed before 1988 (15 years into the dictatorship and long after its most violent period). Okay, but he still has to go to Spain and, what with the new charges the Spanish magistrates send as a consequence of the ruling, the torture and kidnapping counts would easily suffice to make him spend his remaining years behind bars. And if that's not enough, magistrates from Belgium, France and Switzerland get in on the act as well, with their own accounts to settle. After more legal challenges and medical exams, Pinochet's extradition hearing finally takes place and he is committed for extradition on 35 charges on 8 October 1999.

Within a week, the anti-impunity paladins of the UK government raise an entirely new obstacle to justice for Pinochet, an alleged 'recent and significant deterioration in Senator Pinochet's health.'[99] Home Secretary Jack Straw commissions a medical examination, which, according to Straw, 'indicated that Senator Pinochet was unfit to stand trial and that no significant improvement could be expected.'[100] Ordered by a court to disclose the medical report, in strict confidence, to Spain, Belgium, France and Switzerland, Straw gives them a week to reply, and then, after considering 'all this material,' declares himself 'satisfied that the conclusion of the original report was correct.'[101] On 3 March 2000, Pinochet is set free and put on a plane back to Chile.

In fact, the leaked medical report is immediately demolished by experts in geriatrics as 'skimpy and unconvincing.'[102] Pinochet demonstrates to the whole world the bogus nature of his medical excuse only minutes after setting foot, or rather wheelchair, on Chilean soil to a hero's welcome, complete with military band, when this 'diminished little man' who 'London pardoned for human pity' suddenly 'stretched to full size, the dull-witted smile dissolved into a vigilant expression, and ... once again on his feet, saluted the first row of three hundred big shots who were waiting on the runway ... with a lucidity that appeared to belie the medical–political hypocrisy of liberating him for lapses in memory.'[103]

In Chile it takes little time for investigating magistrate Juan Guzman to conclude that Pinochet is, in fact, perfectly fit to stand trial, but his attempts to put Pinochet on trial, or even under house arrest, are blocked by higher courts. In March of 2001 an appeals court grants what amounts to a complete acquittal, without benefit of any trial, on all the charges of murder in the 'Caravan of Death' case – the murder of 75 Leftists in the aftermath of the 1973 coup that brought Pinochet to power – despite the fact that 'former army generals have repeatedly testified that murders committed in their areas of jurisdiction were carried out on the direct orders of General Pinochet.'[104] In July 2002 the farce comes to an end when the case is definitively stopped by the Chilean Supreme Court, in a 4–1 decision, on the grounds of Pinochet's unfitness to stand trial.[105]

So the British Home Secretary was quite right when he said in his official statement letting Pinochet go back to Chile that 'I am all too aware that the practical consequence of refusing to extradite Senator Pinochet to Spain is that he will probably not be tried anywhere.' That he simultaneously expressed confidence in the Spanish justice system – 'their principles for determining the fitness of an accused to stand trial [are] similar to ours'

– amounted to a clumsy admission that he expected a miscarriage of justice to occur in Chile – otherwise why would it make any difference to the outcome whether Pinochet was sent to Spain or to Chile? And no doubt he was telling the truth when he admitted that he was acting against public opinion, citing 70,000 letters and emails from all over the world: 'almost all have urged me to allow the extradition proceedings to take their course, so that the allegations made against Senator Pinochet could be tried.' On the other hand, few believed his claim that '[a]ll the decisions which I have taken have been mine alone, and have not been decisions of her majesty's government,' much less that he acted for the stated compassionate grounds of a sudden health deterioration. On the contrary, British newspapers immediately denounced what turned out to be a deal reached many months earlier between the governments of Blair, Aznar of Spain, and Frei of Chile.[106] At crucial moments the Spanish judiciary had been betrayed by the Aznar government, so eager a participant in America's wars from Kosovo to Iraq. The government of Bill Clinton was also said to have exerted 'considerable pressure to persuade Britain to release Pinochet.'[107] Nor did it escape attention that the deal had been put together and approved by the anti-impunity gang, fresh from their Kosovo crusade and still howling for the arrest of Milosevic. Maurizio Matteuzzi of Rome's *Il Manifesto* wrote that, if the governments concerned had

> a minimum of decency, they would be ashamed of themselves. And with them also other champions of the blah-blah-blah about human rights ... like Clinton (implacable with Castro, Saddam, and Milosevic, but so soft with 'our own son of a bitch' from Chile) and his Mrs. Albright.

Matteuzzi called the decision the 'triumph of the worst mixture of realpolitik and business.'[108] In fact Madrid had staked much of the country's economic growth on commercial ventures in Latin America – Chile above all – and was not anxious to champion an initiative that smacked of neo-colonialism.[109]

So we have a purely self-interested decision taken by hypocrites of the first rank. This did not prevent these very same hypocrites and the human rights professionals from going on ad nauseam about the 'milestone' and the 'landmark' and the 'legacy' and the 'precedent.' Even as he announced he was guaranteeing Pinochet's impunity, Jack Straw pronounced the House of Lords decision 'a landmark judgment in human rights law, whose impact has been felt far beyond our shores. It will be a permanent legacy of the Pinochet case.'[110] 'Regardless Of Outcome, Pinochet Case Sets Precedent,' read one *Washington Post* headline over an article quoting the always quotable Richard Dicker of Human Rights Watch:

The legal point has been made: There is no immunity for crimes against humanity and torture committed by a former head of state ... What happens now has no bearing on the legal significance, or the practical significance, or the symbolic significance of the case.[111]

Another 'human rights activist' quoted in the *Post* article actually had the vacuity to 'pair' Pinochet with Milosevic:

Speaking of the Milosevic and Pinochet cases, and the launching of US-led air strikes against Yugoslavia on humanitarian grounds last spring, Mr. Pisar said the doctrine had been progressing relentlessly 'to a point where the very underpinnings of the sovereign state have given way to human rights. That progress has been steady, and it will continue regardless of what happens to Pinochet.'

But what does pairing these two cases really show? Milosevic, the enemy of the United States and the United Kingdom, winds up at The Hague, extradited by the government in violation of the Yugoslav Constitution and Criminal Code, and despite a decision of Yugoslavia's highest court to the contrary. Pinochet, the friend of the United States and the United Kingdom, winds up free, despite the fact that England's highest court approved his extradition, because the government blocked it. This is the same UK government that would not stop at killing Bosnian Serbs in order to arrest them, or at beggaring Yugoslavia with sanctions until it handed over Milosevic. And you didn't hear anyone say, 'It doesn't matter what happens to Milosevic so long as the precedent is established.' The precedent established by Pinochet was, in fact: commit your war crimes on the right side and your impunity is guaranteed, whatever the law says; commit them on the wrong side and, whatever the law says, you're in for it.

Even after the Chilean courts had let the old man off, the human rights groups were still inexplicably celebrating the 'precedent.' Human Rights Watch, while lamenting the injustice to his victims, nevertheless claimed his case was 'a permanent advance in the cause of human rights' marking 'the beginning of the end of impunity for the worst state crimes' because it 'helped to establish the principle that grave human rights crimes are subject to "universal jurisdiction" and can be prosecuted anywhere in the world' without immunity even for former heads of state.[112] But if you read the House of Lords decision you will find that it's more of a precedent in *favor* of impunity than against it, and this *despite* the Nuremberg precedent. For one thing, the Lords decided that former heads of state had immunity for their crimes unless their states had relinquished it by treaty. That's why the only crimes for which Pinochet could be extradited were those of torture committed from late 1988, because that's the date by which Spain and Chile and the United Kingdom had all ratified the *Convention Against Torture*. Pinochet's immunity was complete for crimes committed before that date, and for any crimes that fell outside the treaty. In a willful misreading of the Nuremberg precedent, the Law Lords held that the Military Tribunal's decision to the contrary was based not on customary international law, but on the explicit removal of immunity in Article 7 of the Nuremberg Charter.[113] In fact, the Nuremberg judges had characterized their Charter as being just a restatement of customary international law – in other words, applicable whether or not it was contained in the Charter or in any treaty. This was precisely to avoid the claim of *ex post facto* law:

> The Charter is not an arbitrary exercise of power on the part of the victorious nations, but, in the view of the Tribunal, as will be shown, it is the expression of international law existing at the time of its creation.[114]

And they explicitly held:

> The principle of international law, which under certain circumstances, protects the representatives of a state, cannot be applied to acts which are condemned as criminal by international law.[115]

This became Principle III of the International Law Commission's 'Principles of International Law recognized in the Charter of the Nürnberg Tribunal and in the Judgement of the Tribunal.'[116]

The Lords' retreat from Nuremberg was based on a complete lack of precedent. Almost all the cases cited were not criminal cases at all, but rather *civil* cases, where the issue was the very different one of whether a state *as well*, and not *solely* the official who perpetrated the act, should be liable in damages.[117] The only criminal case that could be found on point was the case of former Philippine president Ferdinand Marcos and his wife Imelda (she of the 3,000 pairs of shoes), charged in the United States with theft of public property while in office. Faced with a request for assistance from Swiss authorities, the Federal Tribunal of Switzerland had to decide whether the Marcos's had immunity under international law. The Court in fact *denied* the Marcos's their immunity because it had been waived by the Philippines. However, it upheld it in theory on an unconvincing analogy from *diplomatic* immunity, a very different matter. The diplomat is forced for practical reasons to be present in the foreign territory. Why should that exempt a former head of state or any other official from the jurisdiction of a country where they are not present for any official reason, or for crimes committed when they were not officially engaged in any foreign country?[118] Besides, the Marcos case was about garden-variety property crime – the farthest thing from the grave international crimes for which Nuremberg had declared there was no immunity.[119]

At several points in the Pinochet judgment, the Lords pointed to the ICC as an example of an express exclusion of state immunity, and a real effect of the decision was to undermine national jurisdiction in favor of the ICC.[120] In fact, mainstream lawyers have been very suspicious of claims to national jurisdiction over international crimes, considering them 'extravagant' and certainly inferior to the ICC in their protection of the rights of accused international criminals 'who will suffer the main hardship from this new exotic jurisdiction.'[121] Indeed. This is another argument by US supporters of the ICC:

> Enforcement of international criminal law by different states is ad hoc and uneven at best, determined through a system of national courts whose motives we cannot always trust and whose procedures we do not control.... In contrast, the Treaty of Rome provides the United States with an opportunity to shape a fair and consistent international court system that will honor American concerns.[122]

That didn't prevent the many ignorant claims that Pinochet would have had a harder time escaping justice had the ICC been in force. For instance, Rome conference president Giovanni Conso argued that, had the ICC 'already been operational during Pinochet's regime ... perhaps Chile's ordeal would never have assumed such tragic proportions.'[123] But since Pinochet's crimes were all committed on Chilean soil, it would only have applied had Chile ratified the treaty, and only to crimes committed *after ratification*.[124] We have to imagine a regime like Pinochet's ratifying the treaty – or if it had already ratified, cooperating – when the statute itself does not even provide any sanctions for non-cooperation.[125] As of September 2003, Chile had *still* not ratified the treaty. Furthermore, the principle of 'complementarity' would have provided very good arguments for anyone who wanted to leave the whole thing up to Chile. Finally, Article 98 of the Rome Statute would have given Britain an even better excuse to send Pinochet home instead of to The Hague, not only because it allowed for 'impunity agreements,' but also because it explicitly incorporated the immunity applied by the House of Lords.[126] So the Pinochet decision legitimated the subordination of unpredictable national jurisdictions to the discipline of the ICC, and thus decidedly improved chances of impunity. Some anti-interventionists approved of Pinochet being sent home to be tried by a local court.[127] But they got the precedent wrong, too. First, because the US-installed dictator would never be tried – partly because he had been able, with the help of some supreme criminals, to transform Chile in his own image. Second, because the whole point of holding him as long as he was held was to legitimate the seminal military 'humanitarian intervention' that was Kosovo. When Pinochet was arrested, NATO had for several months been planning an attack whose justification was essentially that Milosevic was an international criminal; Pinochet was held throughout the war as an example of the impartiality of the movement that NATO was leading; and he was released when the war had been over for almost a year. The real Pinochet precedent is that international criminal law, for all its dramatic pronouncements and precedents, will always know how to distinguish between useful and troublesome prosecutions, between friend and foe, between 'our' war criminals and theirs.

BELGIUM

Another example of the way the ICC has operated to prevent 'extravagant' exercises of jurisdiction from getting out of hand is the sad story of Belgium's universal jurisdiction law. Following the setting up of the ICTY Tribunal in 1993, Belgium enacted its own war crimes law covering grave violations of the Geneva Conventions of 1949 and Protocols 1 and 2 of 1977. These crimes became punishable in Belgium wherever they had been committed.[128] In February 1999, with NATO priming for its Kosovo war, Belgium – not only a NATO country but the home of NATO headquarters – expanded the scope of the law to include genocide and crimes against humanity, and above all to expressly remove official immunity: 'The immunity attached to the official quality of a person does not prevent the application of this law.'[129] This was Belgium's particular contribution to the propaganda campaign against Milosevic, and was published the day before the NATO bombing of Yugoslavia commenced. But the law was not used against Milosevic. In fact, under it, high-profile investigations would be opened up into the criminal activities of such distinctly unusual suspects as Ariel Sharon, George Bush (Sr.), Colin Powell and General Tommy Franks (the American commander of the 2003 war against Iraq). Not that any of these men would ever actually be charged under the law, much less convicted. The honor of the only trials, convictions and sentences went to some highly *usual* suspects: four Rwandan Hutus (two Catholic nuns, a university professor and a businessman) found to be complicit in the same Rwandan massacres of 1994 for which the ICTR had been prosecuting Hutus since 1995. The accused, who had fled to Belgium in 1994, were sentenced to terms of imprisonment ranging from twelve to 20 years in June 2001. The papers were full of stories of the 'Blood Sisters.' Michael Ignatieff, never one to miss an opportunity to hammer a usual suspect, outdid himself commenting for the *New York Times* on a photo of the nuns on trial as 'a study in the unimaginable disguises of evil':

> What mixture of terror and hatred led these nuns to betray the promise of their faith? The Rwandan massacres left in their wake hundreds of disturbing questions like that one – How does mass violence suddenly erupt? Are we all capable of murdering our neighbours? Where does evil come from?[130]

But others weren't so puzzled. They put these events, and these trials of Africans by European courts, right in their context of 100 years of colonial rule, 80 of them by these same Belgians who now presumed to try their colonial subjects for crimes that they did plenty to encourage and nothing to prevent. In the courtroom, Hutus and Tutsis seemed agreed on the nature of the proceedings: 'Quite frankly, this is a totally political process,' said a Hutu observer. 'What about the French and the Belgians?' asked a Tutsi. 'They are the ones who brought tribalism between the Hutus and the Tutsis. They brought colonialism. They have to put themselves on trial.'[131]

In Belgium the trial was seen as serving purely Belgian interests – an attempt to expiate Belgian guilt for pulling out of the peacekeeping force in the midst of the Rwandan massacres, while at the same time bolstering the reputation of Belgium's scandal-ridden justice system: 'The government wants to improve the country's image and restore faith in its institutions, no doubt about it,' according to a lawyer for relatives of the victims in the trial.[132] Hence the rapid about-face when attempts were made to use the process on unusual suspects. The publicity given to the cases of the Hutus gave some Palestinians living in Belgium the idea of bringing charges against Israeli Prime Minister Ariel Sharon for his part in the 1982 massacre at the Sabra and Shatila refugee camps in Lebanon. The complainants were survivors of the massacre. In July 2001 Sharon had to cancel a trip to Belgium because a Belgian magistrate had opened a criminal investigation against him. In retaliation for the charges, Israelis also filed a complaint in Belgium against Yasser Arafat. Other complaints from the political Right followed against Fidel Castro and Saddam Hussein. Israel also began to threaten Belgium with diplomatic consequences. The Attorney General of Belgium referred the case to the appeals court for a preliminary judgment. Before it could be delivered, however, the International Court of Justice at The Hague – not the ICTY, not the ICC, but the long-established ICJ – gave Ariel Sharon a Valentine's Day present by striking another blow against 'extravagant jurisdiction.' The case was about the Belgian law, but it concerned a rather more usual suspect, charged with the usual crime of inciting hatred against the Tutsis. The accused was Abdulaye Yerodia

Ndombasi, Congolese Foreign Minister.[133] The Congo objected that the charge violated their sovereign immunity, and the ICJ agreed because the warrant had been issued while the accused was still Foreign Minister. The ICJ judges followed the *Pinochet* approach of extending diplomatic immunity by analogy to a non-analogous context and, more importantly, confining the Nuremberg precedent to cases where the express terms of a treaty or other binding instrument had removed immunity – contrary, as we've seen, to the way the Nuremberg Tribunal and the United Nations General Assembly saw things.[134] After giving an expansive reading to immunity (punishment could only be imposed 'in respect of acts committed during that period of office *in a private capacity*'), the ICJ judges also reminded everyone that incumbent and former ministers could be subject to criminal proceedings before 'certain international criminal courts' such as the ICTY, the ICTR and the ICC.[135]

In other words, the case was another vote against 'extravagant' jurisdiction in favor of the domesticated and predictable ICC. This was the beginning of the end for the Belgian law. In February 2003 the Belgian Supreme Court ruled that no proceedings could be taken against Sharon until he left office. The Israelis were still angry, but what counted more was American anger at complaints by Iraqi Belgians laid in March 2003, with bombs again falling on Baghdad, against Bush Sr., Powell and Cheney for 403 lives' worth of collateral damage in the First Gulf War.[136] The Americans were already fed up with Belgium for not joining the war against Iraq and even opposing NATO involvement. Now they declared that if Belgium wanted to keep its status as an international center, let alone the headquarters of NATO, it would simply have to change its law.[137] This was the signal for the Belgian Parliament, in mid-war, to pass an amendment to the war crimes law that not only tempered it to the (new) immunities declared by the ICJ, but, more importantly, took the decision to investigate foreign war crimes out of the hands of the relatively independent Belgian judiciary, and put it firmly into the hands of the government.[138] Proceedings could now only be commenced on the application of the federal prosecutor, who was directed to send the case to an international court, or the place where the crime took place, or where the accused could be found, whenever it was 'in the interests of the good administration of justice and respect for Belgium's international obligations' to do so. So when, during the Iraq war of 2003, some Iraqis announced they would seek charges against General Tommy Franks in Belgium for war crimes during 'Operation Iraqi Freedom,' the response was swift: within a week the Belgian government decided to pass the case on to American prosecutors, in accordance with the law.[139] The domestication of the Belgian law brought it in line with the less-celebrated

Canadian law enacted in 2000, on the heels of my country's ratification of the Rome Statute. Though the Canadian law makes every crime in the Rome Statute a crime punishable in Canada, proceedings cannot be commenced without 'the personal consent in writing of the Attorney General of Canada or Deputy Attorney general of Canada' – in other words, the government of Canada.[140] No wonder nobody has heard of this law.

But the changes to the Belgian law still weren't good enough for the Americans, because they couldn't stop the embarrassing charges from being filed in the first place. The law's fate was sealed when more charges were filed against Bush Jr. and Rumsfeld himself, for war crimes during 'Operation Iraqi Freedom.' America put its foot down, right on $352 million that had been earmarked for the renovation of NATO headquarters in Brussels, and threatened a diplomatic boycott of the country.[141] They would accept only the complete repeal of the law, and the Belgian government rushed to oblige with an 'extraordinary session' of the Belgian House of Representatives on 22 July 2003.[142]

JUSTICE

The history of international criminal law seems to vindicate Judge Pal's skepticism about 'victor's justice.' With a track record like this, it would be *unscientific* to expect anything better from this movement in the future. The only rational assumptions are that international criminal law will be firmly subordinated to power, that impunity will be a perk of economic and military hegemony, and that the usual suspects will continue to be rounded up while America gets away with murder.

In *Casablanca*, the usual suspects were innocent, as was the real-life Alfred Dreyfus (see below). That's not necessarily the case with modern international criminal law. The fact that the Americans and their allies have been the supreme criminals in Yugoslavia, Afghanistan and Iraq does not mean their enemies are innocent. The fact that the Americans and the Europeans were directly and indirectly complicit in the atrocities of Rwanda, and the fact that their Tutsi clients in the RPF committed them too, does not mean that the Hutu government and militias did not. On the other hand, the fact that these usual suspects are pronounced guilty by the kind of kangaroo courts that the victors have established doesn't mean they're guilty either; the antics at the Milosevic trial should suffice to raise doubts about that. And it's not only the big-fish trials that suffer from these judicial deficits. They seem to be pervasive, as even an enthusiast like Michael Scharf reveals in his study of the ICTY's first case.[143] A Canadian trial lawyer who acts on behalf of Hutus charged by the Rwanda Tribunal describes his experience as one of a *systematic* miscarriage of justice, which he attributes to the impossible double harness of international criminal trials: 'History and justice cannot be written at the same time, with the same pen, without distorting both.'[144]

Is systematic miscarriage of justice against accused persons the destiny of international criminal law? Perhaps not. The ICC, unlike the ICTY, has not been handcrafted for the specific task of legitimating aggressive war. Though it will always have its public relations radar locked on Washington, there is a far bigger world constituency to satisfy, and this may require really fair trials for accused persons. Time will tell. However, the ICC does have a built-in systematic miscarriage of justice against *victims*, because it leaves a great swath of international crime untouched – namely, supreme crimes and crimes of the supreme powers.

Now, this would seem to pose a big problem for a movement that prides itself on 'universal justice' and 'anti-impunity.' The official guide to the Rome Statute quotes Kofi Annan on the significance of an International Criminal Court:

> In the prospect of an international criminal court lies the promise of universal justice. That is the simple and soaring hope of this vision ... our struggle to ensure that no ruler, no State, no junta and no army anywhere can abuse human rights with impunity. Only then will the innocents of distant wars and conflicts know that they, too, may sleep under the cover of justice; that they, too, have rights, and that those who violate those rights will be punished.[145]

'*Universal* justice'; '*no* state'; '*no* army.' But what if there is a huge, gaping exception for the victims of supreme crimes committed by supreme criminals? What if there is *selective* impunity? One of the very arguments for the ICC was that the ad hoc tribunals were exercises in 'selective justice.' Louise Arbour made this point in the midst of the Kosovo war:

> Irrationally selective prosecutions undermine the perception of justice as fair and even-handed, and therefore serve as the basis for defiance and contempt. The ad hoc nature of the existing Tribunals is indeed a severe fault line in the aspirations of a universally applicable system of criminal accountability. There is no answer to the complaint of those who have been called to account for their actions that others, even more culpable, were never subjected to scrutiny. Why Yugoslavia? Why Rwanda? Why the 1990s? Why only 1994?[146]

Naturally, Arbour was only talking about 'irrationally' selective prosecutions, and she hastened to point out that this didn't affect the validity of the selective punishment of usual suspects:

> Not that the impunity of some makes others less culpable, but it makes it less just to single them out. It therefore runs the risk of giving credence to their claim of victimisation, and even if it does not cast doubt on the legitimacy of their punishment, it taints the process that turns a blind eye to the culpability of others.[147]

To practitioners of the system like Arbour, the problem of selective justice is essentially a matter of public relations. It runs the risk of *giving credence* to these (false) claims of victimization. It isn't really *un*just, only *'less just.'* Still just, in other words. Arbour herself personified selective justice. At the moment she gave this speech, she was putting the finishing touches to the Milosevic indictment, with her NATO patrons committing the supreme crime and a bunch of lesser ones within her very jurisdiction. In Rwanda she confessed that she had to ignore RPF crimes, or the RPF government would shut her down. Supporters of international criminal law want to argue in the face of facts like these that 'half a loaf is better than none.' It would be much better, of course – it would especially *look* better – if they could get all the culprits; but since that is not going to happen, what harm is there in getting some of them?

Now if you study the theory of justice you will find no tolerance for selective justice. That's because justice is based in equality, and it is a serious violation of equality to voluntarily leave some wrongdoers unpunished. It's unjust to their victims and a blow to the whole idea. ICTY insiders Morris and Scharf like this quote from *Gulag Archipelago*, by Alexander Solzhenitsyn (an opponent of the Kosovo war): 'When we neither punish nor reproach evildoers, we are not simply protecting their trivial old age, we are thereby ripping the foundations of justice from beneath new generations.'[148] The French writer Anatole France famously condemned the law's 'majestic equality' for forbidding 'the rich as well as the poor to sleep under bridges, to beg in the streets, and to steal bread.'[149] No doubt he'd lay the same charge against a law that, in its majestic equality, forbade the Americans as well as the Iraqis to use fake surrenders as a war tactic, but left out using overwhelming firepower to conquer a country illegally and with impunity from conventional means of defense. Anatole France adhered to the famous *J'accuse!* manifesto of Emile Zola, provoked by the Dreyfus Affair of the 1890s. Captain Alfred Dreyfus was a Jewish officer in the French army convicted of treason on forged evidence, the truth of his innocence having been covered up by an anti-Semitic military hierarchy. As enduring as the memory of Dreyfus himself was that of the world-famous article on the affair by the novelist Zola, entitled *J'accuse!* – an open letter to the President of the Republic published in 1898. *J'accuse!* is often meant nowadays to evoke an official frame-up where the accusers are really the guilty ones, and in fact one Canadian Serb activist used it as a kind of masthead for her anti-NATO emails during the Kosovo war, arguing that NATO, the real criminal, was framing Serbia. But what sparked Zola's piece was not the conviction of Dreyfus, but the subsequent corrupt acquittal of the real culprit by a special tribunal:

> A military tribunal comes, on orders, to dare to acquit Esterhazy, a supreme affront to all truth, to all justice ... There you have, Mr. President, the Esterhazy affair: a guilty man who they work to acquit. We've been watching this pretty piece of work for almost two months ... a villainous inquest where rogues emerge transfigured and honest people soiled ... The first military tribunal might have acted unwittingly, the second is perforce criminal ... I accuse, finally, the first military tribunal of having violated the law, convicting an accused on secret evidence, and I accuse the second military tribunal of having covered up this illegality, on orders, committing, in its turn, the juristic crime of knowingly acquitting a guilty person.[150]

The classical justice theorist Immanuel Kant considered it equally unjust to leave wrongdoers unpunished as to punish the innocent. For Kant, punishment was a 'categorical imperative' (a whether-you-like-it-or-not thing),

> and woe to him who rummages around in the winding paths of a theory of happiness looking for some advantage to be gained by releasing the criminal from punishment or by reducing the amount of it ... Even if a civil society were to dissolve itself by common agreement of all its members ... the last murderer remaining in prison must first be executed, so that everyone will duly receive what his actions are worth ...[151]

So the idea that international criminal law serves justice by punishing some of the lesser criminals, even if it grants impunity to the supreme criminals for their supreme crimes, is already dubious. But the Kantian approach is rather rigid for most tastes. Sane people prefer protection from war crimes to justice for them once they are committed. Kofi Annan's promises of justice from the new ICC statute turn out on close examination to be rather meager: 'Only then will the innocents of distant wars and conflicts know that they, too, may sleep under the cover of justice; that they, too, have rights, and that those who violate those rights will be punished.'[152]

But you sleep a lot more soundly knowing you are going to wake up than merely knowing somebody is going to be punished if you don't. During World War II, the Jews of Poland didn't ask for a war crimes tribunal to give justice to the murdered; they wanted the allies to bomb the concentration camps *and* German cities immediately, to put a stop to what the Germans were doing.[153]

DETERRENCE

What does international criminal law have to say about the really important question of *preventing* war crimes of the supreme and lesser variety? The classic technique used by the ordinary criminal law to prevent crime is deterrence. According to the American judge and theorist O. W. Holmes:

> The law threatens certain pains if you do certain things, intending thereby to give you a new motive for not doing them. If you persist in doing them, it has to inflict the pains in order that its threats may continue to be believed.[154]

There are quite a few adherents to the view that international criminal law can deter war crimes: 'Effective deterrence is a primary objective of those working to establish the international criminal court,' says the official commentary to the Rome Statute. In the struggle over bringing Milosevic to The Hague, two American professors intoned: 'If Milosevic soon finds himself in the custody of the tribunal, other autocrats contemplating ethnic slaughter will think twice before following through.'[155] The first prosecutor, Richard Goldstone, also expressed considerable faith in the deterrent effect of his tribunal in an interview with Michael Scharf in July 1996:

> Indeed, Richard Goldstone believes the existence of the tribunal may have already deterred human rights violations in the former Yugoslavia during the Croatian army offensive against Serb rebels in August 1995. 'Fear of prosecution at The Hague,' he said, 'prompted Croat authorities to issue orders to their soldiers to protect Serb civilian rights when Croatia took control of the Krajina and western Slavonia regions of the country.'[156]

But the only thing this shows is how badly informed by his American handlers Goldstone had been about the Croatians' Krajina operation. In July 2001, in a belated attempt to pretend to some impartiality (with President Tudjman conveniently dead), an indictment was finally issued by the ICTY against Croatian commander Ante Gotovina ('acting individually and/or in concert with others, including President Franjo Tudjman') for war crimes and crimes against humanity in the 'ethnic cleansing' of 200,000 Serbs from August to November 1995. The counts included persecutions, murder, plunder, wanton destruction of cities, towns and villages, deportation, forced displacement, and other inhumane acts.[157] A *New York Times* story of the time referred to the notorious American military involvement in the action; but being supreme criminals, no indictments were issued against them.[158]

So no deterrence there. And if the interview were held now, the prosecutor would have trouble reconciling the supposed deterrent effect of the Tribunal with the Tribunal's own theory that Milosevic continued to commit his crimes even after the indictment of his colleagues, and even after his *own* indictment, right up until the conquest of Kosovo by NATO in June 1999. Nor does the arrest of Milosevic himself seem to have deterred all the war crimes and crimes against humanity that have occurred since July 2001, in New York, in Afghanistan, in Iraq, and so on. The idea that the threat of ultimate prosecution – to be precise, the *extra* threat from the slightest chance of *international law* prosecution – would work as a deterrent to war criminals should have been laid to rest with World War II. If Mussolini wasn't deterred by what the partisans were sure to do to him if he lost power, why would he fear a war crimes tribunal? Hitler knew exactly what was in store for him should he lose the war; it didn't stop him from slaughtering tens of millions of people. Did he even slow down the death camps after the Moscow Declaration on War Crimes of November 1943? Over 400,000 Hungarian Jews were murdered after March 1944 alone.[159] Anne Frank and her family were only betrayed and deported to their deaths in August 1944. Could there possibly have been even more war crimes in the second half of the twentieth century had there been no Nuremberg or Tokyo?[160] Judge Pal got this right in his dissenting judgment at Tokyo:

> *When the fear of punishment attendant upon particular conduct does not depend upon law but only upon the fact of defeat in war,* I do not think that law adds anything to the risk of defeat already there in any preparation for war. There is already a greater fear – namely the power, the might of the victor.[161]

In other words, if you're not going to punish the Americans for pulverizing a country with bombs – whether because they're in the right or because they are blessed with selective impunity – what conceivable deterrent purpose can there be in punishing the leaders of the country they're bombing after it's over? After all the years of America threatening Saddam Hussein with war crimes prosecution, do you think he was more worried about that or about the precision weapons being aimed at him by American bombers in March and April 2003?

And that's the losing side. What about the winners? ICC enthusiast Hans Corell, United Nations Under-Secretary-General for Legal Affairs, hit the nail on the head when he said, 'From now on, all potential warlords must know that, depending on how a conflict develops, there might be established an international tribunal before which those will be brought who violate the laws of war and humanitarian law...' Precisely, *depending on how a conflict develops* – better yet on how it *turns out*; but most importantly, on which side the war criminal happens to be. The accompanying commentary says things will surely be different, 'Once it is clear that the international community will no longer tolerate such monstrous acts without assigning responsibility and meting out appropriate punishment ...'[162] But nothing could be clearer than that the 'international community' will indeed tolerate them – will *have to* tolerate them, if they come from a superpower, or one of its allies or clients. And what this means is that the rational thing to do is not cease committing crimes, but to commit them on the right side. The 'lesson' is 'that serving U.S. interests allows you to do whatever you want with your ethnic minorities.'[163] As George W. Bush might put it: either you're with us, or you're a war criminal.

Look at the case of Israel. It has been in unbroken, illegal occupation of the Palestinian territories, home to about two million Palestinians, since June 1967. It has been settling these territories, by force, with its own citizens since 1968. The very settlements are 'grave breaches' of the 1977 Protocols of the Geneva Conventions, and *war crimes* under the Rome Statute, Belgian law and Canadian law – as are many of the practices Israel uses to maintain these settlements against the will of the occupied people.[164] But Israel has nothing to fear from international criminal law because it is under the protection of the United States, which provides it with both military invincibility and war-crime impunity.

TRUTH

Another claim that is impossible to accept is that these tribunals somehow serve the function of establishing historical truth. Advocates see themselves as bulwarks against the Holocaust deniers of the future. Michael Scharf makes this claim in his study of the ICTY's first trial:

> The record of the trial provides an authoritative and impartial account to which future historians may turn for truth, and future leaders for warning. While there are various means to achieve an historic record of abuses after a war, the most authoritative rendering is possible only through the crucible of a trial that accords full due process ... By carefully

establishing these facts one witness at a time in the face of vigilant cross-examination by distinguished defense counsel, the Tadic trial produced a definitive account that can endure the test of time and resist the forces of revisionism.[165]

Sometimes you think you read these books more carefully than their authors, because only seven pages earlier Scharf wrote this:

Nor did the defense ever really attempt to dispute the second question ['Did there exist widespread and systematic abuses against non-Serbs?']. Its strategy was to acknowledge that atrocities occurred throughout Bosnia, but to deny that Tadic had any involvement in them. Thus the defense rarely challenged the testimony of the fourteen policy witnesses presented by the prosecution who described the widespread and systematic abuses committed by the Serbs against Bosnian Muslims and Croats in the summer of 1992.... Instead, the defense sought to turn this liability into an asset by suggesting that the evidence given by prosecution witnesses was unreliable because in many cases it was prejudiced testimony of Muslim victims who saw all Serbs as their oppressors.[166]

In other words, the defense strategy was not at all to challenge the historical claims by 'vigilant cross-examination by distinguished defense counsel,' but rather to concede the prosecution version of history and try instead to cast doubt on the individual guilt of the accused. David Paciocco reports precisely the same phenomenon occurring at the ICTR ('tactically there can be no point or premium in arguing that there was no genocide').[167] The conventional historical wisdom never really gets challenged because it is not in the interests of the accused to do so. Even if your only experience with a criminal trial were the O. J. Simpson trial on TV, you'd know how bad criminal trials are at establishing what actually happened. That's not their point. Their point is to determine whether a particular person is going to be punished, and carriage of that task is assigned to parties having a huge stake in the outcome. To justify the punishment, the trial bends over backwards with artificial rules such as the presumption of innocence, a very high burden of proof (beyond a reasonable doubt), and the right to remain silent – things that nobody interested in establishing historical fact would ever dream of using. 'On the contrary, their reductionist, bipolar logic and inherent barriers to the truth conceal and distort history.'[168] If there is a 'truth' that criminal trials are meant to establish, it must be kept firmly within quotation marks, because it is a very different one from the factual, historical truth – it is an *ideological* truth. Criminal law always means to teach us something, to 'make a point.' Part of the point is the deterrent one: this is the kind of thing that can get you in trouble. That's what ordinary criminal courts teach because they exist in the context of operating law enforcement systems that devote enormous resources to ensuring the detection and prosecution of a significant proportion of the crimes committed, especially of those regarded as serious. Now the point about international criminal tribunals is that, given their tiny workload, they can't possibly be aimed at fulfilling this 'truth' function. That's why the ICC insists on 'complementarity.' In the eight years following its first indictment in February 1995, the ICTY completed a total of 70 cases, roughly six per year.[169] In Canada, a country with 50 percent more people than the former Yugoslavia but with no apparent civil war in the 1990s, and a moderate (Western European) rate of crime and punishment, the adult criminal courts decided 450,000 cases in 2001 alone, 120,000 involving violence, 540 of them homicide cases.[170] In its first eight years of activity, the ICTR completed 13 cases relating to the violence in Rwanda of 1994.[171] Yet in the four years from 1996 to 2000, the Rwandan government's domestic 'genocide courts' tried 2,406 and executed 22 (in soccer stadiums before large crowds).[172] Rwanda was holding 112,000 in detention in atrocious conditions before the provisional release of 25,000 in 2003. Amnesty International reports that 11,000 had died in custody.[173]

But, as the British judge Sir James Fitzjames Stephen wrote long ago, the criminal law has another 'truth' function:

> [I]f in all cases criminal law were regarded only as a direct appeal to the fears of persons likely to commit crimes, it would be deprived of a large part of its efficiency, for it operates not only on the fears of criminals, but upon the habitual sentiments of those who are not criminals.... In short, the infliction of punishment by law gives definite expression and a solemn ratification and justification to the hatred which is excited by the commission of the offence ... The criminal law thus proceeds upon the principle that it is morally right to hate criminals, and it confirms and justifies that sentiment by inflicting upon criminals punishments which express it ...[174]

The 'truth' criminal law seeks to teach is one about who is to blame for what has happened; and that person is the person found guilty. That person is not only to be blamed, but to be *hated*. And that means the crime has to be detached from its social and political context and located squarely within the heart of the accused as an inexplicable evil, so that the natural, indeed only possible solution is punishment. That's how Michael Ignatieff could absolve the trial of the Hutu nuns for not resolving 'disturbing questions' such as 'Where does evil come from?'. 'None of them were resolved by the

Belgian court. Justice is built to establish the facts of evil. It cannot explain them.'[175] But Ignatieff did not think through the implications of this the way Judge Pal did at the end of his long dissent on the Tokyo Tribunal:

> [I]n times of trial and stress like those the international world is now passing through, it is easy enough to mislead the people's mind by pointing to false causes as the fountains of all ills and thus persuading it to attribute all the ills to such causes ... no other moment is more propitious for whispering into the popular ear the means of revenge while giving it the outward shape of the only solution demanded by the nature of the evils.[176]

Pal argued that the trials of the war criminals wasted precious attention that should have been devoted to the search for peace in the only way possible:

> 'We must begin systematically to reduce and eliminate all *chief causes* of war.'... The trials should not be allowed to use up the precious little thought that a peace-bound public may feel inclined to spare in order to find the way to 'conquer the doubts and the fears, the ignorance and the greed, which made this horror possible.'[177]

PEACE

And here we have a key to the complicated relationship between peace and international criminal law. Take this statement by ICC campaigner and former Nuremberg prosecutor Benjamin Ferencz: 'There can be no peace without justice, no justice without law and no meaningful law without a Court to decide what is just and lawful under any given circumstance.' The official commentary adds that punishment for war crimes not only deters conflict, but also

> enhances the possibility of bringing a conflict to an end. Two ad hoc international criminal tribunals, one for the former Yugoslavia and another for Rwanda, were created in this decade with the hope of hastening the end of the violence and preventing its recurrence.[178]

But could anyone have picked worse examples? By the time the tribunal was set up for Rwanda, the killing of Tutsis had already been stopped by the victory of the invading Tutsi RPF. In 1998 the Rwandan regime, now a Washington client, with the ICTR and its own genocide courts in operation, had embroiled itself in a war in the Congo that would take millions of lives over the next four and a half years. As for Yugoslavia, Tribunal president Cassese made the same claim in 1995:

> Justice is an indispensable ingredient of the process of national reconciliation. It is essential to the restoration of peaceful and normal relations especially for people who have had to live under a reign of terror. It breaks the cycle of violence, hatred and extra-judicial retribution. Thus peace and justice go hand in hand.[179]

But, like Del Ponte after him, Cassese was willing to have justice wag the dog of 'peaceful and normal relations,' and demanded severe economic sanctions to punish Serb civilians until the ICTY's arrest warrants were executed.[180] This was, as insider Scharf reminded us in 1999, the 'public relations' role for which the Americans had designed the Tribunal in the first place. Indictments 'would serve to isolate offending leaders diplomatically, strengthen the hand of their domestic rivals and fortify the international political will to employ economic sanctions or use force.'[181] And virtually everything the Tribunal has done can best be understood on this one organizing principle: *the legitimation of force*. In late 1992, Eagleburger's spontaneous speech kicking off the Tribunal by naming Serb war criminals was aimed directly at scuttling the Vance–Owen peace initiative in favor of NATO muscle, and at justifying the 'more aggressive measures' he announced in the same breath.[182] The indictments of Karadzic and Mladic on 25 July 1995 were a prelude to the NATO bombing of late August and September 1995. That was followed, it is true, by the Dayton accords, but these were only made possible by letting peace trump 'justice' through the deliberate non-indictment of Milosevic, the alleged 'mastermind' of Bosnia. In 1998, not only did Arbour, McDonald and company supply the necessary Holocaust analogizing for the Kosovo war, they even successfully opposed the establishment of a 'truth and reconciliation commission' for Bosnia, on the grounds that it might undermine their work and draw funds away from the ICTY.[183] Such a commission had been implemented in South Africa as part of the peaceful transition from apartheid to majority rule, generously using its broad powers of amnesty – too generously according to some victims. Imagine how ludicrous it would have been, though, for some NATO court to have insisted on prosecutions and to have told South Africans that they couldn't have peace without justice. Throughout 1999, the ICTY devoted itself almost full-time to the war effort, starting with Racak, which it helped turn into a pretext for war, through to the indictment of Milosevic ('a useful tool in their efforts to demonize the Serbian leader and maintain public support for Nato's bombing campaign against Serbia'[184]), so that

European peace efforts could be derailed and the bombing could continue a few more weeks until it ended on terms favorable to NATO.

The ICTY was par excellence an instrument for the legitimation of war and the undermining of peace. But the ICTY is just one example. It was preceded, remember, by the first Gulf War, where Bush Sr. invoked Nuremberg to paint the Iraqis, falsely, as Nazi-like monsters who threw babies out of incubators. When the Americans decided not to overthrow Saddam Hussein, war crime prosecutions ceased to be a moral imperative. The idea was only revived periodically to remind Americans why the US continued to bomb and sanction Iraq.[185] On 16 March 2003, three days prior to launching its war, the US released a list of Iraqi leaders to be charged with war crimes. The excuse for the list was that it had been intended as a way to *avoid* war, by inducing Iraqi leaders to leave Iraq and escape charges, but that this had unfortunately fallen through – as if that's all the Iraqi leadership had to worry about, and as if America was not already irrevocably committed to war. All the list really did was provide another chance to justify the war by expounding on the fiendishness of the Iraqi leaders:

> In his radio address, Mr. Bush reminded his listeners that it was the 15th 'bitter anniversary' of Mr. Hussein's chemical weapons attack on the Iraqi Kurdish village of Halabja. The attack, Mr. Bush said, 'provided a glimpse of the crimes Saddam Hussein is willing to commit, and the kind of threat he now presents to the entire world.' Using some of his most graphic language yet in describing Mr. Hussein's Iraq, Mr. Bush added: 'We know from human rights groups that dissidents in Iraq are tortured, imprisoned and sometimes just disappear. Their hands, feet and tongues are cut off, their eyes are gouged out, and female relatives are raped in their presence.' Mr. Bush, seeming to prepare the nation for war ...[186]

When the war was over, the victorious Americans earnestly debated how best to use the war crimes approach to justify what they had done. Quickly ruled out was anything in the nature of an international trial that could allow the other side to 'make a point': 'there's no way they're going to let these guys stand there on some platform in a space-age courtroom, justifying themselves before the world the way Milosevic has for years on end.'[187] An American military court would also send the wrong message – besides, the problem from the start was: What had they done to the Americans? The approach that soon found the most favor was the one most consistent with the impression the Americans wanted to give that they had conquered Iraq not for its oil, credibility or strategic value, but for the Iraqis themselves. They had to justify American imperialism by denying it. Ergo, the idea was to hand the matter over to (carefully US-trained and selected) Iraqi courts:

'It allows a group of Arabs to try Arab war criminals. It would address the dangerous perception that this is US imperialism.'[188] As one of its first official acts, following hard on the important business (in a country without water and electricity) of declaring a national holiday to celebrate America's victory, America's hand-picked Iraqi 'Governing Council' announced that this was precisely what would be done.[189] The law was ready by the time of Saddam's capture in December 2003, an event so widely seen by the US media as vindicating the whole continuing bloody fiasco of Iraq that it was considered a major boost for George W. Bush's re-election chances.

Fiat justitia, ruat coelum – Let justice be done, though the heavens should fall. This is the classic philosophical move of anyone who advocates a solution that does more harm than good to most people. But ask yourself whether justice, let alone the selective justice promised by the international criminal law movement, is worth sacrificing any given quantity of peace. Ask yourself whether Hitler's pathetic head on a platter would have been worth the life of even one Jewish child. Kant was driven to his abstract theory of justice in order to try and defend the institution of capital punishment from the charge that it did not prevent crime. Capital punishment as 'justice' is meant to detach violence artificially from its powerful social causes and locate it in the perpetrator alone. The international criminal law movement tries desperately to do the same thing. In October 2002, Human Rights Watch issued a report condemning Palestinian suicide bombers for 'crimes against humanity,' whether the bombings took place in Israel proper or in the occupied territories. 'What about the occupation?' Palestinians protested, criticizing the report for 'fail[ing] to take account of Israel's military superiority,' and for withholding the same label from Israel's activity in the territories. But Human Rights Watch replied that the one had nothing to do with the other. The ban on harming civilians, they said, was 'absolute and unconditional.' Naturally, they also relied on the familiar distinction between murder and collateral damage, holding that there was a difference between what Israel did and 'suicide terror attacks … perpetrated with a deliberate aim of harming civilians.'[190] The fact that Israel had killed almost three times the number of Palestinians, and almost four times the number of children, than vice versa was irrelevant.[191]

In claiming that justice is a precondition to peace, the international criminal law movement is attempting to appropriate the very different idea in the familiar activist slogan of 'no peace without justice,' or as Ontario unions like to say, 'No justice, no peace.' But these slogans have nothing to do with criminal justice; they are about social justice. When Palestinians say 'no peace without justice,' they're not saying there can be no peace without Ariel Sharon in jail.[192] They're talking about the injustices they have no choice but to struggle against, the violent and illegal occupation of their land and everything that flows from it. This is also the sense in which the Pope meant it in his New Year message for 2002: 'True peace therefore is the fruit of justice, that moral virtue and legal guarantee which ensures full respect for rights and responsibilities, and the just distribution of benefits and burdens.'[193] This is the opposite of international criminal law's attempts to detach consequences from causes, which is absolutely of the same cloth as the Bush administration's attempts to detach 'terrorism' from its causes.

Another version of the peace and justice connection is the idea of international criminal law as an alternative to war. At a meeting of practitioners in the field held in May 2003, the head of the International Defense Bar put it this way:

> The policy of the American administration is to oppose the objectives of the ICC and to promote war as the only instrument capable of dealing with crimes against humanity. It's working hard to convince other countries to join it in this doubtful and dangerous enterprise. The best means for the ICC to confront these contestations is to get itself going right away.[194]

This expresses a sentiment widely held, especially among lawyers, that these international legal processes offer a realistic alternative to war. One example often cited is the criminal trial of two Libyans suspected of blowing up Pan Am Flight 103 over Lockerbie, Scotland in 1988, and causing the deaths of 270 people. The trial in the Netherlands was accepted by the US and the UK as a quid pro quo for agreeing to the removal of the Security Council sanctions imposed at their insistence. But there is absolutely nothing to suggest that the trial was seen by the Americans as an alternative to war with Libya, as opposed to an alternative to sanctions, support for which was already eroding in the international community.[195] The war on Afghanistan showed clearly enough that when the Americans are bent on war, no amount of remonstrating with them to accept a trial instead will work. The Taliban were anxious to negotiate bin Laden's extradition, and the whole peace camp – including the Pope – shouted 'fight terror through law, not war.'[196] The US rejected this out of hand and attacked Afghanistan as soon as it was ready. The problem with the fight-terror-through-law-not-war approach is that it assumes that the *justifications* for war ('fighting terror' or 'dealing with crimes against humanity') are the same as the *reasons*.

It's true that a lot of the people who made these claims were not trying to appeal to the peace-loving hearts of the American leaders, but to embarrass them, to 'make a point' and rally opposition. They were trying to use international criminal law to weaken the American case for going to war: 'If you really only wanted justice like you say you do, you'd go to court and not to war.' This is the value many see in the ICC, as providing an institution and standards by reference to which war can be opposed. As William Schabas, a distinguished cheerleader for the ICC, upbraided a co-panelist recently: 'If we're so harmless to the Americans, then why do they fight so hard against us?'[197] But, of course, it's because of the fight the Americans have picked with the ICC that it has been pushed into the inoffensive corner it is in. International criminal law may be a double-edged sword when it comes to making a point, but the edge pointing inward is much the duller one. Above all, it says that the crime the imperialists uniquely commit, the supreme crime of aggressive war, is not a crime at all. So the critical value of international criminal law is reduced to saying which side fights more according to the rules of war. It puts the aggressor and aggressed-against on an equal footing and leaves out entirely the questions of who and what started the war in the first place.

Remember how, during the Iraq war of 2003, the anti-impunity campaigners at Human Rights Watch and Amnesty International periodically issued statements condemning both sides for violations of the Geneva Conventions, both sides for parading prisoners of war on television, the Americans for not taking enough care to avoid injuries to civilians, the Iraqis for 'perfidy' in the use of fake surrenders and suicide bombs. All these they meticulously condemned as war crimes, but neither said *anything* about the supreme crime of aggressive war that made all of these other crimes inevitable; let alone the inherent criminality of every act of violence by the aggressor in an illegal war – even against soldiers. Even lawyers' groups who were declared partisans against the war could not seem to find a way to make this point. When Public Interest Lawyers of the UK and the American Center for Constitutional Rights issued their pre-war warnings to their respective governments in January 2003, the most they could threaten was a complaint to the ICC for the *way* the war might be fought.[198] Supporters of the ICC are right to make its symbolic value central, because these courts can only be symbolic (except for the real violence they sporadically visit on usual suspects). But supporters in the peace camp underestimate the extent to which the international criminal law preaches what it practices. A picture is worth far more than a thousand words nowadays. Milosevic in a glass booth means he's to blame for the Balkan wars; nuns in a glass booth means they're to blame for the killing in Rwanda.

Michel Foucault said many important things about criminal law. One was that criminal law is 'not intended to eliminate offences, but rather to distinguish them, to distribute them, to use them':

Penality would then appear to be a way of handling illegalities, of laying down the limits of tolerance, of giving free rein to some, of putting pressure on others ... And, if one can speak of class justice, it is not only because the law itself or the way of applying it serves the interests of a class, it is also because the differential administration of illegalities through the mediation of penality forms part of those mechanisms of domination.[199]

Criminal law distinguishes between 'true crimes' and mere 'offenses' against the rules, between *criminals* and mere *offenders*. The criminals are the ones who wind up being punished. They are the ones to blame. The unprosecuted complicity of others and the 'causes' are not only irrelevant, they are 'imponderable': 'Justice is built to establish the facts of evil. It cannot explain them.'[200]

VISION

In practice, international criminal law has been very good at legitimating war and very bad at promoting peace; yet some, at least, seem to think that it nevertheless contains a vision worth preserving and working for, a 'vision of a more hopeful future where the rule of law prevails over the rule of violence.'[201] But in fact the vision is a bleak one of permanent war and perpetual war crimes, where the best we can do – the most we can even *dream* of doing – is putting a regular succession of war criminals on trial. So Amnesty International, a group formed two generations ago primarily to oppose punishment as a response to political conflict – hence the name – now finds itself typically *opposing amnesties* in its new-found obsession with 'anti-impunity':

> Amnesty International believes that the Sierra Leone government should repeal the 1999 amnesty so that the national courts of Sierra Leone are able to address impunity for those cases which will not be tried before the Special Court.[202]

In February 2001 Amnesty issued a statement celebrating what it termed a 'landmark' decision by the ICTY, which 'acknowledged' rape and sexual enslavement as crimes against humanity: 'This verdict is a significant step for women's human rights.'[203] But did this really need 'acknowledgment'? And wouldn't a 'significant step for women's human rights' mean actually doing something about putting an end to war rape? However, that would mean actually doing something about putting an end to war, because – despite Amnesty's jejune claim that the ICTY decision 'challenges widespread acceptance that the torture of women is an intrinsic part of war' – accept it or not, where there's war, there's rape. And the international criminal law movement is, in practice, about *encouraging* war by legitimating illegal war-making and declaring – all logic, morality, law and precedent to the contrary – that the supreme criminals, the warmongers, are not criminals at all. This ensures that there will always be plenty of war rape to 'recognize' as crime.

In the new vision of human rights, there is nothing that can be done about their violation other than for the civilized peoples of the North – the ones complicit in the violations in the first place – to send their lawyers and their courts to show the locals how to designate the proper culprits, 'a deluxe international bureaucracy equipped with satellite telephones, state-of-the-art computers and late-model Land Cruisers.'[204] In short, a new 'White Man's Burden,' complete with its 'savage wars of peace,' 'the blame of those ye better' and 'the hate of those ye guard.'[205] Not only 'an imbalanced, one-sided institution through which the North lectures the South about how to do the right thing,'[206] but one in which the North conquers the South and then *puts it on trial*. The punitive vision of international human rights seems like nothing more than globalized American law-and-order politics, like music videos and jeans: what they used to call the 'Coca Colonization' of the world; a distinctly American vision in which there is no 'middle option between moral inertia and moral hysteria, indifference and punishment,' with a total disregard for 'the commonplaces of modern criminology like the need to focus on the character of society that engenders depraved acts, rather than fixating on a supposed depraved few.... Once a hallmark of conservative thinking, the degree of disinterest ICC proponents show in causal theory is striking.'[207] In fact the human-rights-as-punishment vision of the international criminal law movement seems to come straight out of the Bush family's Texas, which despite the 'freedom' everyone hates America for, has the world's largest per capita prison population, and on top of that executes one of its 'own people' by lethal injection roughly every other week. It's also a state, by no coincidence, with enormous inequality: fabulous oil wealth on the one hand, and among the highest rates of poverty on the other, with lots of violent crime as the predictable product.[208] The Texas vision is first to create social conditions that, while to the benefit of a tiny elite, are so intolerable to others that people wind up killing each other in great numbers, and then to self-righteously kill the killers, as if you had nothing to do with it – or rather, to show that you had nothing to do with it.

A Canadian colleague has called this phenomenon the 'criminalization of politics in which social, economic, cultural, and political problems are primarily addressed through the use of the criminal sanction.'[209] In other words, punishment as human rights. Specifically concerning Canada, Kent Roach writes:

> Women's groups might have preferred national day care, equal pay, employment equity, better social services, and quality-based education, but what they got in the 1980s and 1990s were new laws and policies targeting sexual and wife assault, prostitution and pornography. Criminal laws targeting the sexual abuse of children, and hate and war crimes against minorities, were easier to obtain than the more expensive and radical interventions required to come to grips with the causes of these ugly problems.[210]

In 'criminalized politics' all questions of the social causes of violence, lying usually in social inequality itself, are marginalized and rendered irrelevant by a single-minded punitive strategy, which treats all explanations other than the free-floating guilt of the offender as an attempt to evade responsibility. That the punitive strategy was adopted because it was less 'expensive' is just the phony banner under which elites oppose changes in a system that works very well for them, even if it imposes enormous costs on everyone else in inequality, insecurity, violence and repression. International criminal law can be understood to be the globalization of this phenomenon: the rich countries, for reasons of pure greed, create intolerable conditions throughout the world and then selectively use the strife produced by these conditions as an excuse to use violence in the furthering of their own interests. The rich countries find it 'less expensive' to create conditions in which human rights are bound to be violated and then to come crashing in to punish the violators, than to create conditions in which human rights can flourish in the first place.

The concept of 'criminalized politics' is derived from that of '*legalized politics*,' deployed to try and grasp the modern tendency to resolve political questions in legal forums, with lawyers and judges. Legalized politics is often thought of as a democratic development because it can hold governments to account, and certainly there are many examples of the judicial advancement of human rights and democracy. But the historical record is also full of anti-democratic, repressive tendencies, and the phenomenon has often been sponsored as a check on the democratic dangers presented by legislatures representing more radical forces than could be found on any bench. It is not necessary to elaborate this here, but it might be worth pondering the example of the US itself, where the original Constitution entrenched both slavery and debt, and the Supreme Court fought a rear-guard action on behalf of racism and against social welfare policies right up until the

1950s. The brief progressive period that then set in was eclipsed within a generation; since the mid-1970s, the United States Supreme Court has been a force for political reaction.[211] We may even have it to thank for the Bush administration, for whom it cast the decisive vote in December 2000. Another example close to home is Pinochet's Chile, where it was the senior judiciary who helped delegitimate Salvador Allende's reformist government and put the seal of approval on Pinochet's American-sponsored coup, to the extent that in his memoirs, Henry Kissinger could justify the coup by maintaining that the government had been declared unconstitutional by its own Supreme Court.[212] And it was the senior Chilean judiciary, groomed and appointed under Pinochet's dictatorship, who ensured his ultimate personal impunity.

Where does the international criminal law movement fit into all this? The end of the Cold War left only America standing in the ring as the world's unchallengeable military power, but it found its ambitions seriously hampered by the international legal order enshrined in the Charter of the United Nations.[213] This order was based on the sovereign equality of states and the prohibition of the use of force except in narrowly defined circumstances, with the broadly representative Security Council as a guarantor and the even more representative International Court of Justice as the supreme authority on the law. This order had to be overthrown, and it was. As is frequently the case with revolutionary movements, the revolutionaries appealed to 'higher law' notions of 'human rights' (of the victims of the repressive regimes America sought to overthrow), and 'inherent rights' (America's own inherent right to self-defense), and this has led some thoughtful commentators to speak of a 'tyranny of human rights'[214] and of the 'international human rights movement' as being 'part of the problem.'[215] However, the problem is not with the rights, but with the concrete actions they were meant to justify – in this case, bloody war in defiance of the principles and institutions of the Charter of the United Nations. The Charter sought to defend human rights by making borders inviolable, because of the obvious lessons of World War II – lessons corroborated many times in Kosovo, Afghanistan and Iraq, that peaceful, collective solutions to human rights problems are always more successful than violent, unilateral ones. That was the system that was concretely challenged when international criminal law advocates argued, 'Outmoded traditions of State sovereignty must not derail the forward movement ... The silent voices of "We the Peoples" – who are the true sovereigns of today – cry out for enforceable law to protect the universal human interest.'[216] But in practice all the abolition of the sovereign equality of states and the prohibitions on the use of force does is ensure that the conception of human rights most congenial to the most powerful states is the one that gets accepted. There is no question of the new interventionism, like the new right of self-defense, being used against the US, no matter how badly it abuses the human rights of its own people. Exactly like the other elements of 'globalization,' the globalization ('universalization') of human rights is just a euphemism for the strong calling the shots.

But it was not enough that the New World Order be established in theory and in practice, it had to be established in law. Enter the international criminal law movement, in the form of the ICTY, bristling with judges even as its prosecutors, acting as a Supreme Court of the World, where no mere nation's law could possibly stand in its way; a criminal and constitutional court all bound up in one, more powerful than any other court, including the World Court, because it didn't depend on anyone's consent, and could actually arrest people at NATO's gunpoint. When the history of the overthrow of the United Nations is written, a lot of credit will have to be given to the ICTY for its role in Kosovo, because Kosovo gave unilateralism an enormous boost. It allowed the United States, through NATO, to break free of the limits of international law by fashioning a higher legality. As Diana Johnstone has observed, the war over Kosovo 'marked a turning point in the expansion of U.S. military hegemony,' 'rehabilitating' war as 'once again an acceptable instrument of politics,' and overturning the psychological and legal barrier entrenched in the Charter of the United Nations.[217] This was the historic mission of the international criminal law movement, to legalize aggression and the whole repressive apparatus of the New World Order – an order the Americans like to describe as 'freedom,' but one that, in practice, only means freedom for the most powerful countries; freedom from the democratic obstacles that shore up the freedom of the rest. However undemocratic the world's states may be – including naturally the US, which has perfected the democracy of 'one dollar, one vote' – the substitution of American rule for the pluralism of the United Nations cannot be regarded as anything but an epochal democratic setback. Nor is it possible any longer to romanticize as 'autonomy' or 'self-determination' the firm subordination of post-war Yugoslavia, Afghanistan and Iraq to the military and economic rule of what Peter Gowan calls the 'Dollar Wall Street Regime.'[218]

What is the future of international criminal law? It may already have outlived its usefulness to the sole remaining superpower, and certainly any hint of an adversarial role will spell its doom. If the US can delegitimate and marginalize an institution like the United Nations, think how little trouble it would have with an upstart ICC. But, because the results would be so predictable, this is very unlikely to happen. If the ICC is to survive

– and it wants badly to survive – it will continue to ignore the crimes of the US and to round up the usual suspects, to regulate (the way Catherine McKinnon described rape law as 'regulating rape'), but not prohibit – indeed, to legitimate – the use of violence in international affairs. Given the well known tendencies of everyday criminal law to be 'strong with the weak and weak with the strong,' like corporate and police criminals, what could make us think it would change its nature when it went global? The attitude of the peace movement to these courts should be one of extreme skepticism. With some well known exceptions, judges and lawyers as a class are not known for rocking the boat. They should be judged by their practice and not by their rhetoric, the way Tokyo Tribunal Judge B. V. A. Röling said we should judge the Nuremberg principles:

> It is true that both trials had sinister origins; that they were misused for political purposes; and that they were somewhat unfair. But they also made a very constructive contribution to the outlawing of war and the world is badly in need of a fundamental change in the political and legal position of war in international relations.... Yes, notwithstanding all the justifiable criticism, I have reached a favourable opinion of the trials. The evaluation is, of course, provisional. One never knows what role the judgements will play in later events.[219]

So far these principles have failed us very badly, but I suppose we have to keep an open mind.

Notes

CHAPTER 1: IRAQ 2003

1. 'No matter what the whip count is, we're calling for the vote … It's time for people to show their cards …' Associated Press; '"We're Calling for the Vote" at U.N., Bush Says', *Washington Post*, 7 March 2003, p. A18.
2. *Toronto Star*, 24 June 2003, p. D18.
3. Iraq Body Count, *Adding indifference to injury*, 7 August 2003 <www.iraqbodycount. net/editorial_aug0703.htm>.
4. Laura King, 'Baghdad's Death Toll Assessed,' *Los Angeles Times*, 18 May 2003 <www. latimes.com/la-war-iraqidead18may18,1,5937098>.
5. Reuters, 'Casualties so far,' *Guardian*, 23 April 2003 <www.guardian.co.uk/Iraq/ Story/0,2763,928043,00.html>.
6. John M. Broder, 'A Nation at War: The Casualties; Number of Iraqis Killed May Never Be Determined,' *New York Times*, 10 April 2003, p. B1; The Project on Defense Alternatives estimated the total Iraqi death toll up to only 20 April 2003 at between 11,000 and 15,000 Iraqis, of which 3,200 to 4,300 were 'noncombatant civilians': Carl Conetta, *The Wages of War: Iraqi Combatant and Noncombatant Fatalities in the 2003 Conflict*, Project on Defense Alternatives, 20 October 2003 <www.comw. org/pda/0310rm8.html>.
7. Alissa J. Rubin and Patrick J. McDonnell, 'U.S. Gunships Target Insurgents in Iraq Amid Copter Crash Inquiry,' *Los Angeles Times*, 19 November 2003 <www.latimes. com/news/nationworld/world/la-fg-iraq19nov19,1,436097.story).
8. Associated Press, 'At Least 4 Killed in Bombing in Northern Iraq', 20 November 2003 <www.nytimes.com/2003/11/20/international/middleeast/20WIRE-IRAQ. html>.
9. Borzou Daragahi, 'Major assault targets Saddam loyalists,' *Toronto Star*, 13 June 2003, p. A12.
10. 'America's Image Further Erodes, Europeans Want Weaker Ties,' *Pew Center for the People and the Press*, 18 March 2003 <people-press.org/reports/display. php3?ReportID=175>.
11. Mo Mowlam, 'The real goal is the seizure of Saudi oil', *Guardian*, 4 September 2002 <www.guardian.co.uk/Print/0,3858,4494686,00.html>.
12. Jay Bookman, 'The President's real goal in Iraq', *The Atlanta Journal-Constitution*, 29 September 2002, p. F1.
13. Remark attributed to Michael Ledeen, holder of the Freedom Chair at the American Enterprise Institute, by his friend and colleague, *National Review* editor Jonah Goldberg, 'Baghdad Delenda Est, Part Two,' *National Review Online*, 23 April 2002 <www.nationalreview.com/goldberg/goldberg042302.asp>.
14. *Nuremberg Tribunal Judgment*, 1946, p. 26.
15. Robert H. Jackson, *The Nuremberg Case as Presented by Robert H. Jackson, Chief of Counsel for the United States, Together With Other Documents* (New York: Cooper Square Publishers Inc., 1971), pp. 82–4 (emphasis added).
16. <www.un.org/law/ilc/texts/nurnberg.htm>.
17. Bernard D. Meltzer, 'Comment: A Note on some aspects of the Nuremberg Debate,' *University of Chicago Law Review* 14 (1946–7) pp. 460–1 (emphasis added).
18. Human Rights Watch, 'Iraq: Warring Parties Must Uphold Laws Of War,' New York, 19 March 2003 <www.hrw.org/press/2003/03/us031903ltr.htm>; Amnesty International Press Release, 'Iraq: military action could trigger civilian and human

rights catastrophe,' AI INDEX: MDE 14/029/2003, 20 March 2003 <web.amnesty. org/library/Index/engMDE140292003?Open?Open>.

19. Amnesty International Press Release, 'United States of America, International standards for all,' AI INDEX: AMR 51/045/2003, 25 March 2003.

20. United States Department of Defense, News Transcript, 'Briefing on Geneva Convention, EPW's and War Crimes,' 7 April 2003 <www.defenselink.mil/news/ Apr2003/t04072003_t407genv.html>.

21. Human Rights Watch, 'Iraq: Feigning Civilian Status Violates the Laws of War,' 31 March 2003, New York <www.hrw.org/press/2003/03/iraq033103.htm>.

22. Brian Knowlton, 'Army Defends Soldiers Who Killed Civilians at Checkpoint', *International Herald Tribune*, 1 April 2003, <www.nytimes.com/2003/04/01/ international/middleeast/01CND-CIVIL.html?ex=1054353600&en=50150403e2b3 1cba&ei=5070>; William Branigin, 'A Gruesome Scene on Highway 9,' *Washington Post*, 1 April 2003, p. A01.

23. The newspaper account does not mention self-defense; I'm quoting from my notes of the televised press conference.

24. BBC News World Edition, 'Iraqis killed in Falluja protest', 29 April 2003 <news. bbc.co.uk/2/hi/middle_east/2984663.stm>.

25. '[A]lthough the details of the doctrine may vary from state to state, virtually every jurisdiction precludes aggressors from claiming self-defense.' *Woods v. Solem* 891 F.2d 196 1989 (United States Court of Appeals); see also John S. Baker, Jr., 'Criminal Law – Defenses – The Aggressor Doctrine,' *Louisiana Law Review* (1984), vol. 45, p. 251, and Christine Gray, *International Law and the Use of Force* (Oxford University Press, 2000), pp. 101–2.

26. Robert Fisk, 'Were these deaths mishap, or murder?, Attacks don't reflect well on the U.S.,' *Toronto Star*, 9 April 2003, p. A10.

27. John Pilger, 'Iraq. Crime Against Humanity,' Znet, 10 April 2003 <www.zmag. org/content/showarticle.cfm?SectionID=15&ItemID=3426>.

28. Human Rights Watch, 'Letter to US Regarding the Creation of a Criminal Tribunal for Iraq.' Press Release, 15 April 2003 <www.hrw.org/press/2003/04/ iraqtribunal041503ltr.htm>; Timothy Garton Ash, 'What's to be done now?' *Guardian Weekly*, 17–23 April 2003, p. 13.

29. Elisabeth Bumiller, 'U.S. Names Iraqis Who Would Face War Crimes Trial,' *New York Times*, 16 March 2003, <www.nytimes.com>; Security Council Resolution 1483 of 22 May 2003, Preamble and paragraph 3.

30. Agence France Presse, 'Greek lawyers to sue Britain for Iraq crimes against Humanity,' 23 May 2003 <www.ptd.net/webnews/wed/cy/Qiraq-greece-britain-icj.RPfR_DyN.html>.

31. 'International Appeal against the Pre-emptive Use of Force Signed by 350 Jurists and Lawyers from 40 countries,' <www.peacelawyers.ca/Documents/IALANA_ appeal_Fb_2003.pdf>; International Commission of Jurists: 'This Illegal War Must be Conducted Lawfully: The ICJ condemns the illegal invasion of Iraq in the clear absence of Security Council authority – this constitutes a great leap backward in the international rule of law,' <www.icj.org/news.php3?id_article=2774&lang=en>; Canadian professors of international law, 'Military action in Iraq without Security Council authorization would be illegal,' <www.peacelawyers.ca/Documents/ Iraq_Canadian_law_profs_English.pdf>; British and French Lawyers Statement, 'War would be illegal,' *Guardian*, 7 March 2003, <www.guardian.co.uk/Iraq/ Story/0,2763,909314,00.html>; European Association of Lawyers for Democracy and World Human Rights, 'Appeal to the European Governments and the UN Security Council,' <www.ejdm.de/stop%20the%20war.htm>; Richard Norton-Taylor, 'A large majority of international lawyers reject the government's claim that UN Resolution 1441 gives legal authority for an attack on Iraq,' *Guardian*, 14 March 2003 <www.guardian.co.uk/analysis/story/0,3604,914021,00.html>; Contra: BBC News World Edition, 'Attorney General's Iraq response,' 17 March 2003 <news.bbc.co.uk/2/hi/uk_news/politics/2857347.stm>.

32. Preamble to the Charter of the United Nations.
33. Article 2.2 of the Charter of the United Nations.
34. 'Bush: Leave Iraq within 48 hours,' 17 March 2003 <www.cnn.com/2003/WORLD/meast/03/17/sprj.irq.bush.transcript>.
35. Emphasis added.
36. Emphasis added.
37. United Nations Security Council, 'Identical Letters Dated 6 April 1991 from the Permanent Representative of Iraq to the United Nations, Addressed Respectively to the Secretary-General and President of the Security Council.' S/22456, 6 April 1991.
38. 'The UN Resolution on Iraq,' *Guardian*, 3 October 2002 <www.guardian.co.uk/Iraq/Story/0,2763,803467,00.html> (emphasis added).
39. Julian Borger and Rory McCarthy, 'Shift on inspections in bid to win over France,' *Guardian*, 18 October 2002 <www.guardian.co.uk/Iraq/Story/0,2763,814509,00.html>.
40. Campaign Against Sanctions on Iraq, 'UN Security Council Resolutions relating to Iraq: 1441,' 8 November 2002 <www.casi.org.uk/info/scriraq.html>; US/UK draft of 25 October 2002 <www.casi.org.uk/info/usdraftscr021025.pdf>.
41. Vienna Convention on the Law of Treaties, Articles 60 and 62(a) <www.un.org/law/ilc/texts/treaties.htm>; Glen Rangwala, 'Does a "material breach" of SCR687 justify an invasion?' Campaign Against Sanctions on Iraq, 22 August 2002 <www.casi.org.uk/discuss/2002/msg01239.html>.
42. Associated Press, '"We're Calling for the Vote" at U.N., Bush Says.'
43. 'Text of the U.S.–British–Spanish draft Resolution on Iraq,' 24 February 2003 <www.caci.com/homeland_security/un_res_2–24–03.shtml>.
44. Global Policy Forum, 'Changing Patterns in the Use of the Veto in the Security Council' <www.globalpolicy.org/security/data/vetotab.htm>.
45. See Chapter 3
46. 'Diplomacy fails to break deadlock on Iraq,' *Guardian*, 11 March 2003 <www.guardian.co.uk/Iraq/Story/0,2763,912050,00.html>; Giles Tremlett, 'Taking diplomacy to the wire,' *Guardian*, 17 March 2003 <www.guardian.co.uk/Iraq/Story/0,2763,916137,00.html>.
47. Christine Gray, 'From Unity to Polarization: International Law and the Use of Force against Iraq' (2002), 13 *European Journal of International Law* 1, p. 9.
48. Christine Gray, 'After the Ceasefire: Iraq, the Security Council and the Use of Force' (1994), 65 *British Yearbook of International Law* 135; *International Herald Tribune*, 20 February 2001, p. 1.
49. Bradley Graham, 'Air Defense Units in Southern Iraq Hit Hard. U.S. "No-Fly" Patrols Have Struck All Fixed Sites, Commander Says,' *Washington Post*, 9 March 2003, p. A21; Peter Baker, 'Casualties of an "Undeclared War": Civilians Killed and Injured as U.S. Airstrikes Escalate in Southern Iraq,' *Washington Post*, 22 December 2002, p. A01; Michael R. Gordon, 'U.S. Attacked Iraqi Defenses Starting in '02,' *New York Times*, 20 July 2003, p. 1.
50. Security Council Resolution 1154 of 2 March 1998; Phyllis Bennis, 'Déjà Vu All Over Again...,' 15 October 2002 <www.zmag.org/ZNET.htm>.
51. United States Congress, Authorization for Use of Military Force Against Iraq Resolution of 2002, Joint Resolution H.J. Res. 114, 10 October 2002, Section 3(a)(2) <www.usembassy.it/file2002_10/alia/a2101002.htm>.
52. *Doonesbury*, 8 October 2002: 'Hey Mr. President, How'd That Great Line Of Yours Go? The One That Cracked Up The Joint Chiefs Today?' 'No. Karl, No...' 'Tell! Tell!' 'Okay, Okay. I Told Them We Had To Invade Iraq Because I Was Worried Sick About The U.N.'s Credibility.' 'Ha!! Ha! Ha! Ha! Ha! Ha!' 'He Killed The Chiefs With That One! Killed!' 'Well, Everyone Was Being Soo Serious.'
53. Associated Press, '"We're Calling for the Vote" at U.N., Bush Says.'
54. 'This is not pre-emptive war; there is a crucial difference. Pre-emptive war has a meaning, it means that, for example, if planes are flying across the Atlantic to bomb

the United States, the United States is permitted to shoot them down even before they bomb and may be permitted to attack the air bases from which they came.' Noam Chomsky and V. K. Ramachandran, 'Iraq is a trial run,' *Frontline India*, 2 April 2003 <www.zmag.org/content/showarticle.cfm?SectionID=15&ItemID=3369>.

55. 'Text of Bush's Speech at West Point,' the *New York Times* on the Web, 1 June 2002 <www.nytimes.com/2002/06/01/international/02PTEX-WEB.html?pagewanted= print&position=top>.

56. *The National Security Strategy of the United States of America*, September 2002, <www. whitehouse.gov/nsc/nss.pdf>.

57. 'Bush: Leave Iraq within 48 hours.'

58. Associated Press, '"We're Calling for the Vote" at U.N., Bush Says.'

59. 'Bush: Leave Iraq within 48 hours.'

60. Thomas L. Friedman, 'The Meaning of a Skull,' *New York Times*, 27 April 2003, section 4, p. 13.

61. 'Blair's Address to a Joint Session of Congress,' 17 July 2003 <www.nytimes. com/2003/07/17/international/worldspecial/17WEB-BTEX.html>.

62. Alan Freeman, 'Rumsfeld takes victory tour,' *Globe and Mail*, 1 May 2003, pp. A1, A14.

63. Fernando R. Tesón, *Humanitarian Intervention: An Inquiry into Law and Morality* (New York: Transnational Publishers, Inc., 1997), pp. 121–2.

64. Robert Fisk, 'Americans defend two untouchable ministries from the hordes of looters,' *Independent*, 14 April 2003 <www.robert-fisk.com/articles229.htm>.

65. Susan Sachs and Edmund L. Andrews, 'Iraq's Slide Into Lawlessness Squanders Good Will for U.S.' *New York Times*, 18 May 2003, section 1, p. 1.

66. Tesón, *Humanitarian Intervention*, pp. 121–2.

67. UNICEF, 'Iraq survey finds child health sliding,' 13 May 2003 <www.unicef.org/ newsline/2003/03pr34iraq.htm>.

68. Mark MacKinnon, 'Children's Health in Crisis, Iraqi doctors say,' *Globe and Mail*, 28 June 2003: A13.

69. Patrick E. Tyler, 'Barrels Looted at Nuclear Site Raise Fears for Iraqi Villagers,' *New York Times*, 8 June 2003, p. 1.

70. Agence France Presse, 'Power restoration to take two years,' *Dawn* (Pakistan) 14 September 2003 <www.dawn.com/2003/09/14/int1.htm>.

71. Neela Banerjee, 'No Power, No Rebirth in Iraqi Business,' *New York Times*, 25 May 2003, p. BU 1.

72. Rajiv Chandrasekaran, 'Troubles Temper Triumphs in Iraq,' *Washington Post*, 18 August 2003, p. A01.

73. Walter Pincus, 'Skepticism About U.S. Deep, Iraq Poll Shows Motive for Invasion Is Focus of Doubts,' *Washington Post*, 12 November 2003, p. A18.

74. Tesón, *Humanitarian Intervention*, p. 122.

75. Chandrasekaran, 'Troubles Temper Triumphs in Iraq'; Patrick E. Tyler, 'Iraqis Will Join Governing Council U.S. Is Setting Up,' *New York Times*, 8 July 2003 <www. nytimes.com/2003/07/08/international/worldspecial/08IRAQ.html>.

76. William Booth and Rajiv Chandrasekaran, 'Occupation Forces Halt Elections Throughout Iraq,' *Washington Post*, 28 June 2003, p. A20.

77. L. Paul Bremer III, 'The Road Ahead in Iraq – and How to Navigate It,' *New York Times*, 13 July 2003, p. WK13 (emphasis added).

78. Rajiv Chandrasekaran, 'Top Cleric Faults U.S. Blueprint For Iraq,' *Washington Post*, 27 November, 2003, p. A01; 'Alternatives to Iraqi Council Eyed,' *Washington Post*, 9 November 2003, p. A01; Joel Brinkley, 'Iraqis in Accord on Fast Schedule to Regain Power,' *New York Times*, 16 November 2003, p. 1.

79. On complicity in war crimes see Peter Stoett, 'Unpunished Complicities of Genocide,' *Conference: The Canadian Highway to the International Criminal Court* (Canadian Institute for the Administration of Justice: Montreal, 1 May 2003).

80. Matthew White, 'Death Tolls for the Man-made Megadeaths of the Twentieth Century' <users.erols.com/mwhite28/warstat2.htm#Iran-Iraq>.

81. Kenneth Roth, 'Indict Saddam,' *Wall Street Journal*, 22 March 2002 <hrw.org/editorials/2002/iraq_032202.htm>; Glen Rangwala, 'Who armed Saddam?' *Labour Left Briefing*, October 2002 <middleeastreference.org.uk/llb020916a.html>.

82. Research Unit for Political Economy, 'Behind the War on Iraq,' *Monthly Review*, vol. 55 no. 1, May 2003, page 20 at 31; David Morgan, 'Ex-U.S. official says CIA aided Baathists,' *Toronto Star*, 20 April 2003, p. F3; Michael Dobbs, 'U.S. Had Key Role in Iraq Buildup,' *Washington Post*, 30 December 2002, p. A01.

83. Rahul Mahajan, *The New Crusade: America's War on Terrorism* (New York: Monthly Review Press, 2002), p. 106; Peter Gowan, *The Global Gamble: Washington's Faustian Bid for World Dominance* (London: Verso, 1999), pp. 156–7.

84. Matthew White, 'Death Tolls for the Man-made Megadeaths of the Twentieth Century.'

85. William M. Arkin, 'America Cluster Bombs Iraq,' *Washington Post online*, 26 February 2001; Michael Smith, '100 jets join attack on Iraq,' *Daily Telegraph*, 6 September 2002 <www.telegraph.co.uk/news/main.jhtml?xml=/news/2002/09/06/wirq06.xml&sSheet=/portal/2002/09/06/ixport.html>.

86. Michael Byers, 'The Shifting Foundations of International Law: A Decade of Forceful Measures against Iraq,' (2002), *European Journal of International Law*, vol. 13, p. 21. Security Council Resolution 986 (1995), paragraph 3.

87. United Nations Press Release, 'Secretary-General's Address at the University of Bordeaux' (SG/SM 4560 24 April 1991), p. 5.

88. *New York Times*, 29 October 1996, p. A8.

89. Mohamed M. Ali and Iqbal H. Shah, 'Sanctions and Childhood Mortality in Iraq,' *Lancet*, vol. 355, No. 9,218, 27 May 2000, p. 1851.

90. *La Repubblica*, 22 February 2001, p. 18.

91. Tariq Ali, 'Our Herods,' *New Left Review*, second series, no. 5, p. 13 (Sept.–Oct. 2000).

92. 'Editorial: Iraq's Children,' *Lancet*, vol. 355, no. 9,218, 27 May 2000, p. 1,837.

93. John Pilger, 'The great charade,' *Observer*, Sunday 14 July 2002 <www.guardian.co.uk/Archive/Article/0,4273,4461028,00.html>.

94. Chandrasekaran, 'Troubles Temper Triumphs in Iraq.'

95. Anthony Shadid, 'A Villager Attacks U.S. Troops, but Why?' *Washington Post*, 11 August 2003, p. A01.

96. Rossana Rossanda, 'Ritirateli' ('Withdraw Them'), *Il Manifesto*, 13 November 2003, p. 1 (my translation).

97. Ken Roth, *War in Iraq: Not a Humanitarian Intervention* (New York: Human Rights Watch, January 2004) <http://hrw.org/wr2k4/3.htm#_Toc58744952>; see, to the same effect, Antonio Cassese, 'A Follow-Up: Forcible Humanitarian Countermeasures and Opinio Necessitatis,' *European Journal of International Law*, vol. 10 (1999), p. 791.

98. Michael J. Glennon, 'How War Left the Law Behind,' *New York Times*, 21 November 2002, p. A37.

99. Anthony Westell, 'Another League of Nations,' *Globe and Mail*, 21 September 2002, p. A19.

100. Richard Perle, 'Thank God for the death of the UN,' *Guardian*, 21 March 2003 <www.guardian.co.uk/comment/story/0,3604,918764,00.html>.

CHAPTER 2: AFGHANISTAN 2001

1. John F. Burns, 'Villagers Say U.S. Should have Looked not Leapt,' *New York Times*, 17 February 2002, p. 12.

2. Nahlah Ayed, 'Forces set 50 Afghans free, decide to keep five,' *Globe and Mail*, 31 May 2002, p. A18; 'We were better off under the Russians,' *Time Magazine*, 17 June 2002, vol. 159, no. 23 <www.time.com/time/europe/magazine/article/0,13005,901020624-262916,00.html>.

3. Rory McCarthy, 'US planes rain death on the innocent,' *Guardian*, 1 December 2001 <www.guardian.co.uk/afghanistan/story/0,1284,610052,00.html>. Marc W. Herold, 'A Dossier on Civilian Victims of United States' Aerial Bombing of Afghanistan: A Comprehensive Accounting' (Database at <www.cursor.org/stories/civilian_deaths. htm>).

4. Dexter Filkins, 'Flaws in U.S. Air War Left Hundreds of Civilians Dead,' *New York Times*, 21 July 2002, p. 1.

5. Michael E. O'Hanlon, 'A Flawed Masterpiece,' *Foreign Affairs*, vol. 81, no. 3, March/April 2002, p. 47 at p. 59; Rahul Mahajan, *The New Crusade: America's War on Terrorism* (New York: Monthly Review Press, 2002), pp. 46–7.

6. Herold, 'A Dossier on Civilian Victims of United States' Aerial Bombing of Afghanistan'; Marc W. Herold, 'Counting the dead,' *Guardian*, 8 August 2002 <www.guardian.co.uk/comment/story/0,3604,770915,00.html>.

7. Carl Conetta, *Operation Enduring Freedom: Why a Higher Rate of Civilian Bombing Casualties?*, Project on Defense Alternatives, Briefing Report #11 (18 January 2002) <www.comw.org/pda/0201oef.html>. See Mahajan, *The New Crusade*, p. 50 for why the Herold figure is more likely to be accurate.

8. Michael Finkel, 'To Wait Or To Flee,' *New York Times Magazine*, 17 February 2002: p. 34 at pp. 36, 37, and 68. See also *Globe and Mail*, 11 December 2001, p. A10.

9. Jonathan Steele, 'Forgotten victims,' *Guardian*, 20 May 2002, <www.guardian. co.uk/Archive/Article/0,4273,4416837,00.html>; see also Paul Koring, 'Voices of war dissent grow louder as starvation stalks Afghanistan,' *Globe and Mail*, 3 November 2001, p. A4.

10. Eric Schmitt, 'Afghans Link Civilian Deaths to U.S. Bomb,' *New York Times*, 2 July 2002, section A, p. 1; Carlotta Gall, 'Hunt for Taliban Leaves Village with Horror,' *New York Times*, 8 July 2002, section A, p. 1; and 'U.S. Plans Investigation Into Afghan Strike,' *New York Times*, 14 July 2002, p. 10.

11. April Witt, 'U.S. Bomb Kills 11 Civilians in Afghanistan,' *Washington Post*, 10 April 2003, p. A25.

12. 'US bombing kills two Taliban, 10 civilians in southern Afghanistan,' *Hindustan Times*, 20 September 2003 <www.hindustantimes.com/news/181_383350,00050004. htm>; '6 children die in raid on Afghan compound,' *Toronto Star*, 11 December 2003, p. A3.

13. The Project on Defense Alternatives puts the Taliban fighters killed at 3,000–4,000 (Conetta, *Operation Enduring Freedom*). A much higher figure (8,000–12,000) can be found in O'Hanlon, 'A Flawed Masterpiece,' p. 55. About 3,000 Taliban prisoners appear to have been massacred at Mazar Al Sharif alone: 'Film indicts US over massacre of 3000,' *Herald* (Glasgow), 19 December 2002, p. 11.

14. Dexter Filkins with Barry Bearak, 'A Tribe Is Prey to Vengeance After Taliban's Fall in North,' *New York Times*, 7 March 2002 <www.nytimes.com>. David Filipov, 'Warlord's men commit rape in revenge against Taliban,' *Boston Globe*, 24 February 2002 <www.boston.com/globe/search>.

15. O'Hanlon, 'A Flawed Masterpiece,' pp. 48, 57.

16. State of the Union Address to Congress on 29 January 2002 <www.state.gov/g/wi/ rls/14573.htm>.

17. See Secretary of Defense Donald Rumsfeld, 4 December 2001, 'Department of Defense News Briefing' <www.defenselink.mil/news/Dec2001/t12042001_t1204sd. html>.

18. A RAWA video of the public execution of an Afghan woman by the Taliban in the Kabul Sports Stadium on 16 November 1999 was aired by CNN and helped to fuel disgust with the Taliban.

19. These statements can all be found on the RAWA website <rawa.fancymarketing. net>.

20. Countries surveyed whose peoples were in favor of the war were the US (88 percent in favor to 7 percent opposed), Canada (66:23), the UK (65:19), France (60:25), Germany (60:32), Italy (58:30), and Japan (49:44); countries opposed were South

Korea (50:43), Spain (52:31), China (52:28), Turkey (70:18), and Argentina (77:13). 'G-7 countries Find Their Public Supportive of U.S. Military Action in Afghanistan, But Serious Opposition Appears in Other Countries, New Global Poll Finds' <www. ipsos-reid.com/media/dsp_displaypr_cdn.cfm?id_to_view=1385>. An international poll done by the Swiss firm Isopublic a week after 11 September found only the Americans and Israelis in favor of military action against states shown to be 'harboring terrorism,' with most of the world in favor of judicial solutions: 'Around 80 percent of Europeans and around 90 percent of South Americans favor extradition and a court verdict,' Reuters, 'Israel, U.S. only countries where majority backs military strike' *Haaretz English Edition*, 22 September 2001 <www. haaretzdaily.com/hasen/pages/ShArt.html?itemNo=76377>; David Miller, 'Blair should read the polls,' *Guardian*, 3 October 2001 <www.guardian.co.uk/comment/story/0,3604,562145,00.html>.

21.   Christine Gray, 'From Unity to Polarization: International Law and the Use of Force against Iraq' (2002), *European Journal of International Law*, vol. 13, p. 1 at p. 9.

22.   Resolution 661 of 6 August 1990.

23.   Mahajan, *The New Crusade*, p. 26.

24.   John Bassett Moore, *A Digest of International Law*, Vol. II (1906), p. 412; also at www.yale.edu/lawweb/avalon/diplomacy/britian/br-1842d.htm>.

25.   *Nuremberg Tribunal Judgment*, pp. 57–60.

26.   *Nicaragua v. United States of America*, 1986, paragraph 237.

27.   Ibid. at paragraph 195 (emphasis added).

28.   Christine Gray, *International Law and the Use of Force* (Oxford University Press, 2000), p. 118. Speaking of earlier reprisals by Israel and the US against terrorist attacks, she states: 'the actions look more like reprisals, because they were punitive rather than defensive ... given that the attacks on the nationals had already taken place. The USA and Israel aimed to retaliate and deter and said their actions were pre-emptive. The problem for the USA and Israel is that all states agree that in principle forcible reprisals are unlawful.' On the effect of Article 51, see also ibid., pp. 92–6; Albrecht Randelzhofer, 'Article 51' in Bruno Simma, (ed.) *The Charter of the United Nations: A Commentary* (Oxford: Oxford University Press, 1994), pp. 661–78; and Thomas Franck, 'Symposium on the Gulf War,' (1991), *American Journal of International Law*, vol. 85, p. 63.

29.   See for example Oscar Schachter, 'United Nations Law in the Gulf Conflict,' (1991), *American Journal of International Law* vol. 85, p. 452, and Vietnam War Under-Secretary of State Eugene Rostow, 'Until What? Enforcement action or Self-Defense?' (1991), *American Journal of International Law* vol. 85, p. 506.

30.   'Taleban leader protests Bin Laden's innocence,' BBC News, 19 September 2001 <news.bbc.co.uk/1/hi/world/south_asia/1552483.stm>.

31.   'Osama Bin Laden should choose another place,' *Guardian*, 21 September 2001 <www.guardian.co.uk/waronterror/story/0.1361,555694,00.html>.

32.   Speech to Joint session of US Congress, 20 September 2001 (emphasis added), CNN Newsroom, 21 September 2001 <www.cnn.com/TRANSCRIPTS/0109/21/nr.00. html>.

33.   Mahajan, *The New Crusade*, p. 29.

34.   Ibid., pp. 30–1.

35.   John Pilger, 'An unconscionable threat to humanity,' in P. Scraton, (ed.) *Beyond September 11: An Anthology of Dissent* (London: Pluto Press, 2002), p. 19 at p. 24.

36.   See Security Council Resolution 138, 23 June 1960.

37.   Carl Conetta, *Strange Victory: A Critical Appraisal of Operation Enduring Freedom and the Afghanistan War* (Project on Defense Alternatives, 30 January 2002 <www. comw.org/pda/0201strangevic.html>.

38.   See Isabel Hilton, 'Now we pay the warlords to tyrannise the Afghan people,' *Guardian*, 31 July 2003 <www.guardian.co.uk/comment/story/0,3604,1009416,00. html>; Human Rights Watch, *'Killing You is a Very Easy Thing For Us': Human Rights Abuses in Southeast Afghanistan*, July 2003 Vol. 15, No. 05 (C) <www.hrw.org/

reports/2003/afghanistan0703); Noreen S. Ahmed-Ullah, 'Afghan laws still repress women. Refusing suitor, leaving husband bring jail time,' *Chicago Tribune*, 28 April 2002 <rawa.fancymarketing.net/jail.htm>; Geoffrey York, 'Holy war engulfs Afghan feminist,' *Globe and Mail*, 7 August 2002: A1; RAWA Statement on International Women's Day, 8 March 2002, 'Let Us Struggle Against War and Fundamentalism and for Peace and Democracy!' <rawasongs.fancymarketing.net/mar8-02en.htm>; United Nations Development Programme, *Afghanistan Recovery. Needs Assessment Report* <www.undp.org/afghanistan/needsreports/needsreport2.html>.

39. A shopkeeper in the town of Spin Boldak, quoted in Mark MacKinnon, 'Afghan peace now crumbling,' *Globe and Mail*, 2 February 2002: p. A13.

40. F. Chipaux, 'Hamid Karzai, un Pachtoune nommé président. Le nouvel homme fort de l'Afghanistan connait bien le monde occidental,' *Le Monde*, 13 December 2001; 'Afghan pipeline given go-ahead,' BBC News, 30 May 2002 <news.bbc.co.uk/hi/english/business/newsid_2017000/2017044.stm>.

41. Marcus Gee, 'Why they bomb Afghanistan,' *Globe and Mail*, 3 November 2001, p. A15.

42. Mark MacKinnon, 'Afghanistan in need of promised donations,' *Globe and Mail*, 18 June 2002, p. A14.

43. 'Two Norwegian peacekeepers injured in attack on ISAF patrol,' *Agence France-Presse*, 13 May 2003; <sg.news.yahoo.com/030513/1/3aya1.html>; Zvi Bar'el, 'Tribal and strife,' *Haaretz*, 22 April 2003 <www.haaretzdaily.com>; 'US bombing kills two Taliban, 10 civilians in southern Afghanistan'; James Astill, 'Plea for security rethink as French aid worker is buried UN says relief work in Afghanistan cannot continue on existing terms,' *Guardian*, 21 November 2003 <www.guardian.co.uk/international/story/0,3604,1089805,00.html>; Zahid Hussain, 'Afghan president seeks help as Taleban attacks Continue,' *The Times*, 1 October 2003 <www.timesonline.co.uk/article/0,,3-837325,00.html>.

44. Chris Wattie and Sheldon Alberts, 'Canadian troops to be deployed to Afghanistan; 2,000 soldiers to join NATO force in Kabul,' *National Post*, 6 May 2003 <www.nationalpost.com/national/story.html?id=AE317391-4C23-48EF-9AA4-6DEE96D44201>.

45. David Johnston, Don Van Natta Jr. and Judith Mill, 'Qaeda's New Links Increase Threats From Global Sites,' *New York Times*, 16 June 2002, pp. 1, 10.

46. See Gray, *International Law and the Use of Force*, p. 111ff.

47. RAWA, 'Let Us Struggle Against War and Fundamentalism and for Peace and Democracy!'

48. Ahmed Rashid, *Taliban: Militant Islam, Oil and Fundamentalism in Central Asia* (New Haven: Yale University Press, 2000), p. 146; Pilger, 'An unconscionable threat to humanity,' p. 28; testimony by John J. Maresca, Vice President, International Relations, Unocal Corporation To House Committee On International Relations Subcommittee On Asia And The Pacific, 12 February 1998 <www.house.gov/international_relations/105th/ap/wsap212982.htm>; 'Caspian Diplomacy,' *International Herald Tribune*, 17 April 2001, p. 8.

49. Lewis H. Lapham, 'Notebook: Mythography,' *Harper's Magazine*, February 2002, p. 6 at p. 9.

50. Naomi Klein, 'Game Over', *The Nation*, 15 September 2001 <www.thenation.com>.

51. John Powers, 'On Media Fundamentalism,' *LA Weekly*, 21–27 September 2001 <www.laweekly.com/ink/01/44/on-powers.php>.

52. See United Nations Development Programme, *Human Development Report 1999*, p. 38 <hdr.undp.org/reports/global/1999/en/default.cfm>; *Human Development Report 2003* <www.undp.org/hdr2003/pdf/hdr03_HDI.pdf>, pp. 237, 339.

53. International Energy Association, *Key World Energy Statistics* <www.iea.org/statist/keyworld/keystats.htm>.

54. United Nations Development Programme, *Human Development Report 1999*, pp. 134–7.

55. Doug Saunders, 'The Pope, Picasso, Mandela and Q,' *Globe and Mail*, 20 October 2001, p. R8.
56. 'Our best point the way,' *Globe and Mail*, 7 December 2001, p. A21.
57. 'Department of Defense News Briefing,' 4 December 2001 <www.defenselink. mil/news/Dec2001/t12042001_t1204sd.html>.
58. Tom Tomorrow, 'Are you a Real American? Take this quiz and find out!,' *New York Times*, 30 June 2002, p. WK3.
59. 'A Day Of Terror: Bush's Remarks to the Nation on the Terrorist Attacks,' *New York Times*, 12 September 2001, section A, p. 4.
60. See Chapter 3, Note 240.
61. United Nations General Assembly, *Report of the Ad Hoc Committee on International Terrorism*, UN GAOR, 28th Sess., Supp. No. 28 (A/9028) (1973).
62. *U.N.G.A. Resolution on Measures to Prevent International Terrorism*, 18 December 1972/RES/3034 (XXVII).
63. United Nations Security Council Resolution 1160, 31 March 1998.
64. United Nations General Assembly, *Report of the Ad Hoc Committee on International Terrorism*.
65. Noam Chomsky and Edward S. Herman, *The Political Economy of Human Rights: The Washington Connection and Third World Fascism* (Montreal: Black Rose Books, 1979).
66. Tom Harris, 'How Apache Helicopters Work' <fitness.howstuffworks.com/apache-helicopter.htm>.
67. David Barsamian, 'The United States is a Leading Terrorist State: An Interview with Noam Chomsky,' *Monthly Review*, vol. 53, no. 6 (November 2001), p. 10.
68. Michael Walzer, 'Can There Be a Decent Left?' *Dissent*, Spring 2002, p. 19.
69. See the public relations reasons offered by Donald Rumsfeld: 'Secretary of Defense Donald Rumsfeld updates the world on the war against terrorism,' *NewsHour with Jim Lehrer Transcript*, 7 November 2001 <www.pbs.org/newshour/bb/military/july-dec01/rumsfeld2_11-7.html>.
70. Department of Defense Dictionary of Military Terms as amended up until 19 December 2001 <www.dtic.mil/doctrine/jel/doddict>.
71. T. C. Schelling, 'Dispersal, Deterrence, and Damage,' *Operations Research*, vol. 9, no. 3 (1961), p. 363.
72. NATO Press Briefing, 26 March 1999.
73. NATO Press Briefing, 10 May 1999.
74. NATO Press Briefing, 13 April 1999.
75. NATO Press Briefing, 1 June 1999.
76. NATO, 'The Conduct of the Air Campaign,' 30 October 2000 <www.nato.int/ kosovo/repo2000/conduct.htm> visited 29 May 2003.
77. Julian Borger, 'McVeigh brushes aside deaths,' *Guardian*, 30 March 2001 <www. guardian.co.uk/Archive/Article/0,4273,4162150,00.html>; Carolyn Thompson, 'Book: remorseful McVeigh calls kids "collateral damage",' *SouthCoast Today*, 29 March 2001 <www.s-t.com/daily/03-01/03-29-01/a02wn014.htm>.
78. Air Force Gen. Richard B. Myers, Chairman of the U.S. Joint Chiefs of Staff, 15 October 2001. Office of International Information Programs, U.S. Department of State <usinfo.state.gov; www.usis-australia.gov/hyper/2001/1016/epf206.htm>.
79. Robert Fisk, 'It was an outrage, an obscenity,' *Independent*, 27 March 2003 <argument. independent.co.uk/commentators/story.jsp?story=391165>.
80. Dexter Filkins and Michael Wilson, 'Marines, Battling in Streets, Seek Control of City in South', *New York Times*, 25 March 2003, p. A1.
81. Associated Press, '"We're Calling for the Vote" at U.N., Bush Says,' *Washington Post*, 7 March 2003, p. A18.
82. Kenneth Anderson, 'Who Owns the Rules of War?,' *New York Times Magazine*, 13 April 2003, p. 38 at p. 42.
83. Legality of the Threat or Use of Nuclear Weapons (Advisory Opinion of 8 July 1996), [1996] ICJ Reports 226, p. 491.

84. William Safire, 'On Language: "Regime Changes",' *New York Times Magazine*, 10 March 2002, p. 20.
85. Richard L. Berke and Janet Elder, 'Poll Finds Strong Support for U.S. Use of Military Force,' *New York Times*, 16 September 2001, p. 6.
86. United States Department of Defense, 15 October 2001 (Office of International Information Programs, US Department of State – <usinfo.state.gov>).
87. 'Department of Defense News Briefing,' 4 December 2001.
88. Denise Duclaux and Charles Aldinger, 'Afghan Government Protests Attack; Inquiry Launched,' *Miami Herald*, 2 July 2002 <www.miami.com/mld/miami/3583640. htm>.
89. Khalid Amyreh, 'Killing Deliberately "By Mistake",' *Palestine Chronicle*, 4 September 2002 <palestinechronicle.com/article.php?story=20020904045000206>.
90. O'Hanlon, 'A Flawed Masterpiece,' pp. 48, 57.
91. Exodus XXI: 28–9, J. H. Hertz, ed., *The Pentateuch and Haftorahs*, second edition (London: Soncino Press, 1988), p. 310 (emphasis added).
92. 'Couple guilty in killer dogs case.' BBC News, 22 March 2002 (emphasis added), <news.bbc.co.uk/hi/english/world/americas/newsid_1886000/1886638.stm>.
93. Evelyn Nieves, 'Woman's Murder Conviction in Mauling Case Is Overturned,' *New York Times*, 18 June 2002, section A , p. 12 (emphasis added).
94. Associated Press, 'Dog Owner in Mauling due Retrial,' 17 June 2002 <www. intercountynews.com/site/news.cfm?newsid=4473278&BRD=1994&PAG=461& dept_id=226369&rfi=6>.
95. Douglas N. Husak, 'Transferred Intent,' *Notre Dame Journal of Law, Ethics and Public Policy* (1996), vol. 10, p. 65.
96. 2 Plowden, p. 473 at p. 474.
97. 29 P. 3d 209, 220 n9 (Sup. Ct of Calif.). Another example is *Commonwealth v. Fisher* 742 N.E.2d 61 (Mass. 2001).
98. Article 125.25 and .27.
99. Section 229(b).
100. See for example Husak, 'Transferred Intent,' p. 87.
101. *Hyam v. DPP* [1974] 2 All ER 41, p. 56. Andrew Ashworth, *Principles of Criminal Law* (Oxford University Press, 1999), p. 179.
102. Glanville Williams, 'Oblique Intention' [1987] *Cambridge Law Journal* 417, at pp. 419 and 421.
103. Wayne R. LaFave, *Criminal Law*, third edition (St. Paul: West, 2000), pp. 229, 231.
104. Ibid., p. 661.
105. Penal Code of Texas, revised 31 May 2002, Section 19.02 (b), *Texas Legislature Online* <www.capitol.state.tx.us/statutes/petoc.html> (emphasis added).
106. Article 19.03.
107. The American Law Institute, *Model penal code and commentaries* (Philadelphia, PA.: American Law Institute, 1980), pp. 14 and 226. See also the *Canadian Criminal Code*, sections 229 (a) and (c).
108. Illinois Compiled Statutes, Criminal Code of 1961 (720 ILCS 5/9–1), Criminal Offenses, section 9.1 (emphasis added).
109. *New York Penal Code*, Articles 125.25 and .27.
110. Borger, 'McVeigh brushes aside deaths'; Thompson, 'Book: Remorseful McVeigh calls kids "collateral damage".'
111. William Walker, 'Lawyer says transcript vindicates F-16 pilot blamed in deaths,' *Toronto Star*, 19 July 2002, p. A1.

CHAPTER 3: KOSOVO 1999

1. Richard Perle, 'Thank God for the death of the UN,' *Guardian*, 21 March 2003 <www.guardian.co.uk/comment/story/0,3604,918764,00.html>.

2. 'Oh what a lovely war!' *Economist*, 24 April 1999, p. 50 (emphasis added); BBC News, 23 April 1999 <news.bbc.co.uk/2/hi/europe/326481.stm#map>. In Taiwan, opponents outnumbered supporters by about two to one, though a third had no opinion.

3. Noam Chomsky, *The New Military Humanism: Lessons from Kosovo* (Vancouver: New Star Books, 1999), p. 142; United Nations, Security Council Press Release, 'Security Council rejects demand for cessation of use of force against Federal Republic of Yugoslavia' (SC/6659; 26 March 1999).

4. 'Majority in Greece wants Clinton tried for war crimes,' *Irish Times*, 27 May 1999.

5. Michael Ignatieff, *Virtual War: Kosovo and Beyond* (Toronto: Viking Books, 2000), p. 193.

6. *Declaration of the Group of 77*, South Summit, Havana, Cuba, 10–14 April 2000, paragraph 54 <www.g77.org/Docs/Declaration_G77Summit.htm>.

7. Human Rights Watch, 'Civilian Deaths in the NATO Air Campaign,' vol. 12, no. 1 (D), February 2000.

8. Federal Republic of Yugoslavia, Federal Ministry for Foreign Affairs, *Economic Survey*, (Belgrade, 10 November 1999, no. 2), p. 1: 'more than 1,800 killed.'

9. *Washington Post* investigative reporter Michael Dobbs estimated 'from independent sources' that 1,600 civilians had been killed in the bombing: Michael Dobbs, 'A War-Torn Reporter Reflects,' *Washington Post Magazine*, 11 July 1999, p. B1. The figure of 1,200 is given in Marc Herold, *Blown Away: The Myth and Reality of Precision Bombing in Afghanistan* (Monroe, Maine: Common Courage Press, 2004), p. 30.

10. Michael E. O'Hanlon, 'A Flawed Masterpiece,' *Foreign Affairs*, vol. 81, no. 3 (March/April 2002) p. 47 at p. 55; Federal Republic of Yugoslavia, *Economic Survey*: '5,000 wounded ... some 2,000 wounded persons will remain disabled for life.'

11. Dobbs estimates 1,000 military dead: Dobbs, 'A War-Torn Reporter Reflects.'

12. 'Danube study questions warfare that bombs polluting targets,' *Guardian*, 27 October 1999, p. 15.

13. Joan McQueeney Mitric, 'L'eredità ambientale di una guerra sporca,' in Francesco Strazzari et al., *La pace intrattabile. Kosovo 1999/2000: radiografia del dopo-bombe.* (Trieste: Asterios editore, 2000), p. 186.

14. 'The EIU Estimates War Damage in Yugoslavia at $60bn,' *Economist Intelligence Unit*, 23 August 1999 <www.economistgroup.com/new/Yucrq399.html>.

15. Ibid.

16. Gabriela Arcadu, 'I rifugiati,' in Strazzari, *La pace intrattabile*, p. 63; Organization for Security and Co-operation in Europe, *Kosovo/Kosova As Seen, As Told* (1999), chapter 14, www.osce.org/kosovo/documents/reports/hr/part1/ch14.htm.

17. 'Many have fled terror but some of those Ward spoke to said they were fleeing the NATO bombs.' Audrey Gillan, 'What's the story?' *London Review of Books*, vol. 21, no. 11 (27 May 1999) p. 15 at p. 16.

18. 'Report of the Secretary-General prepared pursuant to Resolutions 1160 (1998), 1199 (1998) and 1203 (1998) of the Security Council,' (S/1998/1221, 24 December 1998).

19. Gillan, 'What's the story?' p. 16.

20. 'Erasing History: Ethnic cleansing in Kosovo.' (U.S. Department of State, Washington D.C., May 1999) <www.state.gov/www/regions/eur/rpt_9905_ethnic_ksvo_2.html>.

21. Ignatieff, *Virtual War*, p. 200 (emphasis added).

22. Chomsky, *New Military Humanism*, p. 92.

23. Ibid., p. 21; Ignatieff, *Virtual War*, p. 96.

24. Mick Hume, 'Nazifying the Serbs, from Bosnia to Kosovo,' in Philip Hammond and Edward S. Herman (eds), *Degraded Capability: The Media and the Kosovo Crisis* (London, Pluto Press, 2000), p. 71.

25. CBS *Face the Nation*, 16 May 1999 (Burrelle's Information Services, 1999).

26. Gillan, 'What's the Story?'

27. Pablo Ordaz, 'Policías y forenses españoles no hallan pruebas de genocidio al norte de Kosovo,' *El Pais*, 23 septiembre 1999 <www.elpais.es/archivo>.

28. *Globe and Mail*, 12 October 1999, p. A2.

29. 'The Truth About Rajmonda,' *CBC Television*, 8 September 1999 <www.cbc.ca/national/pgminfo/kosovo3/-rajmonda.html>.

30. 'U.S. government support was essential to the project [but] convergence with the views of the U.S. government is purely coincidental,' *Political Killings in Kosova/Kosovo March–June 1999* (American Bar Association Central and East European Law Institute, 2000), p. 11 <shr.aaas.org/kosovo/pk/xi>.

31. Geoffrey Nice, for the Prosecution, in his opening statement at Milosevic's trial. *Milosevic Trial Transcript*, 12 February 2002, p. 14 (emphasis added).

32. See above, Note 16.

33. See Maria Koinova and Luis Rodriguez-Pinero Royo, 'La condizione dei diritti umani e delle minoranze,' in Strazzari, *La pace intrattabile*.

34. Ibid., p. 135; 'Kosovo Serbs Urge West to Defend Their Rights,' by Richard Murphy, Vienna (Reuters), 31 May 2001 <news.suc.org/bydate/2001/May_31/0.html>.

35. Koinova e Rodriguez-Pinero Royo, 'La condizione dei diritti umani e delle minoranze', pp. 135–6.

36. Aleksandar Mitic, 'The destiny of the Serbs of Kosovo,' in Strazzari, *La pace intrattabile*, p. 149.

37. Koinova e Rodriguez-Pinero Royo, 'La condizione dei diritti umani e delle minoranze', pp. 140–1. 'Bomb Kills 7 Serbs in Kosovo Convoy Guarded by NATO,' *New York Times*, 17 February 2001, p. A1.

38. Vanessa Gera, 'Ethnic-related violence surges again in Kosovo,' (Associated Press), *Seattle Times*, 2 September 2003 <seattletimes.nwsource.com>.

39. Steven Erlanger, 'No Solution in Sight To Balkan Tensions,' *International Herald Tribune*, 17 April 2001, p. 9.

40. Koinova e Rodriguez-Pinero Royo, 'La condizione dei diritti umani e delle minoranze,' p. 142.

41. Marco Montanari, 'Strutture economiche kosovare,' in Strazzari, *La pace intrattabile*, p. 99.

42. Susanna Minezzi, 'Traffico di donne. Un mercato in espansione,' in Strazzari, *La pace intrattabile*, p. 181.

43. Lord Robertson of Port Ellen, 'Kosovo One Year On: Achievement and Challenge,' 21 March 2000 <www.nato.int/kosovo/repo2000/index.htm>.

44. Ignatieff, *Virtual War*, p. 207.

45. By far the most compelling account of American hypocrisy over 'military humanism' you'll ever read can be found in Chomsky, *New Military Humanism*.

46. Ignatieff, *Virtual War*, p. 155.

47. Robertson, 'Kosovo One Year On.'

48. See generally, Diana Johnstone, *Fools' Crusade: Yugoslavia, NATO and Western Delusions* (New York: Monthly Review Press); David Owen, *Balkan Odyssey* (London: Victor Gollancz, 1995); Susan L. Woodward, *Balkan Tragedy: Chaos and Dissolution after the Cold War* (Washington, D.C.: Brookings Institution, 1995); Peter Gowan, *The Global Gamble: Washington's Faustian Bid for World Dominance* (London: Verso, 1999); Bob Allen, *Why Kosovo? The Anatomy of a Needless War* (Ottawa: Canadian Centre for Policy Alternatives, 1999); Steve Terrett, *The Dissolution of Yugoslavia and the Badinter Arbitration Commission: A Contextual Study of Peace-Making Efforts in the Post-Cold War World* (Ashgate: Dartmouth, 2000). Andrea Kathryn Talentino, 'Bosnia,' in Michael E. Brown and Richard N. Rosecrance (eds), *The Costs of Conflict: Prevention and Cure in the Global Arena* (Rowman and Littlefield Publishers, Inc., 1999); John Williams, *Legitimacy in International Relations and the Rise and Fall of Yugoslavia* (New York: St. Martin's Press, 1998); David Chandler, 'Western Intervention and the Disintegration of Yugoslavia, 1989–1999,' in Hammond and Herman, *Degraded Capability*.

49. Deuteronomy XV: 6, in J. H. Hertz, ed., *The Pentateuch and Haftorahs*, second edition (London: Soncino Press, 1988), p. 812.
50. Jeffrey Sachs, 'Beyond Bretton Woods: A New Blueprint,' *Economist*, 1 October 1994, p. 23 at p. 24.
51. There are enormous discrepancies in estimates of the number of casualties in the Bosnian civil war, which range from 25,000 to 250,000 dead: Owen, *Balkan Odyssey*, p. 80 and Chandler, 'Western Intervention and the Disintegration of Yugoslavia, 1989–1999,' p. 26. For the dubious bases of the high casualty counts, see Johnstone, *Fools' Crusade*, pp. 54–5.
52. Owen, *Balkan Odyssey*.
53. Quoted in Paul Phillips, 'Why Were We Bombing Yugoslavia?' (1999), *Studies in Political Economy*, vol. 60, p. 85 at p. 94.
54. Warren Zimmerman, 'The Last Ambassador: A Memoir of the Collapse of Yugoslavia,' *Foreign Affairs*, March/April 1995, p. 13.
55. David Binder, 'U.S. Policymakers on Bosnia Admit Errors in Opposing Partition in 1992,' *New York Times*, 29 August 1993, p. 10.
56. *New York Times*, 3 February 1993, p. 1; Owen, *Balkan Odyssey*, p. 110.
57. See Security Council Resolutions 816 of 31 March 1993 and 836 of 4 June 1993.
58. Owen, *Balkan Odyssey*, p. 339.
59. Chandler, 'Western Intervention and the Disintegration of Yugoslavia, 1989–1999,' p. 29; see also David Owen, 'Lessons from Bosnia and Kosovo,' extract from a lecture delivered at the University of Geneva, 7 November 2000, (in the possession of the author) p. 5 ('Bosnia ... is now basically a NATO/EU protectorate').
60. Boutros Boutros-Ghali, *Unvanquished: A U.S.–U.N. Saga* (New York: Random House, 1999), p. 247.
61. David Binder, 'In Yugoslavia, Rising Ethnic Strife Brings Fears of Worse Civil Conflict,' *New York Times*, 1 November 1987, p. 14.
62. Zimmerman, 'The Last Ambassador', p. 3.
63. Marco Montanari, 'Strutture economiche kosovare,' p. 99 (my translation).
64. Robertson, 'Kosovo One Year On.'
65. Woodward, *Balkan Tragedy*, p. 382.
66. Ragazzi, 'Introduzione' in Strazzari, *La pace intrattabile*, p. 25 (my translation).
67. Ignatieff, *Virtual War*, p. 21.
68. Amnesty International reported thousands dead in protracted ethnic and political violence during 1998 in each of the Congo, Sierra Leone, Rwanda, Algeria, and, of course, Afghanistan, and more than a thousand each in Indonesia and Colombia (where 3,500 would die in 1999). *Amnesty International, Annual Report 1999*; *Annual Report 2000* <www.web.amnesty.org>.
69. UN Security Council Resolution 1160, 16 March 1998.
70. Robertson, 'Kosovo One Year On.'
71. Ibid.
72. Ignatieff, *Virtual War*, p. 28.
73. See also Security Council Resolution 1199, 23 September 1998.
74. Report of the Secretary General Prepared Pursuant to Resolutions 1160 (1998), 1199 (1998) and 1203 (1998) of the Security Council (United Nations Security Council S/1998/1221, 24 December 1998), paragraphs 11–14.
75. *News Hour with Jim Lehrer*, 'Return to Violence', Online News Hour, 18 January 1999 <www.pbs.org/newshour/bb/europe/jan-june99/kosovo_1-18.html>.
76. 'Clinton Voices Anger and Compassion at Serbian Intransigence on Kosovo,' *New York Times*, 20 March 1999, p. A7.
77. Confirmed by the ranking OSCE officer in Racak, testifying before the ICTY, *Milosevic Trial Transcript*, 30 May 2002, p. 5874.
78. See Johnstone, *Fools' Crusade*, pp. 238–44 and citations therein.
79. Professor Dusan Dunjic 'The (Ab)use of Forensic Medicine,' Serbian Unity Congress Website <http:www.suc.org/politics/kosovo/documents/Dunjic0499.html>.

80. 'Serbs set new conditions for Kosovo peace accord,' CNN.com, 16 March 1999 <europe.cnn.com/WORLD/europe/9902/28/kosovo.02/index.html>.
81. Written communication to me from Dr. Ranta, 6 July 2001.
82. Helena Ranta, *Report of the EU Forensic Expert Team on the Racak Incident* (Press Release, Pristina, 17 March 1999), p. 1.
83. Ibid., p. 2 (emphasis added).
84. Ibid., p. 1.
85. 'Clinton Voices Anger and Compassion.'
86. Ranta, *Report of the EU Forensic Expert Team*, p. 3.
87. Ibid.
88. 'Serbs's Killing of 40 Albanians Ruled a Crime Against Humanity,' *The New York Times*, 18 March 1999: A13; Anthony Loyd, 'Kosovo killings "a crime against humanity",' *The Times*, 18 March 1999, p. 18.
89. Ranta, *Report of the EU Forensic Expert Team*, p. 3.
90. Written communication to me from Dr. Ranta, 12 July 2001.
91. *Milosevic Trial Transcript*, 12 March 2003, pp. 17723–5, 17770, 17806–8.
92. J. Rainio, K. Lalua and A. Penttila, 'Independent forensic autopsies in an armed conflict: investigation of the victims from Racak, Kosovo,' (2001), *Forensic Science International*, vol. 116, p. 171.
93. Ibid., p. 184.
94. Ibid.
95. Ignatieff, *Virtual War*, p. 58.
96. 'Woefully unprepared for war, the KLA seems instead to have had the deliberate strategy of provoking an international intervention.' (Independent International Commission on Kosovo, *The Kosovo Report: conflict, international response, lessons learned* (New York : Oxford University Press, 2000), p. 52.
97. William E. Ratliff, '"Madeleine's War" and the Costs of Intervention. The Kosovo Precedent,' *Harvard International Review*, vol. 22, no. 4 (Winter 2001), p. 71; see also Christopher Layne and Benjamin Schwarz, 'Was it a Mistake? We Were Suckers For the KLA,' *Washington Post*, 26 March 2000, p. B1.
98. See Lawrence E. Walsh, *Final report of the Independent Counsel for Iran/Contra Matters* (Washington, D.C.: U.S. Court of Appeals for the District of Columbia Circuit, 1993), vol. 1, chapter 25; *In Re: Oliver L. North (Walker Fee Application)*, United States Court of Appeals of for the District of Columbia Circuit Division No. 86-6 (1996) <www.ll.georgetown.edu/federal/judicial/dc/opinions/9_opinions/86–00061. html>.
99. Elizabeth Shogren, 'William Walker, once criticized for his inaction in El Salvador, is treated like a hero by ethnic Albanian refugees,' *Los Angeles Times*, 14 April 1999, p. 15.
100. *Milosevic Trial Transcript*, 12 June 2002, p. 6851.
101. Ambassador William Walker, U.S. Department of State, On-the-record briefing on the Kosovo Verification Mission, 8 January 1999 (Released by the Office of the Spokesman, Washington, DC, 8 January 1999) <www.state.gov/www/policy_ remarks/1999/990108_walker_kosovo.html>.
102. Reuters, 'U.N. plan to disarm Iraq "doomed to fail",' *Toronto Star*, 27 June 2000, p. A16.
103. In fact, Walker was telling NATO military Chief Klaus Naumann at this time that most of the violations were by the KLA, not the Serbs. *Milosevic Trial Transcript*, 12 June 2002, p. 6853.
104. Ignatieff, *Virtual War*, pp. 59–60.
105. Allan Little, 'How NATO was sucked into Kosovo conflict,' *Sunday Telegraph*, 27 February 2000, p. 29.
106. United States Republican Policy Committee, 'Bosnia II: The Clinton Administration Sets Course for NATO Intervention in Kosovo' (12 August 1998) <www.senate. gov/~rpc/releases/1998/kosovo.htm>.
107. *Milosevic Trial Transcript*, 12 June 2002, pp. 6895–6.

108.   Ibid., p. 6803.
109.   Ibid., p. 6804.
110.   Letter dated 30 January 1999 from the Secretary-General of the North Atlantic Treaty Organization, addressed to the President of the Federal Republic of Yugoslavia, Appendix (United Nations Security Council S/1999/107, 2 February 1999).
111.   Owen, 'Lessons from Bosnia and Kosovo,' p. 6.
112.   Little, 'How NATO was Sucked into Kosovo Conflict.' See also Ignatieff, *Virtual War*, p. 56.
113.   Mr. Paul Heinbecker (Assistant Deputy Minister, Department of Foreign Affairs and International Trade), testifying before The Standing Committee on National Defence And Veterans Affairs of the Canadian House of Commons (*Hansard*, 9 February 1999, p. 1536).
114.   *Interim Agreement for Peace and Self-Government in Kosovo* (23 February 1999), Article 8.I.3, 'Kosovo & Yugoslavia: Law in Crisis,' *Jurist* <jurist.law.pitt.edu/ramb.htm>.
115.   Seth Ackerman, 'What Reporters Knew about Kosovo Talks – But Didn't Tell,' 2 June 1999 (Fairness & Accuracy In Reporting, New York, NY) <www.fair.org/press-releases/kosovo-talks.html>.
116.   Robertson, 'Kosovo One Year On.'
117.   *Interim Agreement for Peace and Self-Government in Kosovo*, Art. 1.1.
118.   Steven Erlanger, 'Serb View: A Victory,' *New York Times*, 24 February 1999, p. A10.
119.   *Rambouillet Accords: Co-Chairmen's Conclusions*, 23 February 1999 (Office of the High Representative – www.ohr.int/docu/d990223a.htm>.
120.   See 'Attacks on Iraq come under fire at Security Council,' CNN.com, 3 March 1999 <www.cnn.com/WORLD/meast/9903/03/iraq>); William M. Arkin, 'America Cluster Bombs Iraq,' washingtonpost.com, 26 February 2001 <washingtonpost.com/wp-dyn/articles/A46524-2001Feb23.html>; 'Iraq says Western planes kill 3 civilians,' 13 February 1999 <www.cnn.com/WORLD/meast/9902/13/iraq.01/index.html>.
121.   'Kosovo Albanians sign accord; Serbs brace for NATO attack,' CNN.com, 18 March 1999 <cnn.co.il/WORLD/europe/9903/18/kosovo.05>.
122.   Rollie Keith, 'The Diplomatic Failure of Kosovo,' *The Democrat*, vol. 39, no. 3 (May 1999) p. 10 (also at www.bc.ndp.ca); Eric Canepa, 'The Aftermath of the Publication of the German Government Documents,' ZNet <www.zmag.org/crisescurevts/germandocsmore.htm>.
123.   *Rambouillet Accords: Co-Chairmen's Conclusions*, paragraph 5; 'Bloody ambush marks anniversary of Kosovo war's start,' CNN.com, 28 February 1999 <europe.cnn.com/WORLD/europe/9902/28/kosovo.02/index.html>; 'Tension in Kosovo high after killings of Serbs,' CNN.com, 4 March 1999 <europe.cnn.com/WORLD/europe/9903/04/kosovo.02/index.html>.
124.   United Nations Security Council, Resolution 1244, 10 June 1999, Annex 2, paragraphs 3 and 4.
125.   Chomksy, *New Military Humanism*, pp. 111, 115.
126.   Robertson, 'Kosovo One Year On.'
127.   Independent International Commission on Kosovo, *The Kosovo Report*, p. 157.
128.   Robertson, 'Kosovo One Year On.'
129.   Craig R. Whitney, 'Allies Expecting "Many More Weeks" of Air Campaign,' *New York Times*, 11 April 1999, p. 10.
130.   John Goetz and Tom Walker, 'Serbian ethnic cleansing scare was a fake, says general,' *Sunday Times*, 2 April 2000, p. 21.
131.   Chomsky, *New Military Humanism*, p. 36.
132.   Ibid., p. 26.
133.   Peter Gowan, 'Making Sense of NATO's War on Yugoslavia' in L. Panitch and C. Leys (eds.), *Socialist Register 2000: Necessary And Unnecessary Utopias* (London: Merlin Press, 1999), p. 261.
134.   Ibid., p. 262.

135. Peter Gowan, 'From Rambouillet to the Chinese Embassy Bombing. Whose Stupid War Was this?' *Against the Current* <www.igc.apc.org/solidarity/atc/81NatoGowan. html>.

136. George Monbiot, 'A discreet deal in the pipeline,' *Guardian*, 15 February 2001 <www.guardian.co.uk/Archive/Article/0,4273,4136440,00.html>.

137. Johnstone, *Fools' Crusade*, p. 162.

138. 'Clinton Voices Anger and Compassion.' See also Chomsky, *New Military Humanism*, p. 134; Robertson, 'Kosovo One Year On'; and Independent International Commission on Kosovo, *The Kosovo Report*, pp. 157–8.

139. Johnstone, *Fools' Crusade*, p. 236.

140. Chomsky, *New Military Humanism*, p. 137.

141. Thomas L. Friedman, 'A Manifesto for the Fast World,' *New York Times Magazine*, 28 March 1999, p. 40 at p. 49.

142. Chomsky, *New Military Humanism*, p. 138; Nicola Butler, 'NATO at 50: Papering Over The Cracks', *Ploughshares Monitor*, December 1999 <www.ploughshares.ca/ content/MONITOR/mond99d.html>.

143. David E. Sanger, 'Bush, in Kosovo, Tells U.S. Troops Role Is Essential,' *New York Times*, 25 July 2001, p. A1.

144. Johnstone, *Fools' Crusade*, p. 250.

145. Robertson, 'Kosovo One Year On'; Editorial, 'Kosovo as a war game,' *Globe and Mail*, 19 June 1999, p. A6.

146. 'Clinton Voices Anger and Compassion.'

147. 'The Road to War: A Special Report: How a President, Distracted by Scandal, Entered Balkan War,' *New York Times*, 18 April 1999.

148. Gregory Shank, 'Commentary: Not a Just War, Just a War – NATO's Humanitarian Bombing Mission,' (1999), *Social Justice*, vol. 26, no. 1, p. 4 at p. 37.

149. See UNAIDS Fact Sheets, *Sub-Saharan Africa* (December 2003) and *Access to HIV Treatment and Care* (December 2003) <www.unaids.org/en/media/fact+sheets. asp>.

150. Gowan, 'Making Sense of NATO's War on Yugoslavia,' p. 272.

151. Ibid., pp. 276–7.

152. Ibid., pp. 276–8.

153. John Seaman, 'The international system of humanitarian relief,' in Harriss, *Politics of Humanitarian Intervention*, p. 28.

154. After the war this thesis seems to have gained support even among supporters of the bombing: 'NATO ... seemed prepared to circumvent the UN ... possibly because of an ancillary interest in constructing a new post-cold war security architecture in Europe based on a renovated NATO.' Independent International Commission on Kosovo, *The Kosovo Report*, p. 175.

155. Ignatieff, *Virtual War*, p. 17.

156. Ibid., p. 31.

157. Antonio Cassese, 'Ex iniuria ius oritur: Are We Moving towards International Legitimation of Forcible Humanitarian Countermeasures in the World Community?' *European Journal of International Law* (1999), vol. 10, no. 1, p. 24.

158. Robertson, 'Kosovo One Year On.'

159. For example, Julie Mertus, 'Human Rights Should Know No Boundaries,' *Washington Post*, 11 April 1999, p. B1 at p. B5.

160. Christine Gray, 'From Unity to Polarization: International Law and the Use of Force against Iraq,' (2002), *European Journal of International Law*, vol. 13, p. 1 at p. 9.

161. Independent International Commission on Kosovo, *The Kosovo Report*, p. 173.

162. Willams and Scharf, 'NATO Intervention on Trial: The Legal Case That Was Never Made,' *Human Rights Review*, January–March 2000, p. 106.

163. Address by Adolf Hitler, Chancellor of the Reich, before the Reichstag, 1 September 1939, The Avalon Project at the Yale Law School <www.yale.edu/lawweb/avalon/ wwii/gp2.htm>.

164. Letter to Chamberlain of 23 September 1938, quoted in John Rosenthal, 'Kosovo and "The Jewish Question",' *Monthly Review*, vol. 51, no. 9 (2000), p. 24.
165. Address to the Canadian Parliament on 29 April 1999 <www.parl.gc.ca/36/1/parlbus/chambus/house/debates/218_1999-04-29/han218_1110-e.htm>, p. 1035 at 1110.
166. *Nuremberg Tribunal Judgement*, 1946, pp. 79–80.
167. 'Definition of "Aggression," suggested by American Delegation as Basis of Discussion, 19 July 1945,' in *Report of Robert H. Jackson United States Representative to the International Conference on Military Trials, London 1945* (Washington: Department of State, 1949), pp. 294, 375.
168. Ibid., pp. 295–302 and 375–97.
169. Lucy S. Dawidowicz, *The War against the Jews, 1933–45* (London: Penguin Books, 1987), pp. 447–8, 480.
170. United Nations General Assembly, Resolution 3314 (XXIX) (Definition of Aggression), 14 December 1974, Article 5.
171. See Chapter 2 for this aspect of the case.
172. *Nicaragua v. United States of America, 1986*, p. 14.
173. The dissenters were the American, British and Japanese judges, rather neatly representing the 'Trilateral' axis of the 1980s.
174. *Nicaragua v. United States of America*, 1986, pp. 146–7.
175. *Nicaragua v. United States of America* (Jurisdiction and Admissibility), vol. 1984, ICJ Reports, p. 392.
176. For a catalog of US crimes against peace in Latin America before and after the Nicaragua case, see Max Hilaire, *International Law and the United States Military Intervention in the Western Hemisphere* (The Hague: Kluwer Law International, 1997).
177. *Nicaragua v. United States of America*, 1986, pp. 134–5.
178. Fernando R. Tesón, *Humanitarian Intervention: An Inquiry into Law and Morality* (New York: Transnational Publishers, Inc., 1997).
179. Tesón, *Humanitarian Intervention*, p. 166.
180. This and the following passages are from ibid., pp. 121–2.
181. Williams and Scharf, 'NATO Intervention on Trial,' p. 105.
182. Rodriguez and Pinero Royo, 'La condizione dei diritti umani e delle minoranze,' p. 140 (my translation).
183. See, for example, Mertus 'Human Rights Should Know No Boundaries,' at p. B5.
184. Williams and Scharf, 'NATO Intervention on Trial,' p. 105.
185. Tesón, *Humanitarian Intervention*, p. 121.
186. David E. Sanger, 'Bush, in Kosovo, Tells U.S. Troops Role Is Essential,' *New York Times*, 25 July 2001, pp. A1, A6.
187. *Convention on the Prevention and Punishment of the Crime of Genocide*, 1948, 9 December 1948, 78 U.N.T.S., p. 277.
188. Ibid., Article 8 (emphasis added).
189. *Nicaragua v. United States of America, 1986*, p. 134.
190. Case Concerning Legality of Use of Force (*Yugoslavia v. Belgium; Canada; France; Germany; Italy; Netherlands; Portugal; United Kingdom; United States of America*). Request for The Indication of Provisional Measures, Order (International Court of Justice 2 June 1999, General List No. 105–14) <www.icj-cij.org/icjwww/idecisions.htm>.
191. Yugoslavia appeared ready to drop the case when Milosevic was ousted, but the matter had still not been resolved in August 2003. See International Court of Justice, Press Release, 2002/10, 22 March 2002 <www.icj-cij.org/icjwww/ipresscom/ipress2002/ipresscom2002-10_yugo_20020322.htm>.
192. United Nations Press Release, 'Secretary-General's Address at the University of Bordeaux,' (SG/SM 4560 24 April 1991), pp. 3, 6.
193. Charter of the United Nations, Article 1.1 and Preamble (emphasis added).

194. See Security Council Resolutions 794 of 3 December 1992, 816 of 31 March 1993, 918 of 17 May 1994, 929 of 22 June 1994, and 940 of 31 July 1994.

195. Williams and Scharf, 'NATO Intervention on Trial,' p. 105.

196. Cassese, 'Ex iniuria ius oritur.'

197. Ibid., p. 27.

198. Sydney D. Bailey and Sam Daws, *The Procedure of the UN Security Council*, third edition (Oxford: Clarendon Press, 1998), p. 239.

199. S/18250, 31 July 1986, and S/18428, 28 October 1986. It had already vetoed two resolutions condemning the naval attacks on Nicaragua when they occurred (S/14941, 2 April 1982; S/16463, 4 April 1982). The US also vetoed resolutions condemning its invasions of Grenada in 1983 (S/16077/Rev.1, 27 October 1983) and Panama in 1989 (S/21048, 23 December 1989). Anjali V. Patil, *The UN Veto in World Affairs 1946–1990: A Complete Record and Case Histories of the Security Council's Veto* (Sarasota: UNIFO Publishers, 1992).

200. See for example Security Council Press Release, 'Draft Resolution on Middle East Situation Rejected by Security Council,' 27 March 2001 <www0.un.org/News/Press/docs/2001/sc7040.doc.htm>.

201. Ignatieff, *Virtual War*, pp. 78–9.

202. Ibid., pp 60–1.

203. *Rwanda: The Preventable Genocide. Special Report by the International Panel of Eminent Personalities* (Organization of African Unity, 2000), p. 100. See also Harriss, 'Introduction: a time of troubles', p. 12.

204. *Rwanda: The Preventable Genocide*, pp. 31–2; Andrea Kathryn Talentino, 'Rwanda' in Brown and Rosecrance, *The Costs of Conflict*, pp. 56–7.

205. See generally Robin Philpot, *Ça ne s'est pas passé comme ça à Kigali* (Montréal: Les Éditions des Intouchables, 2003); Peter Uvin, *Aiding Violence: The Development Enterprise in Rwanda* (Kumarian Press, 1998); L. R. Melvern, *A People Betrayed: The Role of the West in Rwanda's Genocide* (London: Zed Books, 2000).

206. Presidential Decision Directive 25, 'Administration Policy on Reforming Multilateral Peace Operations,' *International Legal Materials* vol. 33, p. 795 (May 1994).

207. Boutros-Ghali, *Unvanquished*, pp. 135–6.

208. Security Council Resolution 914 of 27 April 1994.

209. Testimony of Wayne Madsen before the Subcommittee on International Operations and Human Rights, Committee on International Relations, US House of Representatives, 17 May 2001 <www.house.gov/intenrational_realtions/mads0517.htm>; also Lynne Duke, 'U.S. Military Role in Rwanda Greater Than Disclosed,' *Washington Post*, 16 August 1997, p. A01.

210. Editorial, 'Whose genocide was it?', *Globe and Mail*, 10 July 2000, p. A12.

211. Bailey and Daws, *Procedure of the UN Security Council*, pp. 270–2.

212. Anthony McDermott, *The New Politics of Financing the UN* (New York: Macmillan, 2000), pp. 104–6, p. 96.

213. Boutros-Ghali, *Unvanquished*, p. 333.

214. Ibid., pp. 89–91.

215. Ibid., p. 69.

216. Ibid., p. 124.

217. Ibid., p. 298.

218. Johnstone, *Fools' Crusade*, p. 307, n.1; 'Kofi Annan,' *NewsHour*, 18 October 1999 (MacNeil-Lehrer Productions, PBS Online) <www.pbs.org/newshour/bb/international/july-dec99/annan_bio_10-18.html>. See also 'NATO heads for Bosnia's front lines' (CNN, 21 December 1995, <www.cnn.com/WORLD/Bosnia/updates/dec95/12-20/handove/inmdex.html>.

219. Secretary General of the United Nations, 'Secretary-General Reflects On "Intervention" In Thirty-Fifth Annual Ditchley Foundation Lecture,' press release, 26 June 1998 (SG/SM/6613).

220. Simma, Bruno, 'NATO, the UN and the Use of Force: Legal Aspects,' (1999), *European Journal of International Law*, vol. 10, p. 8.

221. Douglas Hamilton, 'Annan Backs NATO Military Threat Over Kosovo,' (Reuters, 28 January 1999, alb-net.com/kcc/29janar.htm#annan).

222. Simma, 'NATO, the UN and the Use of Force,' p. 8.

223. 'The Blair Doctrine,' 22 April 1999, *NewsHour with Jim Lehrer*, transcript, PBS online <www.pbs.org/newshour/bb/international/jan-june99/blair_doctrine4-23.html>.

224. Ignatieff, *Virtual War*, p. 72.

225. 'Will fight for "just" cause, Eggleton says,' *Globe and Mail*, 2 October 1999, p. A22.

226. *Financial Times*, 10 January 2000, p. 19.

227. Resolutions 1160 of 31 March 1998, 1199 of 23 September 1998, 1203 of 24 October 1998 and 1239 of 14 May 1999.

228. See Jules Lobel and Michael Ratner, 'Bypassing the Security Council: Ambiguous Authorizations to Use Force, Ceasefires and the Iraqi Inspection Regime,' (1999), *American Journal of International Law*, vol. 93, p. 124 at pp. 135 and 153.

229. Lewis Mackenize, 'There's no risk-free way to keep peace,' *Globe and Mail*, 14 September 2000, p. A17 (emphasis added).

230. General Assembly Resolution No. 377A, 3 November 1950 (Uniting for Peace), adopted at the 302nd Plenary Mtg., Fifth Sess., p.10.

231. Independent International Commission on Kosovo, *The Kosovo Report*, p. 174. John F. Murphy, 'Force and Arms,' in Christopher C. Joyner, ed., *The United Nations and International Law* (American Society of International Law and Cambridge University Press, 1997), p. 109.

232. Christiane Amanpour and James Rubin were married on 9 August 1998 (BBC online network, news.bbc.co.uk/hi/english/world/americas/newsid_147000/147813. stm).

233. Hammond and Herman, *Degraded Capability*; Owen, *Balkan Odyssey*, p. 100; John Simpson, *Strange Places, Questionable People* (London: Macmillan, 1998), pp. 444 ff.; Johnstone, *Fools' Crusade*, pp. 68–70.

234. Annan, 'The legitimacy to intervene,' p. 19.

235. Vaclav Havel, Address to the Canadian Parliament, p. 1110.

236. Shalom, 'Reflections on NATO and Kosovo,' p. 12.

237. Diana Johnstone, 'NATO and the New World Order: Ideals and Self-Interest,' in Hammond and Herman, *Degraded Capability*, p. 12.

238. The US ranked at the very bottom of the 'Human Poverty Index' in the 17 ranked 'High Human Development' countries, with the highest proportion of its population living on less than 50 percent of the median income: United Nations Development Programme, *Human Development Report 1999* (New York: Oxford University Press, 1999), pp. 134, 149.

239. The Death Penalty Information Center, 'The Death Penalty: An International Perspective' <penalreform.org/english/nlececa9_1.htm>.

240. The US had previously vied with Russia, but a recent Russian amnesty made the US the undisputed leader: *Newsletter of the Penal Reform Project in Eastern Europe and Central Asia*, Issue No. 9 (Spring-Summer 2000) <penalreform.org/english/nlececa9_1.htm>; Marc Mauer 'Americans Behind Bars – A Comparison of International Rates of Incarceration,' in Ward Churchill and J. J. Vander Wall, *Cages of Steel: The Politics of Imprisonment in the United States* (Washington, D.C.: Maisonneuve Press, 1992). The US population behind bars was officially 1,860,520 at mid-year 1999 (U.S. Bureau of Justice Statistics, 'Nation's Prison And Jail Population Reaches 1,860,520' www.ojp.usdoj.gov/bjs/pub/press/pjim99.pr); by mid-2002 it had passed the 2 million mark (U.S. Bureau of Justice Statistics, 'Nation's Prison And Jail Population Exceeds 2 Million Inmates For First Time' <www.ojp.usdoj.gov/bjs/pub/press/pjim02pr.htm>).

241. Sourcebook of criminal justice statistics online, Table 3, pp. 120 <www.albany.edu/sourcebook/1995/pdf/t3120.pdf>.

242. Téson, *Humanitarian Intervention*, pp. 123–6.

243. Shalom, 'Reflections on NATO and Kosovo,' p. 14.
244. The Corfu Channel Case [1949] ICJ Reports 4, p. 35.
245. Antonio Cassese, 'A Follow-Up: Forcible Humanitarian Countermeasures and Opinio Necessitatis,' (1999), *European Journal of International Law*, vol. 10, pp. 791, 792 and 796.
246. *Declaration of the Group of 77*.
247. Christine Gray, *International Law and the Use of Force* (Oxford: OUP, 2000), pp. 24–42; Peter Hilpold, 'Humanitarian Intervention: Is There a Need for a Legal Reappraisal?' (2001) *European Journal of International Law* 12, p. 437. Nico Krisch, Review Essay: 'Legality, Morality and the Dilemma of Humanitarian Intervention after Kosovo,' (2002) *European Journal of International Law* 13, p. 323.
248. *The Responsibility to Protect. Report of the International Commission on Intervention and State Sovereignty* (Canada: Ministry of Foreign Affairs, 2001), pp. 54–5; Independent International Commission on Kosovo, *The Kosovo Report*, pp. 170–2.
249. Thomas L. Friedman, 'The End of NATO?' *New York Times*, 3 February 2002, p. WK15.
250. Timothy Garton Ash, 'Russia's Eventual Place in NATO,' *New York Times*, 22 July 2001, p. 13.
251. Richard Perle, 'Thank God for the death of the UN.' Emphasis added.
252. 'Progressive Governance Summit, 13–14 July 2003 Communiqué' <www.number-10.gov.uk/output/page4146.asp>.

CHAPTER 4: THE WAR CRIMES TRIBUNAL

1. 'Milosevic: "That's your problem"' <www.guardian.co.uk/audioarchive/letter/template/0,7138,345012,00.html>; *Milosevic Trial Transcript*, 3 July 2001, p. 2.
2. Ibid., p. 5.
3. Michael P. Scharf, *Balkan Justice: The Story Behind the First International War Crimes Trial Since Nuremberg* (Carolina Academic Press: Durham North Carolina, 1997), p. xiv.
4. Michael Scharf, 'Indicted For War Crimes, Then What?' *Washington Post*, 3 October 1999, p. B1.
5. 'Serbs must be stopped now,' CNN.Com, 23 March 1999 <www.cnn.com/US/9903/23/u.s.kosovo.04/index.html#1>.
6. 'Serb atrocities in Kosovo reported as Nato resumes air strikes,' Guardian Unlimited, 27 March 1999; <www.guardian.co.uk/Archive/Article/0,4273,3845533,00.html>.
7. Mick Hume, 'Nazifying the Serbs, from Bosnia to Kosovo,' in Philip Hammond and Edward S. Herman, eds, *Degraded Capability: The Media and the Kosovo Crisis* (London: Pluto Press, 2000), p. 72.
8. Ibid.
9. Apt Organizations of Israel, USA, Canada and Brazil, *Apt: A Town Which Does Not Exist Any More* (Tel Aviv: Committee of the Apt Memorial Book, 1966), pp. 11, 20.
10. Julie Burchill, 'Forty Reasons Why the Serbs Are Not the New Nazis and the Kosovars Are Not the New Jews,' *Guardian*, 10 April 1999 <www.guardian.co.uk/weekend/story/0,3605,307097,00.html>.
11. Vaclav Havel, Address to the Canadian Parliament on 29 April 1999 <www.parl.gc.ca/36/1/parlbus/chambus/house/debates/218_1999-04-29/han218_1035-e.htm, p. 1035 at 1110>.
12. David S. Wyman, *The Abandonment of the Jews: America and the Holocaust 1941–1945* (New York: Pantheon Books, 1984), chapter 15.
13. Diana Johnstone, *Fools' Crusade: Yugoslavia, Nato and Western Delusions* (New York: Monthly Review Press, 2003), p. 69.

14. Letter from Bosnia and Herzegovina Permanent Representative to the President of the Security Council, 29 July 1992 (S/24365).
15. *New York Times,* 2 August 1992, p. L14.
16. Roy Gutman, 'Witness' Tale of Death and torture in six-week spree, at least 3,000 killed' *Newsday,* 2 August 1992, p. 5.
17. *The Prosecutor v. Jelisic,* ICTY, Decision of 14 December 1999 <www.un.org/ICTY/brcko/trialc1/judgement/index.htm>.
18. Anthony Lewis, 'Yesterday's Man,' *New York Times,* 3 August 1992, p. A19.
19. *New York Times,* 5 August 1992, p. A12.
20. Anthony Lewis, 'Will Bush Take Real Action?' *New York Times,* 7 August 1992, p. A27.
21. *New York Times,* 5 August, p. A14.
22. *New York Times,* 4 August, p. A18.
23. Margaret Thatcher, 'Stop the Excuses. Help Bosnia Now,' *New York Times,* 6 August, p. A23.
24. Walter Goodman, 'TV Images of Bosnia Ignite Passions and Politics,' *New York Times,* 6 August 1992, p. C20.
25. *The Times,* 7 August 1992, p. 1.
26. Matt Wells, 'LM closes after losing libel action,' *Guardian,* 31 March 2000 <www.guardian.co.uk/itn/article/0,2763,181259,00.html>. See also John Simpson, *Strange Places, Questionable People* (London: Macmillan, 1998), pp. 444–6.
27. *Prosecutor v. Tadic,* (Tadic IT-94–1 'Prijedor'), ICTY Trial Chamber (7 May 1997, 14 July 1997, 11 November 1999); Appeals Chamber (27 January 2000) <www.un.org/ICTY/tadic/trialc2/judgement/index.htm>.
28. *Prosecutor v. Delalic et al.,* IT-96–21 'Celebici Camp' <www.un.org/ICTY/celebici/trialc2/judgement/index.htm>.
29. *Time,* 24 August 1992, p. 46.
30. *New York Times,* 2 August 1992, p. 14; see also 'The Push for National "Purity",' *Newsweek,* 3 August 1992, p. 37; Chuck Sudetic, 'Red Cross Cites Violations,' *New York Times,* 4 August 1992, p. A6.
31. Johnstone, *Fools' Crusade,* p. 29.
32. Scharf, *Balkan Justice,* p. 23.
33. Ibid., p. 37.
34. ISecurity Council Resolution 764, 13 July 1992, paragraph 10.
35. Scharf, *Balkan Justice,* p. 38.
36. 'United Kingdom Material on International Law,' 1990, *British Yearbook of International Law,* vol. 61, p. 602.
37. 'Gulf War Stories the Media Loved – Except They Aren't True' <www.fair.org/extra/best-of-extra/gulf-war-not-rue.html>; Chris Hedges, 'Freed Kuwaitis Tell of Iraqi Abuse Including Some Cases of Torture,' *New York Times,* 28 February 1991, p. A1.
38. President Bush, from a speech in Dallas on 15 October 1990, *US Department of State Dispatch,* 22 October 1990, p. 205.
39. *The Times,* 26 September 1990, p. 8.
40. UN General Assembly, 88th plenary meeting, 29 December 1989 (A/RES/44/240); Noam Chomsky, *Deterring Democracy* (New York: Verso, 1991), pp. 164–5; Max Hillaire, *International Law and the United States Military Intervention in the Western Hemisphere* (London: Kluwer Law International, 1997), p. 109ff.
41. Marc Weller, 'When Saddam is brought to court...' *The Times,* 3 September 1990, p. 10.
42. *The Path to The Hague: Selected documents on the origins of the ICTY* (The Hague: United Nations, International Criminal Tribunal for the former Yugoslavia, 2001), Document 8 (26 August 1992) <www.un.org/icty/publication/path.htm>.
43. Ibid., Document 9.
44. *New York Times,* 8 August 1992, p. 9.

45. Elie Wiesel, *And the Sea is Never Full. Memoirs 1969–* (New York: Alfred A Knopf, 1999), p. 392.
46. *The Path to The Hague*, Document 18 (Letter of Mr. Elie Wiesel to Mr. Antonio Cassese, 28 June 1996).
47. *New York Times*, 5 August 1992, p. A1, and 26 August 1992, p. A1.
48. Owen, *Balkan Odyssey*, (CD-ROM appendix) 'Specific Decisions by the London Conference,' 27 August 1992, Document 10.
49. *The Path to The Hague*, Document 12 ('Statement at the international conference on the former Yugoslavia, Geneva Switzerland, 16 December 1992'); Elaine Sciolino, 'U.S. Names Figures to be Prosecuted Over War Crimes,' *New York Times International*, 17 December 1992, p. A1.
50. Carol Off, *The Lion, the Fox and the Eagle: A Story of Generals and Justice in Rwanda and Yugoslavia* (Random House Canada, 2000), pp. 263–4; Carla Anne Robbins, 'World Again Confronts Moral Issues Involved in War Crimes Trials,' *Wall Street Journal*, 13 July 1993, p. A1; Scharf, *Balkan Justice*, p. 44.
51. Peter S. Canellos, 'Amnesty Plan Worries UN War-Crimes Prosecutor,' *Boston Globe*, 1 October 1994, p. 8.
52. Scharf, *Balkan Justice*, p. 87.
53. Off, *The Lion, the Fox and the Eagle*, pp. 274–5.
54. Ibid., p. 264.
55. Scharf, *Balkan Justice*, p. 44.
56. Christopher Hitchens, *The Trial of Henry Kissinger* (London: Verso, 2001), pp. 101–6, 123; *New York Times*, 6 August 1992, p. A9.
57. Scharf, *Balkan Justice*, pp. 44–5.
58. Virginia Morris and Michael P. Scharf, *An Insider's Guide to the International Criminal Tribunal for the Former Yugoslavia: a documentary history and analysis* (Irvington-on-Hudson, N.Y.: Transnational Publishers, 1995), volume II, p. 451ff; Scharf, *Balkan Justice*, p. 55ff.
59. Security Council Resolution 827, paragraph 5.
60. Johnstone, *Fools' Crusade*, p. 103.
61. Morris and Scharf, *An Insider's Guide to The International Criminal Tribunal for the Former Yugoslavia*, vol. I, p. 337; ICTY Key Figures <www.un.org/icty/glance/keyfig-e.htm>. Scharf, *Balkan Justice*, pp. 82–3; Richard J. Goldstone, *For Humanity: Reflections of a War Crimes Investigator* (New Haven: Yale University Press, 2000), pp. 83, 87–8.
62. *Report of the International Tribunal for the Prosecution of Persons Responsible for Serious Violations of International Humanitarian Law Committed in the Territory of the Former Yugoslavia since 1991*, 23 August 1995 <www.un.org/icty/rappannu-e/1995).
63. Arthur Jay Klinghoffer, *The International Dimension of Genocide in Rwanda* (New York: NYU Press, 1998), p. 117 ff.
64. Off, *The Lion, the Fox and the Eagle*, p. 331; see also an interview broadcast on CBC on 9 November 1999: *A Passion For Justice: The Life & Times Of Louise Arbour*.
65. Felicity Barringer, 'United Nations: Annan Asks For New Rwanda Prosecutor,' *New York Times*, 30 July 2003, p. A4; Colum Lynch, 'U.N. Prosecutor Fights To Keep Her Job Intact,' *Washington Post*, 9 August 2003, p. A12; Security Council Resolution 1503 of 28 August 2003, paragraphs 8 and 9.
66. Off, *The Lion, the Fox and the Eagle*, pp. 315, 330; see also Klinghoffer, *The International Dimension of Genocide in Rwanda*, p. 121.
67. The legal arguments against the tribunal, as opposed to the other legitimacy arguments, were rather weak. See Scharf, *Balkan Justice*, p. 47.
68. Ibid., p. 55.
69. Morris and Scharf, *An Insider's Guide to The International Criminal Tribunal for The Former Yugoslavia*, volume II, pp. 479–80.
70. Scharf, *Balkan Justice*, p. 63.
71. Ibid., pp. 76–8.
72. Goldstone, *For Humanity*, p. 78.

73. Ibid., p. 80.
74. Ibid., p. 82.
75. Ibid., pp. 84–5.
76. Off, *The Lion, the Fox and the Eagle*, p. 290.
77. Goldstone, *For Humanity*, p. 100.
78. Cedric Thornberry, 'Saving the War Crimes Tribunal,' *Foreign Policy* 104 (Fall 1996), p. 79.
79. Scharf, *Balkan Justice*, p. 85.
80. Off, *The Lion, the Fox and the Eagle*, p. 276.
81. Ibid., p. 289.
82. Ibid., p. 287.
83. Scott Taylor, 'Review: The lion, the glitch and the warlords,' *Globe and Mail*, 18 November 2000, p. D13.
84. Off, *The Lion, the Fox and the Eagle*, p. 289.
85. *Who is Who at NATO?* <www.nato.int/cv/saceur/clark.htm>.
86. Off, *The Lion, the Fox and the Eagle*, p. 305.
87. 'Kosovo In Crisis,' *The NewsHour with Jim Lehrer*, transcript, 12 June 1998 <www.pbs.org/newshour/bb/europe/jan-june98/kosovo_6-12.html>.
88. ICTY Press Release, 7 July 1998.
89. NATO Press Release, 12 August 1998, 'Statement by the Secretary General of NATO' <www.nato.int/docu/pr/1998/p98-094e.htm>.
90. ICTY Press Release, 9 September 1998.
91. Scharf, *Balkan Justice*, pp. 63–6.
92. ICTY Press Release, 9 September 1998.
93. Security Council Resolution 1199 of 23 September1998.
94. ICTY Press Release, 2 October 1998.
95. ICTY Press Release, 15 October 1998.
96. ICTY Press Release, 5 November 1998.
97. Security Council Resolution 1207 of 17 November 1998.
98. ICTY Press Release, 19 November 1998.
99. ICTY Press Release, 16 January 1999.
100. Off, *The Lion, the Fox and the Eagle*, p. 345.
101. ICTY Press Release, 20 January 1999; Elaine Sciolino And Ethan Bronner, 'How a President, Distracted by Scandal, Entered Balkan War,' *New York Times*, 18 April 1999, p. 1.
102. James Hooper of the Balkan Action Council, 'Return to Violence,' *The NewsHour with Jim Lehrer*, 18 January 1999 <www.pbs.org/newshour/bb/europe/jan-june99/kosovo_1-18.html>.
103. Letter dated 30 January 1999 from the Secretary-General of the North Atlantic Treaty Organization addressed to the President of the Federal Republic of Yugoslavia, Appendix (United Nations Security Council S/1999/107, 2 February 1999).
104. ICTY Press Release, 18 March 1999.
105. 'Serb atrocities in Kosovo reported as NATO resumes air strikes,' *Guardian*, 27 March 1999 <www.guardian.co.uk/Archive/Article/0,4273,3845533,00.html>.
106. ICTY Press Release, 24 March 1999.
107. Public discussion of the Kosovo investigations was later described as the 'only exception' to the no-comment rule: ICTY Weekly Press Briefing, 5 May 1999.
108. ICTY Press Release, 26 March 1999.
109. ICTY Press Release, 31 March 1999 (CC/PIU/391-E).
110. ICTY Press Release, 31 March 1999 (CC/PIU/392-E).
111. ICTY Press Release, 31 March 1999 (CC/PIU/391-E).
112. *Complaint of the Belgrade Law Faculty*, 3 April 1999 (in the author's possession).
113. ICTY Press Briefing, 14 April 1999.
114. ICTY Press Briefing, 21 April 1999.
115. See Chapter 6 for a detailed analysis of these incidents.

116. Marcus Gee, 'Doubts raised over impartiality of prosecutor,' *Globe and Mail*, 21 April 1999, p. A14.
117. ICTY Press Release, 19 April 1999.
118. *New York Times*, 28 December 1995 <www.newstimes.com/archive95/dec28 95/naa. htm>; ICTY Press Briefings of 28 April 1999 and 11 October 2000.
119. US Department of State Office of the Spokesman, Secretary of State Madeleine K. Albright, Press Remarks on the 'Ethnic Cleansing in Kosovo Report,' Washington, D.C., 10 May 1999 <secretary.state.gov/www/statements/1999/990510.html>.
120. ICTY Press Release, 13 May 1999 (emphasis added).
121. See Chapter 6.
122. ICTY Press Briefing, 7 April 1999.
123. 'Serbia Democratization Act of 1999,' 106th Congress, 1st Session, H.R. 1373, Section 401 (b) and (c).
124. ICTY Press Briefing, 28 April 1999 (emphasis added).
125. ICTY Press Releases, 27 May 1999 (JL/PIU/403-E and JL/PIU/404-E).
126. *Prosecutor v. Milosevic, Milutinovic, Sainovic, Ojdanic and Stojiljkovic*, ICTY, Indictment, 22 May 1999 <www.un.org/icty/indictment/english/mil-ii990524e.htm>.
127. Chomsky, *The New Military Humanism*, p. 87.
128. ICTY Press Release, 27 May 1999 (JL/PIU/404-E).
129. Ibid.
130. ICTY Press Release, 29 September 1999.
131. ICTY Press Release, 27 May 1999 (JL/PIU/404-E).
132. Ibid.
133. Roger Cohen, 'Warrants Served For Serbs' Leader And 4 Assistants,' *New York Times*, 28 May 1999, p. A1.
134. Scharf, 'Indicted For War Crimes, Then What?'
135. Chomsky, *The New Military Humanism*, p. 86.
136. ICTY Press Briefing, 19 May 1999.
137. Chomsky, *The New Military Humanism*, p. 104.
138. Off, *The Lion, the Fox and the Eagle*, p. 348.
139. Ibid., p. 351.
140. Ibid., p. 352. Cohen, 'Warrants Served For Serbs' Leader,' confirms that the Americans were at least informed before the indictment was made public.
141. US Department Of State, Office of the Spokesman, *Interview Of Secretary Of State Madeleine K. Albright On CBS' This Morning*, 28 May 1999 <usembassy-australia. state.gov/hyper/wf990528/epf504.htm>.
142. NATO, Operation Allied Force Update, 31 May 1999 <www.nato.int/kosovo/press/ u990531a.htm>; Human Rights Watch, *Civilian Deaths in the NATO Air Campaign*, Appendix A; Federal Republic of Yugoslavia, *NATO Crimes in Yugoslavia*, volume II, pp. 262, 400.
143. Goldstone, *For Humanity*, p. 108.
144. Scharf, *Balkan Justice*, p. 89.
145. Goldstone, *For Humanity*, p. 92.
146. *Declaration of the Stockholm International Forum on the Holocaust*, 28 January 2000 <www.holocaustforum.gov.se/conference/official_documents/declaration/index. htm>.
147. 'Lessons for the Future' <www.holocaustmemorialday.gov.uk/sections/1/lessons. htm>.
148. 'Commemorative Programme' <www.holocaustmemorialday.gov.uk/2004/sections/ national/progs/2001.pdf>.

CHAPTER 5: THE TRIAL OF MILOSEVIC

1. *Serbia Democratization Act of 1999*, HR 1373 (12 April 1999) passed as S 720, 4 November 1999, sections 301(5)(c) and 302.

2. 'Constitution Watch: Yugoslavia,' *East European Constitutional Review*, vol. 9 no. 4 (Autumn 2000) <www.law.nyu.edu/eecr/vol9num4/constitutionwatch/yugoslavia. html>; Roger Cohen, 'Who Really Brought Down Milosevic?' *New York Times Magazine*, 26 November 2000, p. 43.

3. *Foreign Operations, Export Financing, and Related Programs Appropriations, 2001 Act*, Public Law 106–429, 6 November 2000, section 594.

4. Jon Swain, 'Carla the cool prosecutor looks her enemy straight in the eye,' *Sunday Times*, 8 July 2001, 4GN, p. News 27.

5. Jurgen Elsässer, 'Carla Del Ponte und die Albanermafia,' *Konkret*, December 2002, <www.juergen-elsaesser.de/html/template.php?inhalt=../de/inhalt_archiv1. html#>.

6. *La Repubblica*, 6 February 2001, p. 22.

7. *La Repubblica*, 26 January 2001, p. 18.

8. Steven Erlanger, 'U.S. Makes Arrest of Milosevic a Condition of Aid to Belgrade,' *New York Times*, 10 March 2001, p. A1.

9. Editorial, 'Yugoslavia's Appeal,' *International Herald Tribune*, 27 March 2001, p. 10.

10. *La Repubblica*, 10 February 2001, p. 21 and 9 March 2001, p. 20.

11. *International Herald Tribune*, 4 April 2001, p. 4.

12. Marco Ansaldo, 'Amato: Usa decisive,' *La Repubblica*, 1 April 2001, p. 7.

13. *International Herald Tribune*, 2 April 2001, p. 4.

14. Ibid.

15. *Toronto Star*, 29 June 2001, p. A10.

16. Constitution of the Federal Republic of Yugoslavia, Article 17 (3).

17. 'Constitution Watch: Yugoslavia,' *East European Constitutional Review*, vol. 10, no. 2/3 (Spring Summer 2001) <www.law.nyu.edu/eecr/vol10num2_3/constitutionwatch/ index.html>. In Canada, even on requests from the ICTY, the period is 30 days (*Extradition Act*, S.C. 1999, c.18, section 50).

18. Federal Constitutional Court, Decisions nos. 150/01 and 152/01, 6 November 2001.

19. *Globe and Mail*, 29 June 2001, p. A9.

20. *National Post*, 29 June 2001, p. A4.

21. Roger Cohen, 'From Bosnia to Berlin to The Hague, On a Road Toward a Continent's Future,' *New York Times*, 15 July 2001, p. WK 7.

22. Editorial, 'Milosevic to The Hague,' *Globe and Mail*, 29 June 2001, p. A12.

23. *Toronto Star*, 29 June 2001, p. A10.

24. *Globe and Mail*, 29 June 2001, p. A1.

25. *National Post*, 29 June 2001, p. A1.

26. *Globe and Mail*, 29 June 2001, p. A9.

27. The Yugoslav decision was five judges to one. Official Gazette, FRY, No. 19, 12 April 2002 (translation by Vladimir Krsljanin).

28. Constitution of the Federal Republic of Yugoslavia, Articles 23 and 67.

29. Ibid., Article 16.

30. *Cheung v. The King* [1939] A.C. 160, 161 (House of Lords, England); *Eichmann* (1962) 36, *International Law Reports*, 277 (Supreme Court of Israel); *The United States v. Alvarez-Machin* 112 S.Ct. 2188 (1992) (Supreme Court of the United States).

31. Dusan Stojanovic, 'Yugoslavia skirting bankruptcy,' (Associated Press) *Toronto Star*, 3 July 2001, p. A13. The US continued to apply the aid pressure, demanding and getting more extraditions, as well as access to Yugoslav government archives to help in the flagging prosecution of Milosevic. See *Foreign Operations, Export Financing, and Related Programs Appropriations Act, 2002*, Public Law 107–115, sections 581 and 584; 'U.S.: Yugoslavia Aid Resuming,' CBSNews.com, 21 May 2002; Steven Erlanger, 'Did Serbia's Leader Do the West's Bidding Too Well?' *New York Times*, 16 March 2003, p. WK4.

32. Dmitri Rogozin, Chair of Russian State Duma's Committee for International Affairs, quoted in *La Repubblica*, 2 April 2001, p. 7.

33. Johnstone, *Fools' Crusade*, p. 258.
34. *Milosevic Trial Transcript*, 3 July 2001, p. 2.
35. Guido Rampoldi, 'Kosovo, le fosse dell'orrore che fanno paura all'Occidente, *La Repubblica*, 3 November 1999, p. 1 (my translation).
36. *Milosevic Trial Transcript*, 12 February 2002, p. 14.
37. See *Prosecutor of the Tribunal v. Milosevic et al.*, ICTY Case No. IT-99-37-PT, second amended indictment, 16 October 2001, paragraph 66.
38. Ibid., paragraph 66 and Appendix.
39. Elie Wiesel, 'The Question of Genocide,' *Newsweek*, 12 April 1999, p. 37.
40. *Prosecutor v. Krstic*, IT-98-33 'Srebrenica-Drina Corps' Trial Chamber Judgement (2 August 2001) <www.un.org/icty/krstic/TrialC1/judgement/index.htm>.
41. A careful review of the evidence can be found in Diana Johnstone, *Fools' Crusade: Yugoslavia, NATO and Western Delusions* (New York: Monthly Review Press, 2002), pp. 109–18.
42. *Report of the Secretary-General Pursuant to General Assembly Resolution 53/35: The Fall of Srebrenica*, UN Doc. A/54/549, 15 November 1999.
43. Ibid., paragraphs 109, 111, 497.
44. Johnstone, *Fools' Crusade*, p. 32.
45. *Report of the Secretary-General*, paragraph 506 (emphasis added).
46. Ibid., paragraph 502.
47. Ibid., paragraph 491.
48. *Prosecutor v. Krstic*, paragraphs 425 and 427.
49. Ibid., paragraph 426.
50. Ibid., paragraphs 73 and 547.
51. Ibid., paragraph 75, emphasis added.
52. Ibid., paragraphs 81 and 82, emphasis added.
53. UN General Assembly Resolution 96(I), 11 December 1946.
54. Raphael Lemkin, *Axis rule in occupied Europe: laws of occupation, analysis of government, proposals for redress* (New York: H. Fertig, 1973 [originally published 1944]), p. 79.
55. *Prosecutor v. Krstic*, paragraph 593.
56. Ibid., 562.
57. Ibid., paragraph 589, note 1,306 citing UN Doc. AG/Res.37/123D (16 December 1982).
58. Ibid., paragraph 590.
59. Ibid., paragraphs 593, 595, emphasis added.
60. *Department of Defense News Briefing, 25 October 2001,* United States Department of Defense News Transcript <www.defenselink.mil/news/Oct2001/t10252001_ t1025rum.html>.
61. *Prosecutor v. Milosevic*, IT-99–37-AR73; IT-01–50-AR73; IR-01–51-AR73, Decision on prosecution's motion for joinder, 13 December 2001 <www.org/icty/milosevic/ tricalc/decision-e/11213JD5516912.htm>; Decision on Prosecution interlocutory Appeal for refusal to order joinder, 1 February 2002 <www.org/icty/appeal/decision-e/20201JD317089.htm>.
62. Letter to the editor of the *Globe and Mail*, 12 July 2001 (in the possession of the author – emphasis added).
63. 'Richard May: The man judging Milosevic,' *BBC News*, 3 July 2001 <news.bbc. co.uk/1/hi/world/europe/1829056.stm>.
64. See the ICTY's Fourth and Ninth *Annual Reports* <www.un.org/icty/rappannu-e/ 1998/index.htm>, paragraphs 7–10; <www.un.org/icty/rappannu-e/2002/index. htm>, paragraphs 47–54.
65. Security Council Resolutions 1191 of 27 August 1998 and 1340 of 8 February 2001; Kwon was only assigned to the Milosevic case in November 2001.
66. *Milosevic Trial Transcript*, 3 July 2001, pp. 2–5.
67. *Milosevic Trial Transcript*, 30 August 2001, p. 25.
68. *Milosevic Trial Transcript*, 29 October 2001, p. 66.

69. *Milosevic Trial Transcript*, 30 October 2001, pp. 63–4.
70. Ramsey Clark once said to me that calling The Hague Tribunal a 'kangaroo court' was 'unfair to kangaroos.'
71. This and subsequent quotations, Edward L. Greenspan, 'This is a lynching,' *National Post*, 13 March 2002, p. A20.
72. Milosevic Trial Video Archive <hague.bard.edu/video.html>.
73. Rosie Di Manno, 'Doing time at war-crimes trial,' *Toronto Star*, 20 July 2002, p. A12. Di Manno has mixed up the name of two witnesses. The testimony she recounts is actually that of Xhevahire Syla, not Merifidete Selmani. Syla testified on 17 July 2002, and the relevant passages can be found at p. 8209 of the transcript.
74. *Milosevic Trial Transcript*, 17 July 2002, pp. 8209–11.
75. Ibid., p. 8197.
76. This episode and the next are discussed in the online article 'Extreme Prejudice: The Hague Tribunal and the Trial of Slobodan Milosevic' by Ian Johnson <www.onlineopinion.com.au/2002/Jul02/johnson.htm>.
77. *Milosevic Trial Transcript*, 6 June 2002, p. 6380.
78. This and following passages from *Milosevic Trial Transcript*, 7 June 2002, pp. 6563–7.
79. See above, Chapter 3.
80. *Milosevic Trial Transcript*, 11 June 2002, p. 6786.
81. Ibid., p. 6790. In this respect, the prosecutors were allowed rather more leeway than Milosevic, who was forbidden by May from asking General J. O. M. Maisonneuve whether he 'personally' believed Racak was a 'massacre.' Ibid., 30 May 2002, p. 5891.
82. The comma is misleading. May spat out the words in staccato fashion to show he would hear no argument. Later May extended the time limit by 15 minutes, which he declared to be 'considerably more.' Ibid., 12 June 2002, p. 6880.
83. Ibid., pp. 6817–18.
84. Ibid., p. 6818.
85. Ibid., p. 6848.
86. Ibid., p. 6864.
87. Ibid., p. 6865.
88. Ibid., p. 6870.
89. Ibid., p. 6871.
90. Ibid., p. 6889.
91. Ibid.
92. Ibid., p. 6827.
93. Ibid., p. 6851.
94. Ibid., p. 6765.
95. Ibid., p. 6881.
96. Ibid., p. 6899.
97. Ibid., pp. 6823–4.
98. Ibid., pp. 6894–5.
99. Ibid., p. 6895.
100. Ibid., pp. 6895–6, quoted in Chapter 3, above.
101. Ibid., pp. 6896–7.
102. Ibid., pp. 6911–12.
103. Ibid., p. 6912.
104. Ibid., p. 6913.
105. Ibid., p. 6914.
106. *Milosevic Trial Transcript*, 15 December 2003, p. 30407.
107. Ibid., p. 30413.
108. Ibid., pp. 30417–18.
109. Sandro Contenta, 'U.N. rests its case against Milosevic', *Toronto Star*, 26 February 2004, p. A12.
110. *Milosevic Trial Transcript*, 26 July 2002, pp. 8711ff.
111. Ibid., p. 8725.

112. Ibid., p. 8765.
113. Ian Fischer, 'A Coldly Pointed Finger As Milosevic's Defense,' *New York Times*, 17 February 2002, p. 10.

CHAPTER 6: AMERICA GETS AWAY WITH MURDER

1. *Complaint to the ICTY by the University of Belgrade Law School*, 3 April 1999 (translation, in the possession of the author).
2. Personal communication from Michael Scharf dated 31March 2003 (in the possession of the author).
3. House of Commons Debates for 13 April 1999, Column 32 <www.publications. parliament.uk/pa/cm199899/cmhansrd/vo990413/debtext/90413-09.htm>.
4. 'Clinton: NATO won't back down,' 15 April 1999 <www.cnn.com/US/9904/15/ clinton.kosovo>.
5. Madeleine K. Albright and Robin Cook, 'Our campaign is working,' *Washington Post*, 16 May 1999, B7.
6. NATO Press Briefing, 8 May 1999.
7. NATO Morning Briefing, 1 June 1999.
8. Robert H. Jackson, *The Nuremberg Case as Presented by Robert H. Jackson, Chief of Counsel for the United States, Together With Other Documents* (New York: Cooper Square Publishers Inc., 1971), pp. 82–4.
9. It is sometimes possible in criminal law, and international criminal law too, to justify an otherwise illegal act on the basis of 'necessity,' of which the defense of a third person from serious criminal victimization is a branch; but any claim to necessity in Kosovo would fail for essentially the same reasons the claim of humanitarian intervention would fail.
10. *Geneva Convention Relative to the Protection of Civilian Persons in Time of War, Convention IV*, Article 4, in Adam Roberts and Richard Guelff, eds, *Documents on the Laws of War* (third edition; Oxford University Press, 2000), p. 303.
11. Jean Pictet (gen. ed.), *Commentary, Geneva Convention Relative to the Protection of Civilian Persons in Time of War, Convention IV* (ICRC, Geneva, 1958), p. 47, quoted in *Prosecutor v. Tadic* (ICTY Trial Chamber, Opinion and Judgment of 7 May 1997), paragraph 579.
12. NATO Press Briefing, 3 May 1999. William Drozdiak, 'Commander of Air War Says Kosovo Victory Near, Belgrade Seen Giving in Within Two Months,' *Washington Post*, 24 May 1999, p. A01.
13. *Sansregret v. The Queen* [1985], 1 S.C. R. 570 (Supreme Court of Canada); *R. v. Buzzanga and Durocher* (1979), 49 C.C.C. (2d) 369, (Ontario Court of Appeal); Andrew Ashworth, *Principles of Criminal Law* (Oxford University Press, 1999), pp. 195–7; Wayne R. LaFave, *Criminal Law*, third edition (West Publishing Company, 2000), p. 232.
14. Michael Ignatieff, *Virtual War: Kosovo and beyond* (Toronto: Viking Books, 2000), p. 100.
15. Jean Pictet, *Development and Principles of International Humanitarian Law* (Dordrecht: Martinus Nijhoff, 1985), p. 72.
16. International Committee of the Red Cross, *Geneva Conventions of 12 August 1949 and Additional Protocols of 8 June 1977: ratifications, accessions and successions* <www. icrc.org/eng/party_gc>.
17. Roberts and Guelff, *Documents on the Laws of War*, p. 7.
18. Ibid., pp. 9–10.
19. John Pilger, 'Moral tourism,' *Guardian*, 15 June 1999 <www.guardian.co.uk/ comment/story/0,3604,288528,00.html>.
20. NATO Press Briefing, 8 May 1999.
21. Dana Priest, 'Divided, They Withstood,' *Washington Post*, 4 October 1999.

22. 'Bodies litter village after scores killed in disputed attack,' *Globe & Mail*, 15 May 1999, p. A22.
23. Stephen Chapman, 'Under Fire: The Right Way to Kill Enemy Civilians,' *Chicago Tribune*, 27 May 1999, p. 27.
24. Drozdiak, 'Commander of Air War Says Kosovo Victory Near.'
25. NATO Press Briefing, 24 April 1999.
26. NATO Press Briefing, 3 May 1999.
27. Ibid.
28. NATO Press Briefing, 25 May 1999.
29. NATO Press Briefing, 31 May 1999.
30. NATO Press Briefing, 1 June 1999.
31. Charles Trueheart, 'War crimes court looks at NATO commanders,' *Toronto Star*, 29 December 1999, p. A27.
32. Rowan Scarborough, 'U.S. Denounces U.N. Probe of NATO Bombing,' *Washington Times*, 30 December 1999, p. A1.
33. Jan Cienski and Hoel-Denis Bellavance, 'We will never hand NATO pilots to Arbour, U.S. official says,' *National Post*, 22 May 1999, p. A1.
34. ICTY Press Release, 30 December 1999.
35. Security Council Press Release, 2 June 2000 (SC/6870); ICTY Press Release, 20 June 2000.
36. Charles Trueheart, 'U.N. Tribunal Rejects Calls for Probe of NATO,' *Washington Post*, 3 June 2000, p. A9.
37. ICTY Press Release, 13 June 2000.
38. Trueheart, 'U.N. Tribunal Rejects Calls for Probe of NATO.'
39. ICTY Press Briefing, 7 June 2000 (admitting awareness of contents of Amnesty's report).
40. NATO Press Release, 7 June 2000 <www.nato.int/docu/pr/2000/p00-060e.htm>.
41. *Toronto Star*, 14 June 2000, p. A19.
42. The link was still there on 20 April 2000 (I have the printout), a full year after the complaints against NATO had been lodged with the ICTY; it was removed sometime between then and 16 February 2001.
43. See Amnesty's press releases of 23 March 1999 (News Service 056/99 AI INDEX: EUR 70/13/99); 23 April 1999 (News Service: 76/99 AI INDEX: EUR 70/43/99) and 10 May 1999 (News Service: 088/99 AI INDEX: EUR 70/57/99).
44. Press Release of 27 May 1999 (News Service: 104/99 AI INDEX: EUR 70/81/99).
45. *Amnesty Report*, pp. 28, 32.
46. Ibid., p. 29.
47. Ibid.
48. Paragraphs 35–42 and 48–50 of the ICTY Report are lifted verbatim from William J. Fenrick, 'Attacking the Enemy Civilian as a Punishable Offense,' 7 Duke J. Comp. & Int'l L. 539, 542–6 (1997), except for one bow to political correctness in the sentence: 'For example, bombing a refugee camp is obviously prohibited if its only military significance is that women in the camp are knitting socks for soldiers' (p. 545); this becomes '*people*' knitting socks in the ICTY Report (paragraph 48).
49. *ICTY Report*, paragraph 90.
50. *Amnesty Report*, p. 72.
51. Compare *ICTY Report*, paragraph 68, with Human Rights Watch, *Civilian Deaths in the NATO Air Campaign* (February 2000): 'Case Studies of Civilian Deaths – Refugees on the Djakovica-Decane Road, Kosovo' <www.hrw.org/reports/2000/nato/Natbm200-01.htm#P328_90536).
52. Ibid. ('Summary'). Human Rights Watch itself treads a very fine line, finding 'no evidence of war crimes' but concluding that 'NATO violated international humanitarian law' (the ICTY Report denied even this). The war crimes conclusion is not argued in the report, but it may have been based on the notion that NATO's killings were not 'willful.' However, this is contradicted by Human Rights Watch's own findings.

53. *ICTY Report*, paragraph 90.
54. Ibid., paragraph 12.
55. Ibid., paragraph 53.
56. *ICTY Report*, paragraph 56.
57. See, for example, 'Magistratura' in Luciano Violante, ed., *Dizionario delle istituzioni e dei diritti del cittadino* (Roma: Riuniti, 1996), p. 164.
58. Article 18.4 (emphasis added).
59. *Prosecutor v. Milosevic et al.*, ICTY Case IT-99–37-I, Decision on Review of Indictment and Application for Consequential Orders, 24 May 1999 <www.un.org/icty/Supplement/supp5-e/milosevic.htm>.
60. ICTY Press Release, 16 January 1999, quoted more fully in Chapter 4.
61. ICTY Press Release, 20 January 1999.
62. *ICTY Report*, paragraph 5 (emphasis added).
63. Ibid.
64. *ICTY Report*, paragraph 22 (emphasis added).
65. *NATO Crimes in Yugoslvia: Documentary Evidence* (Belgrade: Federal Ministry of Foregin Affairs, 1999), pp. 257ff.
66. NATO Press Briefing, 13 April 1999.
67. *ICTY Report*, paragraph 59.
68. Ibid.
69. Ibid.
70. Ibid.
71. Ekkehard Wenz, *Comment on ICTY's Final Report to the Prosecutor by the Committee Established to Review the NATO Bombing Campaign Against the Federal Republic of Yugoslavia* (12 July 2000) <www.balkanpeace.org/lan/lan10.shtml>.
72. 'Pentagon says it did not intentionally manipulate Kosovo war tape,' CNN.com, 6 January 2000 <www.cnn.com/2000/US/01/06/nato.train.video/index.html>.
73. *ICTY Report*, paragraph 61.
74. Wenz, *Comment on ICTY's Final Report to the Prosecutor*, paragraph 12.
75. *ICTY Report*, paragraph 62.
76. *Amnesty Report*, p. 36.
77. *ICTY Report*, paragraphs 74–9.
78. Ibid., paragraph 78 (emphasis added).
79. ICTY Report, paragraph 77.
80. 'Yugoslav TV chief jailed,' CNN.com, 21 June 2002 <www.cnn.com/2002/WORLD/europe/06/21/yugo.tv.jail/index.html>.
81. *Amnesty Report*, p. 50.
82. Lord Robertson of Port Ellen, 'Kosovo One Year On: Achievement and Challenge,' 21 March 2000 <www.nato.int/kosovo/repo2000/index.htm>.
83. Ignatieff, *Virtual War*, p. 150.
84. 1977 Protocol I, Article 57.
85. Ignatieff, *Virtual War*, p. 101.
86. *ICTY Report*, paragraph 28.
87. See, for example, the 1992 amendment to the *Criminal Code of Canada*, now section 273.2 (b).
88. 1977 Protocol I, Article 86 (2).
89. *R. v. Buzzanga and Durocher*.
90. *ICTY Report*, paragraph 27.
91. A. P. V. Rogers, *Law on the Battlefield* (Manchester: Manchester University Press, 1996).
92. *ICTY Report*, paragraph 38.
93. Rogers, *Law on the Battlefield*, p. 36 (emphasis added).
94. Ibid.
95. *Amnesty Report*, p. 20, quoting A. P. V. Rogers, 'Zero-casualty warfare,' *International Review of the Red Cross*, no. 837, 31 March 2000.
96. Fenrick, 'Attacking the Enemy Civilian as a Punishable Offense,' p. 549.

97. Ibid., p. 565.
98. *ICTY Report*, paragraph 30. The law of war makes a distinction between crimes against peace (*jus ad bellum*) and crimes against the laws and customs of war (*jus in bello*).
99. Ibid., paragraph 32.
100. Jackson, *The Nuremberg Case*, pp. 82–4. Jackson next proceeded to make the point already quoted several times about any resort to war being a resort to means that are inherently criminal.
101. Bernard D. Meltzer, 'Comment: A Note on some aspects of the Nuremberg Debate,' *University of Chicago Law Review* (1946–47), vol. 14, p. 455 at pp. 460–1.
102. Thus the Tribunal decided it had no jurisdiction over crimes against humanity committed before the war. *Nuremberg Tribunal Judgement*, 1946, p. 135.
103. International Military Tribunal for the Far East, *The Tokyo war crimes trial* annotated, compiled and edited by R. John Pritchard and Sonia Magbanua Zaide (New York: Garland Publishing, 1981–1988) Vol. 20, pp. 48452–3. The Tokyo Tribunal's Charter also did not restrict the charge of 'crimes against humanity' to those committed against civilians, the way the Nuremberg Charter and the Statutes of the ICTY, ICTR and ICC would (*Id.* Appendix A-5).
104. Virginia Morris and Michael P. Scharf, *An insider's guide to the international criminal tribunal for the former Yugoslavia: a documentary history and analysis* (Irvington-on-Hudson, N.Y.: Transnational Publishers, 1995), vol. 1, p. 79.
105. *The Prosecutor v. Tadic*, ICTY Appeals Chamber, 15 July 1999, paragraph 285.
106. Another change from Nuremberg to the ICTY, though slight, might also have been used in NATO's defense, though it wasn't. In the Nuremberg Charter, Crimes against Humanity were described as those '*committed* against any civilian population,' while in the ICTY this was changed to '*directed* against any civilian population.' Collateral damage falls more easily within the former than within the latter, though in the case of the NATO bombing of Yugoslavia, a campaign aimed mainly at the 'psychological harassment of the civilian population' (Human Rights Watch, above), the difference would be irrelevant.
107. See, for example, Carol Off, *The Lion, the Fox and the Eagle: A Story of Generals and Justice in Rwanda and Yugoslavia* (Random House Canada, 2000), p. 364; Barbara Crossette, 'At the Hague, It's a Leader on Trial, Not a People,' *New York Times*, 17 February 2002, p. WK3.

CHAPTER 7: ROUNDING UP THE USUAL SUSPECTS WHILE AMERICA GETS AWAY WITH MURDER

1. 'Major Strasser's been shot ... Round up the usual suspects' is a line from the closing minutes of the 1943 American movie *Casablanca*. Cynical-opportunist-with-a-heart-of-gold Captain Renault (Claude Rains) has just witnessed good guy Humphrey Bogart kill Nazi bad guy Major Strasser in order to allow Ingrid Bergman to escape with the Czech resistance leader. But instead of denouncing Bogart to the arriving gendarmes, Renault covers up his crime by directing them to the 'usual suspects,' the poor saps ('refugees, liberals and beautiful young girls') always rounded up for harassment when there's an unsolved crime. Though the phrase has now acquired a sinister connotation, you can't help feeling good when Renault utters these words in *Casablanca*, because this time the real American culprit is a *good* guy, acting for noble (and not geopolitical) motives, and his victim is indeed a Nazi, killed, after being given fair warning, with one remarkably clean shot and no collateral damage.
2. Rome Statute of the International Criminal Court, 17 July 1998, Preamble <www.un.org/law/icc/statute/romefra.htm>.

3. *Statement By The United Nations Secretary-General Kofi Annan At The Ceremony Held At Campidoglio Celebrating The Adoption Of The Statute Of The International Criminal Court,* 18 July 1998 <www.un.org/icc/index.htm>.
4. Rome Statute, Articles 5(2) and 121.
5. Giovanni Conso, 'Epilogue: Looking to the Future,' in Roy S. Lee (ed.), *The International Criminal Court. The Making of the Rome Statute: Issues, Negotiations, Results* (The Hague: Kluwer Law International, 1999), p. 475.
6. David J. Scheffer, 'Developments at Rome Treaty Conference,' Testimony Before the Senate Foreign Relations Committee, Washington, DC, 23 July 1998 <www.state.gov/www/policy_remarks/1998/980723_scheffer_icc.html>.
7. David J. Scheffer 'The United States and the International Criminal Court,' (1999), *American Journal of International Law*, vol. 93, pp. 12–13.
8. Scheffer, 'Developments at Rome Treaty Conference.'
9. Scheffer, 'Developments at Rome Treaty Conference'; Lee, 'Introduction' in Lee, *The International Criminal Court*, p. 25, footnote 46.
10. Rome Statute, Articles 12 and 13. The statute is only prospective, so it could only apply to crimes committed on or after 1 July 2002.
11. Ibid., Article 13 (b).
12. Michael P. Scharf, 'The ICC's Jurisdiction over the Nationals of Non-party States: Critique of the U.S. Position,' *Law and Contemporary Problems*, vol. 64, no. 7 (2001), p. 85.
13. Sharon Williams, 'The Rome Statute on the International Criminal Court: From 1947–2000 and Beyond,' (2000), 38 *Osgoode Hall Law Journal* 297 at 319.
14. Human Rights Watch, *Bilateral Immunity Agreements* (March 2003) <hrw.org/campaigns/icc/docs/bilateralagreements.pdf 2003>.
15. American Servicemembers' Protection Act 2002, Title II of Public Law 107–206, section 2007(c); there are certain exceptions for NATO member countries and any 'major non-NATO ally.'
16. Reuters, 'U.S. cuts military aid to 35 countries,' *Toronto Star*, 2 July 2003, p. A4.
17. Sections 2004 and 2008.
18. USA for the International Criminal Court, *The American Servicemembers Protection Act (AKA The Hague Invasion Act)* <www.usaforicc.org/facts_ASPA.html>.
19. Amnesty International Press Release, 9 March 2002 (IOR 30/007/2002); The Coalition for the International Criminal Court, *CICC Questions and Answers on U.S. So-Called 'Article 98' Agreements,* 'Documents on Impunity Agreements,' March 2003 <www.iccnow.org/documents/otherissuesimpunityagreem.html>; *Human Rights Watch,* 'A Background Briefing,' March 2003 <www.hrw.org/campaigns/icc/docs/bilateralagreements.pdf>. Hans-Peter Kaul and Claus Kress, 'Jurisdiction and Cooperation in the Statute of the International Criminal Court: Principles and Compromises,' *Yearbook of International Humanitarian Law* (1999) 2, pp. 143, 165. See also European Union, Council of Ministers, Council Session 2,450 (External Relations), Press Release 12,134/02, 30 September 2002, suggesting a compromise to allow European Union members to enter into such agreements.
20. Section 2005.
21. Paul Knox, 'Peacekeeping dispute hints at bigger issues,' *Globe and Mail*, 4 July 2002, p. A15.
22. It was renewed by Security Council Resolution 1487 of 12 June 2003.
23. Scheffer, 'Developments at Rome Treaty Conference.'
24. Rome Statute, Article 8.2.b (xviii) and (xx); Philippe Kirsch and John T. Holmes, 'The Rome Conference on an International Criminal Court: The Negotiating Process,' (1999), *American Journal of International Law*, vol. 93, p. 2 at p. 7.
25. Rome Statute, Article 28(b).
26. Ibid., Article 8.2(f).
27. Röling, B.V.A., *The Tokyo Trial and Beyond: Reflections of a Peacemonger*, Antonio Cassese (ed.), (Cambridge: Polity Press: 1993), p. 55.

28. Associated Press, 'Clinton's Words: "The Right Action",' *New York Times*, 1 January 2001, p. A6.
29. Ibid.
30. *Vienna Convention on the Law of Treaties*, 23 May 1969, Article 18 (a), 1155 U.N.T.S. 331.
31. *United Nations Treaties*, Part I, Chapter XVIII, 10. Rome Statute of the International Criminal Court, Declarations, note 6.
32. ICTY Press Release 13 May 1999 (JL/PIU/401-E). Emphasis added.
33. Scheffer, 'Developments at Rome Treaty Conference.'
34. Scharf, 'The ICC's Jurisdiction over the Nationals of Non-party States.'
35. American Servicemembers' Protection Act, Section 2002 (7).
36. United States Department of Defense Military Commission Order No. 1 of 21 March 2002 <jurist.law.pitt.edu/issues/militarytrials.htm>.
37. Marc Grossman, Under Secretary for Political Affairs, 'American Foreign Policy and the International Criminal Court,' Remarks to the Center for Strategic and International Studies, Washington, DC, 6 May 2002 <www.state.gov/p/9949. htm>.
38. Ibid.
39. Henry A. Kissinger, 'The Pitfalls of Universal Jurisdiction: Risking Judicial Tryanny,' *Foreign Affairs*, vol. 80, no. 4 (July/August 2001), p. 86 at pp. 93–4.
40. Scheffer, 'The United States and the International Criminal Court,' pp. 12, 19.
41. Scheffer, 'Developments at Rome Treaty Conference.'
42. Associated Press, 'Clinton's Words.'
43. Scheffer, 'Developments at Rome Treaty Conference.'
44. Wedgewood, 'The International Criminal Court.'
45. Law Reform Commission of Canada, *Our Criminal Law* (Ottawa: Information Canada, 1976), pp. 3–6.
46. Scharf, 'Indicted For War Crimes, Then What?' *Washington Post*, 3 October 1999, p. B1.
47. Lawrence Eagleburger before the House of Representatives Committee on International Relations, 25 July 2000 (Serial No. 106–176).
48. Fairness and Accuracy In Reporting, 'In Iraq Crisis, Networks Are Megaphones for Official Views,' 18 March 2003 <www.fair.org/reports/iraq-sources.html>.
49. Grossman, 'American Foreign Policy and the International Criminal Court.'
50. Scharf, 'The ICC's Jurisdiction over the Nationals of Non-party States,' p. 71.
51. ICTY Statute, Articles 13 and 16.
52. Rome Statute, Articles 36.6 and 42.4.
53. Wedgewood, 'The International Criminal Court,' p. 106.
54. Scharf, 'The ICC's Jurisdiction over the Nationals of Non-party States,' p. 71, note 21.
55. Marlise Simons, 'Court With a Growing Docket, but No Chief Prosecutor Yet,' *New York Times*, 16 March 2003, p. 4.
56. *Toronto Star*, 4 April 2003, p. A8.
57. James C. O'Brien, 'Courting Trouble,' *Globe and Mail*, 12 July 2002, p. A19.
58. UN Press Release, United Nations Diplomatic Conference of Plenipotentiaries on the Establishment of an International Criminal Court, Biographical Note L/ROM/4, 15 June 1998 <www.un.org/icc/pressrel/lrom4.htm>.
59. See *Yugoslavia v. Canada*, International Court of Justice, Verbatim Record of 10 May 1999 <www.icj-cij.org/icjwww/idocket/iyca/iycaframe.htm>.
60. Ministry of Foreign Affairs, the Netherlands, 'The Netherlands as Host State for the ICC' <www.minbuza.nl/default.asp?CMS_ITEM=0D4D40EFA54C411897CA6 C14625C7914X3X62822X25>.
61. Rome Statute, Article 53.
62. Ibid., Articles 15.3, 17.1 (a) and (d), 19, 39(2) and 57 2(a).
63. Simons, 'Court With a Growing Docket.'

64. Transparency International Press Release, 22 April 2003 <www.transparency.org/pressreleases_archive/2003/2003.04.22.secret_bank_accounts.html>.
65. <www.transparency.org/about_ti/donors.html>.
66. Associated Press, 'War Crimes Prosecutor Vows to Win Trust,' *New York Times*, 23 April 2003 <www.nytimes.com>.
67. Wedgewood, 'The International Criminal Court,' pp. 103–4.
68. Elliott Roosevelt, *As He Saw It* (New York: Duell, Sloan and Pearce, 1946), pp. 188–9.
69. Sir Winston S. Churchill, *The Second World War, Volume V: Closing the Ring* (London: Cassell & Co. Ltd., 1952), p. 330.
70. Arieh J. Kochavi, *Prelude To Nuremberg: Allied War Crimes Policy and the Question of Punishment* (University of North Carolina Press, 1998), p. 83.
71. Ibid.
72. Ibid., p. 84.
73. Ibid., pp. 84–5.
74. Ibid., p. 85.
75. Frank M. Buscher, *The U.S. War Crimes Trial Program in Germany, 1946–1955* (New York: Greenwood Press, 1989), p. 12.
76. Kochavi, *Prelude To Nuremberg*, pp. 81, 87.
77. Bradley F. Smith, *The American Road to Nuremberg: The Documentary Record 1944–1945* (Stanford, California: Hoover Institution Press, 1982), p. 21.
78. Kochavi, *Prelude To Nuremberg*, pp. 88–9; Buscher, *The U.S. War Crimes Trial Program in Germany*, p. 20.
79. Ibid., p. 8.
80. Smith, *The American Road to Nuremberg*, p. 209.
81. Kochavi, *Prelude To Nuremberg*, p. 91.
82. Ibid., p. 247.
83. Gar Alperovitz, *The Decision to Use the Atomic Bomb* (New York: Vintage Books, 1996).
84. Röling, *The Tokyo Trial and Beyond*, p. 113.
85. Ibid., p. 114.
86. Ibid., p. 79.
87. Ibid., p. 84.
88. 'The Dissenting Opinion of the Member for India (Radhabinod B. Pal),' R. John Pritchard and Sonia Magbanua Zaide, eds, International Military Tribunal for the Far East, *The Tokyo War Crimes Trial* (New York: Garland Pub., 1981–1988), vol. 21.
89. Ibid., pp. 12 (quoting exiled Austrian jurist Hans Kelsen) and 1232.
90. Ibid., pp. 137–8.
91. Ibid., p. 128 (emphasis in original).
92. Human Rights Watch, Press Release of 19 October 1998 <www.hrw.org/press98/oct/chile1019.htm>.
93. *Constitution of Chile*, 1980, as amended 1997, Articles 75 and 81; Owen M. Fisk, 'The Limits of Judicial Independence,' *Inter-American Law Review* 25: 1 (1993), pp. 70ff.
94. David Sugarman, 'From Unimaginable to Possible: Spain, Pinochet and the Judicialization of Power,' (2002), *Journal of Spanish Cultural Studies*, vol. 3, p. 107, at p. 109.
95. *Reg. v. Bow Street Magistrate*, Ex p. Pinochet (No. 1) (H.L.(E.)) [2000] 1 A.C. 61.
96. *Reg. v. Bow Street Magistrate*, Ex p. Pinochet (No. 2) (H.L.(E.)) [2000] 1 A.C. 119.
97. Sugarman, *From Unimaginable to Possible*, p. 114.
98. The majority was composed of three judges appointed by Blair and three by Major. The lone dissenter had been appointed by Thatcher herself.
99. 'Edited text of Jack Straw's statement to MPs,' *Guardian*, 3 March 2000 <www.guardian.co.uk/Pinochet_on_trial/Story/0,2763,190573,00.html>.
100. Ibid.

101. Ibid.
102. Hugh O'Shaughnessy, 'Secret UK deal freed Pinochet,' *Guardian*, 7 January 2000 <www.guardian.co.uk/Pinochet_on_trial/Story/0,2763,418915,00.html>.
103. Guido Rampoldi, 'Democracy Humiliated,' *La Repubblica*, 4 March 2000, p. 1 (my translation).
104. Jonathan Franklin, 'Chilean judges reduce charges against Pinochet,' *Guardian*, 9 March 2001 <www.guardian.co.uk/international/story/0,3604,448813,00.html>.
105. Amnesty International, Press Release of 3 July 2002 (AI Index: AMR 22/006/2002 (Public)).
106. O'Shaughnessy, 'Secret UK deal freed Pinochet.'
107. Sugarman, *From Unimaginable to Possible*, pp. 107, 118.
108. Maurizio Matteuzzi, 'Uno Show Osceno,' *Il Manifesto*, 4 March 2000 (my translation).
109. See the Chile Information Project, quoting *El Mercurio* of 20 March 1998 <ssdc.ucsd.edu/news/chip/h98/chip.19980320.html>.
110. 'Edited text of Jack Straw's statement to MPs.'
111. Charles Trueheart 'Regardless Of Outcome, Pinochet Case Sets Precedent,' *Washington Post*, 14 January 2000, p. A22.
112. Human Rights Watch Press Releases of 1 and 9 July 2001 <hrw.org/press/2002/07/pino0701.htm>, <www.hrw.org/press/2001/07/pino0709.htm>.
113. *Pinochet Judgment*, Lord Browne-Wilkinson for the majority, p. 204 E; see, to the contrary, Lord Millett, p. 272 E.
114. Nuremberg Tribunal Judgement, 1946, p. 77.
115. Ibid., p. 84.
116. *Yearbook of the International Law Commission 1950* vol. II, pp. 374–8.
117. *Pinochet Judgment*, p. 254 H, p. 278C.
118. *Pinochet Judgment*, p. 257G.
119. *Marcos and Marcos v. Federal Department of Police*, Switzerland, Federal Tribunal, 2 November 1989, 102 I.L.R., p. 198.
120. *Pinochet Judgment*, pp. 204 E, 244 F and 289 C-E.
121. Sharon Williams, *International Criminal Law*, Tenth revised edition, 2001 (Osgoode Hall Law School), pp. 57–8.
122. William Coblentz and Jeff Bleich, 'We need a World Criminal Court, But U.S. Opposes Treaty Establishing Rule of World Law,' *San Francisco Chronicle*, 5 November 1998, p. A29.
123. Conso, 'Epilogue,' p. 476.
124. Rome Statute, Article 12.
125. Ibid., Article 87.7.
126. Kristina Miskowiak, *The International/Criminal Court: Consent, Complementarity and Cooperation* (Copenhagen: DJOF Publishing, 2000), pp. 63–4.
127. Simon Jenkins, 'The new order that splits the world,' *The Times*, 31 January 2001, p. 20.
128. *Loi du 16 juin 1993 relative à la répression des infractions graves aux conventions internationals de Genève du 12 août 1949 et aux Protocols I et II du juin 1977, additionnels à ces conventions*, Article 7.
129. *Loi relative à la répression des violations graves du droit international humanitaire* (10 February 1999), Article 5.3, 38 Int'l Leg. Mat. 918.
130. Michael Ignatieff, 'Blood Sisters,' *New York Times Magazine*, 9 September 2001, p. 74.
131. Keith B. Richburg, 'Rwandan Nuns Jailed in Genocide,' *Washington Post*, 9 June 2001, p. A01.
132. Marlise Simons, 'An Awful Task: Assessing 4 Roles in Death of Thousands in Rwanda,' *New York Times*, 30 April 2001, p. A3.
133. Case Concerning the Arrest Warrant of 11 April 2000 (*Democratic Republic of the Congo v. Belgium*), International Court of Justice, 14 February 2002, General List No.

121 <www.icj-cij.org./icjwww/idocket/iCOBE/icobejudgment/icobe_ijudgment_20020214.PDF>.

134. Ibid., paragraph 58; see also paragraph 53 for the diplomatic immunity analogy.

135. Ibid., paragraph 61 (emphasis added).

136. 'Belgium rethinks war crimes law,' *BBC World/Europe*, 26 March 2003 <news.bbc. co.uk/1/hi/world/europe/2886931.stm>.

137. Jeffrey T. Kuhner, 'Iraqis target Gen. Franks for war crimes trial,' *Washington Times*, 28 April 2003 <www.washtimes.com/national/20030428-12027619.htm>.

138. Sénat de Belgique, *Projet de loi modifiant la loi du 16 juin 1993* (doc. Chambre, nos 50–2256/10 et 11), 5 avril 2003.

139. Agence France Presse, 'Greek lawyers to sue Britain for Iraq crimes against Humanity,' 23 May 2003 <www.ptd.net/webnews/wed/cy/Qiraq-greece-britain-icj.RPfR_DyN.html>.

140. Crimes Against Humanity Act, S.C. 2000 c. 24, sections 8(b) and 9(3).

141. Ian Black and Ewen MacAskill, 'US threatens Nato boycott over Belgian war crimes law,' *Guardian*, 13 June 2003 <www.guardian.co.uk/international/story/0,3604,976449,00.html>; 'Belgium: Suits Against Bush And Blair,' *New York Times*, 20 June 2003, p. A8; Ian Black, 'Belgium gives in to US on war crimes law,' 24 June 2003 <www.guardian.co.uk/international/story/0,3604,983746,00.html>.

142. Chambre des Représentants de Belgique, Session Extraordinaire 2003, *Projet de loi relative aux violations graves du droit international humanitaire* (DOC 51–0103/001), adopted by the Senate 1 August 2003 <www.senate.be>, restricting jurisdiction in extraterritorial cases to where a Belgian is the accused or, under strict conditions, the victim. Article 27 repeals the 1993 law.

143. Michael P. Scharf, *Balkan Justice: The Story Behind the First International War Crimes Trial Since Nuremberg* (Durham North Carolina: Carolina Academic Press, 1997), p. 212.

144. David M. Paciocco, 'Defending Rwandans before the ICTR: A Venture Full of Pitfalls and Lessons for International Criminal Law,' *Conference: The Canadian Highway to the International Criminal Court* (Canadian Institute for the Administration of Justice, Montreal, 1 May 2003; unpublished paper in the author's possession).

145. United Nations, *The Rome Statute of the International Criminal Court*, 'Overview' <www.un.org/law/icc/general/overview.htm>.

146. ICTY Press Release of 13 May 1999 (JL/PIU/401-E).

147. Ibid.

148. Virginia Morris and Michael P. Scharf, *An insider's guide to the international criminal tribunal for the former Yugoslavia: a documentary history and analysis* (Irvington-on-Hudson, N.Y.: Transnational Publishers, 1995), vol. 1, p. v.

149. *Le lys rouge* (Paris: Calmann-Levy, (no date) [1894]), pp. 117–18 (trans.).

150. Emile Zola, 'J'Accuse...!', *L'Aurore*, 13 January 1898 (my translation).

151. Immanuel Kant, *The Metaphysical Elements of Justice: Part I of The Metaphysics of Morals.* Translated, with an introduction by John Ladd. (Indianapolis: Bobbs-Merrill, 1965), pp. 100–102.

152. United Nations, *The Rome Statute of the International Criminal Court*, 'Overview.'

153. Kochavi, *Prelude To Nuremberg*, pp. 6–26; Wyman, *The Abandonment of the Jews*, pp. 288–307.

154. Oliver Wendell Holmes, *The Common Law*, [1881] (Boston: Little, Brown, 1963), p. 40.

155. Charles Kupchan and Danile Orentlicher, 'Don't let Milosevic retire quietly,' *Toronto Star*, 31 October 2000, p. A24.

156. Scharf, *Balkan Justice*, p. 219.

157. *Prosecutor v. Ante Gotovina* (ICTY Case No: It-01–45-I), Indictment <www.un.org/icty/indictment/english/got-ii010608e.htm>.

158. Carlotta Gall with Marlise Simons, 'Croatia in Turmoil After Agreeing to Send Two to Tribunal,' *New York Times*, 8 July 2001, p. A3.

159. Lucy S. Dawidowicz, *The War Against the Jews 1933–45* (Harmondsworth: Pelican Books, 1987), pp. 455–6.
160. Carrie Gustafson, 'International Criminal Courts: Some Dissident Views on the Continuation of War by Penal Means,' *Houston Journal of International Law* (1998), vol. 21, p. 51 at p. 62.
161. 'The Dissenting Opinion of the Member for India,' pp. 146–7 (emphasis in original).
162. United Nations, *The Rome Statute of the International Criminal Court*, 'Overview.'
163. Stephen R. Shalom, 'Reflections on NATO and Kosovo,' *New Politics* (Summer 1999) 5, p. 12.
164. See the numerous studies and data provided by the joint Jewish/Palestinian rights group *B'Tselem*, The Israeli Information Center for Human Rights in the Occupied Territories <www.btselem.org>. '*The transfer, directly or indirectly, by the occupying power of parts of its own civilian population into the territory it occupies*' is made a war crime by Article 8.2(b)(viii) of the Rome Statute. Israel has acted in lock-step with the Americans on the ICC, voting against it at Rome, signing it symbolically with Clinton, and unsigning it with Bush, having already concluded a reciprocal impunity agreement with the US under Article 98.
165. Scharf, *Balkan Justice*, pp. 215–16.
166. Ibid., pp. 208–9.
167. Paciocco, 'Defending Rwandans before the ICTR,' p. 8.
168. Gustafson, 'International Criminal Courts,' p. 75.
169. Fact sheet on ICTY proceedings (5 May 2003) <www.un.org/icty/glance/index.htm>.
170. Statistics Canada, 'Cases in adult criminal court 2001' <www.statcan.ca/english/Pgdb/legal19a.htm>.
171. ICTR, Completed Cases <www.ictr.org/wwwroot/default.htm>.
172. William A. Schabas, 'Addressing Impunity in Developing Countries: Lessons from Rwanda and Sierra Leone,' *Conference: The Canadian Highway to the International Criminal Court* (unpublished paper in the author's possession), p. 10.
173. Amnesty International News Release of 29 April 2003 (AI INDEX: AFR 47/005/2003).
174. Sir James Fitzjames Stephen, *A History of the Criminal Law of England* (New York: Burt Franklin, 1964; reprint of 1883 edition), volume II, pp. 79–81.
175. Ignatieff, 'Blood Sisters,' p. 74.
176. 'The Dissenting Opinion of the Member for India (Radhabinod B. Pal),' pp. 1232–4.
177. Ibid. Quotes unattributed; emphasis in original.
178. United Nations, *The Rome Statute of the International Criminal Court*, 'Overview' <www.un.org/law/icc/general/overview.htm>.
179. Scharf, *Balkan Justice*, pp. 221–2.
180. Ibid., p. 225.
181. Scharf, 'Indicted For War Crimes, Then What?'
182. Quoted above (Chapter 4).
183. Priscilla B. Hayner, *Unspeakable Truths: Confronting State Terror and Atrocity* (New York: Routledge, 2001), p. 208.
184. Scharf, 'Indicted For War Crimes, Then What?'
185. Associated Press, 'Prosecuting Saddam: Washington Calls for War Crimes Tribunal,' 19 September 2000 <abcnews.go.com/sections/world/DailyNews/saddam000919.html>.
186. Elisabeth Bumiller, 'U.S. Names Iraqis Who Would Face War Crimes Trial,' *New York Times*, 16 March 2003, p. 1.
187. Susan Dominus, 'Their Day in Court,' *New York Times Magazine*, 30 March 2003, pp. 32–3.
188. Ibid., p. 33.
189. 'Iraq moves towards self-rule,' *BBC News World Edition*, 13 July 2003 <news.bbc.co.uk/2/hi/middle_east/3062037.stm>; Richard A. Oppel Jr. and Patrick E. Tyler

'Iraqis Plan War-Crime Court; G.I.'s to Stay Until Elections,' *New York Times*, 16 July 2003, p. A9.

190.   Amira Hass, 'Human Rights Watch blasts Palestinians for war crimes. New report calls suicide strikes against civilians a violation of international law,' *Haaretz*, 1 November 2002 <www.haaretzdaily.com>.

191.   B'Tselem, The Israeli Information Center for Human Rights in the Occupied Territories, *Fatalities in the Al-Aqsa Intifada, 29 September 2000–11 May 2003* <www.btselem.org>.

192.   Cambridge Palestine Solidarity Campaign, 'Palestine – No Peace Without Justice' <www.campalsoc.freeserve.co.uk).

193.   'No Peace Without Justice – No Justice Without Forgiveness,' Message Of His Holiness Pope John Paul II For The Celebration Of The World Day Of Peace, 1 January 2002 <http://www.vatican.va/holy_father/john_paul_ii/messages/peace/documents/hf_jp-ii_mes_20011211_xxxv-world-day-for-peace_en.html>.

194.   Elise Groulx, 'Le Troisieme Pilier: La profession juridique veritable partenaire du système de justice penale internationale' (my translation). *Conference: The Canadian Highway to the International Criminal Court* (unpublished paper in the author's possession).

195.   Michael Plachta, 'The Lockerbie Case: The Role of the Security Council in Enforcing the Principle Aut Dedere Aut Judicare,' (2001), *European Journal of International Law*, vol. 12, p. 125.

196.   Peter Spiro, 'Not War Crimes,' *FindLaw's Legal Commentary*, 19 September 2001 <writ.news.findlaw.com/commentary/20010919_spiro.html>; Marjorie Cohn, 'Bombing of Afghanistan is illegal and must be stopped,' *Jurist* <jurist.law.pitt.edu/forum/forumnew36.htm>; Pope John Paul II, 'No Peace Without Justice – No Justice Without Forgiveness.'

197.   Or something to this effect; I'm quoting from memory from the *Conference: The Canadian Highway to the International Criminal Court.*

198.   The Canadian-based Lawyers Against the War also warned the Canadian government of prosecution at the ICC, but we placed primary emphasis on the illegality of the war itself, and threatened prosecution in Canada under Canadian law for murder (intentional killing without lawful excuse). Canada stayed out of the war, though I'd be surprised if the threats played much part in the decision.

199.   Michel Foucault, *Discipline and Punish: The Birth of the Prison* (New York: Pantheon Books, 1977; trans. Alan Sheridan), p. 272; *Surveiller et punir. Naissance de la prison.* Éditions Gallimard, 1975, p. 277.

200.   Ignatieff, 'Blood Sisters,' p. 74.

201.   Princeton International Law Professor Richard Falk, quoted in 'Global Governance: A Conversation with Richard Falk,' Foreign Policy Association <www.fpa.org/topics_info2414/topics_info_show.htm?doc_id=117024>, 25 July 2002. Admittedly Falk wandered somewhat from the peace camp in supporting America's wars in Yugoslavia and Afghanistan, though not in Iraq.

202.   Amnesty International News Release of 2 April 2003 (AI INDEX: AFR 51/001/2003). The Special Court for Sierra Leone set up in 2000 was the third ad hoc tribunal, after the ICTY and ICTR, set up to prosecute 'usual suspects' – namely, those opposed to the US/UK client regime in this diamond-rich, impoverished country. The Court's prosecutor is a former American Defense Department lawyer, Mr. David M. Crane, who according to the court website 'served for over thirty years in the Government of the United States, most recently as senior Inspector General at the US Department of Defence' <www.sc-sl.org>. The Court's most dramatic action at this writing was the purely propagandistic indictment of Charles Taylor, President of neighboring Liberia, as a prelude to his American-backed ouster in August 2003. Taylor's main crime seems to have been his support for rebels in Sierra Leone.

203.   Amnesty International News Release of 22 February 2001 (AI Index EUR 63/004/2001).

204.   Schabas, 'Addressing Impunity in Developing Countries,' p. 3.

205. Rudyard Kipling, *The White Man's Burden*, first published in *McClure's Magazine*, February 1899.
206. Schabas, 'Addressing Impunity in Developing Countries,' p. 3.
207. Gustafson, 'International Criminal Courts,' pp. 51, 54, 70, 77.
208. Texas is the seventh-worst state for overall poverty in the US, the worst country for poverty in the developed world. Texas also ranks first in the percentage of children without health insurance (US Census Bureau, 'Poverty 2001 – Number and Percent of Children under 19 Years of Age, at or below 200 Percent of Poverty, by State,' <www.census.gov/hhes/poverty/poverty01/table4.pdf>. Despite its inequality, Texas seems to keep from rising above the fifteenth-highest rate of violent crime in the US by virtue of being number one when it comes to the punitive response. Texas has the biggest prison population in the United States (163,190 people in jail out of 20 million population). If it were an independent state it would have the highest per capita prison population in the world. (Justice Policy Institute (Washington, D.C.), *Texas Tough?: An Analysis of Incarceration and Crime Trends in The Lone Star State* <www.cjcj.org/pubs/texas/texas.html>. Texas also leads the country in executions since 1976, accounting for 303 out of 852, with 33 out of 71 in 2002 alone (Death Penalty Information Center Murder Rates 1995–2001: State Execution Rates, <www.deathpenaltyinfo.org>.
209. Kent Roach, *Due Process and Victims' Rights: The New Law and Politics of Criminal Justice* (Toronto: University of Toronto Press, 1999), p. 32.
210. Ibid., pp. 4, 8.
211. For a full discussion of this phenomenon please see my 'A Brief History of the New Constitutionalism, or "How we changed everything so that everything would remain the same"' (1998) 32 *Israel Law Review*, p. 250.
212. Henry Kissinger, *White House Years* (Boston: Little, Brown, c. 1979), p. 683.
213. 'In 2003, the United States will spend more on the Pentagon, about $400 billion, than the next 15 largest militaries combined. And its economy is twice as large as its closest rival, Japan.' James Dao, 'One Nation Plays the Great Game Alone,' *New York Times*, 6 July 2002, p. WK1.
214. Kirsten Sellars, 'The Tyranny of Human Rights,' *Spectator*, 28 August 1999, p. 11.
215. David Kennedy, 'The International Human Rights Movement: Part of the Problem?' [2001] E.H.L.R., p. 245.
216. Address by Benjamin B. Ferencz to the Rome Conference.
217. Johnstone, *Fools' Crusade*, pp. 1–2.
218. Peter Gowan, *The Global Gamble: Washington's Faustian Bid for World Dominance* (London: Verso, 1999).
219. Röling, *The Tokyo Trial and Beyond*, pp. 89–90.

Index

Compiled by Sue Carlton